THE BOOK OF ABIGAIL AND JOHN

The Book of ABIGAIL AND JOHN

Selected Letters of the Adams Family

1762~1784

Edited and with an Introduction by

L. H. BUTTERFIELD

MARC FRIEDLAENDER AND MARY-JO KLINE

Harvard University Press
Cambridge, Massachusetts
and London, England

Fifth printing 1976

Printed in the United States of America

Library of Congress Cataloging in Publication Data

Adams, Abigail Smith, 1744–1818.
The book of Abigail and John.

Includes index.
1. Adams, Abigail Smith, 1744–1818. 2. Adams, John, Pres. U.S., 1735–1826. I. Adams, John, Pres. U.S., 1735–1826, joint author. II. Butterfield, Lyman Henry. III. Friedlaender, Marc, 1905– IV. Kline, Mary-Jo. V. Title.
E322.1.A293 973.4'4'0924 75-17509
ISBN 0-674-07855-1 (cloth)
ISBN 0-674-07854-3 (paper)

CONTENTS

ILLUSTRATIONS

Illustrations

Illustrations

INTRODUCTION

Abigail and John

John and Abigail, Abigail and John—their names are as inseparably linked as those of any human pair in history, or for that matter in legend or literature.

When they met in 1759, John Adams, twenty-three years old and a graduate of Harvard in the class of 1755, had recently returned from keeping school and studying law in Worcester to establish a practice in the village of Braintree on the South Shore of Massachusetts Bay. He had little but his own talents and education to help him, and he felt rather sorry for himself: "It is my Destiny to dig Treasures with my own fingers. No Body will lend me or sell me a Pick axe." But he was aquiver with anxiety to succeed. "Shall I look out for a Cause to Speak to," he asked in his Diary, "and exert all the Soul and all the Body I own, to cut a flash, strike amazement, to catch the Vulgar? . . . A bold Push, a resolute Attempt, a determined Enterprize, or a slow, silent, imperceptible creeping? Shall I creep or fly?"

This tension between determination and self-doubt was to remain central in John Adams' character through most of his life, the source not only of torment to him but also of our fascination with his ample and vivid personal records in the form of diaries and letters. It may not be too much to say that these opposing forces would have pulled him apart and destroyed him if he had not encountered Abigail Smith.

Except by hindsight, one can find nothing in the background of this young woman to suggest the place she would win in history. Her father was a well-to-do parson who, like many others in rural New England, owned a collection of books which his diary shows he lent to friends and neighbors. Her mother was a Quincy and thus related by blood and marriage to many of the families longest established and most respected in the Bay Colony. But Abigail herself, early and late and with some warmth, declared that like other American girls of the time she and her sisters suffered from lack of educational opportunities. "Every assistance and advantage which can be procured is afforded to the Sons, whilst the daughters are wholly neglected in point of Literature," she wrote in 1778, using "Literature" in the broad sense of humane studies. What she learned, as her grandson Charles Francis Adams was later to remark, she "picked up . . . as an eager gatherer" from the books available to her and from social intercourse at the Weymouth parsonage, which was lively and literate and to which young Lawyer Adams contributed from the time they met, when Abigail was in her fifteenth year.

A little circumstance connected with the social life of the Smith girls and their friends in neighboring towns is revealing in itself and had a permanent effect for Abigail Smith and John Adams. Communication by other means being difficult if not impossible, young people wrote lots of letters, for fun and self-improvement even if they had little of consequence to tell each other. It was part of the exercise to avoid signing one's own name and to choose a name from ancient history or classical mythology. This was evidently done not only to display one's literary attainments but also to gain—or pretend to gain—at least temporary freedom from Puritan morals and manners. Thus in some of their earliest letters Abigail and John appear as Diana and Lysander, and readers will agree that the tone of this correspondence is uninhibited. Later Abigail chose Portia as her pen name; John Adams, though he dropped any fanciful disguise for himself, thought Portia—the virtuous Roman matron of history and the learned woman jurist in *The Merchant of Venice*—a perfect sobriquet for his wife, and encouraged her to continue it.

Abigail was not yet Portia when the newly married couple settled at the foot of Penn's Hill in Braintree. But she was on her way. In a prophetic letter written on the eve of their marriage, John Adams told her that their separation for necessary business had thrown him into mental and physical "Disorder." "A month or two more would make me the most insufferable Cynick, in the World. . . . People have lost all their good Properties, or I my Justice, or Discernment." Only her presence, which has "always softened and warmed my Heart, shall restore my Benevolence. . . . You shall polish and refine my sentiments of Life and Manners, banish all the unsocial and ill natured Particles in my Composition, and form me to that happy Temper, that can reconcile a quick Discernment with a perfect Candour."

Allowing for some hyperbole, it was all true, or to become true. Observing the altered tone and substance of the entries in Adams' Diary before and after marriage, Bernard Bailyn has explained in a masterly page or two the radical change in Adams' character that they reflect—from the "tossings and turnings and the corrosive self-examinations" that had gone on for years to "a sudden emergence into maturity." Public events, notably the Stamp Act crisis, played a large part in this transformation, but Abigail was the primary and indispensable agent. After studying her portrait painted by Benjamin Blyth soon after her marriage, Mr. Bailyn writes:

> Abigail's face is extraordinary, not so much for its beauty, which, in a masculine way, is clearly enough there, as for the maturity and the power of personality it expresses. The face is oval in shape, ending in a sharp, almost fleshless, chin; a rather long arched nose; brilliant, piercing, wide-spaced eyes. It is about as confident, controlled, and commanding a face as a woman can have and still remain feminine. The mystery is not so much why Adams no longer poured his soul out into his notebooks as why he did not burn the ones in which he had.

And so this remarkably happy and enduring partnership was launched. Like all others, it suffered strains. But they were imposed from outside, and they never seriously or for long damaged the steady entente between husband and wife over a period of more than half a century. John Adams' life, as he viewed it, was an unrelieved succession of anxieties and arduous labors for inadequate rewards, especially after he entered public service. But Abigail Adams was wholly supportive, as confident of her husband's powers as she was of her own, and unshakably serene in spirit.

Much has recently been made, and with reason, of Abigail Adams as an advocate of equal rights for women. The evidence repeatedly cited is a passage in her letter to John Adams of March 31, 1776, in which, as America moved inexorably toward independence, she urged her husband and his fellow delegates in Congress to "Remember the Ladies" in framing their new government, and to "be more generous and favourable to them than your ancestors. Do not put such unlimited power in the hands of the Husbands." Paraphrasing one of Adams' own political maxims, she reminded him that "all Men would be tyrants if they could," and she did not stop there. "If perticuliar care and attention is not paid to the Laidies," she spiritedly told him, "we are determined to foment a Rebelion, and will not hold ourselves bound by any Laws in which we have no voice, or Representation."

Beneath the good humor of John Adams' reply, one may detect a little uneasiness, and it is clear from letters he wrote to others at the time that he took her position seriously. Married to such a woman, he could not fail to. The cause of women's rights made no overt gains in the Revolutionary era, and no rebellion was fomented. Mrs. Adams occasionally made edged remarks on the subject in later letters, but in practice and normally in expression she accepted things as they were. Since her husband's views were almost always her own, even though—as commonly—she arrived at them independently, she felt no sense of psychological or intellectual subordination, and he had no inclination whatever to give her grounds for feeling any. On the social side she appears to have been happy in the conventional role of a wife dependent on her husband's protection. Readers may be surprised to find that she who adjured her husband to recognize the equal rights of women or risk domestic insurrection did not think she could attend "publick assemblies" without a male to protect her. And that when public duty called John Adams away for months and then years on end, his wife could exclaim, "I can glory in my Sacrifice"—to *his* interest, as he gloried in sacrificing himself to the interest of his country.

Abigail Adams found her role as wife and mother satisfying because both her husband and the times in which she lived gave her unusual opportunities to employ her unusual talents. From the beginning, John Adams was much away from home, in his Boston office and on the court circuits from Maine to Cape Cod. Thus there was no great transition in farm management when he set off for the Continental Congress in the summer of 1774, to return for only brief intervals until late in 1777, and then to set sail for France and a decade of diplomatic missions in Europe. "I hope in time," his wife wrote him in the spring of 1776, "to have the reputation of being as good a *Farmeress* as my partner has of being a good Statesman." Both from her reports and those of friends and neighbors, as well as from his own observation, John Adams knew she fully realized this aim. "I am very happy to learn that you have done such great Things in the Way of paying Debts," he wrote her the next year. "I know not what would become of me, and mine, if I had not such a Friend to take Care of my Interests in my Absence." Her responsibilities expanded again when Adams sailed for France; they continued to be heavy until he was retired by the voters from the presidency, and for that matter afterward. In his "Memoir" of his grandmother, Charles Francis Adams suggested with great plausibility that Abigail Adams' singular capacity, energy, and good judgment in managing the farming and business affairs of the family may very well have saved her husband from the financial ruin suffered by too many of his contemporaries who devoted their lives to public service.

The Letters

It is needless to trace in detail the history of this conjugal relationship. The letters that document it are here to read and are of a quality that makes commentary pallid if not superfluous.

What the letters do for John Adams is to show another and more engaging human being than most of his contemporaries knew. His public face was formidable; with not too many exceptions, the state papers and treatises on government he gave to the world were dull and turgid. He was called "His Rotundity" and "the Duke of Braintree" because he was short, stout, and stood upon his dignity on all public occasions. His family and correspondents, and, best of all, his wife, knew a different John Adams: an over-earnest, moody, often petulant, and sometimes mulishly stubborn man to be sure; but at the same time frank, trusting, and deeply affectionate, readier to forgive others than they were to forgive him (a trait his wife did not share), and endowed with a vein of humor as apt to break out at the expense of himself as of others.

Here in these letters to Abigail Adams is Lawyer Adams, tired of his "wandering, itinerating Life" and longing to see his "Grass and Blossoms and Corn." He wants to have his children and his books around him, and "Pray let the People take Care of the Caterpillars." From Ipswich in June 1774 he sends directions for making the best sort of manure heap, and a fortnight later, in Maine, he worries whether he, or indeed anyone, is qualified to do the business that will come before the assembly of colonial delegates about to meet in Philadelphia. Shall he have "a Suit of new Cloaths" made at Boston or wait until he gets to Congress?

"There is in the Congress," he writes in September, "a Collection of the greatest Men upon this Continent," but he soon discovers that, *because* they are great men, they all talk too much. And Philadelphians eat and drink too much. By the following summer, when open war has broken out in his own province and a Continental army has been put in the field, he is out of all patience with the laggards in Congress who want to go on sending humble petitions to King George in London. He sends letters home about "The Fidgets, the Whims, the Caprice, the Vanity" of some of his colleagues. The letters are intercepted and published in the tory press, parodied, and circulated, with sneers, in England. Briefly apprehensive about this, John Adams is soon rather pleased with his unsought notoriety, because it is now clear that the country is moving steadily with him toward independence. In two remarkable letters sent off the day after this "greatest Question was decided," Adams reviews for his wife the history of this "memorable Epocha" and, casting his eye far into the future, declares he sees "Rays of ravishing Light and Glory" that penetrate the gloomy prospect of toil, privation, and bloodshed immediately faced by his embattled countrymen.

"I begin to suspect that I have not much of the Grand in my Composition," John Adams told his wife early in 1777, continuing the self-analysis that was his lifelong habit. But he was shortly summoned to serve on the grandest stage of the day, the court of His Most Christian Majesty at Versailles. "The Delights of France are innumerable," he reported, even to such a "stern and hauty Republican" as he considered himself. He "could fill Volumes with Descriptions of Palaces and Temples, Paintings, Sculpture," and all the rest, if he would allow himself to—and he did indeed send home some very graphic travel and sightseeing accounts. But he hoped that the taste for such things would not be exported to America for a long time to come, and he was determined that his children—representing the first generation of free and virtuous American citizens—should not be seduced by "the syren songs" of idleness and luxury.

As for himself, he was *en garde* against the "Delights" that Europe spread before him. In a characteristic letter from Spain to his daughter Abigail, he said he was happy to write her whatever might "contribute to your Improvement. . . . But you must remember that my Voyages and Journeys are not for my private Information, Instruction, Improvement, Entertainment or Pleasure; but laborious and hazardous Enterprizes of Business" undertaken in the service of the United States. His letters and diaries during the years 1778–1784 furnish a private view of American diplomacy unrivaled for insights into the character of those he dealt with and into his own. Unfortunately he did not do as well for Mrs. Adams during these years as he did for others. When she reproached him for neglecting her, he offered all kinds of justifications. For one thing, he told her, "You should consider, it is a different Thing to have five hundred Correspondents and but one." Spies infested Paris, the post routes, and the seaports. Enemy cruisers infested the Atlantic, and the captains of threatened vessels threw the mail overboard. Nobody wrote him, he complained, and so he had no news to tell his wife. There was truth in these allegations, but the real reason for Adams' periodic silences to his wife was the sense of isolation and frustration, the not knowing where he would turn next, that from time to time overwhelmed his stout heart and resourceful mind.

Never for long. Abigail Adams saw to that. She might "assume the Signature of Penelope" and confess that "the tears have flowed faster than the Ink" when she took up her pen to write. But her letters kept coming in spite of losses by land or sea, in spite of illnesses of her own and illness all around her. In only one case that we know of did she ask a friend to write for her—when, in the summer of 1777, the daughter she named Elizabeth was stillborn. On that occasion she was back at her wonted tasks, including correspondence with her husband, within days.

She knew her letters were anything but "moddles" of form. Her curiously angular handwriting, almost cuneiform in appearance, confirms her statement that she had never been sent even to a writing school. She could not spell or punctuate. Her clerical habits were dreadful: many of the rough drafts on which we are dependent for texts (because the fair copies were lost) are misdated or not dated at all; and to add to the confusion, she often recorded incorrectly the dates of the letters to which she was replying. Yet one must keep in mind the difficult circumstances, especially during the war years, under which she wrote, in a small and crowded house, with children around her, farms and tenants to manage, help scarce, provisions dear, taxes soaring, local epidemics occurring almost annually. She spoke movingly, not only for herself and her own generation but also for earlier and later generations of married women, when she remarked in a letter of 1776: "I always had a fancy for a closet with a window which I could more peculiarly call my own."

The central and conspicuous fact about Abigail Adams' letters is that she hardly knew how to write a dull paragraph. Signed or unsigned, her letters bear the unmistakable marks of her perceptiveness, her total self-possession, and her artless but captivating personal style. Her reports from home mingle the momentous with the intimate—news of battles with requests for pins or perhaps a green silk umbrella, tart comments on generals and politicians with the prattle of her children, diplomacy with dress goods. In a letter of 1776 that deals with such disparate topics as the condition of the Adamses' house in Boston after the British evacuation and the domestic production of saltpeter to make gunpowder, she also expressed doubts about the "passion for Liberty" among Virginians, since they "have been accustomed to deprive their fellow Creatures of theirs." That her political opinions were usually formed independently rather than absorbed from her husband is indicated by her frequently anticipating him. She was a vigorous advocate of separation from Great Britain as early as the fall of 1775, and in May 1776 she pointedly asked, "Shall we not be dispiced . . . for hesitateing so long at a word?" Well before John Adams in Paris had learned of Silas Deane's explosive public accusations of Arthur Lee and the Congress, she had read them in Braintree and condemned them in terms very like those he would use a month later. This was to be the pattern of their mental relationship through the rest of their lives. With astonishingly few exceptions, they read each other's minds as well as they read each other's letters across any extent of land or water.

Centennial and Bicentennial Versions

Nearly three hundred of the letters exchanged by John and Abigail Adams between May 1774, when news of the Act of Parliament closing the port of Boston reached America, and February 1783, when the terms of peace among the warring powers had been determined, appeared in print in 1876. As the nation's hundredth year approached, Charles Francis Adams, then nearing seventy and about to complete his editorial labors on his father's mammoth diary, had paused to consider what he might draw from the family archives that would especially suit the occasion and appeal to the public mood. The result was a book called *Familiar Letters of John Adams and His Wife, during the Revolution.*

Equally attractive in design and content, the *Familiar Letters* proved one of the enduring legacies of the Centennial year and one of the two or three in literary form that mattered at all. Within a short time, letters selected from the volume began to appear in popular collections and "libraries of choice reading"; and down to our own time—the texts as published in 1876 having long since passed into the public domain—compilers of anthologies for school and college use have reprinted selections from the Adams correspondence.

Charles Francis Adams had calculated, or divined, well. However mixed the reputation of the Adamses as statesmen might be, the letters of his grandparents that he gave to the world established them as the prototypical American couple. By their fortitude, their sacrifices, their public and private wisdom—and yes, by their unexpected charm and humor, too—they had won their way through the long struggle for independence. In the United States at its hundredth birthday, John and Abigail Adams were *everybody*'s grandparents.

Charles Francis Adams would not have put it that way. But he was well aware of the resonant chords of feeling he was striking. He had begun his own intermittent but lifelong career as family archivist and editor by bringing out a series of small and highly selective volumes of his grandparents' correspondence, the first of which was *Letters of Mrs. Adams* (1840). To this he prefixed a "Memoir" of the writer, a concise but brilliant essay which was to serve, with minor revisions, as the editorial introduction throughout the series, including the *Familiar Letters* of 1876. He began it by observing that the "memorials" of the public actors of the Revolutionary era had been or were being made abundantly available. But the materials he was presenting were of a different order. They were contributions to a history of "feeling" rather than of "action." "Our history," he went on in a prescient paragraph,

> is for the most part wrapped up in the forms of office. The great men of the Revolution, in the eyes of posterity, are many of them like heroes of a mythological age. They are seen, chiefly, when conscious

> that they are upon a theatre, where individual sentiment must be sometimes disguised, and often sacrificed, for the public good. Statesmen and Generals rarely say all they think or feel. The consequence is that, in the papers which come from them, they are made to assume a uniform of grave hue, which, though it doubtless exalts the opinion entertained of their perfections, somewhat diminishes the interest with which later generations scan their character. Students of human nature seek for examples of man under circumstances of difficulty and trial; man as he is, not as he would appear; but there are many reasons why they may be often baffled in the search. We look for the workings of the heart, when those of the head alone are presented to us. . . . The solitary meditation, the confidential whisper to a friend, never meant to reach the ear of the multitude, the secret wishes, not blazoned forth to catch applause, the fluctuations between fear and hope that most betray the springs of action,—these are the guides to character, which most frequently vanish with the moment that called them forth, and leave nothing to posterity but those coarser elements for judgment that are found in elaborated results.

In this kind of material, revealing the hidden "springs of action," the human story behind the historic event, the Adams family correspondence is incomparably rich over a period of more than a century, and the correspondence of Abigail and John Adams during the Revolution is the best of all among it, since, to quote the family editor once more, it is "an exact transcript of the feelings" of the writers during "times of no ordinary trial." The editor felt some trepidation about invading the privacy of a generation not long departed, but he need not have worried. There were no equivalents in the surviving papers of other founding fathers and mothers, and readers in 1876 and long afterward have been duly grateful for what the Adamses recorded. In our time, such apologies are altogether needless. For one thing, the findings of modern psychology, and for another, our constant exposure to advertising and public-relations techniques have schooled us to distrust the political speech, the official statement, the news release, the televised press conference, and for that matter their antecedents in the form of self-serving pamphlets and memoirs. We seek contemporaneous, unguarded, unsophisticated testimony, recorded for no more than one reader, to tell us what the men and women of history really were, not what they wanted us to think them. We don't want images but selves.

The Book of Abigail and John is a Bicentennial updating of Charles Francis Adams' contribution to the nation's Centennial. It contains what the present editors consider the *best* letters of John and Abigail Adams, written from their courtship beginning late in 1762 to their reunion in Europe in August 1784, a considerably longer span of time than that encompassed in *Familiar Letters*. To these letters have been added a number of letters to "third parties" and selected diary and autobiographical passages that reveal the two as man and woman, husband and wife, father and mother.

If the present editors have documented the actual wartime years less intensively than their predecessor, they have furnished some things (besides numerous pre- and postwar letters) that he did not. One such thing is a selection of letters more truly representative both of the principal actors and their time. Charles Francis Adams was a gifted and painstaking editor, well in advance of the standards of his day. But he was unwilling to break entirely through the crust of Victorian propriety. In the early editions of his grandparents' correspondence he left out all but one of their remarkable courtship letters, and in *Familiar Letters* he omitted those dealing with subjects that for one reason or another he thought indelicate. Thus he systematically suppressed materials too graphically descriptive of disease, for example nearly all of Abigail Adams' accounts of the dysentery epidemic in 1775 and her own and her children's agonizing experience with smallpox inoculation in 1776. He also deleted every trace of the poignant incident of Abigail Adams' pregnancy and the stillbirth of a daughter. Although it has never been thought polite to air family finances in public, Charles Francis Adams' reluctance to allow anything to appear that touched even remotely on his grandparents' business interests amounted to a phobia, and so he deprived readers of what they most need to know about Abigail Adams' management of domestic affairs in wartime. In so doing he deprived her of some of her stature as a businesswoman. An example is her "Letter wholy Domestic," May 14, 1776, never printed by her grandson, dealing with weather and crops, the scarcity and high wages of laborers, and the bills she has collected and paid. It would be hard to imagine an incident more revealing of the times or of Mrs. Adams than her dispute with old Mr. Hayden, recorded in another letter omitted by Charles Francis Adams. Hayden was her tenant, and the labor of his sons on the Adams farm was supposed to help pay his rent, but in the summer of 1775 his sons were away on military service. Still, as the countryside filled up with families who had fled from Boston, Hayden refused to give up a room in the tenant house, even for a woman who was "in circumstances." "All the art of Man shall not stir him," Mrs. Adams reported to her distant husband. Nor could all her womanly arts.

With the exceptions specified in the Note to the Reader, the letters selected for the present volume are printed with their texts intact. The family editor regularly and silently excised material, varying in length from paragraphs to phrases and single words, that he supposed unfit for reading in a domestic circle. Thus he suppressed most of Abigail Adams' warmer expressions of endearment. He printed her informative letter of July 13–14, 1776, reporting her arrival in Boston with the children for inoculation, but consigned to oblivion the cow driven in from Braintree to supply the family with milk and the favorite mare lamed by an accident. "She was not with foal, as you immagined," Mrs. Adams added in her businesslike way, "but I hope she is now as care has been taken in that Respect." These were not topics for Founding Fathers and their wives to be discussing. Who now, we may ask, is wearing "a uniform of grave hue"? Eating and drinking, too, suggested to the Victorian mind a lack of refinement, and although John Adams is not known to have overindulged in either, his casual allusions to these necessary and agreeable habits were subject to his grandson's vigilant censorship. Less easy to explain is Charles Francis Adams' suppression of much that a fond mother reported to an equally fond father about their children—their chatter, the comfort they furnished her, and the trials they caused her. He must have thought them too trifling for preservation, and there was also the problem of converting the children's remarks to "Mar" and their inquiries about "Par" into conventional English.

For the family editor followed the then universal practice of normalizing according to 19th-century literary standards the spelling, grammar, and punctuation he found in the manuscripts. Curiously, he seems to have had no interest in the history of English pronunciation and usage, and he shunned regional and dialect forms as vulgarisms. The result was a gain in tidiness—and a real loss of individuality of expression. Abigail Adams, unschooled and highly individualistic, suffered most by this treatment. Her "otherways" becomes "otherwise," her "topsa turva" becomes "topsy turvy," her "conster" becomes "construe," and so on and so on. She is not allowed such rustic locutions as "I set down to write you a monday," which is converted to "I sat down to write you on Monday"; nor her Yankee pronunciation of "Canady" and "Frankling"; nor her "tolerably comfortable," which emerges colorlessly as "very comfortable." Some of her spellings were uniquely her own, and when given literally the words they represent are not always recognizable at first glance, for example "Revere" (for reverie), "ridged oeconomy" (rigid economy), "Belcona" (balcony), "bugget" (budget).

The present editors, in order to transmit all they can of the writers' spontaneity and the idiom of their time and place, have followed the readings of the original manuscripts. Only too conscious of her literary shortcomings in the formal sense, Abigail Adams would probably have approved of her grandson's decision to correct her mistakes and touch up her letters stylistically if they were to be printed at all. "I wish you would burn all my Letters," she pleaded in one that even she thought was "a strange Mixture" and knew was very carelessly written. Yet it is surely time to present this written legacy, flawed in spelling and syntax but rich in human spirit, in its true form. For this we could doubtless count on John Adams' support. He replied to his wife's injunction: "The Conclusion of your Letter makes my Heart throb more than a Cannonade would. You bid me burn your Letters. But I must forget you first." Thanks to the record they made and their descendants preserved, neither partner will be forgotten.

Note to the Reader and Acknowledgments

The Book of Abigail and John is a book to be read rather than studied. The letters it includes are drawn from a much larger body of material of the same kind published in The Belknap Press edition of *The Adams Papers*, specifically *Adams Family Correspondence*, vols. 1–4 (Cambridge: Harvard University Press, 1963, 1973), and from a fifth volume now being edited. All the entries from John Adams' diaries and Autobiography and the single entry from Abigail Adams' journal of her voyage to England in 1784 are selected from *Diary and Autobiography of John Adams* (4 vols., 1961), bearing the same imprint. Readers seeking more details about either the principal figures or the lesser ones in the family story during the years covered, or about persons or events alluded to in these documents, should turn to the relevant volumes of *The Adams Papers*, first consulting the indexes, which are very inclusive.

Texts in the present collection are given in complete form, with these exceptions: (1) When a letter was written on two or more days, the editors have felt free to consider that part or those parts bearing particular dates as a complete letter and to ignore less interesting matter written on other dates. (2) Brief and negligible postscripts have been omitted. (3) In diary material the editors have on occasion printed partial entries and ignored less relevant entries between those here printed.

Texts are given literally, with minimal regularization for readability. Words in square brackets are supplied by the editors for missing or illegible matter in the manuscripts, or, if printed in italics, are editorial insertions. Italicized words in angle brackets represent matter the writer struck out but the editors have restored because of its interest. John Adams had an irregular habit of adding several dots or squiggles at the end of a sentence. These appear as dots in the present texts but must be read as Adams' pauses or unwritten thoughts, not as matter omitted by the editors.

Whether or not published hitherto, the manuscript originals of the texts in *The Book of Abigail and John* are in the Adams Papers, given by the Adams family in 1956 to the Massachusetts Historical Society, where the work on the Belknap edition is conducted. The few exceptions are as follows:

Abigail Adams to Isaac Smith Jr., April 20, 1771, in the Massachusetts Historical Society, Smith-Townsend Papers

John Adams to Abigail Adams, July 24, 1775, printed in *Massachusetts Gazette and Boston Weekly News-Letter*, August 17, 1775

John Adams to Abigail Adams the younger, December 12, 1779, in Le Musée de Blérancourt, Aisne, France

Abigail Adams to Elbridge Gerry, July 20, 1781, in the American Philosophical Society

John Adams to Abigail Adams the younger, August 13, 1783, printed in *Journal and Correspondence of Miss Adams, Daughter of John Adams, . . . Edited by Her Daughter* [Caroline Amelia Smith de Windt], New York and London, 1841

Abigail Adams to Elizabeth Smith Shaw, July 10 and July 29, 1784, in the Library of Congress, Shaw Family Papers

Abigail Adams to Mary Smith Cranch, July 20 and July 30, 1784, in the American Antiquarian Society

Abigail Adams the younger, Diary, August 7, 1784, printed in her *Journal and Correspondence*, cited above.

The editors are indebted to the institutions owning the manuscripts in the foregoing list for photoreproductions and for permission to publish them.

They also gratefully acknowledge the contributions to this book of the Adams Papers editor at Harvard University Press, Ann Louise McLaughlin, and of members of the Adams Papers staff: Nancy Koltes, Janet Romaine, and Celeste Walker.

I

OCTOBER 1762~JULY 1774

Now Letter-Writing is, to me, the most agreable Amusement: and Writing to you the most entertaining and Agreable of all Letter-Writing. — John Adams

And — then Sir if you please you may take me.
— Abigail Smith

ABIGAIL ADAMS' BIRTHPLACE IN WEYMOUTH

John Adams' first known reference to the girl who became his wife and made a place for herself in history beside him is in his Diary during the summer of 1759. "Polly and Nabby are Wits," he wrote of Mary and Abigail, the seventeen- and fourteen-year-old daughters of the Reverend William Smith of Weymouth. He pronounced them wanting in the "Tenderness" and "fondness" of another girl, Hannah Quincy, and questioned whether wit was ever compatible with the sisterly, wifely, and motherly graces he admired in Hannah.

He spoke with feeling because he had recently and reluctantly broken off an attachment to Hannah or, rather, had had it broken off for him by an accidental interruption that had dispelled Hannah's wiles, brought him to his senses, and saved him from a marriage that "might have depressed me to absolute Poverty and obscurity, to the End of my Life." So he firmly gave up Hannah, though his Diary shows that he cast many longing glances back in her direction.

Perhaps it was his amiable and versatile friend Richard Cranch who introduced Adams to the family at the Weymouth parsonage. Here was a circle of young people who were at least as fond of reading and writing and fun as they were of Parson Smith's not particularly distinguished Sunday sermons and Thursday lectures. By 1761 Richard Cranch was courting Polly ("Aurelia" in the following letter). They were married late the next year and settled in the Germantown section of Braintree (now part of Quincy), where there were other young people with congenial tastes. By this time John Adams and Abigail Smith were exchanging letters in a style betraying no hint of their Puritan descent or Calvinist upbringing.

JA to AS

Miss Adorable — Octr. 4th. 1762

By the same Token that the Bearer hereof *satt up* with you last night I hereby order you to give him, as many Kisses, and as many Hours of your Company after 9 O'Clock as he shall please to Demand and charge them to my Account: This Order, or Requisition call it which you will is in Consideration of a similar order Upon Aurelia for the like favour, and I presume I have good Right to draw upon you for the Kisses as I have given two or three Millions at least, when one has been received, and of Consequence the Account between us is immensely in favour of yours,

John Adams

JA to AS

Dear Madam Braintree Feby. 14th. 1763

Accidents are often more Friendly to us, than our own Prudence.—I intended to have been at Weymouth Yesterday, but a storm prevented.—Cruel, Yet perhaps blessed storm!—Cruel for detaining me from so much friendly, social Company, and perhaps blessed to you, or me or both, for keeping me at *my Distance.* For every experimental Phylosopher knows, that the steel and the Magnet or the Glass and feather will not fly together with more Celerity, than somebody And somebody, when brought within the striking Distance—and, Itches, Aches, Agues, and Repentance might be the Consequences of a Contact in present Circumstances. Even the Divines pronounce casuistically, I hear, "unfit to be touched these three Weeks."

I mount this moment for that noisy, dirty Town of Boston, where Parade, Pomp, Nonsense, Frippery, Folly, Foppery, Luxury, Polliticks, and the soul-Confounding Wrangles of the Law will give me the Higher Relish for Spirit, Taste and Sense, at Weymouth, next Sunday.

My Duty, w[h]ere owing! My Love to Mr. Cranch And Lady, tell them I love them, I love them better than any Mortals who have no other Title to my Love than Friendship gives, and that I hope he is in perfect Health and she in all the Qualms that necessarily attend ⟨*a beginning*⟩ Pregnancy, and in all other Respects very happy.

Your—(all the rest is inexpressible) John Adams

AS to JA

My Friend Weymouth August th 11 1763

If I was sure your absence to day was occasioned, by what it generally is, either to wait upon Company, or promote some good work, I freely confess my Mind would be much more at ease than at present it is. Yet this uneasiness does not arise from any apprehension of Slight or neglect, but a fear least you are indisposed, for that you said should be your only hindrance.

Humanity obliges us to be affected with the distresses and Miserys of our fellow creatures. Friendship is a band yet stronger, which causes us to [fee]l with greater tenderness the afflictions of our Friends.

And there is a tye more binding than Humanity, and stronger than Friendship, which makes us anxious for the happiness and welfare of those to whom it binds us. It makes their Misfortunes, Sorrows and afflictions, our own. Unite these, and there is a threefold cord—by this cord I am not ashamed to own myself bound, nor do I [believe] that you are wholly free from it. Judg[e you then] for your Diana has she not this day [had sufficien]t cause for pain and anxiety of mind?

She bids me [tell] you that Seneca, for the sake of his Paulina was careful and tender of his health. The health and happiness of Seneca she says was not dearer to his Paulina, than that of Lysander to his Diana.

The Fabrick often wants repairing and if we neglect it the Deity will not long inhabit it, yet after all our care and solisitude to preserve it, it is a tottering Building, and often reminds us that it will finally fall.

Adieu may this find you in better health than I fear it will, and happy as your Diana wishes you.

Accept this hasty Scrawl warm from the Heart of Your Sincere

Diana

JA to AS

My dear Diana — Saturday morning Aug. 1763

Germantown is at a great Distance from Weymouth Meeting-House, you know; The No. of Yards indeed is not so prodigious, but the Rowing and Walking that lyes between is a great Discouragement to a weary Traveller. Could my Horse have helped me to Weymouth, Braintree would not have held me, last Night.—I lay, in the well known Chamber, and dreamed, I saw a Lady, tripping it over the Hills, on Weymouth shore, and Spreading Light and Beauty and Glory, all around her. At first I thought it was Aurora, with her fair Complexion, her Crimson Blushes and her million Charms and Graces. But I soon found it was Diana, a Lady infinitely dearer to me and more charming.—Should Diana make her Appearance every morning instead of Aurora, I should not sleep as I do, but should be all awake and admiring by four, at latest.—You may be sure I was mortifyed when I found, I had only been dreaming. The Impression however of this dream awaked me thoroughly, and since I had lost my Diana, I enjoy'd the Opportunity of viewing and admiring Miss Aurora. She's a sweet Girl, upon my Word. Her breath is wholesome as the sweetly blowing Spices of Arabia, and therefore next to her fairer sister Diana, the Properest Physician, for your drooping — J. Adams

THE REVEREND WILLIAM SMITH, FATHER OF ABIGAIL ADAMS

AS to JA

Weymouth Sepbr. th 12 1763

You was pleas'd to say that the receipt of a letter from your Diana always gave you pleasure. Whether this was designed for a complement, (a commodity I acknowledg that you very seldom deal in) or as a real truth, you best know. Yet if I was to judge of a certain persons Heart, by what upon the like occasion passess through a cabinet of my own, I should be apt to suspect it as a truth. And why may I not? when I have often been tempted to believe; that they were both cast in the same mould, only with this difference, that yours was made, with a harder mettle, and therefore is less liable to an impression. Whether they have both an eaquil quantity of Steel, I have not yet been able to discover, but do not imagine they are either of them deficient. Supposing only this difference, I do not see, why the same cause may not produce the same Effect in both, tho perhaps not eaquil in degree.

But after all, notwithstanding we are told that the giver is more blessed than the receiver I must confess that I am not of so generous a disposition, in this case, as to give without wishing for a return.

Have you heard the News? that two Apparitions were seen one evening this week hovering about this house, which very much resembled you and a Cousin of yours. How it should ever enter into the head of an Apparition to assume a form like yours, I cannot devise. When I was told of it I could scarcly believe it, yet I could not declare the contrary, for I did not see it, and therefore had not that demonstration which generally convinces me, that you are not a Ghost.

The original design of this letter was to tell you, that I would next week be your fellow traveler provided I shall not be any encumberance to you, for I have too much pride to be a clog to any body. You are to determine that point. For your— A. Smith

P S Pappa says he should be very much obliged to Your Cousin if he would preach for him tomorrow and if not to morrow next Sunday. Please to present my complements to him and tell him by complying with this request he will oblige many others besides my pappa, and especially his Humble Servant, A. Smith

In 1761 John Adams had inherited from his father a saltbox cottage at the foot of Penn's Hill, with the arable, orchard, and wood land that went with it. And before long he also found himself advancing well enough in his law practice to think practically about marriage. By 1763 he was formally recognized by the Smiths as Abigail's husband-to-be. Fixing a time for their wedding was complicated by an outbreak of smallpox in Boston early in 1764. As a lawyer, Adams had to travel the court circuits, and so it seemed wise for him to be inoculated before establishing a household of his own. This procedure, which, with its preliminaries and sequels, required a month or more, probably deferred the wedding from spring till fall.

Variolous inoculation (to use its technical name), which infected a patient with a light case of smallpox under carefully controlled conditions to avoid the greater danger of taking the disease "in the natural way," had been introduced in Boston (and America) by Dr. Zabdiel Boylston—an uncle of John Adams' mother—in 1721. The practice had "raised an horrid Clamour" then and did so in later epidemics until after the turn of the century, when William Jenner's discovery of vaccination (infection with a milder but immunizing disease, the cowpox) entirely replaced it.

By 1764 inoculation was widely recognized as much less risky than natural infection, but distrust of physicians' motives (how mercenary were they?) persisted, as did concern about contagion from persons undergoing inoculation and from the "hospitals" (often simply quarantined private houses) where they gathered. Provincial and local authorities therefore prohibited the practice unless there were serious outbreaks and then tried to confine it to a few isolated sites. But in the spring of 1764 the town of Boston became "one great hospital." John Adams' letters to his fiancée furnish full and vivid details on the preparatory treatment, the actual procedure of inoculation, and the course of the disease under good professional oversight.

In the letter immediately following, "My Unkle" can hardly be other than Abigail's uncle (and cousin) who bore the only-in-New-England name of Cotton Tufts. A distinguished physician of Weymouth, he is sometimes referred to as just "the Dr." or as "Dr. Trusty," because he carried messages between the courting couple. He underwent inoculation just ahead of John Adams. In later years he often served the Adamses as adviser and agent in their business affairs.

AS to JA

Sir Weymouth April 7. 1764

How do you now? For my part, I feel much easier than I did an hour ago, My Unkle haveing given me a more particuliar, and favorable account of the Small pox, or rather the operation of the preparation, than I have had before. He speaks greatly in favor of Dr. Perkins who has not, as he has heard lost one patient. He has had since he has been in Town frequent opportunities of visiting in the families where the Doctor practises, and he is full in the persuasion that he understands the Distemper, full as well if not better than any physician in Town, and knows better what to do in case of any dificulty. He allows his patients greater liberty with regard to their Diet, than several other physicians. Some of them (Dr. Lord for one) forbid their patients a mouthful of Bread. My unkle says they are all agreed that tis best to abstain from Butter, and Salt—And most of them from meat.

I hope you will have reason to be well satisfied with the Dr., and advise you to follow his prescriptions as nigh as you find your Health will permit. I send by my unkle some balm. Let me know certainly what Day you design to go to Town, Pappa Says Tom shall go that Day and bring your Horse back.

Keep your Spirits up, and I make no doubt you will do well eno'. Shall I come and see you before you go. No I wont, for I want not again, to experience what I this morning felt, when you left Your

A. Smith

Saturday Evening Eight O'Clock

JA to AS My dear Diana [7 *April* 1764]

For many Years past, I have not felt more serenely than I do this Evening. My Head is clear, and my Heart is at ease. Business of every Kind, I have banished from my Thoughts. My Room is prepared for a Seven Days' Retirement, and my Plan is digested for 4 or 5 Weeks. My Brother retreats with me, to our preparatory Hospital, and is determined to keep me Company, through the Small Pox. Your Unkle, by his agreable Account of the Dr. and your Brother, their Strength, their Spirits, and their happy Prospects, but especially, by the Favour he left me from you, has contributed very much to the Felicity of my present Frame of Mind. For, I assure you Sincerely, that, (as Nothing which I before expected from the Distemper gave me more Concern, than the Thought of a six Weeks Separation from my Diana) my Departure from your House this Morning made an Impression upon me that was severely painfull. I thought I left you, in Tears and Anxiety—And was very glad to hear by your Letter, that your Fears were abated. For my own Part, I believe no Man ever undertook to prepare himself for the Small Pox, with fewer [...] than I have at present. I have considered thoughrououghly, the Diet and Medicine prescribed me, and am fully satisfyed that no durable Evil can result from Either, and any other Fear from the small Pox or it's Appurtenances, in the modern Way of Inoculation I never had in my Life.—Thanks for my Balm. Present my Duty and Gratitude to Pappa for his kind offer of Tom. Next Fryday, for certain, with suitable Submission, We take our Departure for Boston. To Captn. Cunninghams We go — And I have not the least doubt of a pleasant 3 Weeks, notwithstanding the Distemper.—Dr. Savil has no Antimony—So I must beg your Care that John Jenks makes the Pills and sends them by the Bearer. I enclose the Drs. Directions. We shall want about 10 I suppose for my Brother and me. Other Things we have of Savil.

Good Night, my Dear, I'm a going to Bed!

Sunday Morning 1/2 After 10.—The People all gone to Meeting, but my Self, and Companion, who are enjoying a Pipe in great Tranquility, after the operation of our Ipichac. Did you ever see two Persons in one Room Iphichacuana'd together? (I hope I have not Spelled that ineffable Word amiss!) I assure you they make merry Diversion. We took turns to be sick and to laugh. When my Companion was sick I laughed at him, and when I was sick he laughed at me. Once however and once only we were both sick together, and then all Laughter and good Humour deserted the Room. Upon my Word we both felt very sober.—But all is now easy and agreable, We have had our Breakfast of Pottage without salt, or Spice or Butter, as the Drs. would have it, and are seated to our Pipes and our Books, as happily as Mortals, preparing for the small Pox, can desire.

5 o clock afternoon.—Deacon Palmer has been here and drank Tea with me. His Children are to go with us to Cunninghams. He gives a charming Account of the Dr. and your Brother, whom he saw Yesterday. Billy has two Eruptions for certain, how many more are to come is unknown—But is as easy and more [...] (the Deacon says) than he ever saw him in his Life.

Monday. Ten O'Clock.—Papa was so kind as to call and leave your Favor of April the Eighth—For which I heartily thank you. Every Letter I receive from you, as it is an Additional Evidence of your Kindness to me, and as it gives me fresh Spirits and great Pleasure, confers an Additional Obligation upon me. I thank you for your kind and judicious Advice. The Deacon made me the offer Yesterday, which, for the very Reasons you have mentioned, I totally declined. I told you before We had taken our Vomits and last Night We took the Pills you gave me, and we want more. Lent We have kept ever since I left you, as rigidly as two Carmelites. And you may rely upon it, I shall strictly pursue the Drs. Directions, without the least Deviation. Both the Physick and the Abstinence, have hitherto agreed extreamly well with me, for I have not felt freer from all Kinds of Pain and Uneasiness, I have not enjoyed a clearer Head, or a brisker flow of Spirits, these seven Years, than I do this day.

My Garden, and My Farm, (if I may call what I have by that Name) give me now and then a little Regret, as I must leave them in more Disorder than I could wish. But the dear Partner of all my Joys and sorrows, in whose Affections, and Friendship I glory, more than in all other Emoluments under Heaven, comes into my Mind very often and makes me sigh. No other Consideration I assure you, has given me, since I began my Preparation, or will give me I believe, till I return from Boston any Degree of Uneasiness.

Papa informs me that Mr. Ayers goes to Town, tomorrow Morning. Will you be so kind as to write the Dr., that I shall come into Town on Fryday, that I depend on Dr. Perkins and no other. And that I beg he would write me whether Miss Le Febure can take in my Brother and me in Case of Need. For My Unkle writes me, I must bring a Bed, as his are all engaged, it seems. I have written him, this Moment, that I can not carry one, and that he must procure one for me, or I must look out Elsewhere. I shall have an Answer from him to night and if he cannot get a Bed, I will go to Mrs. Le Febures if she can take us.

Should be glad if Tom might be sent over, Fryday Morning. My Love and Duty where owing. Pray continue to write me, by every opportunity, for, next to Conversation, Correspondence, with you is the greatest Pleasure in the World to yr. John Adams

AS to JA

Sir Weymouth April 8. 1764

If our wishes could have conveyed you to us, you would not have been absent to Day. Mr. Cranch and my Sister have been here, where they hoped to have found you. We talk'd of you, they desire to be rememberd to you, and wish you well thro the Distemper. Mr. Cranch told me that the Deacon with his children design for Boston next Saturday and that they propose going by water—that the Deacon would have you go with them, but I would by no means advise you to go by water, for as you are under prepairation you will be much more exposed to take cold, the weather too is so uncertain that tho the morning may look promissing, yet you know it is frequently very raw and cold in the afternoon. Besides if you should wait till then and Saturday should prove an unplasent Day, you will make it so much the longer before you get into Town. Suffer me therefore to injoin it upon you, not to consent to go by water, and that you have no need to do as Tom will wait upon you any day that you desire. Let me know wheather you took your vomit, whether you have got your pills and whether you have begun Lent—how it suits you? I am very fearful that you will not when left to your own managment follow your directions—but let her who tenderly cares for you both in Sickness and Health, intreet you to be careful of that Health upon which depends the happiness of Your A Smith

JA to AS

My ever dear Diana Braintree Ap. 11th. 1764

The Room which I thought would have been an Hospital or a Musæum, has really proved a Den of Thieves, and a scene of Money

Changers. More Persons have been with me about Business, since I *shut up*, than a few, and many more than I was glad to see, for it is a sort of Business that I get nothing by, but Vanity and Vexation of Spirit. If my Imprisonment had been in Consequence of Bankruptcy, I should not have endured much more Mortification and Disquiet. I wish this Day was a Fast, as well as Tomorrow, that I might be sure of two Days Tranquility, before my Departure. I am not very impatient at present: Yet I wish I was at Boston. Am somewhat fearful of foul weather, on Fryday. If it should be, the very first fair Opportunity must be embracd.

Abstinence from all, but the cool and the soft, has hitherto agreed with me very well; and I have not once transgressed in a single Iota. The Medicine we have taken is far from being loathsome or painful or troublesome, as I own I expected. And if I could but enjoy my Retreat in silence and solitude, there would be nothing Wanting but Obliviscence of your Ladyship, to make me as Happy as a Monk in a Cloyster or an Hermit in his Cell. You will wonder, perhaps at my calling in Monks and Hermits, on this Occasion, and may doubt about the Happiness of their situations: Yet give me leave to tell you freely, the former of these are so tottally absorbed in Devotion and the latter in Meditation, and such an Appetite, such a Passion for their Respective Employments and Pleasures grows habitually up in their Minds, that no Mortals, (excepting him who hopes to be bound to your Ladyship in the soft Ligaments of Matrimony) has a better security for Happiness than they.

Hitherto I have written with the Air and in the style of Rattle and Frolick; but now I am about to shift to the sober and the Grave.—My Mamma is as easy and composed, and I think much more so than I expected. She sees We are determined, and that opposition would be not only fruitless, but vexatious, and has therefore brought herself to acquiesce, and to assist in preparing all Things, as conveniently and comfortably as she can. Heaven reward her for her kind Care, and her Labours of Love!

I long to come once more to Weymouth before I go to Boston. I could, well enough. I am as well as ever, and better too. Why should not I come? Shall I come and keep fast with you? Or will you come and see me? I should be glad to see you in this House, but there is another very near it, where I should rejoice much more to see you, and to live with you till we shall have lived enough to ourselves, to Glory, Virtue and Mankind, and till both of us shall be desirous of Translation to a wiser, fairer, better World.

I am, and till then, and forever after will be your Admirer and Friend, and Lover,

John Adams

JA to AS

Dr. Diana Thurdsdy. 5. Oclock. [*12 April*] 1764

I have Thoughts of sending you a Nest of Letters like a nest of Basketts; tho I suspect the latter would be a more genteel and acceptable Present to a Lady. But in my present Circumstances I can much better afford the former than the latter. For, my own Discretion as well as the Prescriptions of the Faculty, prohibit any close Application of Mind to Books or Business—Amusement, Amusement is the only study that I follow. Now Letter-Writing is, to me, the most agreable Amusement ⟨*I can find*⟩: and Writing to you the most entertaining and Agreable of all Letter-Writing. So that a Nest of an hundred, would cost me Nothing at all.—What say you my Dear? Are you not much obliged to me, for making you the cheapest of all possible Presents?

Shall I continue to write you, so much, and so often after I get to Town? Shall I send you, an History of the whole Voyage? Shall I draw You the Characters of all, who visit me? Shall I describe to you all the Conversations I have? I am about to make my Appearance on a new Theatre, new to me. I have never been much conversant in scenes, where Drs., Nurses, Watchers, &c. make the Principal Actors. It will be a Curiosity to me. Will it be so to you? I was always pleased to see human Nature in a Variety of shapes. And if I should be much alone, and feel in tolerable Spirits, it will be a Diversion to commit my Observations to Writing.

I believe I could furnish a Cabinet of Letters upon these subjects which would be exceeded in Curiosity, by nothing, but by a sett describing the Characters, Diversions, Meals, Wit, Drollery, Jokes, Smutt, and Stories of the Guests at a Tavern in Plymouth where I lodge, when at that Court—which could be equalled by nothing excepting a minute History of Close stools and Chamber Potts, and of the Operation of Pills, Potions and Powders, in the Preparation for the small Pox.

Heaven forgive me for suffering my Imagination to straggle into a Region of Ideas so nauseous And abominable: and suffer me to return to my Project of writing you a Journal. You would have a great Variety of Characters—Lawyers, Physicians (no Divines I believe), a Number of Tradesmen, Country Colonells, Ladies, Girls, Nurses, Watchers, Children, Barbers &c. &c. &c. But among all These, there is but one whose Character I would give much to know better than I do at present. In a Word I am an old Fellow, and have seen so many Characters in my Day, that I am almost weary of Observing them.—Yet I doubt whether I understand human Nature or the World very well or not?

There is not much Satisfaction in the study of Mankind to a benevolent Mind. It is a new Moon, Nineteen Twentyeths of it opaque and unenlightened.

Intimacy with the most of People, will bring you acquainted with Vices and Errors, and Follies enough to make you despize them. Nay Intimacy with the most celebrated will very much diminish our Reverence and Admiration.

What say you now my dear shall I go on with my Design of Writing Characters?—Answer as you please, there is one Character, that whether I draw it on Paper or not, I cannot avoid thinking on every Hour, and considering sometimes together and sometimes asunder, the Excellencies and Defects in it. It is almost the only one that has encreased, for many Years together, in Proportion to Acquaintance and Intimacy, in the Esteem, Love and Admiration of your

John Adams

AS to JA

My Dearest Friend — Weymouth April 12. 1764

Here am I all alone, in my Chamber, a mere Nun I assure you, after professing myself thus will it not be out of Character to confess that my thoughts are often employ'd about Lysander, "out of the abundance of the Heart, the mouth speaketh," and why Not the Mind thinketh.

Received the pacquet you so generously bestowed upon me. To say I Fasted after such an entertainment, would be wronging my Conscience and wounding Truth. How kind is it in you, thus by frequent tokens of remembrance to alleviate the pangs of absence, by this I am convinced that I am often in your Thoughts, which is a satisfaction to me, notwithstanding you tell me that you sometimes view the dark side of your Diana, and there no doubt you discover many Spots—which I rather wish were erased, than conceal'd from you. Do not judge by this, that your opinion is an indifferent thing to me, (were it so, I should look forward with a heavey Heart,) but it is far otherways, for I had rather stand fair there, and be thought well of by Lysander than by the greater part of the World besides. I would fain hope that those faults which you discover, proceed more, from a wrong Head, than a bad Heart. E'er long May I be connected with a Friend from whose Example I may form a more faultless conduct, and whose benevolent mind will lead him to pardon, what he cannot amend.

The Nest of Letters which you so undervalue, were to me a much more welcome present than a Nest of Baskets, tho every stran of those had been gold and silver. I do not estimate everything according to the price the world set upon it, but according to the value it is of to me, thus that which was cheapest to you I look upon as highly valuable.

You ask whether you shall send a History of the whole voyage, characters, visits, conversations &c. &c. It is the very thing that I designd this Evening to have requested of you, but you have prevented my asking, by kindly offering it. You will greatly oblige me by it, and it will be no small amusement to me in my State of Seperation. Among the many who will visit, I expect Arpasia will be one, I want her character drawn by your pen (Aurelia says she appears most agreable in her Letters). I know you are a critical observer, and your judgment of people generally plases me. Sometimes you know, I think you too severe, and that you do not make quite so many allowances as Humane Nature requires, but perhaps this may be oweing to my unacquainedness with the World. Your Business Naturly leads you to a nearer inspection of Mankind, and to see the corruptions of the Heart, which I believe you often find desperately wicked and deceitful.

Methinks I have abundance to say to you. What is next? O that I should have been extreemly glad to have seen you to Day. Last Fast Day, if you remember, we spent together, and why might we not this? Why I can tell you, we might, if we had been together, have been led into temptation. I dont mean to commit any Evil, unless setting up late, and thereby injuring our Health, may be called so. To that I could have submitted without much remorse of Conscience, that would have had but little weight with me, had you not bid me adieu, the last time I saw you. The reflexion of what I that forenoon endured, has been ever since sufficient to deter me from wishing to see you again, till you can come and go, as you formerly used to.

Betsy sends her Love to you, says she designd to have kissed you before you went away, but you made no advances, and she never haveing been guilty of such an action, knew not how to attempt it. Know you of any figure in the Mathematicks whereby you can convey one to her? Inclining lines that meet in the same center, will not that figure come as nigh as any?

What think you of the weather. We have had a very promissing afternoon, tho the forenoon threatned a Storm. I am in great hopes that Sol will not refuse his benign influence tomorrow.

To-Morrow you leave Braintree. My best wishes attend you. With Marcia I say

> "O Ye immortal powers! that guard the just
> Watch round his Head, and soften the Disease
> Banish all Sorrow from his Mind
> Becalm his Soul with pleasing thoughts
> And shew Mankind that virtue is your care."

Thus for Lysander prays his A Smith

PS Let me hear from you soon as possible, and as often. By sending your Letters to the Doctor believe you may get conveyance often. I rejoice to hear you feel so comfortable. Still be careful, good folks are scarce. My Mamma has just been up, and asks to whom I am writing. I answerd not very readily. Upon my hesitating—Send my Love say'd she to Mr. Adams, tell him he has my good wishes for his Safty. A good Night to you—my fire is out. Pray be so kind (as to deliver) or send if they dont visit you, these Letters as directed.

Fryday morning

What a Beautiful morning it is, I almost wish I was going with you.—Here [I] send the Books, papa prays [you] would be careful of them. I send you some tobacco to smoke your Letters over, tho I dont imagine you will use it all that way.—A pleasent ride to you. Breakfast calls your A Smith

JA to AS

My dearest [*Boston, 13 April 1764*]

We arrived at Captn. Cunninghams, about Twelve O'Clock and sent our Compliments to Dr. Perkins. The Courrier returned with Answer that the Dr. was determined to inoculate no more without a Preparation preevious to Inoculation. That We should have written to him and have received Directions from him, and Medicine, before We came into Town. I was surprized and chagrined. I wrote, instantly, a Letter to him, and informed him we had been under a Preparation of his prescribing, and that I presumed Dr. Tufts had informed him, that We depended on him, in Preference to any other Gentleman. The Dr. came, immediately with Dr. Warren, in a Chaise—And after an Apology, for his not Recollecting—(I am obliged to break off my Narration, in order to swallow a Porringer of Hasty Pudding and Milk. I have done my Dinner)—for not recollecting what Dr. Tufts had told him, Dr. Perkins demanded my left Arm and Dr. Warren my Brothers. They took their Launcetts and with their Points divided the skin for about a Quarter of an Inch and just suffering the Blood to appear, buried a Thread about ⟨*half*⟩ a Quarter of an Inch long in the Channell. A little Lint was then laid over the scratch and a Piece of a Ragg pressed on, and then a Bandage bound over all—my Coat and waistcoat put on, and I was bid to go where and do what I pleased. (Dont you think the Dr. has a good Deal of Confidence in my Discretion, thus to leave me to it?)

The Doctors have left us Pills red and black to take Night and Morning. But they looked very sagaciously and importantly at us, and ordered my Brother, larger Doses than me, on Account of the Difference in our Constitutions. Dr. Perkins is a short, thick sett, dark Complexioned, Yet pale Faced, Man, (Pale faced I say, which I was glad to see, because I have a great Regard for a Pale Face, in any Gentleman of Physick, Divinity or Law. It indicates search and study). Gives himself the alert, chearful Air and Behaviour of a Physician, not forgeting the solemn, important and wise. Warren is a pretty, tall, Genteel, fair faced young Gentleman. Not quite so much Assurance in his Address, as Perkins, (perhaps because Perkins was present) Yet shewing fully that he knows the Utility thereof, and that he will soon, practice it in full Perfection.

The Doctors, having finished the Operation and left Us, their Directions and Medicines, took their Departure in infinite Haste, depend on't.

I have one Request to make, which is that you would be very careful in making Tom, Smoke all the Letters from me, very faithfully, before you, or any of the Family reads them. For, altho I shall never fail to smoke them myself before sealing, Yet I fear the Air of this House will be too much infected, soon, to be absolutely without Danger, and I would not you should take the Distemper, by Letter from me, for Millions. I write at a Desk far removed from any sick Room, and shall use all the Care I can, but too much cannot be used.

I have written thus far, and it is 45 Minutes Past one O Clock and no more.

My Love to all. My hearty Thanks to Mamma for her kind Wishes. My Regards as due to Pappa, and should request his Prayers, which are always becoming, and especially at such Times, when We are undertaking any Thing of Consequence as the small Pox, undoubtedly, tho, I have not the Least Apprehension att all of what is called Danger.

I am as ever Yr. John Adams

JA to AS

Saturday. Two O Clock [*14 April 1764*]

The Deacon and his Three Children are arrivd and the Operation has been performed, and all well. And now our Hospital is full. There are Ten, of Us, under this Roof, now expecting to be sick. One, of Us, Mr. Wheat, begins to complain of a Pain Under his Arm and in his Knees, and about his Back, so that We expect within a few Hours to see the Course of the Eruption and of the fever that preeceeds and accompanies it.

Your Friends, Miss Paine and Miss Nicholson have been here, and are gone. I delivered your Letters. Arpasia asked me, if you was five feet and six Inches tall? I replyd I had not taken Measure as Yet. You know the Meaning of this Question. She is neither Tall, nor short, neither lean nor fat—pitted with the small Pox—a fine Bloom. Features somewhat like Esther Quincy's. An Eye, that indicates not only Vivacity, but Fire—not only Resolution, but Intrepidity. (Scandal protect me, Candor forgive me.) I cannot say that the Kindness, the softness, the Tenderness, that constitutes the Characteristick Excellence of your sex, and for the Want of which no Abilities can atone, are very conspicuous Either in her Face, Air or Behaviour.

Is it not insufferable thus to remark on a Lady whose face I have once only and then but just seen and with whom I have only exchangd two or three Words? Shes a Buxom Lass however, and I own I longed for a Game of Romps with her, and should infallibly have taken one, only I thought the Dress I was in, the Air I had breathd and especially the Medicine I had taken, would not very greatly please a Lady, a stranger, of much Delicacy. Poll. Palmer and I shall unquestionably go to romping very soon.

Perkins, Sprague and Lord, are the Physicians that attend this House. Each has a few Particulars in Point of Diet, in which he differs from the others, and Each has Pills and Powders, different from the others to administer, different at least in size, and shape and Colour. I like my own vastly the best, tho Dr. Lord is really a Man of sense.

I fear I must write less than I have done. The Drs. dont approve it. They will allow of nothing scarcly but the Card Table, Chequer Bord, Flute, Violin, and singing, unless, Tittle Tattle, Roll and Tumble, shuttle Cock &c.

Pray write as often as you can to yr. John Adams

AS to JA

Sir Sunday Noon Weymouth April th 15 1764

Mr. Cranch informs me that Hones will go to Town tomorrow, and that I may not miss one opportunity, have now taken my pen to thank you for yours by Tom, and also for that which I have just now received by Mr. Ayres. You seem in high Spirits at which you know I rejoice. Your minute description of the persons you have seen, are very entertaining to me. I cannot consent you should omit writing, unless you find it prejudicial to your Health, if so I have not a word more to say. But, if amusement is all they require, why is not one amusement as good as an other, it may be those who forbid you cannot conceive that writing to a Lady is any amusement, perhaps they rank it under the Head of drudgery, and hard Labour.

However all I insist upon is that you follow that amusement which is most agreable to you whether it be Cards, Chequers, Musick, Writing, or Romping.

May not I hear from you by Hones? I shall take all possible care that the Letters I receive be well smoked before I venture upon them, enclose the Letters in a cover, but seal only the out side, Tom makes bungling work opening them, and tares them sadly.

As to any other of the familys being endangerd by them, there is no fear of that, they are very good, and let me enjoy my Letters to myself unless I vouchsafe they should see them. So Miser like I hoard them up, and am not very communicative.

Your Mamma doubtless would rejoice to hear from you, if you write you may enclose to me, I will take good care of it, if you want any thing I can serve you in, let me know, have you milk eno? You have a large number, who I suppose live upon it, write me if it would be agreable to You to have some.

Tis meeting time, the Bell rings. Adieue, my Friend—My —— add what else you please. And always believe me What I really am Your own

A Smith

AS to JA

My Friend

Weymouth April th 16 1764

I think I write to you every Day. Shall not I make my Letters very cheep; don't you light your pipe with them? I care not if you do, tis a pleasure to me to write, yet I wonder I write to you with so little restraint, for as a critick I fear you more than any other person on Earth, and tis the only character, in which I ever did, or ever will fear you. What say you? Do you approve of that Speach? Dont you think me a Courageous Being? Courage is a laudable, a Glorious Virtue in your Sex, why not in mine? (For my part, I think you ought to applaud me for mine.)—Exit Rattle.

Solus your Diana.

And now pray tell me how you do, do you feel any venom working in your veins, did you ever before experience such a feeling?—This Letter will be made up with questions I fancy—not set in order before you neither.—How do you employ yourself? Do you go abroad yet? Is it not cruel to bestow those favours upon others which I should rejoice to receive, yet must be deprived of?

I have lately been thinking whether my Mamma—when I write again I will tell you Something. Did not you receive a Letter to Day by Hones?

This is a right Girls Letter, but I will turn to the other side and be sober, if I can—but what is bred in the bone will never be out of the flesh, (as Lord M would have said).

As I have a good opportunity to send some Milk, I have not waited for your *orders*; least if I should miss this, I should not catch such an other. If you want more balm, I can supply you.

Adieu, evermore remember me with the tenderest affection, which is also borne unto you by Your —— A Smith

To the testimony John Adams gives on the efficacy of inoculation and the risks of refusing it, may be added the figures furnished by the town of Boston when the epidemic had run its course. These show that of those who neither fled nor were inoculated, 699 caught the smallpox and 124 died, that is to say, more than one in six. Of the 4,977 who stayed or flocked into Boston to be inoculated, only 46, or fewer than one in a hundred, died.

JA to AS

Tuesday 17th. April 1764

Yours of April 15th. this moment received. I thank You for it—and for your offer of Milk, but We have Milk in vast Abundance, and every Thing else that we want except Company.

You cant imagine how finely my Brother and I live. We have, as much Bread and as much new pure Milk, as much Pudding, and Rice, and indeed as much of every Thing of the farinaceous Kind as We please—and the Medicine We take is not att all nauseous, or painfull.

And our Felicity is the greater, as five Persons in the same Room, under the Care of Lord And Church, are starved and medicamented with the utmost severity. No Bread, No Pudding, No Milk is permitted them, i.e. no pure and simple Milk, (they are allowed a Mixture of Half Milk and Half Water) and every other Day they are tortured with Powders that make them as sick as Death and as weak as Water. All this may be necessary for them for what I know, as Lord is professedly against any Preparation previous to Inoculation. In which opinion I own I was fully agreed with him, till lately. But Experience has convinced me of my Mistake, and I have felt and now feel every Hour, the Advantage and the Wisdom of the contrary Doctrine.

Dr. Tufts and your Brother have been here to see Us this Morning. They are charmingly well and chearfull, tho they are lean and weak.

Messrs. Quincy's Samuel and Josiah, have the Distemper very lightly. I asked Dr. Perkins how they had it. The Dr. answerd in the style of the Faculty "Oh Lord sir; infinitely light!" It is extreamly pleasing, says he, wherever we go We see every Body passing thro this tremendous Distemper, in the lightest, easiest manner, conceivable.

The Dr. meaned, those who have the Distemper by Inoculation in the new Method, for those who have it in the natural Way, are Objects of as much Horror, as ever. There is a poor Man, in this Neighbourhood, one Bass, now labouring with it, in the natural Way. He is in a good Way of Recovery, but is the most shocking sight, that can be seen. They say he is no more like a Man than he is like an Hog or an Horse—swelled to three times his size, black as bacon, blind as a stone. I had when I was first inoculated a great Curiosity to go and see him; but the Dr. said I had better not go out, and my Friends thought it would give me a disagreable Turn. My Unkle brought up one Vinal who has just recoverd of it in the natural Way to see Us, and show Us. His face is torn all to Pieces, and is as rugged as Braintree Commons.

This Contrast is forever before the Eyes of the whole Town, Yet it is said there are 500 Persons, who continue to stand it out, in spight of Experience, the Expostulations of the Clergy, both in private and from the Desk, the unwearied Persuasions of the select Men, and the perpetual Clamour and astonishment of the People, and to expose themselves to this Distemper in the natural Way!—Is Man a rational Creature think You?—Conscience, forsooth and scruples are the Cause. —I should think my self, a deliberate self Murderer, I mean that I incurred all the Guilt of deliberate self Murther, if I should only stay in this Town and run the Chance of having it in the natural Way.

Mr. Wheat is broke out, and is now at the Card Table to amuze himself. He will not be able to get above a score or two. Badger has been pretty lazy and lolling, and achy about the Head and Knees and Back, for a Day or two, and the Messengers appear upon him, that foretell the compleat Appearance of the Pox in about 24. Hours.

Thus We see others, Under the symptoms, and all the Pains that attend the Distemper, under the present Management, every Hour, and are neither dismayed nor in the least disconcerted, or dispirited. But are every one of Us wishing that his Turn might come next, that it might be over, and we about our Business, and I return to my Farm, my Garden, but above all, to my Diana who is the best of all Friends, And the Richest of all Blessings to her own Lysander

How shall I express my Gratitude to your Mamma and your self, for your Kind Care and Concern for me. Am extreamly obliged for the Milk, and the Apples. But would not have you trouble yourselves any more for We have a sufficient, a plentiful supply, of those, and every other good Thing that is permitted Us. Balm is a Commodity in very great Demand and very scarce, here, and there is a great Number of

Us to drink of its inspiring Infusion, so that my Unkle, Aunt, and all the Patients under their Roof would be obligd, as well as myself, if you could send me some more.

I received Your agreable Favour by Hannes, this Morning, and had but just finished My Answer to it, when I received the other, by Tom.

I never receive a Line from you without a Revivification of Spirits, and a joyful Heart. I long to hear that—something you promissed to tell me, in your next. What can that Thing be? thought I. My busy fancy will be speculating and conjecturing about it, night and day, I suppose, till your next Letter shall unriddle the Mystery. You are a wanton, malicious, what shall I call you for putting me in this Puzzle and Teaze for a day or two, when you might have informd me in a Minute.

You had best reconsider and retract that bold speech of yours I assure You. For I assure you there is another Character, besides that of Critick, in which, if you never did, you always hereafter shall fear me, or I will know the Reason why.

Oh. Now I think on't I am determined very soon to write you, an Account in minute Detail of the many Faults I have observed in you. You remember I gave you an Hint that I had observed some, in one of my former Letters. You'l be surprized, when you come to find the Number of them.

By the Way I have heard since I came to Town an Insinuation to your Disadvantage, which I will inform you off, as soon as you have unravelled Your Enigma.

We have very litle News, and very little Conversation in Town about any Thing, but the Adulterated Callomel that kill'd a Patient at the Castle, as they say. The Town divides into Parties about it, and Each Party endeavours to throw the Blame, as usual, where his Interest, or Affections, prompt him to wish it might go.

Where the Blame will center, or where the Quarrell will terminate, I am not able to foresee.

The Persons talked of are Dr. Gelston, Mr. Wm. Greenleaf, the Apothecary who married Sally Quincy, and the Serjeant, French a Braintree man, who is said to have caried the Druggs from the Apothecary to the Physician. But I think the Serjeant is not much suspected. After all, whether any Body att all is to blame, is with me a dispute.

Make my Compliments to all the formall, give my Duty to all the honourable, and my Love to all the Friendly, whether at Germantown, Weymouth or Elsewhere, that enquire after me, and believe me to be with unalterable Affection Yr. J. Adams

AS to JA

Thursday Eve.—Weymouth April th 19 1764

Why my good Man, thou hast the curiosity of a Girl. Who could have believed that only a slight hint would have set thy imagination a gig in such a manner. And a fine encouragement I have to unravel the Mistery as thou callest it. Nothing less truly than to be told Something to my disadvantage. What an excellent reward that will be? In what Court of justice did'st thou learn that equity? I thank thee Friend such knowledg as that is easy eno' to be obtained without paying for it. As to the insinuation, it doth not give me any uneasiness, for if it is any thing very bad, I know thou dost not believe it. I am not conscious of any harm that I have done, or wished to any Mortal. I bear no Malice to any Being. To my Enimies, (if any I have) I am willing to afford assistance; therefore towards Man, I maintain a Conscience void of offence.

Yet by this I mean not that I am faultless, but tell me what is the Reason that persons had rather acknowledg themselves guilty, than be accused by others. Is it because they are more tender of themselves, or because they meet with more favor from others, when they ingenuously confess. Let that be as it will there is something which makes it more agreeable to condemn ourselves than to be condemned by others.

But altho it is vastly disagreeable to be accused of faults, yet no person ought to be offended when such accusations are deliverd in the Spirit of Friendship.—I now call upon you to fullfill your promise, and tell me all my faults, both of omission and commission, and all the Evil you either know, or think of me, be to me a second conscience, nor put me off to a more convenient Season. There can be no time more proper than the present, it will be harder to erase them when habit has strengthned and confirmd them.

Do not think I triffle. These are really meant as words of Truth and Soberness—for the present good Night.

Fryday Morning April th 20

What does it signify, why may not I visit you a Days as well as Nights? I no sooner close my Eyes than some invisible Being, swift as the Alborack of Mahomet, bears me to you. I see you, but cannot make my self visible to you. That tortures me, but it is still worse when I do not come for I am then haunted by half a dozen ugly Sprights. One will catch me and leep into the Sea, an other will carry me up a precipice (like that which Edgar describes to Lear,) then toss me down, and were I not then light as the Gosemore I should shiver into atoms—an other will be pouring down my throat stuff worse than the witches Broth in Macbeth.—Where I shall be carried next I know not, but I had rather have the small pox by inoculation half a dozen times, than be sprighted about as I am. What say you can you give me any encouragement to come? By the time you receive this hope from experience you will be able to say that the distemper is but a triffle. Think you I would not endure a triffle for the pleasure of seeing Lysander, yes were it ten times that triffle I would.—But my own inclinations must not be followed—to Duty I sacrifice them. Yet O my Mamma forgive me if I say, you have forgot, or never knew—but hush.—And do you Lysander excuse me that something I promis'd you, since it was a Speach more undutifull than that which I Just now stop'd my self in—for the present good by.

Fryday Evening

I hope you smoke your Letters well, before you deliver them. Mamma is so fearful least I should catch the distemper, that she hardly ever thinks the Letters are sufficently purified. Did you never rob a Birds nest? Do you remember how the poor Bird would fly round and round, fearful to come nigh, yet not know how to leave the place —just so they say I hover round Tom whilst he is smokeing my Letters.

But heigh day Mr. whats your Name?—who taught you to threaten so vehemently "a Character besides that of critick, in which if I never did, I always hereafter shall fear you."

Thou canst not prove a villan, imposible. I therefore still insist upon it, that I neither do, nor can fear thee. For my part I know not that there is any pleasure in being feard, but if there is, I hope you will be so generous as to fear your Diana that she may at least be made sensible of the pleasure.

Mr. Ayers will bring you this Letter, and the *Bag*. Do no[t] repine—it is fill'd with Balm.

Here is Love, respects, regards, good wishes—a whole waggon load of them sent you from all the good folks in the Neighbourhood.

To morrow makes the 14th Day. How many more are to come? I dare not trust my self with the thought. Adieu. Let me hear from you by Mr. Ayers, and excuse this very bad writing, if you had mended my pen it would have been better, once more adieu. Gold and Silver have I none, but such as I have, give I unto thee—which is the affectionate Regard of Your A Smith

JA to AS

Boston April 26th. 1764

Many have been the particular Reasons against my Writing for several days past, but one general Reason has prevailed with me more than any other Thing, and that was, an Absolute Fear to send a Paper from this House, so much infected as it is, to any Person lyable to take the Distemper but especially to you. I am infected myself, and every Room in the House, has infected People in it, so that there is real Danger, in Writing.

However I will write now, and thank you for yours of Yesterday. Mr. Ayers told you the Truth. I was comfortable, and have never been otherwise. I believe, None of the Race of Adam, ever passed the small Pox, with fewer Pains, Achs, Qualms, or with less smart than I have done. I had no Pain in my Back, none in my side, none in my Head. None in my Bones or Limbs, no reching or vomiting or sickness. A short shivering Fit, and a succeeding hot glowing Fit, a Want of Appetite, and a general Languor, were all the symptoms that ushered into the World, all the small Pox, that I can boast of, which are about Eight or Ten, (for I have not yet counted them exactly) two of which only are in my Face, the rest scattered at Random over my Limbs and Body. They fill very finely and regularly, and I am as well, tho not so strong, as ever I was in my Life. My Appetite has returned, and is quick enough and I am returning gradually to my former Method of Living.

Very nearly the same may be said of my Brother excepting that, he looks leaner than I, and that he had more sickness and Head Ach about the Time of the Eruption than I.

Such We have Reason to be thankful has been our Felicity. And that of Deacon Palmers Children has been, nearly the same. But others in the same House have not been so happy—pretty high Fevers, and severe Pains, and a pretty Plentiful Eruption has been the Portion of Three at last of our Companions. I join with you sincerely in your Lamentation that you were not inoculated. I wish to God the Dr. would sett up an Hospital at Germantown, and inoculate you. I will come and nurse you, nay I will go with you to the Castle or to Point Shirley, or any where and attend you. You say rightly safety there is not, and I say, safety there never will be. And Parents must be lost in Avarice or Blindness, who restrain their Children.

I believe there will be Efforts to introduce Inoculation at Germantown, by Drs. Lord and Church.

However, be carefull of taking the Infection unawares. For all the Mountains of Peru or Mexico I would not, that this Letter or any other Instrument should convey the Infection to you at unawares.

I hope soon to see you, mean time write as often as possible to yrs.,

John Adams

P.S. Dont conclude from any Thing I have written that I think

Inoculation a light matter.—A long and total Abstinence from every Thing in Nature that has any Taste, Two heavy Vomits, one heavy Cathartick, four and twenty Mercurial and Antimonial Pills, and Three Weeks close Confinement to an House, are, according to my Estimation of Things, no small matters.—However, who would not chearfully submit to them rather than pass his whole Life in continual Fears, in subjection, under Bondage.

Sylvia and Myra send Compliments.

AS to JA

Dear Lysander Weymouth April 30. 1764

Your Friendly Epistle reach'd me a fryday morning, it came like an Infernal Mesenger, thro fire and Brimstone, Yet it brought me tidings of great joy. With gratitude may this month be ever rememberd by Diana. You have been peculiarly favourd, and may be numberd with those who have had the distemper lightest. What would I give that I was as well thro it. I thank you for your offerd Service, but you know that I am not permitted to enjoy the benifit of it.

Yesterday the Dr. returnd to our no small Satisfaction. I think there is but one person upon Earth, the Sight of whom would have more rejoiced me. But "not Sight alone would please." It would therefore be adviseable to keep at an unseeable distance till any approach would not endanger.

I was yesterday at the Meeting of a Gentleman and his Lady. Cloathe[s] all shifted—no danger—and no fear. A how do ye, and a how do ye, was exchanged between them, a Smile, and a good naturd look. Upon my word I believe they were glad to see each other. A tender meeting. I was affected with it. And thought whether Lysander, under like circumstances could thus coldly meet his Diana, and whether Diana could with no more Emotion receive Lysander. What think you. I dare answer for a different meeting on her part were She under no restraint. When may that meeting be? Hear you have sent for your Horse, the Doctor tells me that you rode out a friday, do not venture abroad too soon, very bad winds for invalids tho I hear you stand it like an oak.—O by the way you have not told me that insinuation to my disadvantage which you promised me. Now methinks I see you criticizeing—What upon Earth is the Girl after. Where is the connexion between my standing the distemper like an oak, and an insinuation to her disadvantage?—Why I did not expect that a short sighted mortal would comprehend it, it was a Complex Idea if I may so express myself. And in my mind there was a great connexion. I will show you how it came about. "I did expect this purgation of

Lysander would have set us on a level and have renderd him a Sociable creature, but Ill Luck, he stands it like an oak, and is as haughty as ever." Now mentioning one part of this Sentance, brought to mind the accusation of haughtiness, and your faults naturally lead me to think of my own. But here look yee. I have more than insinuations against you. "An intolerable forbiding expecting Silence, which lays such a restraint upon but moderate Modesty that tis imposible for a Stranger to be tranquil in your presence." What say you to that charge? Deny it not, for by experience I know it to be true. Yes to this day I feel a greater restraint in your Company, than in that of allmost any other person on Earth, but thought I had reasons by myself to account for it, and knew not that others were affected in the same manner till a late complaint was enterd against you. Is there any thing austere in your countanance? Indeed I cannot recollect any thing. Yet when I have been most pained I have throughly studied it, but never could discover one trace of the severe. Must it not then be something in Behaviour, (ask Silvia, (not Arpasia for these are not her complaints) what it is) else why should not I feel as great restraint when I write. But to go on, "Why did he read Grandison, the very reverse in practice. Sir Charles call'd forth every one's excellencies, but never was a thought born in Lysanders presence." Unsociable Being, is an other charge. Bid a Lady hold her Tongue when she was tenderly inquireing after your wellfare, why that sounds like want of Breeding. It looks not like Lysander for it wears the face of ingratitude.—I expect you [to] clear up these matters, without being in the least saucy.

As to the charge of Haughtiness I am certain that is a mistake, for if I know any thing of Lysander, he has as little of that in his disposition, as he has of Ill nature. But for Saucyness no Mortal can match him, no not even His Diana

JA to AS

Boston May 7th. 1764

I promised you, Sometime agone, a Catalogue of your Faults, Imperfections, Defects, or whatever you please to call them. I feel at present, pretty much at Leisure, and in a very suitable Frame of Mind to perform my Promise. But I must caution you, before I proceed to recollect yourself, and instead of being vexed or fretted or thrown into a Passion, to resolve upon a Reformation—for this is my sincere Aim, in laying before you, this Picture of yourself.

In the first Place, then, give me leave to say, you have been extreamly negligent, in attending so little to Cards. You have very litle Inclination, to that noble and elegant Diversion, and whenever you have taken an Hand you have held it but aukwardly and played it, with a very uncourtly, and indifferent, Air. Now I have Confidence enough in your good sense, to rely upon it, you will for the future endeavour to make a better Figure in this elegant and necessary Accomplishment.

Another Thing, which ought to be mentioned, and by all means amended, is, the Effect of a Country Life and Education, I mean, a certain Modesty, sensibility, Bashfulness, call it by which of these Names you will, that enkindles Blushes forsooth at every Violation of Decency, in Company, and lays a most insupportable Constraint on the freedom of Behaviour. Thanks to the late Refinements of modern manners, Hypocrisy, superstition, and Formality have lost all Reputation in the World and the utmost sublimation of Politeness and Gentility lies, in Ease, and Freedom, or in other Words in a natural Air and Behaviour, and in expressing a satisfaction at whatever is suggested and prompted by Nature, which the aforesaid Violations of Decency, most certainly are.

In the Third Place, you could never yet be prevail'd on to learn to sing. This I take very soberly to be an Imperfection of the most moment of any. An Ear for Musick would be a source of much Pleasure, and a Voice and skill, would be a private solitary Amusement, of great Value when no other could be had. You must have remarked an Example of this in Mrs. Cranch, who must in all probability have been deafened to Death with the Cries of her Betcy, if she had not drowned them in Musick of her own.

In the Fourth Place you very often hang your Head like a Bulrush. You do not sit, erected as you ought, by which Means, it happens that you appear too short for a Beauty, and the Company looses the sweet smiles of that Countenance and the bright sparkles of those Eyes.—This Fault is the Effect and Consequence of another, still more inexcusable in a Lady. I mean an Habit of Reading, Writing and Thinking. But both the Cause and the Effect ought to be repented and amended as soon as possible.

Another Fault, which seems to have been obstinately persisted in, after frequent Remonstrances, Advices and Admonitions of your Friends, is that of sitting with the Leggs across. This ruins the figure and the Air, this injures the Health. And springs I fear from the former source vizt. too much Thinking.—These Things ought not to be!

A sixth Imperfection is that of Walking, with the Toes bending inward. This Imperfection is commonly called Parrot-toed, I think, I know not for what Reason. But it gives an Idea, the reverse of a bold and noble Air, the Reverse of the stately strutt, and the sublime Deportment.

Thus have I given a faithful Portraiture of all the Spotts, I have hitherto discerned in this Luminary. Have not regarded Order, but have painted them as they arose in my Memory. Near Three Weeks have I conned and studied for more, but more are not to be discovered. All the rest is bright and luminous.

Having finished the Picture I finish my Letter, lest while I am recounting Faults, I should commit the greatest in a Letter, that of tedious and excessive Length. There's a prettily turned Conclusion for You! from yr. Lysander

AS to JA

Weymouth May. th 9 1764

Welcome, Welcome thrice welcome is Lysander to Braintree, but ten times more so would he be at Weymouth, whither you are affraid to come.—Once it was not so. May not I come and see you, at least look thro a window at you? Should you not be glad to see your Diana? I flatter myself you would.

Your Brother brought your Letter, tho he did not let me see him, deliverd it the Doctor from whom received it safe. I thank you for your Catalogue, but must confess I was so hardned as to read over most of my Faults with as much pleasure, as an other person would have read their perfections. And Lysander must excuse me if I still persist in some of them, at least till I am convinced that an alteration would contribute to his happiness. Especially may I avoid that Freedom of Behaviour which according to the plan given, consists in Voilations of Decency, and which would render me unfit to Herd even with the Brutes. And permit me to tell you Sir, nor disdain to be a learner, that there is such a thing as Modesty without either Hypocricy or Formality.

As to a neglect of Singing, that I acknowledg to be a Fault which if posible shall not be complaind of a second time, nor should you have had occasion for it now, if I had not a voice harsh as the screech of a peacock.

The Capotal fault shall be rectified, tho not with any hopes of being lookd upon as a Beauty, to appear agreeable in the Eyes of Lysander, has been for Years past, and still is the height of my ambition.

The 5th fault, will endeavour to amend of it, but you know I think that a gentleman has no business to concern himself about the Leggs of a Lady, for my part I do not apprehend any bad effects from the practise, yet since you desire it, and that you may not for the future trouble Yourself so much about it, will reform.

The sixth and last can be cured only by a Dancing School.

But I must not write more. I borrow a hint from you, therefore will not add to my faults that of a tedious Letter—a fault I never yet had reason to complain of in you, for however long, they never were otherways than agreeable to your own A Smith

Released from his medical ordeal, John Adams "passed the summer of 1764 in Attending Court and pursuing my Studies with some Amusement on my little farm to which I was frequently making Additions." In September he was occupied in finding and engaging servants, and Abigail was in Boston acquiring house furnishings.

JA to AS

My dear Diana Septr. 30th. 1764

I have this Evening been to see the Girl.—What Girl? Pray, whát Right have you to go after Girls?—Why, my Dear, the Girl I mentioned to you, Miss Alice Brackett. But Miss has hitherto acted in the Character of an House-Keeper, and her noble aspiring Spirit had rather rise to be a Wife than descend to be a Maid.

To be serious, however, she says her Uncle, whose House she keeps cannot possibly spare her, these two Months, if then, and she has no Thoughts of leaving him till the Spring, when she intends for Boston to become a Mantua Maker.

So that We are still to seek. Girls enough from fourteen to four and Twenty, are mentioned to me, but the Character of every Mothers Daughter of them is as yet problematical to me. Hannah Crane (pray dont you want to have her, my Dear) has sent several Messages to my Mother, that she will live with you as cheap, as any Girl in the Country. She is stout and able and for what I know willing, but I fear not honest, for which Reason I presume you will think of her no more.

Another Girl, one Rachael Marsh, has been recommended to me as a clever Girl, and a neat one, and one that wants a Place. She was bred in the Family of one of our substantial Farmers and it is likely understands Country Business, But whether she would answer your Purposes, so well as another, I am somewhat in Doubt.

I have heard of a Number of younger Girls of Fourteen and thereabout, but these I suppose you would not choose.

It must therefore be left with you to make Enquiry, and determine for yourself. If you could hear of a suitable Person at Mistick or Newtown, on many Accounts she would be preferable to one, nearer home.

So much for Maids—now for the Man. I shall leave orders for Brackett, to go to Town, Wednesday or Thurdsday with an Horse Cart. You will get ready by that Time and ship aboard, as many Things as you think proper.

It happens very unfortunately that my Business calls me away at this Juncture for two Weeks together, so that I can take no Care at all about Help or Furniture or any Thing else. But Necessity has no Law.

Tomorrow Morning I embark for Plymouth—with a ⟨*fowl*⟩ disordered stomach, a pale Face, an Aching Head and an Anxious Heart. And What Company shall I find there? Why a Number of bauling Lawyers, drunken Squires, and impertinent and stingy Clients. If you realize this, my Dear, since you have agreed to run fortunes with me, you will submit with less Reluctance to any little Disappointments and Anxieties you may meet in the Conduct of your own Affairs.

I have a great Mind to keep a Register of all the stories, Squibbs, Gibes, and Compliments, I shall hear thro the whole Week. If I should I could entertain you with as much Wit, Humour, smut, Filth, Delicacy, Modesty and Decency, tho not with so exact Mimickry, as a certain Gentleman did the other Evening. Do you wonder, my Dear, why that Gentleman does not succeed in Business, when his whole study and Attention has so manifestly been engaged in the nobler Arts of smutt, Double Ententre, and Mimickry of Dutchmen and Negroes? I have heard that Imitators, tho they imitate well, Master Pieces in elegant and valuable Arts, are a servile Cattle. And that Mimicks are the lowest Species of Imitators, and I should think that Mimicks of Dutchmen and Negroes were the most sordid of Mimicks. If so, to what a Depth of the Profound have we plunged that Gentlemans Character. Pardon me, my dear, you know that Candour is my Characteristick—as it is undoubtedly of all the Ladies who are entertained with that Gents Conversation.

Oh my dear Girl, I thank Heaven that another Fortnight will restore you to me—after so long a separation. My soul and Body have both been thrown into Disorder, by your Absence, and a Month of two more would make me the most insufferable Cynick, in the World. I see nothing but Faults, Follies, Frailties and Defects in any Body, lately. People have lost all their good Properties or I my Justice, or Discernment.

But you who have always softened and warmed my Heart, shall restore my Benevolence as well as my Health and Tranquility of mind. You shall polish and refine my sentiments of Life and Manners, banish all the unsocial and ill natured Particles in my Composition, and form me to that happy Temper, that can reconcile a quick Discernment with a perfect Candour.

Believe me, now & ever yr. faithful Lysander

AS to JA

Sir

Boston Octobr. 4. 1764

I am much obliged to you for the care you have taken about help. I am very willing to submit to some inconveniences in order to lessen your expences, which I am sensible have run very high for these 12 months past and tho you know I have no particuliar fancy for Judah yet considering all things, and that your Mamma and you seem to think it would be best to take her, I shall not at present look out any further.

The cart you mentiond came yesterday, by which I sent as many things as the horse would draw the rest of my things will be ready the Monday after you return from Taunton. And—then Sir if you please you may take me. I hope by that time, that you will have recoverd your Health, together with your formour tranquility of mind. Think you that the phylosopher who laught at the follies of mankind did not pass thro' life with more ease and pleasure, than he who weept at them, and perhaps did as much towards a reformation. Tis true that I have had a good deal of fatigue in my own affair since I have been in town, but when I compare that with many other things that might have fallen to my Lot I am left without any Shadow of complaint. A few things, indeed I have meet with that have really discomposed me, one was haveing a corosive applied when a Lenitive would have answerd the same good purpose. But I hope I have drawn a lesson from that which will be useful to me in futurity, viz. never to say a severe thing because to a feeling heart they wound to deeply to be easily cured.—Pardon me this is not said for to recriminate, and I have only mentiond it, that when ever there is occasion a different method may be taken.

I do not think of any thing further to add, nor any thing new to tell you, for tis an old Story tho I hope as pleasing as it is true, to tell you that I am unfeignedly Your

Diana

Abigail Smith and John Adams were married on October 25, 1764. We have no account of the wedding. They went to live in the farmhouse (now known as the John Quincy Adams Birthplace), separated by a cartway from its very similar neighbor, John Adams' birthplace. Adams cut a doorway where a window had been and set up his law office and growing library on the ground floor. The Stamp Act evoked his first important literary effort, a series of papers published in the *Boston Gazette* in 1765 and later given the collective title *A Dissertation on the Canon and the Feudal Law.* These drew him, willy-nilly, deep into provincial politics.

A daughter, Abigail, was born in July 1765; a son, named for his great-grandfather Colonel John Quincy, the proprietor of Mount Wollaston, was born two years later. A second daughter, Susanna ("Suky"), was born at the end of 1768 but lived only fourteen months. Family—farm—the law—and the politics of protest against British encroachments on American rights engrossed the young parents' minds and energies during the next decade. How these interests jostled with one another and kept John Adams in a state of constant tension is suggested not only by his letters but by the entries here inserted from his Diary in 1771 and 1772 recording some of his moves between Braintree and Boston, where he first took his family and established a law office in 1768. His frequent resolutions to ignore politics during these years were always undone by events.

John Adams to Richard Cranch

Dr. sir September 23. 1767

I have but a few Moments, to congratulate you on the fresh Blessing to your Family.—Another fine Child and Sister comfortable! Oh fine! I know the Feeling as well as you and in Spight of your earlier Marriage, I knew it sooner than you.—Here you must own I have the Advantage of you.—But what shall we do with this young Fry?—In a little while Johnny must go to Colledge, and Nabby must have fine Cloaths, aye, and so must Betcy too and the other and all the rest. And very cleverly you and I shall feel when we recollect that we are hard at Work, over Watches and Lawsuits, and Johnny and Betcy at the same Time Raking and fluttering away our Profits. Aye, and there must be dancing Schools and Boarding Schools and all that, or else, you know, we shall not give them polite Educations, and they wil better not have been born you know than not have polite Educations.—These Inticipations are not very charming to me, and upon the whole I think it of more Consequence to have Children than to make them gay and genteel, so I conclude to proceed in my Endeavours for the former, and to lett the latter happen as it will. I am as ever your faithfull Friend & affectionate Brother, John Adams

JA to AA

Falmouth [29] June [1769],
I know not wt. day but it is
Thurdsday morning the first Week

My dearest

I embrace with Joy, this Opportunity of writing you. Mr. Langdon, who is to be the Bearer, was so good as to call this Morning, to know if I had any Letters to send. You'l therefore of Course, treat him civilly and give him Thanks. We are now but beginning the Business of Falmouth Court. The Weather has been for three days, so hot, as to render the Business of the Court very irksome, indeed, but we are in hopes it will now be cooler. How long I shall be obliged to stay here, I cant say. But you may depend I shall stay here no longer, than absolute Necessity requires. Nothing but the Hope of acquiring some little Matter for my dear Family, could carry me, thro these tedious Excursions.—How my Business at home may suffer I cant tell.—I hope to be in Boston before July C[our]t. If I should not, you will see that my Actions are entered.—Give my Love to my little Babes. Cant you contrive to go to Braintree to kiss my little Suky, for me. Respects, Compliments and Love to all who deserve them, and believe me, unalterably yours, John Adams

From John Adams' Diary

1771. APRIL 16. TUESDAY EVENING.

Last Wednesday my Furniture was all removed to Braintree. Saturday, I carried up my Wife and youngest Child, and spent the Sabbath there, very agreably. On the 20th. or 25th. of April 1768, I removed into Boston. In the 3 Years I have spent in that Town, have received innumerable Civilities, from many of the Inhabitants, many Expressions of their good Will both of a public and private Nature. Of these I have the most pleasing and gratefull Remembrance. I wish all the Blessings of this Life and that which is to come, to the worthy People there, who deserve from Mankind in general much better Treatment than they meet with. I wish to God it was in my Power to serve them, as much as it is in my Inclination.—But it is not.—My Wishes are impotent, my Endeavours fruitless and ineffectual, to them, and ruinous to myself. What are to be the Consequences of the Step I have taken Time only can discover. Whether they shall be prosperous or Adverse, my Design was good, and therefore I never shall repent it.

Monday Morning, I returned to Town and was at my Office before Nine, I find that I shall spend more Time in my Office than ever I did. Now my family is away, I feel no Inclination at all, no Temptation to be any where but at my Office. I am in it by 6 in the Morning—I am in it, at 9 at night—and I spend but a small Space of Time in running down to my Brothers to Breakfast, Dinner, and Tea.

Yesterday, I rode to Town from Braintree before 9, attended my Office till near two, then dined and went over the ferry to Cambridge, attended the House the whole Afternoon, returned, and spent the whole Evening in my Office, alone—and I spent the Time much more profitably, as well as pleasantly, than I should have done at Clubb.

This Evening is spending the same Way. In the Evening, I can be alone at my Office, and no where else. I never could in my family.

1771. FEB. [*i.e.* APRIL] 18. THURSDAY. FASTDAY.

Tuesday I staid at my Office in Town, Yesterday went up to Cambridge. Returned at Night to Boston, and to Braintree, still, calm, happy Braintree—at 9. o Clock at night. This Morning, cast my Eyes out to see what my Workmen had done in my Absence, and rode with my Wife over to Weymouth. There we are to hear young Blake—a pretty fellow.

SATURDAY [20 APRIL].

Fryday morning by 9 o Clock, arrived at my Office in Boston, and this Afternoon returned to Braintree. Arrived just at Tea time. Drank Tea with my Wife. Since this Hour a Week ago I have led a Life Active enough—have been to Boston twice, to Cambridge twice, to Weymouth once, and attended my office, and the Court too. But I shall be no more perplexed, in this Manner. I shall have no Journeys to make to Cambridge—no general Court to attend—But shall divide my Time between Boston and Braintree, between Law And Husbandry. Farewell Politicks.

Abigail Adams' cousin Isaac Smith Jr. had been a favorite correspondent of the Smith girls on bookish subjects for years. However, Abigail did not share, as her letter to him in London reveals, the political inclinations that would lead him ultimately into loyalism. Those inclinations make it doubtful that upon acquaintance he found much in common with Catharine Macaulay, admired by Abigail Adams not only as a woman writer but as a political radical.

Of "obstacles sufficent" to prevent her traveling very far, Abigail Adams now had an increasing number. Her third son, Charles, was born in May 1770; her fourth and last, Thomas Boylston, was to be born in September 1772.

Abigail Adams to Isaac Smith Jr.

Dear Sir | Braintree April the 20 1771

I write you, not from the Noisy Buisy Town, but from my humble Cottage in Braintree, where I arrived last Saturday and here again am to take up my abode.

"Where Contemplation p[l]umes her rufled Wings
And the free Soul look's down to pitty Kings."

Suffer me to snatch you a few moments from all the Hurry and tumult of London and in immagination place you by me that I may ask you ten thousand Questions, and bear with me Sir, tis the only recompence you can make for the loss of your Company.

From my Infancy I have always felt a great inclination to visit the Mother Country as tis call'd and had nature formed me of the other Sex, I should certainly have been a rover. And altho this desire has greatly diminished owing partly I believe to maturer years, but more to the unnatural treatment which this our poor America has received from her, I yet retain a curiosity to know what ever is valuable in her. I thank you Sir for the particular account you have already favourd me with, but you always took pleasure in being communicatively good.

Women you know Sir are considerd as Domestick Beings, and altho they inherit an Eaquel Share of curiosity with the other Sex, yet but few are hardy eno' to venture abroad, and explore the amaizing variety of distant Lands. The Natural tenderness and Delicacy of our Constitutions, added to the many Dangers we are subject too from your Sex, renders it almost imposible for a Single Lady to travel without injury to her character. And those who have a protecter in an Husband, have generally speaking obstacles sufficent to prevent their Roving, and instead of visiting other Countries; are obliged to content themselves with seeing but a very small part of their own. To your Sex we are most of us indebted for all the knowledg we acquire of Distant lands. As to a Knowledg of Humane Nature, I believe it may as easily be obtained in this Country, as in England, France or Spain. Education alone I conceive Constitutes the difference in Manners. Tis natural I believe for every person to have a partiality for their own Country. Dont you think this little Spot of ours better calculated for happiness than any other you have yet seen or read of. Would you exchange it for England, France, Spain or Ittally? Are not the people here more upon an Eaquality in point of knowledg and of circumstances—there being none so immensly rich as to Lord it over us, neither any so abjectly poor as to suffer for the necessaries of life provided they will use the means. It has heretofore been our boasted priviledg that we could sit under our own vine and Apple trees in peace enjoying the fruits of *our own labour*—but alass! the much dreaded change Heaven avert. Shall we ever wish to change Countries; to change conditions with the Affricans and the Laplanders for sure it were better never to have known the blessings of Liberty than to have enjoyed it, and then to have it ravished from us.

But where do I ramble? I only ask your ear a few moments longer. The Americans have been called a very religious people, would to Heaven they were so in earnest, but whatever they may have been I am affraid tis now only a negitive virtue, and that they are only a less vicious people. However I can quote Mr. Whitefield as an authority that what has been said of us is not without foundation. The last Sermon I heard him preach, he told us that he had been a very great traveller, yet he had never seen so much of the real appearence of Religion in any Country, as in America, and from your discription I immagine you join with him in Sentiment. I think Dr. Sherbear in his remarks upon the english Nation has some such observation as this. In London Religion seems to be periodical, like an ague which only returns once in Seven Days, and then attacks the inhabitants with the cold fit only, the burning never succeeds in this Country. Since which it seems they have found means to rid themselves intirely of the ague.—As to news I have none to tell you, nor any thing remarkable to entertain you with. But you Sir have every day new Scenes opening to you, and you will greatly oblige me by a recital of whatever you find worthy notice. I have a great desire to be made acquainted with Mrs. Maccaulays own history. One of my own Sex so eminent in a tract so uncommon naturally raises my curiosity and all I could ever learn relative to her, is this that she is a widdow Lady and Sister to Mr. Sawbridge. I have a curiosity to know her Education, and what first prompted her to engage in a Study never before Exibited to the publick by one of her own Sex and Country, tho now to the honour of both so admirably performed by her. As you are now upon the Spot, and have been entroduced to her acquaintance, you will I hope be able to satisfie me with some account, in doing which you will confer an oblagation upon your assured Friend, Abigail Adams

JA to AA

My Dr. Plymouth May Saturday 1772

I take an opportunity by Mr. Kent, to let you know that I am at Plymouth, and pretty well. Shall not go for Barnstable untill Monday.

There are now signs of a gathering Storm, so I shall make my self easy here for the Sabbath. I wish myself at Braintree. This wandering, itinerating Life grows more and more disagreable to me. I want to see my Wife and Children every Day, I want to see my Grass and Blossoms and Corn, &c. every Day. I want to see my Workmen, nay I almost want to go and see the Bosse Calfs's as often as Charles does. But above all except the Wife and Children I want to see my Books.

None of these Amusements are to be had. The Company we have is not agreable to me. In Coll. Warren and his Lady I find Friends, Mr. Angier is very good, but farther than these, I have very little

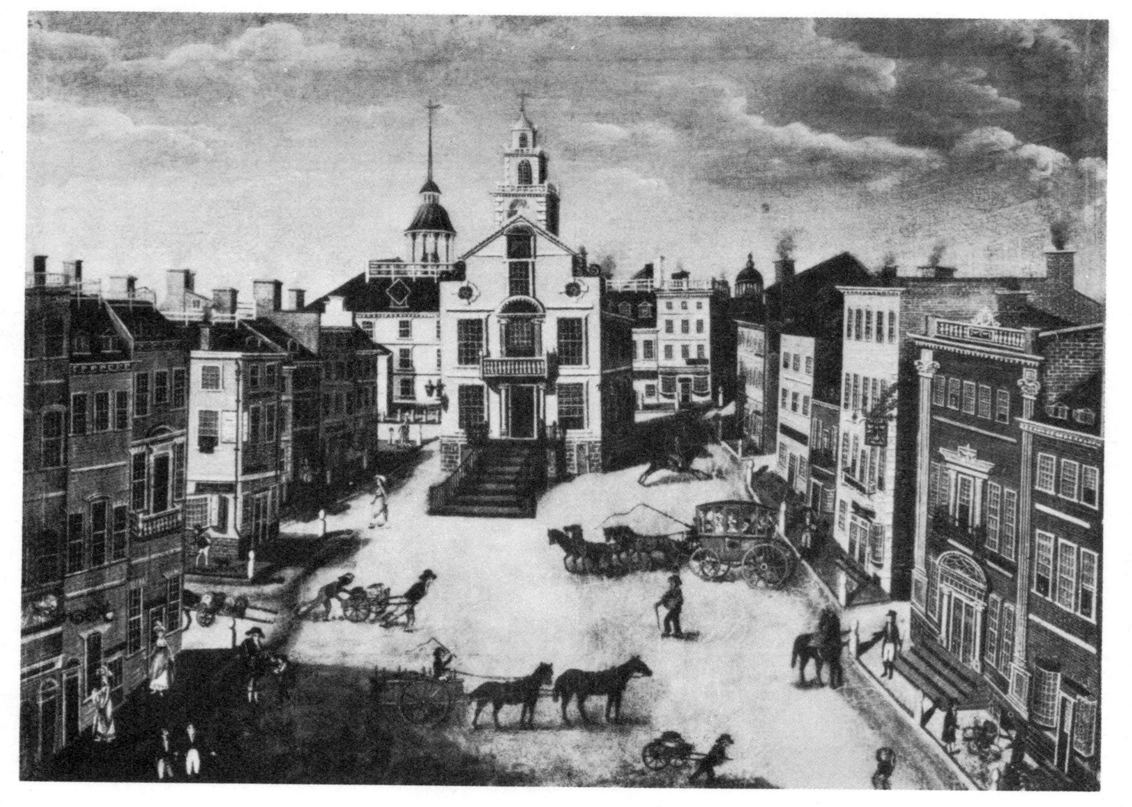

OLD STATE HOUSE, BOSTON

Pleasure in Conversation. Dont expect me, before Saturday.—Perhaps Mrs. Hutchinson may call upon you, in her Return to Boston, the later End of next Week or beginning of the Week after.

Pray let the People take Care of the Caterpillars. Let them go over and over, all the Trees, till there is not the appearance of a nest, or Worm left.

John Adams

From John Adams' Diary

1772. NOVR. 21.

Next Tuesday I shall remove my Family to Boston, after residing in Braintree about 19 Months. I have recovered a Degree of Health by this Excursion into the Country, tho I am an infirm Man yet. I hope I have profited by Retirement and Reflection!—and learned in what manner to live in Boston! How long I shall be able to stay in the City, I know not; if my Health should again decline, I must return to Braintree and renounce the Town entirely. I hope however to be able to stay there many Years! To this End I must remember Temperance, Exercise and Peace of Mind. Above all Things I must avoid Politicks, Political Clubbs, Town Meetings, General Court, &c. &c. &c.

I must ride frequently to Braintree to inspect my Farm, and when in Boston must spend my Evenings in my Office, or with my Family, and with as little Company as possible.

"Last Night," John Adams wrote in his Diary on December 17, 1773, "3 Cargoes of Bohea Tea were emptied into the Sea. . . . This is the most magnificent Movement of all. . . . I cant but consider it as an Epocha in History." Adams held that this first violent response to governmental measures had been absolutely necessary. "To let [the tea] be landed, would be giving up the Principle of Taxation by Parliamentary Authority, against which the Continent have struggled for 10 years." It would subject "ourselves and our Posterity forever to Egyptian Taskmasters." But as he presided among his "little flock" while Abigail visited her parents at Weymouth, he was bound to ask himself, "What Measures will the Ministry take, in Consequence of this?"

Parliament moved swiftly to punish the Bostonians. News of the Boston Port Act, passed March 31, 1774, reached America early in May. The act closed the port to all trade at the beginning of June and thus cut off the town's lifeline to its neighbors and the world. On May 13 General Thomas Gage arrived in Boston harbor to take over as a military governor and enforce a whole panoply of coercive acts.

AA to JA

Weymouth December 30 1773

Alass! How many snow banks devide thee and me and my warmest wishes to see thee will not melt one of them. I have not heard one Word from thee, or our Little ones since I left home. I did not take any cold comeing down, and find my self in better Health than I was. I wish to hear the same account from you. The Time I proposed to tarry has Elapsed. I shall soon be home sick. The Roads at present are impassible with any carriage. I shall not know how to content myself longer than the begining of Next week. [I nev]er left so large a flock of little ones before. You must write me how they all do. Tis now so near the Court that I have no expectation of seeing you here. My daily thoughts and Nightly Slumbers visit thee, and thine. I feel gratified with the immagination at the close of the Day in seeing the little flock round you inquiring when Mamma will come home—as they often do for thee in thy absence.

If you have any news in Town which the papers do not communicate, pray be so good as to Write it. We have not heard one Word respecting the Tea at the Cape or else where.

I have deliverd John the Bearer of this the key of your linnen. I hope you have been able to come at some by taking the Draw above it out. I should be obliged if you would send me that Book of Mr. Pembertons upon the Classicks and the progress of Dulness which is at Mr. Cranchs.

You will not fail in remembring me to our little ones and telling Johnny that his Grand mama has sent him a pair of mittins, and Charlly that I shall bring his when I come home. Our little Tommy you must kiss for Mamma, and bid Nabby write to me. Dont dissapoint me and let John return without a few lines to comfort the heart of Your affectionate

Abigail Adams

JA to AA

My Dear Boston May 12. 1774

I am extreamly afflicted with the Relation your Father gave me, of the Return of your Disorder. I fear you have taken some Cold; We have had a most pernicious Air, a great Part of this Spring. I am sure I have Reason to remember it—my Cold is the most obstinate and threatning one, I ever had in my Life: However, I am unwearied in my Endeavours to subdue it, and have the Pleasure to think I have had some Success. I rise at 5, walk 3 Miles, keep the Air all day and walk again in the Afternoon. These Walks have done me more good than any Thing, tho I have been constantly plied with Teas, and your Specific. My own Infirmities, the Account of the Return of yours, and the public News coming alltogether have put my Utmost Phylosophy to the Tryal.

We live my dear Soul, in an Age of Tryal. What will be the Consequence I know not. The Town of Boston, for ought I can see, must suffer Martyrdom: It must expire: And our principal Consolation is, that it dies in a noble Cause. The Cause of Truth, of Virtue, of Liberty and of Humanity: and that it will probably have a glorious Reformation, to greater Wealth, Splendor and Power than ever.

Let me know what is best for us to do. It is expensive keeping a Family here. And there is no Prospect of any Business in my Way in this Town this whole Summer. I dont receive a shilling a Week.

We must contrive as many Ways as we can, to save Expences, for We may have Calls to contribute, very largely in Proportion to our Circumstances, to prevent other very honest, worthy People from suffering for Want, besides our own Loss in Point of Business and Profit.

Dont imagine from all this that I am in the Dumps. Far otherwise. I can truly say, that I have felt more Spirits and Activity, since the Arrival of this News, than I had done before for years. I look upon this, as the last Effort of Lord Norths Despair. And he will as surely be defeated in it, as he was in the Project of the Tea.—I am, with great Anxiety for your Health your John Adams

Anticipating the civil and domestic commotions ahead, Adams early in 1774 purchased from his brother Peter their father's "Homestead" and the large farm that went with it. "A fine addition . . . of arable, and Meadow," he recorded with satisfaction. Keeping open only his office in his Queen Street house in Boston, he now moved his family back to Braintree and prepared them as best he could for the "Age of Tryal" that was upon them.

Attorney Adams continued on his court rounds during the spring and at the end of June "went for the tenth and last time on the Eastern Circuit" in Maine. He carried with him a new responsibility and a new source of worry. On June 17 the General Court, meeting behind barred doors to prevent a prorogation, elected a delegation from Massachusetts Bay to attend "a Meeting of Committees from the several Colonies . . . to consult upon the present State of the Colonies and the Miseries to which they are reduced by the Operation of certain Acts of Parliament respecting America." John Adams was one of the five delegates chosen to travel to Philadelphia for what became known to history as the First Continental Congress.

"I wander alone, and ponder," Adams wrote in his Diary. "I muse, I mope, I ruminate.—I am often In Reveries and Brown Studies.—The Objects before me, are too grand, and multifarious for my Comprehension.—We have not Men, fit for the Times. We are deficient in Genius, in Education, in Travel, in Fortune—in every Thing. I feel unutterable Anxiety.—God grant us Wisdom, and Fortitude!"

In his letters of late June and July these doubts about both personal and public adequacy, alternate with a kind of Roman resolution: "Vapours avaunt! I will do my Duty, and leave the Event."

JA to AA

My Dr. Ipswich June 23. 1774

I had a tollerable Journey hither, but my Horse trotted too hard. I miss my own Mare—however I must make the best of it.

I send with this an whole Packett of Letters, which are upon a Subject of great Importance, and therefore must intreat the earliest Conveyance of them.

There is but little Business here, and whether there will be more at York or Falmouth is uncertain, but I must take the Chance of them.

My Time, in these tedious Peregrinations, hangs heavily upon me. One half of it is always spent without Business, or Pleasure, or Diversion, or Books or Conversation. My Fancy and Wishes and Desires, are at Braintree, among my Fields, Pastures and Meadows, as much as those of the Israelites were among the Leeks, Garleeks and Onions of the Land of Goshen.

My Sons and Daughter too are missing, as well as their Mother, and I find nothing in any of my Rambles to supply their Place.

We have had a vast Abundance of Rain here this Week and hope you have had a Sufficiency with you. But the Plenty of it, will render the Making of Hay the more critical, and you must exhort Bracket to be vigilant, and not let any of the Grass suffer, if he can help it.

I wish you would converse with Brackett, and Mr. Hayden and Mr. Belcher about a proper Time to get me a few freights of Marsh Mud, Flatts, or Creek Mudd. I must have some If I pay the Cash for getting it, at almost any Price. But I wont be answerable again to Deacon Palmer, for the Schough. Whoever undertakes, shall hire that, and I will be chargeable to no Man but the Undertaker, and Labourers. I want a freight or two, soon, that it may be laid by the wall and mixed with Dust and Dung that it may ferment and mix as soon as may be, now the hot Weather is coming on.

I want to be at Home, at this Time, to consider about Dress, Servant, Carriage, Horses &c. &c. for a Journey. But ——. Kiss my sweet ones for me. Your

John Adams

JA to AA

My Dear York June 29. 1774

I have a great Deal of Leisure, which I chiefly employ in Scribbling, that my Mind may not stand still or run back like my Fortune.—There is very little Business here, and David Sewall, David Wyer, John Sullivan and James Sullivan and Theophilus Bradbury are the Lawyers who attend the Inferiour Courts and consequently conduct the Causes at the Superiour.

I find that the Country is the Situation to make Estates by the Law.

John Sullivan, who is placed at Durham in New Hampshire, is younger, both in Years and Practice than I am; He began with nothing, but is now said to be worth Ten thousand Pounds Lawfull Money, his Brother James allows five or six or perhaps seven thousand Pounds, consisting in Houses and Lands, Notes, Bonds, and Mortgages. He has a fine Stream of Water, with an excellent Corn Mill, Saw Mill, Fulling Mill, Scyth Mill and others, in all six Mills, which are both his Delight and his Profit. As he has earned Cash in his Business at the Bar, he has taken Opportunities, to purchase Farms of his Neighbours, who wanted to sell and move out farther into the Woods, at an Advantageous Rate. And in this Way, has been growing rich, and under the Smiles and Auspices of Governor Wentworth, has been promoted in the civil and military Way, so that he is treated with great Respect in this Neighbourhood.

James Sullivan, Brother of the other, who studied Law under him, without any Accademical Education, (and John was in the same Case,) is fixed at Saco, alias Biddeford in our Province. He began with neither Learning, Books, Estate or any Thing, but his Head and Hands, and is now a very popular Lawyer and growing rich very fast, purchasing great Farms &c., a Justice of the Peace, and Member of the General Court.

David Sewall of this Town never practices out of this County, has no Children, has no Ambition, nor Avarice they say, (however Quære). His Business in this County maintains him very handsomely, and he gets beforehand.

Bradbury at Falmouth, they say, grows rich very fast.

I was first sworn in 1758; My Life has been a continual Scæne of Fatigue, Vexation, Labour and Anxiety. I have four Children. I had a pretty Estate from my Father, I have been assisted by your Father. I have done the greatest Business in the Province. I have had the very richest Clients in the Province: Yet I am Poor in Comparison of others.

This I confess is grievous, and discouraging. I ought however, to be candid enough to acknowledge that I have been imprudent. I have spent an Estate in Books. I have spent a Sum of Money indiscreetly in a Lighter, another in a Pew, and a much greater in an House in Boston. These would have been Indiscretions, if the Impeachment of the Judges, the Boston Port Bill, &c. &c. had never happened; but by the unfortunate Interruption of my Business from these Causes, these Indiscretions become almost fatal to me, to be sure much more detrimental.

John Lowell, at Newbury Port, has built him an House, like the

Palace of a Nobleman and lives in great Splendor. His Business is very profitable. In short every Lawyer who [has] the least Appearance of Abilities makes it do in the Co[untry.] In Town, nobody does, or ever can, who Either is not obstinately determined never to have any Connection with Politicks or does not engage on the Side of the Government, the Administration and the Court.

Let us therefore my dear Partner, from that Affection which we feel for our lovely Babes, apply ourselves by every Way, we can, to the Cultivation of our Farm. Let Frugality, And Industry, be our Virtues, if they are not of any others. And above all Cares of this Life let our ardent Anxiety be, to mould the Minds and Manners of our Children. Let us teach them not only to do virtuously but to excell. To excell they must be taught to be steady, active, and industrious.

I am &c. your John Adams

JA to AA

York July 1st: 1774

I am so idle, that I have not an easy Moment, without my Pen in my Hand. My Time might have been improved to some Purpose, in mowing Grass, raking Hay, or hoeing Corn, weeding Carrotts, picking or shelling Peas. Much better should I have been employed in schooling my Children, in teaching them to write, cypher, Latin, French, English and Greek.

I sometimes think I must come to this—to be the Foreman upon my own Farm, and the School Master to my own Children. I confess myself to be full of Fears that the Ministry and their Friends and Instruments, will prevail, and crush the Cause and Friends of Liberty. The Minds of that Party are so filled with Prejudices, against me, that they will take all Advantages, and do me all the Damage they can. These Thoughts have their Turns in my Mind, but in general my Hopes are predominant.

In a Tryal of a Cause here to Day, some Facts were mentioned, which are worth writing to you. It was sworn, by Dr. Lyman, Elder Bradbury and others, that there had been a Number of Instances in this Town of fatal Accidents, happening from sudden Noises striking the Ears of Babes and young Children. A Gun was fired near one Child, as likely as any; the Child fell immediately into fits, which impaired his Reason, and is still living an Ideot. Another Child was sitting on a Chamber floor. A Man rapped suddenly and violently on the Boards which made the floor under the Child [tremble?]. The Child was so startled, and frightened, that it fell into fits, which never were cured.

This may suggest a Caution to keep Children from sudden Frights and surprizes.

Dr. Gardiner arrived here to day, from Boston, brings us News of a Battle at the Town Meeting, between Whigs and Tories, in which the Whiggs after a Day and an Halfs obstinate Engagement were finally victorious by two to one. He says the Tories are preparing a flaming Protest.

I am determined to be cool, if I can; I have suffered such Torments in my Mind, heretofore, as have almost overpowered my Constitution, without any Advantage: and now I will laugh and be easy if I can, let the Conflict of Parties, terminate as it will—let my own Estate and Interest suffer what it will. Nay whether I stand high or low in the Estimation of the World, so long as I keep a Conscience void of Offence towards God and Man. And thus I am determined by the Will of God, to do, let what will become of me or mine, my Country, or the World.

I shall arouse myself ere long I believe, and exert an Industry, a Frugality, a hard Labour, that will serve my family, if I cant serve my Country. I will not lie down and die in Dispair. If I cannot serve my Children by the Law, I will serve them by Agriculture, by Trade, by some Way, or other. I thank God I have a Head, an Heart and Hands which if once fully exerted alltogether, will succeed in the World as well as those of the mean spirited, low minded, fawning obsequious scoundrells who have long hoped, that my Integrity would be an Obstacle in my Way, and enable them to out strip me in the Race.

But what I want in Comparison of them, of Villany and servility, I will make up in Industry and Capacity. If I dont they shall laugh and triumph.

I will not willingly see Blockheads, whom I have a Right to despise, elevated above me, and insolently triumphing over me. Nor shall Knavery, through any Negligence of mine, get the better of Honesty, nor Ignorance of Knowledge, nor Folly of Wisdom, nor Vice of Virtue.

I must intreat you, my dear Partner in all the Joys and Sorrows, Prosperity and Adversity of my Life, to take a Part with me in the Struggle. I pray God for your Health—intreat you to rouse your whole Attention to the Family, the stock, the Farm, the Dairy. Let every Article of Expence which can possibly be spared be retrench'd. Keep the Hands attentive to their Business, and [let] the most prudent Measures of every kind be adopted and pursued with Alacrity and Spirit.

I am &c.,

John Adams

JA to AA

Falmouth July 6th: 1774

Our J[ustic]e H[utchinso]n is eternally giving his Political Hints. In a Cause, this Morning, Somebody named Captn. Mackay as a Refferee. I said "an honest Man!"—"Yes" says H[utchinso]n, "he's an honest Man, only *misled*.—He he he," blinking, and grinning.—At Dinner, to day, Somebody mentioned Determinations in the Lords House (the Court sitts in the Meeting House).—"I've known many very bad Determinations in the Lords House of late" says he, meaning a Fling upon the Clergy.—He is perpetually flinging about the Fasts, and ironically talking about getting Home to the Fast. A Gentleman told me, that he had heard him say frequently, that the Fast was perfect Blasphemy.—"Why dont they pay for the Tea? Refuse to pay for the Tea! and go to fasting and praying for Direction! perfect Blasphemy!"

This is the Moderation, Candor, Impartiality, Prudence, Patience, Forbearance, and Condescention of our J[ustic]e.

S[amuel] Q[uincy] said Yesterday, as Josa. told me, that he was for staying at home and not going to Meeting as they i.e. the Meetings are now managed.

Such is the Bitterness and Rancour, the Malice and Revenge, the Pride and Vanity which prevails in these Men. And such Minds are possessed of all the Power of the Province.

S. makes no Fortune this Court. There is very little Business here, it is true, but S. gets very little of that little—less than any Body.

Wyer retains his old good Nature and good Humour, his Wit, such as it is, and his Fancy, with its wildness.

Bradbury retains his Anxiety and his plaintive, angry Manner, David Sewal his Softness, and conceited Modesty.

Bradbury and Sewall always roast Dr. Gardiner, at these Courts, but they have done it more now than usual, as Gardiner had not me to protect him.—See how I think of myself!

I believe it is Time to think a little about my Family and Farm. The fine Weather, we have had for 8 or 10 days past I hope has been carefully improved to get in my Hay. It is a great Mortification to me that I could not attend every Step of their Progress in mowing, making and carting. I long to see what Burden.

But I long more still to see to the procuring more Sea Weed and Marsh Mud and Sand &c.

However my Prospect is interrupted again. I shall have no Time. I must prepare for a Journey to Philadelphia, a long Journey indeed! But if the Length of the Journey was all, it would be no burden. But the Consideration of What is to be done, is of great Weight. Great Things are wanted to be done, and little Things only I fear can be done. I dread the Thought of the Congress's falling short of the Expectations of the Continent, but especially of the People of this Province.

Vapours avaunt! I will do my Duty, and leave the Event. If I have the Approbation of my own Mind, whether applauded or censured, blessed or cursed, by the World, I will not be unhappy.

Certainly I shall enjoy good Company, good Conversation, and shall have a fine Ride, and see a little more of the World than I have seen before.

I think it will be necessary to make me up, a Couple of Pieces of new Linnen. I am told, they wash miserably, at N. York, the Jerseys and Philadelphia too in Comparison of Boston, and am advised to carry a great deal of Linnen.

Whether to make me a Suit of new Cloaths, at Boston or to make them at Phyladelphia, and what to make I know not, nor do I know how I shall go—whether on Horse back, in a Curricle, a Phaeton, or altogether in a Stage Coach I know not.

The Letters I have written or may write, my Dear, must be kept secret or at least shewn with great Caution.

Mr. Fairservice goes tomorrow: by him I shall send a Packett.

Kiss my dear Babes for me. Your John Adams

I believe I forgot to tell you one Anecdote: When I first came to this House it was late in the Afternoon, and I had ridden 35 miles at least. "Madam" said I to Mrs. Huston, "is it lawfull for a weary Traveller to refresh himself with a Dish of Tea provided it has been honestly smuggled, or paid no Duties?"

"No sir, said she, we have renounced all Tea in this Place. I cant make Tea, but I'le make you Coffee." Accordingly I have drank Coffee every Afternoon since, and have borne it very well. Tea must be universally renounced. I must be weaned, and the sooner, the better.

Justice Foster Hutchinson, whose jibes at the patriot cause are mentioned in the preceding letter, is to be distinguished from his brother, Governor Thomas Hutchinson, mentioned below. It was the Governor's departure for England that had occasioned an outpouring of expressions of personal respect from those most antipathetic to the patriots. Publication in broadside form of their names, embellished with contemptuous characterizations, provided a handy record of those who supported Hutchinson's views and actions.

The "famous Cause" in which Adams was engaged was as attorney for the plaintiff in King *v.* Stewart *et al.* Richard King, a well-to-do and evidently arrogant storekeeper and timber-exporter, had taken the government's side during the Stamp Act disturbances. On a March night in 1766 a mob of his fellow townsmen, including some who considered themselves harassed by King because they owed him money, vandalized his house. In an emotional appeal to the jury, John Adams denounced all such acts of private vengeance and won a judgment for King.

JA to AA

My Dear Falmouth July 7th: 1774

Have you seen a List of the Addressers of the late Governor? There is one abroad, with the Character, Profession or Occupation of each Person against his Name. I have never seen it but Judge Brown says, against the Name of Andrew Fanuil Phillips, is "Nothing," and that Andrew when he first heard of it said, "Better be nothing with one Side, than every Thing with the other."—This was witty and smart, whether Andrew said it, or what is more likely, it was made for him.

A Notion prevails among all Parties that it is politest and genteelest to be on the Side of Administration, that the *better Sort*, the *Wiser Few*, are on one Side; and that the Multitude, the Vulgar, the Herd, the Rabble, the Mob only are on the other. So difficult it is for the frail feeble Mind of Man to shake itself loose from all Prejudices and Habits. However Andrew, or his Prompter is perfectly Right, in his Judgment, and will finally be proved to be so, that the lowest on the Tory Scale, will make it more for his Interest than the highest on the Whiggish. And as long as a Man Adhers immoveably to his own Interest, and has Understanding or Luck enough to secure and promote it, he will have the Character of a Man of Sense And will be respected by a selfish World. I know of no better Reason for it than this—that most Men are conscious that they aim at their own Interest only, and that if they fail it is owing to short Sight or ill Luck, and therefore cant blame, but secretly applaud, admire and sometimes envy those whose Capacities have proved greater and Fortunes more prosperous.

I am to dine with Mr. Waldo, to day. Betty, as you once said.

I am engaged in a famous Cause: The Cause of King, of Scarborough vs. a Mob, that broke into his House, and rifled his Papers, and terrifyed him, his Wife, Children and Servants in the Night. The Terror, and Distress, the Distraction and Horror of this Family cannot be described by Words or painted upon Canvass. It is enough to move a Statue, to melt an Heart of Stone, to read the Story. A Mind susceptible of the Feelings of Humanity, an Heart which can be touch'd with Sensibi[li]ty for human Misery and Wretchedness, must reluct, must burn with Resentment and Indignation, at such outragious Injuries. These private Mobs, I do and will detest. If Popular Commotions can be justifyed, in Opposition to Attacks upon the Constitution, it can be only when Fundamentals are invaded, nor then unless for absolute Necessity and with great Caution. But these Tarrings and Featherings, these breaking open Houses by rude and insolent Rabbles, in Resentment for private Wrongs or in pursuance of private Prejudices and Passions, must be discountenanced, cannot be even excused upon any Principle which can be entertained by a good Citizen—a worthy Member of Society.

Dined With Mr. Collector Francis Waldo, Esqr. in Company with Mr. Winthrop, the two Quincys and the two Sullivans. All very social and chearfull—full of Politicks. S. Quincy's Tongue ran as fast as any Bodies. He was clear in it, that the House of Commons had no Right to take Money out of our Pocketts, any more than any foreign State—repeated large Paragraphs from a Publication of Mr. Burke's in 1766, and large Paragraphs from Junius Americanus &c. This is to talk and to shine, before Persons who have no Capacity of judging, and who do not know that he is ignorant of every Rope in the Ship.

I shant be able to get away, till next Week. I am concerned only in 2 or 3 Cases and none of them are come on yet. Such an Eastern Circuit I never made. I shall bring home as much as I brought from home I hope, and not much more, I fear.

I go mourning in my Heart, all the Day long, tho I say nothing. I am melancholly for the Public, and anxious for my Family, as for myself a Frock and Trowsers, an Hoe and Spade, would do for my Remaining Days.

For God Sake make your Children, *hardy, active* and *industrious*, for Strength, Activity and Industry will be their only Resource and Dependance.

John Adams

II

AUGUST 1774 ~ MAY 1776

Tis a dreadful time with this whole province.
— Abigail Adams

You are really brave, my dear, you are an Heroine.
— John Adams

PLAN OF THE TOWN AND HARBOUR OF BOSTON AND THE COUNTRY ADJACENT
(Braintree and Weymouth are at lower right)

On his return to Braintree from Maine in mid-July, John Adams went to "mowing, raking, carting, and frolicking with my Workmen." Thus he reported his activities to his intimate friend and correspondent, James Warren of Plymouth, whose literary wife, Mercy Otis Warren, was an equally faithful correspondent of Abigail Adams.

There were other matters requiring attention before he departed for Philadelphia. Confidants such as Abigail's uncle Norton Quincy of Mount Wollaston were to be consulted, family and friends to be seen. Some provision had to be made for the four young men who were reading law with Adams: Edward Hill and Jonathan Williams at his office in Boston, Nathan Rice and John Thaxter in Braintree. Rice would keep the town school before enlisting. Thaxter, a cousin of Mrs. Adams, would become tutor to young John Quincy Adams, thus beginning a relationship that was renewed in Europe during Thaxter's service as secretary to John Adams.

On August 10 four of the delegates from Massachusetts to the Congress set out from Boston "in a coach and four, preceded by two white servants well mounted and arm'd, with four blacks behind in livery, two on horseback and two footmen." The correspondence between Philadelphia and Braintree that ensued was conducted with substantial regularity on both sides, though with occasional interception of letters by the British or tories despite the writers' best efforts to guard against such "foul Play."

AA to JA

Braintree August 19 1774

The great distance between us, makes the time appear very long to me. It seems already a month since you left me. The great anxiety I feel for my Country, for you and for our family renders the day tedious, and the night unpleasent. The Rocks and quick Sands appear upon every Side. What course you can or will take is all wrapt in the Bosom of futurity. Uncertainty and expectation leave the mind great Scope. Did ever any Kingdom or State regain their Liberty, when once it was invaded without Blood shed? I cannot think of it without horror.

Yet we are told that all the Misfortunes of Sparta were occasiond by their too great Sollicitude for present tranquility, and by an excessive love of peace they neglected the means of making it sure and lasting. They ought to have reflected says Polibius that as there is nothing more desirable, or advantages than peace, when founded in justice and honour, so there is nothing more shameful and at the same time more pernicious when attained by bad measures, and purchased at the price of liberty.

I have received a most charming Letter from our Friend Mrs. W[arre]n. She desires me to tell you that her best wishes attend you thro your journey both as a Friend and patriot—hopes you will have no uncommon difficulties to surmount or Hostile Movements to impeade you—but if the Locrians should interrupt you, she hop[e]s you will beware that no future Annals may say you chose an ambitious Philip for your Leader, who subverted the noble order of the American Amphyctions, and built up a Monarchy on the Ruins of the happy institution.

I have taken a very great fondness for reading Rollin's ancient History since you left me. I am determined to go thro with it if posible in these my days of solitude. I find great pleasure and entertainment from it, and I have perswaided Johnny to read me a page or two every day, and hope he will from his desire to oblige me entertain a fondness for it.—We have had a charming rain which lasted 12 hours and has greatly revived the dying fruits of the earth.

I want much to hear from you. I long impatiently to have you upon the Stage of action. The first of September or the month of September, perhaps may be of as much importance to Great Britan as the Ides of March were to Ceaser. I wish you every Publick as well, as private blessing, and that wisdom which is profitable both for instruction and edification to conduct you in this difficult day.—The little flock remember Pappa; and kindly wish to see him. So does your most affectionate

Abigail Adams

JA to AA

My Dr. Prince Town New Jersey Aug. 28th. 1774

I received your kind Letter, at New York, and it is not easy for you to imagine the Pleasure it has given me. I have not found a single Opportunity to write since I left Boston, excepting by the Post and I dont choose to write by that Conveyance, for fear of foul Play. But as We are now within forty two Miles of Philadelphia, I hope there to find some private Hand by which I can convey this.

The Particulars of our Journey, I must reserve, to be communicated after my Return. It would take a Volume to describe the whole. It has been upon the whole an Agreable Jaunt, We have had Opportunities to see the World, and to form Acquaintances with the most eminent and famous Men, in the several Colonies we have passed through. We have been treated with unbounded Civility, Complaisance, and Respect.

We Yesterday visited Nassau Hall Colledge, and were politely treated by the Schollars, Tutors, Professors and President, whom We are, this Day to hear preach. Tomorrow We reach the Theatre of Action. God Almighty grant us Wisdom and Virtue sufficient for the high Trust that is devolved upon Us. The Spirit of the People wherever we have been seems to be very favourable. They universally consider our Cause as their own, and express the firmest Resolution, to abide the Determination of the Congress.

I am anxious for our perplexed, distressed Province—hope they will be directed into the right Path. Let me intreat you, my Dear, to make yourself as easy and quiet as possible. Resignation to the Will of Heaven is our only Resource in such dangerous Times. Prudence and Caution should be our Guides. I have the strongest Hopes, that We shall yet see a clearer Sky, and better Times.

Remember my tender Love to my little Nabby. Tell her she must write me a Letter and inclose it in the next you send. I am charmed with your Amusement with our little Johnny. Tell him I am glad to hear he is so good a Boy as to read to his Mamma, for her Entertainment, and to keep himself out of the Company of rude Children. Tell him I hope to hear a good Account of his Accidence and Nomenclature, when I return. Kiss my little Charley and Tommy for me. Tell them I shall be at Home by November, but how much sooner I know not.

Remember me to all enquiring Friends—particularly to Uncle Quincy, your Pappa and Family, and Dr. Tufts and Family. Mr. Thaxter, I hope, is a good Companion, in your Solitude. Tell him, if he devotes his Soul and Body to his Books, I hope, notwithstanding the Darkness of these Days, he will not find them unprofitable Sacrifices in future.

I have received three very obliging Letters, from Tudor, Trumble, and Hill. They have cheered us, in our Wanderings, and done us much Service.

My Compliments to Mr. Wibirt and Coll. Quincy, when you see them.

Your Account of the Rain refreshed me. I hope our Husbandry is prudently and industriously managed. Frugality must be our Support. Our Expences, in this Journey, will be very great—our only Reward will be the consolatory Reflection that We toil, spend our Time, and tempt Dangers for the public Good—happy indeed, if we do any good!

The Education of our Children is never out of my Mind. Train them to Virtue, habituate them to industry, activity, and Spirit. Make them consider every Vice, as shamefull and unmanly: fire them with

Ambition to be usefull—make them disdain to be destitute of any usefull, or ornamental Knowledge or Accomplishment. Fix their Ambition upon great and solid Objects, and their Contempt upon little, frivolous, and useless ones. It is Time, my dear, for you to begin to teach them French. Every Decency, Grace, and Honesty should be inculcated upon them.

I have [kept] a few Minutes by Way of Journal, which shall be your Entertainment when I come home, but We have had so many Persons and so various Characters to converse with, and so many Objects to view, that I have not been able to be so particular as I could wish.—I am, with the tenderest Affection and Concern, your wandering

John Adams

Rumors, both those without foundation and those that were magnifications of the actual, continually perplexed the colonial leadership. The "dreadfull Catastrophy" in Boston, referred to in the following letter and given wide credence, was in fact no more than the bloodless seizure by Gage's troops of the powder stored in the arsenal in what is now Somerville for transfer to Castle Island in Boston Harbor.

This was increasingly a time of commitment and of a "clashing of parties" even within families. The scene at the home of Colonel Josiah Quincy that Abigail Adams sketches typifies the day. One son, Samuel, solicitor general of the Province, shown in disagreement with others of the family and with his wife on the conflict, became a loyalist exile. His brother Josiah Jr. ("the Patriot") shortly undertook a mission to England to present there the views of the Massachusetts patriots. His death during his return voyage in May 1775 was a great loss to the cause and deeply affected his friends, including John Adams.

JA to AA

My Dear — Phyladelphia Septr. 8. 1774

When or where this Letter will find you, I know not. In what Scenes of Distress and Terror, I cannot foresee.—We have received a confused Account from Boston, of a dreadfull Catastrophy. The Particulars, We have not heard. We are waiting with the Utmost Anxiety and Impatience, for further Intelligence.

The Effect of the News We have both upon the Congress and the Inhabitants of this City, was very great—great indeed! Every Gentleman seems to consider the Bombardment of Boston, as the Bombardment, of the Capital of his own Province. Our Deliberations are grave and serious indeed.

It is a great Affliction to me that I cannot write to you oftener than I do. But there are so many Hindrances, that I cannot.

It would fill Volumes, to give you an Idea of the scenes I behold and the Characters I converse with.

We have so much Business, so much Ceremony, so much Company, so many Visits to recive and return, that I have not Time to write. And the Times are such, as render it imprudent to write freely.

We cannot depart from this Place, untill the Business of the Congress is compleated, and it is the general Disposition to proceed slowly. When I shall be at home I cant say. If there is Distress and Danger in Boston, pray invite our Friends, as many as possible, to take an Assylum with you. Mrs. Cushing and Mrs. Adams if you can.

There is in the Congress a Collection of the greatest Men upon this Continent, in Point of Abilities, Virtues and Fortunes. The Magnanimity, and public Spirit, which I see here, makes me blush for the sordid venal Herd, which I have seen in my own Province. The Addressers, and the new Councillors, are held in universal Contempt and Abhorrence, from one End of the Continent to the other.

Be not under any Concern for me. There is little Danger from any Thing We shall do, at the Congress. There is such a Spirit, thro the Colonies, and the Members of the Congress are such Characters, that no Danger can happen to Us, which will not involve the whole Continent, in Universal Desolation, and in that Case who would wish to live?

Make my Compliments to Mr. Thaxter and Mr. Rice—and to every other of my Friends. My Love to all my dear Children—tell them to be good, and to mind their Books. I shall come home and see them, I hope, the latter End of next Month.

Adieu. John Adams

P.S. You will judge how Things are like to be in Boston, and whether it will not be best to remove the Office entirely to Braintree. Mr. Hill and Williams, may come up, if they choose, paying for their Board.

AA to JA

Dearest Friend Braintree Sepbr. 14 1774

Five Weeks have past and not one line have I received. I had rather give a dollar for a letter by the post, tho the consequence should be that I Eat but one meal a day for these 3 weeks to come. Every one I see is inquiring after you and when did I hear. All my intelligance is collected from the news paper and I can only reply that I saw by that, that you arrived such a day. I know your fondness for writing and your inclination to let me hear from you by the first safe conveyance which makes me suspect that some Letter or other has miscaried, but I hope now you have arrived at Philidelphia you will find means to convey me some inteligance.

We are all well here. I think I enjoy better Health than I have done these 2 years. I have not been to Town since I parted with you there. The Govenor is making all kinds of warlike preperations such as mounting cannon upon Beacon Hill, diging entrenchments upon the Neck, placeing cannon there, encamping a regiment there, throwing up Brest Works &c. &c. The people are much allarmed, and the Selectmen have waited upon him in concequence of it. The county congress have also sent a committee—all which proceedings you will have a more particuliar account of than I am able to give you from the publick papers. But as to the Movements of this Town perhaps you may not hear them from any other person. In consequence of the powders being taken from Charlstown, a general alarm spread thro many Towns and was caught pretty soon here. The report took here a fryday, and a Sunday a Soldier was seen lurking about the common. Supposed to be a Spy, but most likely a Deserter. However inteligence of it was communicated to the other parishes, and about 8 o clock a Sunday Evening there pass[ed] by here about 200 Men, preceeded by a horse cart, and marched down to the powder house from whence they took the powder and carried [it] into the other parish and there secreeted it. I opened the window upon there return. They pass'd without any Noise, not a word among them till they came against this house, when some of them perceiveing me, askd me if I wanted any powder. I replied not since it was in so good hands. The reason they gave for taking it, was that we had so many Tories here they dare not trust us with it. They had taken Vinton in their Train, and upon their return they stoped between Cleverlys and Etters, and calld upon him to deliver two Warrents. Upon his producing them, they put it to vote whether they should burn them and it pass'd in the affirmitive. They then made a circle and burnt them, they then call'd a vote whether they should huzza, but it being Sunday evening it passd in the negative. They call'd upon Vinton to swear that he would never be instrumental in carrying into execution any of these new atcts. They were not satisfied with his answers however they let him rest. A few Days after upon his making some foolish speaches, they assembled to the amount of 2 and [3?] hundred, swore vengance upon him unless he took a solemn oath. Accordingly, they chose a committee and sent [them] with him to Major Miller to see that he complied, and they waited his return, which proving satisfactory they disperced. This Town appear as high as you can well immagine, and if necessary would soon be in arms.

Not a Tory but hides his head. The church parson thought they were comeing after him, and run up garret they say, an other jumpt out of his window and hid among the corn whilst a third crept under his bord fence, and told his Beads.

September 16 1774

I Dined to Day at Coll. Quincys. They were so kind as to send me, and Nabby and Betsy an invitation to spend the Day with them, and as I had not been to see them since I removed to Braintree, I accepted the invitation. After I got there, came Mr. Samll. Quincys wife and Mr. Sumner, Mr. Josiah and Wife. A little clashing of parties you may be sure. Mr. Sam's Wife said she thought it high time for her Husband to turn about, he had not done half so clever since he left her advice. Said they both greatly admired the most excellent and much admired Speach of the Bishop of St. Asaph which suppose you have seen. It meets, and most certainly merrits the greatest encomiums.

Upon my return at night Mr. Thaxter met me at the door with your Letter dated from Prince town New Jersy. It really gave me such a flow of Spirits that I was not composed eno to sleep till one oclock. You make no mention of one I wrote you previous to that you received by Mr. Breck and sent by Mr. Cunningham. I am rejoiced to hear you are well; I want to know many more perticuliars than you wrote me, and hope soon to hear from you again. I dare not trust myself with the thought of how long you may perhaps be absent. I only count the weeks already past, and they amount to 5. I am not so lonely as I should have been, without my two Neighbours. We make a table full at meal times, all the rest of their time they spend in the office. Never were two persons who gave a family less trouble than they do. It is at last determined that Mr. Rice keep the School here. Indeed he has kept ever since he has been here, but not with any expectation that He should be continued, but the people finding no small difference between him and his predecessor chose he should be continued. I have not sent Johnny. He goes very steadily to Mr. Thaxter who I believe takes very good care of him, and as they seem to have a likeing to each other believe it will be best to continue him with him. However when you return we can then consult what will be best. I am certain that if he does not get so much good, he gets less harm, and I have always thought it of very great importance that children should in the early part of life be unaccustomed to such examples as would tend to corrupt the purity of their words and actions that they may chill with horrour at the sound of an oath, and blush with indignation at an obscene expression. These first principal[s] which grow with their growth and strengthen with their strength neither time nor custom can totally eradicate.—You will perhaps be tired. No let it serve by way of relaxation from the more important concerns of the Day, and be such an amusement as your little hermitage used to afford you here. You have before you to express myself in the words of the Bishop the greatest National concerns that ever came before any people, and if the prayers and peti[ti]ons assend unto Heaven which are daily offerd for you, wisdom will flow down as a streem and Rithousness as the mighty waters, and your deliberations will make glad the cities of our God.

I was very sorry I did not know of Mr. Cary's going. It would have been so good an opportunity to have sent this as I lament the loss of. You have heard no doubt of the peoples preventing the court from setting in various counties, and last week in Taunton, Anger [Angier] urged the courts opening, and calling out the action, but could not effect it.

I saw a Letter from Miss Eunice wherein she gives an account of it, and says there were 2000 men assembled round the court house and by a committee of nine presented a petition requesting that they would not set, and with the uttmost order waited 2 hours for there answer, when they disperced.

Your family all desire to be remember'd to you, as well as unkle Quincy who often visits me, to have an hour of sweet communion upon politicks with me. Coll. Quincy desires his complements to you. Dr. Tufts sends his Love and your Mother and Brothers also. I have lived a very recluse life since your absence, seldom going any where except to my Fathers who with My Mother and Sister desire to be rememberd to you. My Mother has been exceeding low, but is a little better.—How warm your climate may be I know not, but I have had my bed warmed these two nights.—I must request you to procure me some watermellon seads and Muskmellon, as I determine to be well stocked with them an other year. We have had some fine rains, but as soon as the corn is gatherd you must release me of my promise. The Drougth has renderd cutting a second crop impracticable, feeding a little cannot hurt it. However I hope you will be at home to be convinced of the utility of the measure.—You will burn all these Letters least they should fall from your pocket and thus expose your most affectionate Friend,

Abigail Adams

JA to AA

Phyladelphia Septr. 16. 1774

Having a Leisure Moment, while the Congress is assembling, I gladly embrace it to write you a Line.

INDEPENDENCE SQUARE, PHILADELPHIA, LOOKING EAST FROM SIXTH STREET

(From the left: County Courthouse, State House, American Philosophical Society, Library Company of Philadelphia, Carpenters' Hall)

When the Congress first met, Mr. Cushing made a Motion, that it should be opened with Prayer. It was opposed by Mr. Jay of N. York and Mr. Rutledge of South Carolina, because we were so divided in religious Sentiments, some Episcopalians, some Quakers, some Aanabaptists, some Presbyterians and some Congregationalists, so that We could not join in the same Act of Worship.—Mr. S. Adams arose and said he was no Bigot, and could hear a Prayer from a Gentleman of Piety and Virtue, who was at the same Time a Friend to his Country. He was a Stranger in Phyladelphia, but had heard that Mr. Duchè (Dushay they pronounce it) deserved that Character, and therefore he moved that Mr. Duchè, an episcopal Clergyman, might be desired, to read Prayers to the Congress, tomorrow Morning. The Motion was seconded and passed in the Affirmative. Mr. Randolph our President, waited on Mr. Duchè, and received for Answer that if his Health would permit, he certainly would. Accordingly next Morning he appeared with his Clerk and in his Pontificallibus, and read several Prayers, in the established Form; and then read the Collect for the seventh day of September, which was the Thirty fifth Psalm.—You must remember this was the next Morning after we heard the horrible Rumour, of the Cannonade of Boston.—I never saw a greater Effect upon an Audience. It seemed as if Heaven had ordained that Psalm to be read on that Morning.

After this Mr. Duche, unexpected to every Body struck out into an extemporary Prayer, which filled the Bosom of every Man present. I must confess I never heard a better Prayer or one, so well pronounced. Episcopalian as he is, Dr. Cooper himself never prayed with such fervour, such Ardor, such Earnestness and Pathos, and in Language so elegant and sublime—for America, for the Congress, for The Province of Massachusetts Bay, and especially the Town of Boston. It has had an excellent Effect upon every Body here.

I must beg you to read that Psalm. If there was any Faith in the sortes Virgilianæ, or sortes Homericæ, or especially the Sortes biblicæ, it would be thought providential.

It will amuse your Friends to read this Letter and the 35th. Psalm to them. Read it to your Father and Mr. Wibirt.—I wonder what our Braintree Churchmen would think of this?—Mr. Duchè is one of the most ingenious Men, and best Characters, and greatest orators in the Episcopal order, upon this Continent—Yet a Zealous Friend of Liberty and his Country.

I long to see my dear Family. God bless, preserve and prosper it. Adieu.

John Adams

JA to AA

My Dear Philadelphia Septr. 20. 1774

I am very well yet:—write to me as often as you can, and send your Letters to the Office in Boston or to Mr. Cranches, whence they will be sent by the first Conveyance.

I am anxious to know how you can live without Government. But the Experiment must be tryed. The Evils will not be found so dreadfull as you a[ppreh]end them.

Frugality, my Dear, Frugality, OEconomy, Parcimony must be our Refuge. I hope the Ladies are every day diminishing their ornaments, and the Gentlemen too.

Let us Eat Potatoes and drink Water. Let us wear Canvass, and undressed Sheepskins, rather than submit to the unrighteous, and ignominious Domination that is prepared for Us.—Tel Brackett, I shall make him leave off drinking Rum. We cant let him fight yet.—My Love to my dear ones.

Adieu. John Adams

JA to AA

My Dear Phyladelphia Septr. 29. 1774

Sitting down to write to you, is a Scene almost too tender for my State of Nerves. It calls up to my View the anxious, distress'd State you must be in, amidst the Confusions and Dangers, which surround you. I long to return, and administer all the Consolation in my Power, but when I shall have accomplished all the Business I have to do here, I know not, and if it should be necessary to stay here till Christmas, or longer, in order to effect our Purposes, I am determined patiently to wait.

Patience, Forbearance, Long Suffering, are the Lessons taught here for our Province, and at the same Time absolute and open Resistance to the new Government. I wish I could convince Gentlemen, of the Danger, or Impracticability of this as fully as I believe it myself.

The Art and Address, of Ambassadors from a dozen belligerant Powers of Europe, nay of a Conclave of Cardinals at the Election of a Pope, or of the Princes in Germany at the Choice of an Emperor, would not exceed the Specimens We have seen.—Yet the Congress all profess the same political Principles.

They all profess to consider our Province as suffering in the common Cause, and indeed they seem to feel for Us, as if for themselves. We have had as great Questions to discuss as ever engaged the Attention of Men, and an infinite Multitude of them.

I received a very kind Letter from Deacon Palmer, acquainting me with Mr. Cranch's designs of removing to Braintree, which I approve very much—and wish I had an House for every Family in Boston, and Abilities to provide for them, in the Country.

I submit it to you, my Dear, whether it would not be best to remove all the Books and Papers and Furniture in the Office at Boston up to Braintree. There will be no Business there nor any where, I suppose, and my young Friends can study there better than in Boston at present.

I shall be kill'd with Kindness, in this Place. We go to congress at Nine, and there We stay, most earnestly engaged in Debates upon the most abstruse Misteries of State untill three in the Afternoon, then We adjourn, and go to Dinner with some of the Nobles of Pensylvania, at four O Clock and feast upon ten thousand Delicacies, and sitt drinking Madeira, Claret and Burgundy till six or seven, and then go home, fatigued to death with Business, Company, and Care.—Yet I hold it out, surprizingly. I drink no Cyder, but feast upon Phyladelphia Beer, and Porter. A Gentleman, one Mr. Hare, has lately set up in this City a Manufactory of Porter, as good as any that comes from London. I pray We may introduce it into the Massachusetts. It agrees with me, infinitely better than Punch, Wine, or Cyder, or any other Spirituous Liquor.—My Love to my dear Children one by one. My Compliments to Mr. Thaxter, and Rice and every Body else. Yours most affectionately,

John Adams

JA to AA

My Dear — Phyladelphia Octr. 9. 1774

I am wearied to Death with the Life I lead. The Business of the Congress is tedious, beyond Expression. This Assembly is like no other that ever existed. Every Man in it is a great Man—an orator, a Critick, a statesman, and therefore every Man upon every Question must shew his oratory, his Criticism and his Political Abilities.

The Consequence of this is, that Business is drawn and spun out to an immeasurable Length. I believe if it was moved and seconded that We should come to a Resolution that Three and two make five We should be entertained with Logick and Rhetorick, Law, History, Politicks and Mathematicks, concerning the Subject for two whole Days, and then We should pass the Resolution unanimously in the Affirmative.

The perpetual Round of feasting too, which we are obliged to submit to, make the Pilgrimage more tedious to me.

This Day I went to Dr. Allisons Meeting in the Forenoon and heard the Dr.—a good Discourse upon the Lords Supper. This is a Presbyterian Meeting. I confess I am not fond of the Presbyterian Meetings in this Town. I had rather go to Church. We have better Sermons, better Prayers, better Speakers, softer, sweeter Musick, and genteeler Company. And I must confess, that the Episcopal Church is quite as agreable to my Taste as the Presbyterian. They are both Slaves to the Domination of the Priesthood. I like the Congregational Way best—next to that the Independant.

This afternoon, led by Curiosity and good Company I strolled away to Mother Church, or rather Grandmother Church, I mean the Romish Chappell. Heard a good, short, moral Essay upon the Duty of Parents to their Children, founded in Justice and Charity, to take care of their Interests temporal and spiritual. This Afternoons Entertainment was to me, most awfull and affecting. The poor Wretches, fingering their Beads, chanting Latin, not a Word of which they understood, their Pater Nosters and Ave Maria's. Their holy Water—their Crossing themselves perpetually—their Bowing to the Name of Jesus, wherever they hear it—their Bowings, and Kneelings, and Genuflections before the Altar. The Dress of the Priest was rich with Lace—his Pulpit was Velvet and Gold. The Altar Piece was very rich—little Images and Crucifixes about—Wax Candles lighted up. But how shall I describe the Picture of our Saviour in a Frame of Marble over the Altar at full Length upon the Cross, in the Agonies, and the Blood dropping and streaming from his Wounds.

The Musick consisting of an organ, and a Choir of singers, went all the Afternoon, excepting sermon Time, and the Assembly chanted—most sweetly and exquisitely.

Here is every Thing which can lay hold of the Eye, Ear, and Imagination. Every Thing which can charm and bewitch the simple and ignorant. I wonder how Luther ever broke the spell.

Adieu. John Adams

AA to JA

My Much Loved Friend Braintree october 16 1774

I dare not express to you at 300 hundred miles distance how ardently I long for your return. I have some very miserly Wishes; and cannot consent to your spending one hour in Town till at least I have had you 12. The Idea plays about my Heart, unnerves my hand whilst I write, awakens all the tender sentiments that years have encreased and matured, and which when with me were every day dispensing to you. The whole collected stock of ⟨*nine*⟩ ten weeks absence knows not how to brook any longer restraint, but will break forth and flow thro my pen. May the like sensations enter thy breast, and (in spite of all the weighty cares of State) Mingle themselves with those I wish to communicate, for in giving them utterance I have felt more sincere pleasure than I have known since the 10 of August.—Many have been the anxious hours I have spent since that day—the threatning aspect of our publick affairs, the complicated distress of this province, the Arduous and perplexed Buisness in which you are engaged, have all conspired to agitate my bosom, with fears and apprehensions to which I have heretofore been [a] stranger, and far from thinking the Scene closed, it looks [as] tho the curtain was but just drawn and only the first Scene of the infernal plot disclosed and whether the end will be tragical Heaven alone knows. You cannot be, I know, nor do I wish to see you an inactive Spectator, but if the Sword be drawn I bid adieu to all domestick felicity, and look forward to that Country where there is neither wars nor rumors of War in a firm belief that thro the mercy of its King we shall both rejoice there together.

I greatly fear that the arm of treachery and voilence is lifted over us as a Scourge and heavy punishment from heaven for our numerous offences, and for the misimprovement of our great advantages. If we expect to inherit the blessings of our Fathers, we should return a little more to their primitive Simplicity of Manners, and not sink into inglorious ease. We have too many high sounding words, and too few actions that correspond with them. I have spent one Sabbeth in Town since you left me. I saw no difference in respect to ornaments, &c. &c. but in the Country you must look for that virtue, of which you find but small Glimerings in the Metropolis. Indeed they have not the advantages, nor the resolution to encourage our own Manufactories which people in the country have. To the Mercantile part, tis considerd as throwing away their own Bread; but they must retrench their expenses and be content with a small share of gain for they will find but few who will wear their Livery. As for me I will seek wool and flax and work willingly with my Hands, and indeed their is occasion for all our industry and economy.

You mention the removal of our Books &c. from Boston. I believe they are safe there, and it would incommode the Gentlemen to remove them, as they would not then have a place to repair to for study. I suppose they would not chuse to be at the expence of bording out. Mr. Williams I believe keeps pretty much with his mother. Mr. Hills father had some thoughts of removing up to Braintree provided he could be accommodated with a house, which he finds very difficult.

Mr. Cranch's last determination was to tarry in Town unless any thing new takes place. His Friends in Town oppose his Removal so much that he is determind to stay. The opinion you have entertaind of General Gage is I believe just, indeed he professes to act only upon the Defensive. The People in the Co[untr]y begin to be very anxious for the congress to rise. They have no Idea of the Weighty Buisness you have to transact, and their Blood boils with indignation at the Hostile prepairations they are constant Witnesses of. Mr. Quincys so secret departure is Matter of various Specculation—some say he is deputed by the congress, others that he is gone to Holland, and the Tories says he is gone to be hanged.

I rejoice at the favourable account you give me of your Health; May it be continued to you. My Health is much better than it was last fall. Some folks say I grow very fat.—I venture to write most any thing in this Letter, because I know the care of the Bearer. He will be most sadly dissapointed if you should be broke up before he arrives, as he is very desirous of being introduced by you to a Number of Gentlemen of respectable characters. I almost envy him, that he should see you, before I can.

Mr. Thaxter and Rice present their Regards to you. Unkle Quincy too sends his Love to you, he is very good to call and see me, and so have many other of my Friends been. Coll. Warren and Lady were here a monday, and send their Love to you. The Coll. promiss'd to write. Mrs. Warren will spend a Day or two on her return with me. I told Betsy to write to you. She says she would if you were her *Husband.*

Your Mother sends her Love to you, and all your family too numerous to name desire to be rememberd. You will receive Letters from two, who are as earnest to write to Pappa as if the welfare of a kingdom depended upon it. If you can give any guess within a month let me know when you think of returning to Your most Affectionate

Abigail Adams

Between his journey to Braintree following adjournment of the First Continental Congress in late October and his departure six months later in anticipation of the convening of the Second Congress, John Adams was at home with his family. He was active enough but within an area that allowed daily returns to Braintree. In November and December Adams attended the sessions of the first Provincial Congress in Cambridge, and from January to April he probably was often in Boston seeing to the publication of his "Novanglus" essays in the *Boston Gazette.*

The Second Continental Congress convened in May 1775 in an atmosphere that had changed markedly during the long hiatus. Events had begun to shape deliberations; blood had been spilled at Lexington and Concord. Passions in Massachusetts were further inflamed by the newspaper publication of selections from Governor Hutchinson's ransacked papers that were thought incriminating. Resentment swelled over Governor Gage's proclamation addressed to "the infatuated multitudes" and offering pardon to those who ceased their resistance to royal authority, excepting only the "incendiaries and traitors" who were their leaders.

The colonials laid Gage's forces under siege in Boston. Refugees streamed out from that unhappy town. Houses, including the Adamses' on Queen Street, were abandoned to the British army and the reverse tide of loyalist refugees streaming in from other towns and the countryside

The conflict came to Braintree when the British raided Grape Island to take off hay for their horses. Both of John Adams' brothers shouldered muskets in the counterattack. Like other South Shore towns, Braintree began to fill up with displaced Bostonians. Some took over houses abandoned by loyalists. One such house was the Vassall-Borland place, into which the James Bowdoins moved and which later became the home of four generations of Adamses. (It is now the Adams National Historic Site.)

JA to AA

My Dear — Hartford May 2d. 1775

Mr. Eliot of Fairfield, is this Moment arrived in his Way to Boston. He read us a Letter from the Dr. his Father dated Yesterday Sennight being Sunday. The Drs. Description of the Melancholly of the Town, is enough to melt a Stone. The Tryals of that unhappy and devoted People are likely to be severe indeed. God grant that the Furnace of Affliction may refine them. God grant that they may be relieved from their present Distress.

It is Arrogance and Presumption in human Sagacity to pretend to penetrate far into the Designs of Heaven. The most perfect Reverence and Resignation becomes us. But, I cant help depending upon this, that the present dreadfull Calamity of that beloved Town is intended to bind the Colonies together in more indissoluble Bands, and to animate their Exertions, at this great Crisis in the Affairs of Mankind. It has this Effect, in a most remarkable Degree, as far as I have yet seen or heard. It will plead, with all America, with more irresistable Perswasion, than Angells trumpet tongued.

In a Cause which interests the whole Globe, at a Time, when my Friends and Country are in such keen Distress, I am scarcely ever interrupted, in the least Degree, by Apprehensions for my Personal Safety. I am often concerned for you and our dear Babes, surrounded as you are by People who are too timorous and too much susceptible of allarms. Many Fears and Jealousies and imaginary Dangers, will be suggested to you, but I hope you will not be impressed by them.

In Case of real Danger, of which you cannot fail to have previous

Intimations, fly to the Woods with our Children. Give my tenderest Love to them, and to all.

AA to JA

Braintree May 4. 1775

I have but little news to write you. Every thing of that kind you will learn by a more accurate hand than mine; things remain much in the same situation here that they were when you went away, there has been no Desent upon the sea coast. Guards are regularily kept, and people seem more settled, and are returning to their husbandry.—I feel somewhat lonesome. Mr. Thaxter is gone home, Mr. Rice is going into the Army as captain of a company. We have no School. I know not what to do with John.—As Goverment is assumed I suppose Courts of Justice will be established, and in that case there may be Buisness to do. If so would it not be best for Mr. Thaxter to return? They seem to be discouraged in the study of Law, and think there never will be any buisness for them. I could have wishd they had consulted you upon the subject before you went away. Mr. Rice has asked my advice? I tell him I would have him act his pleasure. I dont chuse to advise him either way.—I suppose you will receive 2 or 3 Vol. of that forlorn Wretches Hutchisons Letters. Among many other things I hear he wrote in 1772 that Deacon Philips and you had like to have been chosen into the Counsel, but if you had you should have shared the same fate with Bowers. May the fate of Mordeca be his.—There is no body admitted into Town yet. I have made two or 3 attempts to get somebody in, but cannot succeed, so have not been able to do the Buisness you left in charge with me.—I want very much to hear from you, how you stood your journey, and in what state you find yourself now. I felt very anxious about you tho I endeavourd to be very insensible and heroick, yet my heart felt like a heart of Led. The same Night you left me I heard of Mr. Quincys Death, which at this time was a most melancholy Event, especially as he wrote in minets which he left behind that he had matters of concequence intrusted with him, which for want of a confident must die with him.—I went to see his distressed widdow last Saturday at the Coll. and in the afternoon from an allarm they had, she and her sister, with three others of the family took refuge with me, and tarried all night. She desired me to present her regards to you, and let you know she wished you every blessing, should always esteem you as a sincere Friend of her deceased husband. Poor afflicted woman, my heart was wounded for her.—I must quite the subject, and intreet you to write me by every opportunity. Your

Mother desires to be rememberd to you. She is with me now. The children send Duty, and their Mamma unfeigned Love.

Yours, Portia

AA to JA

24 May B[raintre]e 1775

Suppose you have had a formidable account of the alarm we had last Sunday morning. When I rose about six oclock I was told that the Drums had been some time beating and that 3 allarm Guns were fired, that Weymouth Bell had been ringing, and Mr. Welds was then ringing. I immediatly sent of an express to know the occasion, and found the whole Town in confusion. 3 Sloops and one cutter had come out, and droped anchor just below Great Hill. It was difficult to tell their design, some supposed they were comeing to Germantown others to Weymouth. People women children from the Iron Works flocking down this Way—every woman and child above or from below my Fathers. My Fathers family flying, the Drs. in great distress, as you may well immagine for my Aunt had her Bed thrown into a cart, into which she got herself, and orderd the boy to drive her of to Bridgwater which he did. The report was to them, that 300 hundred had landed, and were upon their march into Town. The allarm flew [like] lightning, and men from all parts came flocking down till 2000 were collected—but it seems their expidition was to Grape Island for *Levet's* hay. There it was impossible to reach them for want of Boats, but the sight of so many persons, and the fireing at them prevented their getting more than 3 ton of Hay, tho they had carted much more down to the water. At last they musterd a Lighter, and a Sloop from Hingham which had six port holes. Our men eagerly jumpt on board, and put of for the Island. As soon as they perceived it, they decamped. Our people landed upon [the] Island, and in an instant set fire to the Hay which with the Barn was soon consumed, about 80 ton tis said. We expect soon to be in continual alarms, till something decisive takes place. We wait with longing Expectation in hopes to hear the best accounts from you with regard to union and harmony &c. We rejoice greatly on the Arival of Doctor Franklin, as he must certainly be able to inform you very perticuliarly of the situation of affairs in England. I wish you would [write] if you can get time; be as perticuliar as you *may*, when you write—every one here abouts come[s] to me to hear what accounts I have. I was so unlucky as not to get the Letter you wrote at New York. Capn. Beals forgot it, and left it behind. We have a flying report here with regard to New York, but cannot give any credit to, as yet, that they had been engaged with the Ships which Gage sent there and taken them with great looss upon both sides.

Yesterday we have an account of 3 Ships comeing in to Boston. I believe it is true, as there was a Salute from the other Ships, tho I have not been able to learn from whence they come. Suppose you have had an account of the fire which did much damage to the Warehouses, and added greatly to the distresses of the inhabitants whilst it continued. The bad conduct of General Gage was the means of its doing so much damage.

Tis a fine growing Season having lately had a charming rain, which was much wanted as we had none before for a fortnight. Your meadow is almost fit to mow. Isaac talks of leaving you, and going into the Army. I believe he will. Mr. Rice has a prospect of an *adjutant* place in the Army. I believe he will not be a very hardy Soldier. He has been sick of a fever above this week, and has not been out of his chamber. He is upon the recovery now.

Our House has been upon this alarm in the same Scene of confusion that it was upon the first—Soldiers comeing in for lodging, for Breakfast, for Supper, for Drink &c. &c. Sometimes refugees from Boston tierd and fatigued, seek an assilum for a Day or Night, a week—you can hardly imagine how we live.

"Yet to the Houseless child of want
our doors are open still.
And tho our portions are but scant
We give them with good will."

I want to know how you do? How are your Eyes? Is not the weather very hot where you are? The children are well and send Duty to Pappa. This day Month you set of. I have never once inquired when you think it posible to return; as I think you could not give me any satisfactory answer. I have according to your direction wrote to Mr. Dilly, and given it to the care of Capn. Beals who will deliver it with his own hand; I got Mr. Thaxter to take a coppy for me, as I had not time amidst our confusions; I send it to you for your approbation. You will be careful of it as I have no other coppy. My best wishes attend you both for your Health and happiness, and that you may be directed into the wisest and best measures for our Safety, and the Security of our posterity. I wish you was nearer to us. We know not what a day will bring forth, nor what distress one hour may throw us into. Heitherto I have been able to mantain a calmness and presence of Mind, and hope I shall, let the Exigency of the time be what they will.

Mrs. W[arre]n desires to be rememberd to you with her sincere regards. Mr. C[ranc]h and family send their Love. He poor man has a fit of his old disorder. I have not heard one Syllable from Providence since I wrote you last. I wait to hear from you, then shall act accordingly. I dare not discharge any debts with what I have except to Isaac, least you should be dissapointed of the remainder. Adieu Breakfast calls your affectionate Portia

AA to JA

Weymouth June [16?] 1775

I set down to write to you a monday, but really could not compose my-self sufficently: the anxiety I sufferd from not hearing one syllable from you for more than five weeks; and the new distress ariseing from the arrival of recruits agitated me more than I have been since the never to be forgotten 14 of April.

I have been much revived by receiving two letters from you last Night, one by the servant of your Friend and the other by the Gentleman you mention, tho they both went to Cambridge, and I have not seen them. I hope to send this as a return to you.

I feard much for your Health when you went away. I must intreat you to be as careful as you can consistant with the Duty you owe your Country. That consideration alone prevaild with me to consent to your departure, in a time so perilous and so hazardous to your family, and with a body so infirm as to require the tenderest care and nursing. I wish you may be supported and devinely assisted in this most important crisis when the fate of Empires depend upon your wisdom and conduct. I greatly rejoice to hear of your union, and determination to stand by us.

We cannot but consider the great distance you are from us as a very great misfortune, when our critical situation renders it necessary to hear from you every week, and will be more and more so, as difficulties arise. We now expect our Sea coasts ravaged. Perhaps, the very next Letter I write will inform you that I am driven away from our, yet quiet cottage. Necessity will oblige Gage to take some desperate steps. We are told for Truth, that he is now Eight thousand strong. We live in continual expectation of allarms. Courage I know we have in abundance, conduct I hope we shall not want, but powder—where shall we get a sufficient supply? I wish we may not fail there. Every Town is fill'd with the distressd inhabitants of Boston—our House among others is deserted, and by this time like enough made use of as a Barrack.—Mr. Bowdoin with his Lady, are at present in the house of Mrs. Borland, and are a going to Middlebouragh to the house of Judge

Oliver. He poor Gentleman is so low, that I apprehend he is hastening to an house not made with Hands—looks like a mere skelliton, speaks faint and low, is racked with a voilent cough, and I think far advanced in a consumption. I went to see him last Saturday. He is very inquisitive of every person with regard to the times, beged I would let him know of the first inteligence I had from you, is very unable to converse by reason of his cough. He rides every pleasent Day, and has been kind enough to call at the Door, (tho unable to get out) several times. Says the very name of Hutchinson distresses him. Speaking of him the other day he broke out, "religious Rascal, how I abhor his Name."

We have had very dry weather not a rainy day since you left us. The english Grass will not yeald half so great a crop as last year. Fruit promisses well, but the Cattepillars have been innumerable.

I wrote you with regard to the money I had got from Providence. I have since that obtain'd the rest. I have done as you directed with regard to the payment of some you mentiond, but it incroachd some upon your Stock. You will write me with regard to what you have necessity for and how I shall convey to you.—Mr. Rice is dissapointed of his place in the Army but has hopes of joining a company much talked of here under Mr. Hancock when he returns. I came here with some of my cousin Kents who came to see me a day, or two ago, and have left company to write you this afternoon least I should fail of conveyance. Pray be perticuliar when you write as possible—every body wants to hear, and to know what is doing, and what may be communicated, do not fail to inform me. All our Friends desire to be kindly rememberd to you. Gage'es proclamation you will receive by this conveyance. All the records of time cannot produce a blacker page. Satan when driven from the regions of bliss, Exibeted not more malice. Surely the father of lies is superceded.—Yet we think it the best proclamation he could have issued.

I shall when ever I can, receive and entertain in the best Manner I am capable the Gentlemen who have so generously proferd their Service in our Army. Goverment is wanted in the army, and Else where. We see the want of it more from so large a body being together, than when each individual was imployd in his own domestick circle.—My best regards attend every Man you esteem. You will make my complements to Mr. Miflin and Lady. I do not now wonder at the regard the Laidies express for a Soldier—every man who wears a cockade appears of double the importance he used to, and I feel a respect for the lowest Subaltern in the Army.—You tell me you know not when you shall see me. I never trust myself long with the terrors which sometimes intrude themselves upon me.

I hope we shall see each other again and rejoice together in happier Days. The little ones are well, and send Duty to Pappa. Dont fail of letting me hear from you by every opportunity, every line is like a precious Relict of the Saints. Pray dont Expose me by a communication of any of my Letters—a very bad Soar upon the middle finger of my right hand has prevented my writing for 3 weeks. This is the 5 Letter I have wrote you. I hope they have all come to hand.—I have a request to make you. Something like the Barrel of Sand suppose you will think it, but really of much more importance to me. It is that you would send out Mr. Bass and purchase me a bundle of pins and put in your trunk for me. The cry for pins is so great that what we used to Buy for 7.6 are now 20 Shillings and not to be had for that. A bundle contains 6 thousand for which I used to give a Dollor, but if you can procure them for 50 [*shillings*] or 3 pound, pray let me have them. Mr. Welch who carries this to head Quarters waits which prevents my adding more than that I am with the tenderest Regard your

Portia

John Adams entered upon the deliberations of the first session of the Second Continental Congress with the highest hopes for its accomplishments. "No Assembly ever had a greater Number of great Objects before them. Provinces, Nations, Empires are small Things, before Us," he wrote. As the weeks went by, however, his spirits drooped. He was plagued by a variety of physical ailments. The enervating weather of the summer months during which the Congress sat made Philadelphia all but unbearable. Those in the Congress who, under the lead of John Dickinson of Pennsylvania, sought compromise with Great Britain established at least a temporary dominance that enabled them to secure passage of the Olive Branch Petition. Goaded into impatience and imprudence, Adams wrote a letter to his wife (the letter is that below dated July 24) and another to James Warren on the same day containing comments that disparaged his colleagues, Dickinson in particular, and asserted the need to form a "Constitution" and establish a "Naval Power." Both letters were intercepted and published in the tory press to the discomfiture of Adams, but without lasting damage. Despite momentary frustrations, the Congress during this brief session established an army, adopted a plan for its administration, appointed a commander-in-chief and a corps of general officers, established a postal system, and took steps to provide finances for the struggle by the issuance of bills of credit.

In Massachusetts, meanwhile, the anguish, pride, and bereavement that followed the Bunker's Hill battle on June 17 and the destruction of Charlestown by fire were balanced by the confidence stimulated by the appearance in their midst of General Washington and of the riflemen who brought evidence that there was indeed Continental support for the hard-pressed Yankees.

JA to AA

[*Philadelphia*] June 17 [*1775*]

I can now inform you that the Congress have made Choice of the modest and virtuous, the amiable, generous and brave George Washington Esqr., to be the General of the American Army, and that he is to repair as soon as possible to the Camp before Boston. This Appointment will have a great Effect, in cementing and securing the Union of these Colonies.—The Continent is really in earnest in defending the Country. They have voted Ten Companies of Rifle Men to be sent from Pensylvania, Maryland and Virginia, to join the Army before Boston. These are an excellent Species of Light Infantry. They use a peculiar Kind of [... ca]ll'd a Rifle—it has circular or [...] Grooves within the Barrell, and carries a Ball, with great Exactness to great Distances. They are the most accurate Marksmen in the World.

I begin to hope We shall not sit all Summer.

I hope the People of our Province, will treat the General with all that Confidence and Affection, that Politeness and Respect, which is due to one of the most important Characters in the World. The Liberties of America, depend upon him, in a great Degree.

I have never been able to obtain from our Province, any regular and particular Intelligence since I left it. Kent, Swift, Tudor, Dr. Cooper, Dr. Winthrop, and others wrote me often, last Fall—not a Line from them this Time.

I have found this Congress like the last. When We first came together, I found a strong Jealousy of Us, from New England, and the Massachusetts in Particular. Suspicions were entertained of Designs of Independency—an American Republic—Presbyterian Principles—and twenty other Things. Our Sentiments were heard in Congress, with great Caution—and seemed to make but little Impression: but the longer We sat, the more clearly they saw the Necessity of pursuing vigorous Measures. It has been so now. Every Day We sit, the more We are convinced that the Designs against Us, are hostile and sanguinary, and that nothing but Fortitude, Vigour, and Perseverance can save Us.

But America is a great, unwieldy Body. Its Progress must be slow. It is like a large Fleet sailing under Convoy. The fleetest Sailors must wait for the dullest and slowest. Like a Coach and six—the swiftest Horses must be slackened and the slowest quickened, that all may keep an even Pace.

It is long since I heard from you. I fear you have been kept in continual Alarms. My Duty and Love to all. My dear Nabby, Johnny, Charly and Tommy come here and kiss me.

We have appointed a continental Fast. Millions will be upon their

Knees at once before their great Creator, imploring his Forgiveness and Blessing, his Smiles on American Councils and Arms.

My Duty to your Uncle Quincy—your Papa, Mama and mine—my Brothers and sisters and yours.

Adieu.

AA to JA

Dearest Friend Sunday June 18 1775

The Day; perhaps the decisive Day is come on which the fate of America depends. My bursting Heart must find vent at my pen. I have just heard that our dear Friend Dr. Warren is no more but fell gloriously fighting for his Country—saying better to die honourably in the field than ignominiously hang upon the Gallows. Great is our Loss. He has distinguished himself in every engagement, by his courage and fortitude, by animating the Soldiers and leading them on by his own example. A particuliar account of these dreadful, but I hope Glorious Days will be transmitted you, no doubt in the exactest manner.

The race is not to the swift, nor the battle to the strong, but the God of Israel is he that giveth strength and power unto his people. Trust in him at all times, ye people pour out your hearts before him. God is a refuge for us.—Charlstown is laid in ashes. The Battle began upon our intrenchments upon Bunkers Hill, a Saturday morning about 3 o clock and has not ceased yet and tis now 3 o'clock Sabbeth afternoon.

Tis expected they will come out over the Neck to night, and a dreadful Battle must ensue. Almighty God cover the heads of our Country men, and be a shield to our Dear Friends. How [many ha]ve fallen we know not—the constant roar of the cannon is so [distre]ssing that we can not Eat, Drink or Sleep. May we be supported and sustaind in the dreadful conflict. I shall tarry here till tis thought unsafe by my Friends, and then I have secured myself a retreat at your Brothers who has kindly offerd me part of his house. I cannot compose myself to write any further at present. I will add more as I hear further.

Tuesday afternoon [20 *June*]

I have been so much agitated that I have not been able to write since Sabbeth day. When I say that ten thousand reports are passing vague and uncertain as the wind I believe I speak the Truth. I am not able to give you any authentick account of last Saturday, but you will not be destitute of inteligence. Coll. Palmer has just sent me word that he has an opportunity of conveyance. Incorrect as this scrawl will be, it shall go. I wrote you last Saturday morning. In the afternoon I received your kind favour of the 2 june, and that you sent me by Captn. Beals at the same time.—I ardently pray that you may be supported thro the arduous task you have before you. I wish I could contradict the report of the Doctors Death, but tis a lamentable Truth, and the tears of multitudes pay tribute to his memory. Those favorite lines [of] Collin continually sound in my Ears

How sleep the Brave who sink to rest,
By all their Countrys wishes blest?
When Spring with dew'ey fingers cold
Returns to deck their Hallowed mould
She their shall dress a sweeter Sod
Than fancys feet has ever trod.
By fairy hands their knell is rung
By forms unseen their Dirge is sung
Their [There] Honour comes a pilgrim grey
To Bless the turf that wraps their Clay
And freedom shall a while repair
To Dwell a weeping Hermit there.

I rejoice in the prospect of the plenty you inform me of, but cannot say we have the same agreable veiw here. The drought is very severe, and things look but poorly.

Mr. Rice and Thaxter, unkle Quincy, Col. Quincy, Mr. Wibert all desire to be rememberd, so do all our family. Nabby will write by the next conveyance.

I must close, as the Deacon w[aits.] I have not pretended to be perticuliar with regard to what I have heard, because I know you will collect better intelligence. The Spirits of the people are very good. The loss of Charlstown affects them no more than a Drop in the Bucket.—I am Most sincerely yours, Portia

JA to AA

My Dear Philadelphia June 23. 1775

I have this Morning been out of Town to accompany our Generals Washington, Lee, and Schuyler, a little Way, on their Journey to the American Camp before Boston.

The Three Generals were all mounted, on Horse back, accompanied by Major Mifflin who is gone in the Character of Aid de Camp. All the Delegates from the Massachusetts with their Servants, and Carriages attended. Many others of the Delegates, from the Congress—a large Troop of Light Horse, in their Uniforms. Many Officers of Militia besides in theirs. Musick playing &c. &c. Such is the Pride and Pomp of

War. I, poor Creature, worn out with scribbling, for my Bread and my Liberty, low in Spirits and weak in Health, must leave others to wear the Lawrells which I have sown; others, to eat the Bread which I have earned.—A Common Case.

We had Yesterday, by the Way of N. York and N. London, a Report, which distresses us, almost as much as that We had last fall, of the Cannonade of Boston. A Battle at Bunkers Hill and Dorchester Point—three Colonels wounded, Gardiner mortally. We wait to hear more particulars. Our Hopes and our Fears are alternately very strong. If there is any Truth in this Account, you must be in great Confusion. God Almightys Providence preserve, sustain, and comfort you.

June 27

This Moment received two Letters from you. Courage, my dear! We shall be supported in Life, or comforted in Death. I rejoice that my Countrymen behaved so bravely, tho not so skillfully conducted as I could wish. I hope this defect will be remedied by the new modelling of the Army.

My Love every where.

AA to JA

Dearest Friend June 25 1775 Braintree

My Father has been more affected with the distruction of Charlstown, than with any thing which has heretofore taken place. Why should not his countanance be sad when the city, the place of his Fathers Sepulchers lieth waste, and the gates thereof are consumed with fire, scarcly one stone remaineth upon an other. But in the midst of sorrow we have abundant cause of thankfulness that so few of our Breathren are numberd with the slain, whilst our enimies were cut down like the Grass before the Sythe. But one officer of all the Welch fuzelers remains to tell his story. Many poor wretches dye for want of proper assistance and care of their wounds.

Every account agrees in 14 and 15 hundred slain and wounded upon their side nor can I learn that they dissemble the number themselves. We had some Heroes that day who fought with amazing intrepidity, and courage—

> "Extremity is the trier of Spirits—
> Common chances common men will bear;
> And when the Sea is calm all boats alike
> Shew mastership in floating, but fortunes blows
> When most struck home, being bravely warded, crave
> A noble cunning." *Shakespear.*

I hear that General *How* should say the Battle upon the plains of Abram was but a Bauble to this. When we consider all the circumstances attending this action we stand astonished that our people were not all cut of. They had but one hundred foot intrenched, the number who were engaged, did not exceed 800, and they [had] not half amunition enough. The reinforcements not able to get to them seasonably, the tide was up and high, so that their floating batteries came upon each side of the causway and their row gallies keeping a continual fire. Added to this the fire from fort hill and from the Ship, the Town in flames all round them and the heat from the flames so intence as scarcely to be borne; the day one of the hottest we have had this season and the wind blowing the smoke in their faces—only figure to yourself all these circumstances, and then consider that we do not count 60 Men lost. My Heart overflows at the recollection.

We live in continual Expectation of Hostilities. Scarcely a day that does not produce some, but like Good Nehemiah having made our prayer with God, and set the people with their Swords, their Spears and their bows we will say unto them, Be not affraid of them. Remember the Lord who is great and terible, and fight for your Breathren, your sons and your daughters, your wives and your houses.

I have just received yours of the 17 of june in 7 days only. Every line from that far Country is precious. You do not tell me how you do, but I will hope better. Alass you little thought what distress we were in the day you wrote. They delight in molesting us upon the Sabbeth. Two Sabbeths we have been in such Alarms that we have had no meeting. This day we have set under our own vine in quietness, have heard Mr. Taft, from psalms. The Lord is good to all and his tender mercies are over all his works. The good man was earnest and pathetick. I could forgive his weakness for the sake of his sincerity—but I long for a *Cooper* and an *Elliot.* I want a person who has feeling and sensibility who can take one up with him

> "And in his Duty prompt at every call
> Can watch, and weep, and pray, and feel for all."

Mr. Rice joins General Heaths regiment to morrow as adjutant. Your Brother is very desirous of being in the army, but your good Mother is really voilent against it. I cannot persuaid nor reason her into a consent. Neither he nor I dare let her know that he is trying for a place. My Brother has a Captains commission, and is stationd at Cambridge. I thought you had the best of inteligence or I should have taken pains to have been more perticuliar. As to Boston, there are many persons yet there who would be glad to get out if they could. Mr.

Boylstone and Mr. Gill the printer with his family are held upon the black list tis said. Tis certain they watch them so narrowly that they cannot escape, nor your Brother Swift and family. Mr. Mather got out a day or two before Charlstown was distroyed, and had lodged his papers and what else he got out at Mr. Carys, but they were all consumed. So were many other peoples, who thought they might trust their little there; till teams could be procured to remove them. The people from the Alms house and work house were sent to the lines last week, to make room for their wounded they say. Medford people are all removed. Every sea port seems in motion.—O North! may the Groans and cryes of the injured and oppressed Harrow up thy Soul. We have a prodigious Army, but we lack many accomadations which we need. I hope the apointment of these new Generals will give satisfaction. They must be proof against calumny. In a contest like this continual reports are circulated by our Enimies, and they catch with the unwary and the gaping croud who are ready to listen to the marvellous, without considering of consequences even tho there best Friends are injured.—I have not venturd to inquire one word of you about your return. I do not know whether I ought to wish for it—it seems as if your sitting together was absolutely necessary whilst every day is big with Events.

Mr. Bowdoin called a fryday and took his leave of me desiring I would present his affectionate regards to you. I have hopes that he will recover—he has mended a good deal. He wished he could have staid in Braintree, but his Lady was fearful.

I have often heard that fear makes people loving. I never was so much noticed *by some people* as I have been since you went out of Town, or rather since the 19 of April. Mr. W[inslo]ws family are determined to be sociable. Mr. A——n are quite Friendly.—Nabby Johny Charly Tommy all send duty. Tom says I wish I could see *par.* You would laugh to see them all run upon the sight of a Letter—like chickens for a crum, when the Hen clucks. Charls says *mar* What is it any good news? and who is for us and who against us, is the continual inquiry.—Brother and Sister Cranch send their Love. He has been very well since he removed, for him, and has full employ in his Buisness. Unkel Quincy calls to hear most every day, and as for the Parson, he determines I shall not make the same complaint I did last time, for he comes every other day.

Tis exceeding dry weather. We have not had any rain for a long time. Bracket has mowed the medow and over the way, but it will not be a last years crop.—Pray let me hear from you by every opportunity till I have the joy of once more meeting you. Yours ever more,

Portia

JA to AA

My Dear Philadelphia July 7. 1775

I have received your very agreable Favours of June 22d. and 25th. They contain more particulars than any Letters I had before received from any Body.

It is not at all surprizing to me that the wanton, cruel, and infamous Conflagration of Charlestown, the Place of your Fathers Nativity, should afflict him. Let him know that I sincerely condole with him, on that melancholly Event. It is a Method of conducting War long since become disreputable among civilized Nations: But every Year brings us fresh Evidence, that We have nothing to hope for from our loving Mother Country, but Cruelties more abominable than those which are practiced by the Savage Indians.

The account you give me of the Numbers slain on the side of our Enemies, is affecting to Humanity, altho it is a glorious Proof of the Bravery of our Worthy Countrymen. Considering all the Disadvantages under which they fought, they really exhibited Prodigies of Valour.

Your Description of the Distresses of the worthy Inhabitants of Boston, and the other Sea Port Towns, is enough to melt an Heart of stone. Our Consolation must be this, my dear, that Cities may be rebuilt, and a People reduced to Poverty, may acquire fresh Property: But a Constitution of Government once changed from Freedom, can never be restored. Liberty once lost is lost forever. When the People once surrender their share in the Legislature, and their Right of defending the Limitations upon the Government, and of resisting every Encroachment upon them, they can never regain it.

The Loss of Mr. Mathers Library, which was a Collection, of Books and Manuscripts made by himself, his Father, his Grandfather, and Greatgrandfather, and was really very curious and valuable, is irreparable.

The Family picture you draw is charming indeed. My dear Nabby, Johnny, Charly and Tommy, I long to see you, and to share with your Mamma the Pleasures of your Conversation.

I feel myself much obliged to Mr. Bowdoin, Mr. Wibirt, and the two Families you mention, for their Civilities to you. My Compliments to them. Does Mr. Wibirt preach against Oppression, and the other Cardinal Vices of the Times? Tell him the Clergy here, of every Denomination, not excepting the Episcopalian, thunder and lighten every sabbath. They pray for Boston and the Massachusetts—they thank God most explicitly and fervently for our remarkable Successes —they pray for the American Army. They seem to feel as if they were among you.

You ask if every Member feels for Us? Every Member says he does

—and most of them really do. But most of them feel more for themselves. In every Society of Men, in every Clubb, I ever yet saw, you find some who are timid, their Fears hurry them away upon every Alarm—some who are selfish and avaricious, on whose callous Hearts nothing but Interest and Money can make Impression. There are some Persons in New York and Philadelphia, to whom a ship is dearer than a City, and a few Barrells of flower, than a thousand Lives—other Mens Lives I mean.

You ask, can they reallize what We suffer? I answer No. They cant, they dont—and to excuse them as well as I can, I must confess I should not be able to do it, myself, if I was not more acquainted with it by Experience than they are.

I am grieved for Dr. Tufts's ill Health: but rejoiced exceedingly at his virtuous Exertions in the Cause of his Country.

I am happy to hear that my Brothers were at Grape Island and behaved well. My Love to them, and Duty to my Mother.

It gives me more Pleasure than I can express to learn that you sustain with so much Fortitude, the Shocks and Terrors of the Times. You are really brave, my dear, you are an Heroine. And you have Reason to be. For the worst that can happen, can do you no Harm. A soul, as pure, as benevolent, as virtuous and pious as yours has nothing to fear, but every Thing to hope and expect from the last of human Evils.

Am glad you have secured an Assylum, tho I hope you will not have occasion for it.

Love to Brother Cranch and sister and the Children.

There is an amiable, ingenious Hussy, named Betcy Smith, for whom I have a very great Regard. Be pleased to make my Love acceptable to her, and let her know, that her elegant Pen cannot be more usefully employed than in Writing Letters to her Brother at Phyladelphia, tho it may more agreably in writing Billet doux to young Gentlemen.

The other Day, after I had received a Letter of yours, with one or two others, Mr. William Barrell desired to read them. I put them into his Hand, and the next Morning had them returned in a large Bundle packed up with two great Heaps of Pins, with a very polite Card requesting Portias Acceptance of them. I shall bring them with me [when] I return: But when that will be is uncertain.—I hope not more than a Month hence.

I have really had a very disagreable Time of it. My Health and especialy my Eyes have been so very bad, that I have not been so fit for Business as I ought, and if I had been in perfect Health, I should have had in the present Condition of my Country and my Friends, no Taste for Pleasure. But Dr. Young has made a kind of Cure of my Health and Dr. Church of my Eyes.

Have received two kind Letters from your Unkle Smith —do thank him for them—I shall forever love him for them. I love every Body that writes to me.

I am forever yours—

The incident recounted in the following letter would in today's terms be called the brass tacks of the American Revolution. Not without its comic aspects, it involves a crusty old New England character named Hayden who happened to be the Adamses' tenant in the adjoining house (the John Adams Birthplace); two families, one local and one in flight from occupied Boston, in each of which there was an expectant mother; and Abigail Adams, for once pushed beyond her powers to cope with a domestic problem. A compromise was worked out, but it satisfied no one, and there were to be disagreeable sequels over several years.

AA to JA

Dearest Friend Braintree July 12. 1775

I have met with some abuse and very Ill treatment. I want you for my protector and justifier.

In this Day of distress for our Boston Friends when every one does what in them lyes to serve them, your Friend Gorge Trott and family moved up to Braintree, went in with her two Brothers and families with her Father, but they not thinking themselves so secure as further in the Country moved away. After they were gone Mr. Church took the house and took a number of borders. Mr. Trott had engaged a house near his Friends but being prevented going quite so soon as he designd, and the great distress people were in for houses, the owner had taken in a family and dissapointed Mr. Trott, nor could he procure a house any where, for the more remote from the sea coast you go the thicker you find the Boston people. After this dissapointment, he had his Goods without unloading brought back to Braintree, and he with all his family were obliged to shelter themselves in your Brothers house till he could seek further. You know, from the situation of my Brothers family it was impossible for them to tarry there, Mrs. Trots circumstances requiring more rooms than one. In this extremity he applied to me to see if I would not accommodate him with the next house, every other spot in Town being full. I sent for Mr. Hayden and handsomely asked him, he said he would try, but he took no pains to procure himself a place. There were several in the other parish which were to be let, but my Gentleman did not chuse to go there. Mr. Trot upon account of his Buisness which is in considerable demand wanted

JOHN AND ABIGAIL ADAMS' FIRST HOME
("THE JOHN QUINCY ADAMS BIRTHPLACE")
AND ITS NEAR NEIGHBOR, THE JOHN ADAMS BIRTHPLACE

to be here. Mr. Trott, finding there was no hopes of his going out said he would go in with him, provided I would let him have the chamber I improved for a Dairy room and the lower room and chamber over it which Hayden has. I then sent and asked Mr. Hayden to be so kind as to remove his things into the other part of the house and told him he might improve the kitchen and back chamber, the bed room and the Dairy room in which he already had a bed. He would not tell me whether he would or not, but said I was turning him out of Door to oblige Boston folks, and he could not be stired up, and if you was at home you would not once ask him to go out, but was more of a Gentleman. (You must know that both his Sons are in the army, not but one Days Work has been done by any of them this Spring.) I as mildly as I could represented the distress of Mr. Trot and the difficulties to which he had been put—that I looked upon it my Duty to do all in my power to Oblige him—and that he Hayden would be much better accommodated than hundreds who were turnd out of Town—and I finally said that Mr. Trott should go in. In this State, Sister Adams got to bed and then there was not a Spot in Brothers house for them to lie down in. I removed my dairy things, and once more requested the old Man to move into the other part of the house, but he positively tells me he will not and all the art of Man shall not stir him, even dares me to put any article out of one room into an other. Says Mr. Trot shall not come in—he has got possession and he will keep it. What not have a place to entertain his children in when they come to see him. I now write you an account of the matter, and desire you to write to him and give me orders what course I shall take. I must take Mr. Trott in with me and all his family for the present, till he can look out further or have that house. It would make your heart ake to see what difficulties and distresses the poor Boston people are driven to. Belcher has two families with him. There are 3 in Veses [Veasey's] house, 2 in Etters, 2 in Mr. Savils, 2 in Jonathan Bass'es and yet that obstinate Wretch will not remove his few things into the other part of that house, but live there paying no rent upon the distresses of others.

It would be needless to enumerate all his impudence. Let it suffice to say it moved me so much that I had hard Work to suppress my temper. I want to know whether his things may be removed into the other part of the house, whether he consents or not? Mr. Trott would rejoice to take the whole, but would put up with any thing rather than be a burden to his Friends. I told the old Man I believed I was doing nothing but what I should be justified in. He says well tis a time of war get him out if I can, but cannon Ball shall not move him. If you think you are able to find 3 houses, for 3 such tenents as you have they must abide where they are, tho I own I shall be much mortified if you do not support me.

I feel too angry to make this any thing further than a Letter of Buisness. I am most sincerely yours, Abigail Adams

AA to JA

Dearest Friend Braintree July 16 1775

I have this afternoon had the pleasure of receiving your Letter by your Friends Mr. Collins and Kaighn and an English Gentle man his Name I do not remember. It was next to seeing my dearest Friend. Mr. Collins could tell me more perticuliarly about you and your Health than I have been able to hear since you left me. I rejoice in his account of your better Health, and of your spirits, tho he says I must not expect to see you till next spring. I hope he does not speak the truth. I know (I think I do, for am not I your Bosome Friend?) your feelings, your anxieties, your exertions, &c. more than those before whom you are obliged to wear the face of chearfulness.

I have seen your Letters to Col. Palmer and Warren. I pity your

Embaresments. How difficult the task to quench out the fire and the pride of private ambition, and to sacrifice ourselfs and all our hopes and expectations to the publick weal. How few have souls capable of so noble an undertaking—how often are the lawrels worn by those who have had no share in earning them, but there is a future recompence of reward to which the upright man looks, and which he will most assuredly obtain provided he perseveres unto the end.—The appointment of the Generals Washington and Lee, gives universal satisfaction. The people have the highest opinion of Lees abilities, but you know the continuation of the popular Breath, depends much upon favorable events.

I had the pleasure of seeing both the Generals and their Aid de camps soon after their arrival and of being personally made known to them. They very politely express their regard for you. Major Miflin said he had orders from you to visit me at Braintree. I told him I should be very happy to see him there, and accordingly sent Mr. Thaxter to Cambridge with a card to him and Mr. Read [Reed] to dine with me. Mrs. Warren and her Son were to be with me. They very politely received the Message and lamented that they were not able to upon account of Expresses which they were that day to get in readiness to send of.

I was struck with General Washington. You had prepaired me to entertain a favorable opinion of him, but I thought the one half was not told me. Dignity with ease, and complacency, the Gentleman and Soldier look agreably blended in him. Modesty marks every line and feture of his face. Those lines of Dryden instantly occurd to me

> "Mark his Majestick fabrick! he's a temple
> Sacred by birth, and built by hands divine
> His Souls the Deity that lodges there.
> Nor is the pile unworthy of the God."

General Lee looks like a careless hardy Veteran and from his appearence brought to my mind his namesake Charls the 12, king of Sweeden. The Elegance of his pen far exceeds that of his person. I was much pleased with your Friend Collins. I persuaded them to stay coffe with me, and he was as unreserved and social as if we had been old acquaintances, and said he was very loth to leave the house. I would have detaind them till morning, but they were very desirous of reaching Cambridge.

You have made often and frequent complaints that your Friends do not write to you. I have stired up some of them. Dr. Tufts, Col. Quincy, Mr. Tudor, Mr. Thaxter all have wrote you now, and a

Lady whom I am willing you should value preferable to all others save one. May not I in my turn make complaints? All the Letters I receive from you seem to be wrote in so much haste, that they scarcely leave room for a social feeling. They let me know that you exist, but some of them contain scarcely six lines. I want some sentimental Effusions of the Heart. I am sure you are not destitute of them or are they all absorbed in the great publick. Much is due to that I know, but being part of the whole I lay claim to a Larger Share than I have had. You used to be more communicative a Sundays. I always loved a Sabeth days letter, for then you had a greater command of your time —but hush to all complaints.

I am much surprized that you have not been more accurately informd of what passes in the camps. As to intelegance from Boston, tis but very seldom we are able to collect any thing that may be relied upon, and to report the vague flying rumours would be endless. I heard yesterday by one Mr. Rolestone [Roulstone] a Goldsmith who got out in a fishing Schooner, that there distress encreased upon them fast, their Beaf is all spent, their Malt and Sider all gone, all the fresh provisions they can procure they are obliged to give to the sick and wounded. 19 of our Men who were in Jail and were wounded at the Battle of Charlstown were Dead. No Man dared now to be seen talking to his Friend in the Street, they were obliged to be within every evening at ten o clock according to Martial Law, nor could any inhabitant walk any Street in Town after that time without a pass from Gage. He has orderd all the melasses to be stilld up into rum for the Soldiers, taken away all Licences, and given out others obligeing to a forfeiture of ten pounds L M if any rum is sold without written orders from the General. He give much the same account of the kill'd and wounded we have had from others. The Spirit he says which prevails among the Soldiers is a Spirit of Malice and revenge, there is no true courage and bravery to be observed among them, their Duty is hard allways mounting guard with their packs at their back ready for an alarm which they live in continual hazard of. Doctor Eliot is not on bord a man of war, as has been reported, but perhaps was left in Town as the comfort and support of those who cannot escape, he was constantly with our prisoners. Mr. Lovel and Leach with others are certainly in Jail. A poor Milch cow was last week kill'd in Town and sold for a shilling stearling per pound. The transports arrived last week from York, but every additional Man adds to their distress.—There has been a little Expidition this week to Long Island. There has been before several attempts to go on but 3 men of war lay near, and cutters all round the Island that they could not succeed. A number of whale boats lay at Germantown; 300 volenters commanded by one Capt. Tupper came on monday evening and took the boats, went on and brought of 70 odd Sheep, 15 head of cattle, and 16 prisoners 13 of whom were sent by Simple Sapling to mow the Hay which they had very badly executed. They were all a sleep in the house and barn when they were taken. There were 3 women with them. Our Heroes came of in triumph not being observed by their Enimies. This spiritted up other[s]. They could not endure the thought that the House and barn should afford them any shelter. They did not distroy them the night before for fear of being discoverd. Capt. Wild of this Town with about 25 of his company, Capt. Gold [Gould] of Weymouth with as many of his, and some other volenters to the amount of an 100, obtaind leave to go on and distroy the Hay together with the House and barn and in open day in full view of the men of war they set of from the Moon so call'd coverd by a number of men who were placed there, went on, set fire to the Buildings and Hay. A number of armed cutters immediately Surrounded the Island, fired upon our Men. They came of with a hot and continued fire upon them, the Bullets flying in every direction and the Men of Wars boats plying them with small arms. Many in this Town who were spectators expected every moment our Men would all be sacrificed, for sometimes they were so near as to be calld to and damnd by their Enimies and orderd to surrender yet they all returnd in safty, not one Man even wounded. Upon the Moon we lost one Man from the cannon on board the Man of War. On the Evening of the same day a Man of War came and anchord near Great Hill, and two cutters came to Pig Rocks. It occasiond an alarm in this Town and we were up all Night. They remain there yet, but have not ventured to land any men.

This Town have chosen their Representative. Col. Palmer is the Man. There was a considerable musture upon Thayers side, and Vintons company marched up in order to assist, but got sadly dissapointed. Newcomb insisted upon it that no man should vote who was in the army—he had no notion of being under the Military power—said we might be so situated as to have the greater part of the people engaged in the Military, and then all power would be wrested out of the hands of the civil Majestrate. He insisted upon its being put to vote, and carried his point immediately. It brought Thayer to his Speach who said all he could against it. —As to the Situation of the camps, our Men are in general Healthy, much more so at Roxbury than Cambridge, and the Camp in vastly better order. General Thomas has the character of an Excelent officer. His Merit has certainly been overlook'd, as modest merrit generally is. I hear General Washington is much pleased with his conduct.

Every article here in the West india way is very scarce and dear. In six week[s] we shall not be able to purchase any article of the kind. I wish you would let Bass get me one pound of peper, and 2 yd. of black caliminco for Shooes. I cannot wear leather if I go bare foot the reason I need not mention. Bass may make a fine profit if he layes in a stock for himself. You can hardly immagine how much we want many common small articles which are not manufactured amongst ourselves, but we will have them in time. Not one pin is to be purchased for love nor money. I wish you could convey me a thousand by any Friend travelling this way. Tis very provoking to have such a plenty so near us, but tantulus like not able to touch. I should have been glad to have laid in a small stock of the West India articles, but I cannot get one copper. No person thinks of paying any thing, and I do not chuse to run in debt. I endeavour to live in the most frugal manner posible, but I am many times distressed.—Mr. Trot I have accommodated by removeing the office into my own chamber, and after being very angry and sometimes persuaideding I obtaind the mighty concession of the Bed room, but I am now so crouded as not to have a Lodging for a Friend that calls to see me. I must beg you would give them warning to seek a place before Winter. Had that house been empty I could have had an 100 a year for it. Many person[s] had applied before Mr. Trot, but I wanted some part of it my self, and the other part it seems I have no command of.—We have since I wrote you had many fine showers, and altho the crops of grass have been cut short, we have a fine prospect of Indian corn and English grain. Be not afraid, ye beasts of the field, for the pastures of the Wilderness do spring, the Tree beareth her fruit, the vine and the olive yeald their increase.

We have not yet been much distressed for grain. Every thing at present looks blooming. O that peace would once more extend her olive Branch.

> "This Day be Bread and peace my lot
> All Else beneath the Sun
> Thou knowst if best bestowed or not
> And let thy will be done."
>
> But is the Almighty ever bound to please
> Ruild by my wish or studious of my ease.
> Shall I determine where his frowns shall fall
> And fence my Grotto from the Lot of all?
> Prostrate his Sovereign Wisdom I adore
> Intreat his Mercy, but I dare no more.

Our little ones send Duty to pappa. You would smile to see them all gather round mamma upon the reception of a letter to hear from pappa, and Charls with open mouth, What does par say—did not he write no more. And little Tom says I wish I could see par. Upon Mr. Rice's going into the army he asked Charls if he should get him a place, he catchd at it with great eagerness and insisted upon going. We could not put him of. he cryed and beged, no obstical we could raise was sufficent to satisfy him, till I told him he must first obtain your consent. Then he insisted that I must write about it, and has been every day these 3 weeks insisting upon my asking your consent. At last I have promised to write to you, and am obliged to be as good as my word.—I have now wrote you all I can collect from every quarter. Tis fit for no eye but yours, because you can make all necessary allowances. I cannot coppy.

There are yet in Town 4 of the Selectmen and some thousands of inhabitants tis said.—I hope to hear from you soon. Do let me know if there is any prospect of seeing you? Next Wedensday is 13 weeks since you went away.

I must bid you adieu. You have many Friends tho they have not noticed you by writing. I am sorry they have been so neglegent. I hope no share of that blame lays upon your most affectionate

Portia

JA to AA

My Dear

July 23 1775

You have more than once in your Letters mentioned Dr. Franklin, and in one intimated a Desire that I should write you something concerning him.

Dr. Franklin has been very constant in his Attendance on Congress from the Beginning. His Conduct has been composed and grave and in the Opinion of many Gentlemen very reserved. He has not assumed any Thing, nor affected to take the lead; but has seemed to choose that the Congress should pursue their own Principles and sentiments and adopt their own Plans: Yet he has not been backward: has been very usefull, on many occasions, and discovered a Disposition entirely American. He does not hesitate at our boldest Measures, but rather seems to think us, too irresolute, and backward. He thinks us at present in an odd State, neither in Peace nor War, neither dependent nor independent. But he thinks that We shall soon assume a Character more decisive.

He thinks, that We have the Power of preserving ourselves, and that even if We should be driven to the disagreable Necessity of assuming a total Independency, and set up a separate state, We could maintain it. The People of England, have thought that the Opposition in America, was wholly owing to Dr. Franklin: and I suppose their scribblers will attribute the Temper, and Proceedings of this Congress to him: but there cannot be a greater Mistake. He has had but little share farther than to co operate and assist. He is however a great and good Man. I wish his Colleagues from this City were All like him, particularly one, whose Abilities and Virtues, formerly trumpeted so much in America, have been found wanting.

There is a young Gentleman from Pensylvania whose Name is Wilson, whose Fortitude, Rectitude, and Abilities too, greatly outshine his Masters. Mr. Biddle, the Speaker, has been taken off, by Sickness. Mr. Mifflin is gone to the Camp, Mr. Morton is ill too, so that this Province has suffered by the Timidity of two overgrown Fortunes. The Dread of Confiscation, or Caprice, I know not what has influenced them too much: Yet they were for taking Arms and pretended to be very valiant.—This Letter must be secret my dear—at least communicated with great Discretion. Yours, John Adams

Here follows the text of one of John Adams' intercepted letters (mentioned earlier in this chapter) that gave him a good deal more public attention than, at the time, he wanted. Although innumerable copies were made and circulated, the original manuscript has never been found. It is reprinted here from the *Massachusetts Gazette and Boston Weekly News-Letter*, a tory paper, of August 17, 1775.

Philadelphia July 24th, 1775.

JA to AA

My Dear,

It is now almost three Months since I left you, in every Part of which my Anxiety about you and the Children, as well as our Country, has been extreme.

The Business I have had upon my Mind has been as great and important as can be intrusted to [One] Man, and the Difficulty and Intricacy of it is prodigious. When 50 or 60 Men have a Constitution to form for a great Empire, at the same Time that they have a Country of fifteen hundred Miles extent to fortify, Millions to arm and train, a Naval Power to begin, an extensive Commerce to regulate, numerous Tribes of Indians to negotiate with, a standing Army of Twenty seven Thousand Men to raise, pay, victual and officer, I really shall pity those 50 or 60 Men.

I must see you e'er long.———Rice, has wrote me a very good Letter, and so has Thaxter, for which I thank them both.———Love to the Children. J. A.

I wish I had given you a compleat History from the Beginning to the End of the Journey, of the Behaviour of my Compatriots.——No Mortal Tale could equal it.——I will tell you in Future, but you shall keep it secret.———The Fidgets, the Whims, the Caprice, the Vanity, the Superstition, the Irritability of some of us, is enough to ———

Addressed To Mrs Abigail Adams Braintrie, to the Care of Col. Warren, favor d by Mr. Hichborne.

The Second Continental Congress stood in recess during August and early September 1775. John Adams, on returning to Massachusetts on August 10, went directly to Watertown where, as a member of the Council, he attended the sessions of the General Court. Visits with his wife were confined to weekends in Braintree and to the final three days of the session, when she joined him in Watertown. The Massachusetts delegates arrived in Philadelphia on September 12 in time for the reconvening of the Congress, now enlarged by the presence of representatives from all thirteen colonies.

Almost immediately following her husband's departure, Abigail Adams fell victim, along with others in the household, to the virulent dysentery, then epidemic. "Our House is an hospital in every part." Before the pestilence abated, her husband's brother Elihu and his child as well as her own mother succumbed. "So sickly and so Mortal a time the oldest Man does not remember."

In this unhappy time John Adams, absorbed in public matters and all unaware that the dire sickness had reached so close, wrote no letter home until three weeks had passed. Word of his family's troubles took more than a month to reach him.

AA to JA

Dearest Friend — Braintree August 10 1775

Tis with a sad Heart I take my pen to write to you because I must be the bearer of what will greatly afflict and distress you. Yet I wish you to be prepaired for the Event. Your Brother Elihu lies very dangerously sick with a Dysentery. He has been very bad for more than a week, his life is despaired of. Er'e I close this Letter I fear I shall write you that he is no more.

We are all in great distress. Your Mother is with him in great anguish. I hear this morning that he is sensible of his Danger, and calmly resigned to the will of Heaven; which is a great Satisfaction to his mourning Friend's. I cannot write more at present than to assure you of the Health of your own family. Mr. Elisha Niles lies very bad with the same disorder.—Adieu.

August 11

I have this morning occasion to sing of Mercies and judgments.

May I properly notice each—a mixture of joy and grief agitate my Bosom. The return of thee my dear partner after a four months absence is a pleasure I cannot express, but the joy is overclouded, and the Day is darkened by the mixture of Grief and the Sympathy I feel for the looss of your Brother, cut of in the pride of life and the bloom of Manhood! in the midst of his usefulness; Heaven san[c]tify this affliction to us, and make me properly thankful that it is not my sad lot to mourn the loss of a Husband in the room of a Brother.

May thy life be spaired and thy Health confirmed for the benefit of thy Country and the happiness of thy family is the constant supplication of thy Friend.

AA to JA

Dearest Friend — Braintree Sepbr. 25 1775

I set down with a heavy Heart to write to you. I have had no other since you left me. Woe follows Woe and one affliction treads upon the heal of an other. My distress for my own family having in some measure abated; tis excited anew upon the distress of my dear Mother. Her kindness brought her to see me every day when I was ill and our little Tommy. She has taken the disorder and lies so bad that we have little hopes of her Recovery. She is possess'd with the Idea that she shall not recover, and I fear it will prove but too true.

In this Town the distemper seems to have abated. We have none now so bad as Patty. She has lain 21 days, each day we had reason to think would be her last, but [a] good Constitution, and youth for ought I know will finally conquer the distemper. She is not able to get out of Bed, nor can she help herself any more than a new born infant. Yet their are symptoms which now appear in her favour.

The desolation of War is not so distressing as the Havock made by the pestilence. Some poor parents are mourning the loss of 3, 4 and 5 children, and some families are wholy striped of every Member.

Wherefore is it that we are thus contended with? How much reason have I for thankfulness that all my family are spaired whilst so many others are striped of their parents, their children, their husbands.

O kind Heaven spair my parents, spair my Dearest Friend and grant him Health. Continue the lives and health of our dear children. Sister Elihu Adams lost her youngest child last night with this disorder. I can add no more than Supplications for your welfare, and an ardent desire to hear from you by every opportunity. It will alleviate every trouble thro which it may be my Lot to pass. I am most affectionately your distress'd

Portia

AA to JA

Weymouth october. 1 1775

Have pitty upon me, have pitty upon me o! thou my beloved for the Hand of God presseth me soar.

Yet will I be dumb and silent and not open my mouth becaus thou o Lord hast done it.

How can I tell you (o my bursting Heart) that my Dear Mother has Left me, this day about 5 oclock she left this world for an infinitely better.

After sustaining 16 days severe conflict nature fainted and she fell asleep. Blessed Spirit where art thou? At times I almost am ready to faint under this severe and heavy Stroke, seperated from *thee* who used to be a comfortar towards me in affliction, but blessed be God, his Ear is not heavy that he cannot hear, but he has bid us call upon him in time of Trouble.

I know you are a sincere and hearty mourner with me and will pray for me in my affliction. My poor father like a firm Believer and a Good christian sets before his children the best of Examples of patience and submission. My sisters send their Love to you and are greatly afflicted. You often Express'd your anxiety for me when you left me before, surrounded with Terrors, but my trouble then was as the small dust in the balance compaird to what I have since endured. I hope to be properly mindful of the correcting hand, that I may not be rebuked in anger.—You will pardon and forgive all my wanderings of mind. I cannot be correct.

Tis a dreadful time with this whole province. Sickness and death are in almost every family. I have no more shocking and terible Idea of any Distemper except the Plague than this.

Almighty God restrain the pestilence which walketh in darkness and wasteth at noon day and which has laid in the dust one of the dearest of parents. May the Life of the other be lengthend out to his afflicted children and Your distressd

Portia

JA to AA

My Dear

Philadelphia Octr. 1. 1775

This Morning, I received your two Letters of September 8th. and September 16th.—What shall I say?—The Intelligence they contain, came upon me by Surprize, as I never had the least Intimation before, that any of my Family was ill, excepting in a Card from Mrs. Warren received a few days ago, in which she informed me that Mrs. Adams had been unwell but was better.

You may easily conceive the State of Mind, in which I am at present.—Uncertain and apprehensive, at first I suddenly thought of setting off, immediately, for Braintree, and I have not yet determined otherwise. Yet the State of public Affairs is so critical, that I am half afraid to leave my Station, Altho my Presence here is of no great Consequence.

I feel—I tremble for You. Poor Tommy! I hope by this Time, however, he has recovered his plump Cheeks and his fine Bloom. By your Account of Patty I fear—but still I will hope she has been supported, and is upon the Recovery.

I rejoice to learn that Nabby and her Brothers have hitherto escaped and pray God that his Goodness may be still continued to them.—Your Description of the distressed State of the Neighbourhood is affecting indeed.

It is not uncommon for a Train of Calamities to come together. Fire, Sword, Pestilence, Famine, often keep Company, and visit a Country in a Flock.

At this Distance I can do no good to you nor yours. I pray God to support you—I hope our Friends and Neighbours are kind as usual. I feel for them, in the general Calamity.

I am so far from thinking you melancholly, that I am charmed with that Admirable Fortitude, and that divine Spirit of Resignation which appears in your Letters. I cannot express the Satisfaction it gives me, nor how much it contributes to support me.

You have alarmed me however, by mentioning Anxieties which you do not think it prudent to mention to any one. I am wholly at a Loss to conjecture what they can be. If they arise from the Letters, be assured that you may banish them forever. These Letters have reached Philadelphia, but have produced Effects very different from those which were expected from the Publication of them. These Effects I will explain to you sometime or other. As to the Versification of them, if there is Wit or Humour in it laugh—if ill Nature, sneer—if mere Dullness, why you may even yawn or nod. I have no Anger, at it, nay even scarcly contempt. It is impotent.

As to Politicks, We have nothing to expect but the whole Wrath and Force of G. Britain. But your Words are as true as an oracle "God helps them, who help them selves, and if We obtain the divine Aid by our own Virtue, Fortitude and Perseverance, We may be sure of Relief."

It may amuse you to hear a Story. A few days ago, in Company with Dr. Zubly, somebody said, there was nobody on our side but the Almighty. The Dr. who is a Native of Switzerland, and speaks but broken English, quickly replied "Dat is enough.—Dat is enough," and turning to me, says he, it puts me in mind of a fellow who once said, The Catholicks have on their side the Pope, and the K. of France and the K. of Spain, and the K. of Sardinia, and the K. of Poland and the Emperor of Germany &c. &c. &c. But as to them poor Devils the Protestants, they have nothing on their side but God Almighty.

JA to AA My Dear Octr: 19. 1775

It is some Time since I wrote you, and I have nothing, now, to write but Repetitions of Respect and Affection.—I am anxious to hear from you. I hope, the Family is better, and that your Grief for the great Loss We have all sustained is somewhat abated. I hope your Father and Sister Betcy, are well, tho they must be greatly afflicted. Give my Love to Betcy, and let her know that I feel, most intimately for her, as well as for myself, and the rest. I consider the Stroke must fall heavier upon her, as it was nearer to her. Her Prosperity is near my Heart—I wish her every Blessing which she can possibly wish for herself.

Really it is very painfull to be 400 Miles from ones Family and Friends when We know they are in Affliction. It seems as if It would be a Joy to me to fly home, even to share with you your Burdens and Misfortunes. Surely, if I were with you, it would be my Study to allay your Griefs, to mitigate your Pains and to divert your melancholly Thoughts.

When I shall come home I know not. We have so much to do, and it is so difficult to do it right, that We must learn Patience. Upon my Word I think, if ever I were to come here again, I must bring you with me. I could live here pleasantly if I had you, with me. Will you come and have the small Pox here? I wish I could remove all the Family, our little Daughter and Sons, and all go through the Distemper here.—What if We should? Let me please myself with the Thought however.

Congress has appointed Mr. Wythe, Mr. Deane and me, a Committee to collect an Account of the Hostilities committed by the Troops and Ships, with proper Evidence of the Number and Value of the Houses and other Buildings destroyed or damaged, the Vessells captivated and the Cattle, Sheep, Hogs &c. taken. We are about writing to all the general assemblies of New England, and to many private Gentlemen in each Collony to assist Us in making the Collections. The Gentlemen with me are able Men. Deane's Character you know. He is a very ingenious Man and an able Politician. Wythe is a new Member from Virginia, a Lawyer of the highest Eminence in that

Province, a learned and very laborious Man: so that We may hope this Commission will be well executed. A Tale of Woe it will be! Such a scene of Distress, and Destruction and so patiently and magnanimously born. Such a Scene of Cruelty and Barbarity, so unfeelingly committed.—I mention this to you my dear, that you may look up and transmit to me a Paper, which Coll. Palmer lent me containing a Relation of the Charlestown Battle, which was transmitted to England by the Committee of Safety. This Paper I must have, or a Copy of it.

I wish I could collect from the People of Boston or others, a proper Set of Paintings of the Scenes of Distress and Misery, brought upon that Town from the Commencement of the Port Bill. Posterity must hear a Story that shall make their Ears to Tingle.

Yours—yours—yours—

As the time of general sickness passed, John and Abigail Adams' absorption in the losses they and their circle had sustained gradually gave way to reflections upon topics that transcended the personal and the immediate.

JA to AA

Octr. 29. 1775

There is, in the human Breast, a social Affection, which extends to our whole Species. Faintly indeed; but in some degree. The Nation, Kingdom, or Community to which We belong is embraced by it more vigorously. It is stronger still towards the Province to which we belong, and in which We had our Birth. It is stronger and stronger, as We descend to the County, Town, Parish, Neighbourhood, and Family, which We call our own.—And here We find it often so powerfull as to become partial, to blind our Eyes, to darken our Understandings and pervert our Wills.

It is to this Infirmity, in my own Heart, that I must perhaps attribute that local Attachment, that partial Fondness, that overweening Prejudice in favour of New England, which I feel very often and which I fear sometimes, leads me to expose myself to just Ridicule.

New England has in many Respects the Advantage of every other Colony in America, and indeed of every other Part of the World, that I know any Thing of.

1. The People are purer English Blood, less mixed with Scotch, Irish, Dutch, French, Danish, Sweedish &c. than any other; and descended from Englishmen too who left Europe, in purer Times than the present and less tainted with Corruption than those they left behind them.

2. The Institutions in New England for the Support of Religion, Morals and Decency, exceed any other, obliging every Parish to have a Minister, and every Person to go to Meeting &c.

3. The public Institutions in New England for the Education of Youth, supporting Colledges at the public Expence and obliging Towns to maintain Grammar schools, is not equalled and never was in any Part of the World.

4. The Division of our Territory, that is our Counties into Townships, empowering Towns to assemble, choose officers, make Laws, mend roads, and twenty other Things, gives every Man an opportunity of shewing and improving that Education which he received at Colledge or at school, and makes Knowledge and Dexterity at public Business common.

5. Our Laws for the Distribution of Intestate Estates occasions a frequent Division of landed Property and prevents Monopolies, of Land.

But in opposition to these We have laboured under many Disadvantages. The exorbitant Prerogatives of our Governors &c. which would have overborn our Liberties, if it had not been opposed by the five preceding Particulars.

AA to JA

November 27 1775

Tis a fortnight to Night since I wrote you a line during which, I have been confined with the Jaundice, Rhumatism and a most voilent cold; I yesterday took a puke which has releived me, and I feel much better to day. Many, very many people who have had the dysentery, are now afflicted both with the Jaundice and Rhumatisim, some it has left in Hecticks, some in dropsies.

The great and incessant rains we have had this fall, (the like cannot be recollected) may have occasiond some of the present disorders. The Jaundice is very prevelant in the Camp. We have lately had a week of very cold weather, as cold as January, and a flight of snow, which I hope will purify the air of some of the noxious vapours. It has spoild many hundreds of Bushels of Apples, which were designd for cider, and which the great rains had prevented people from making up. Suppose we have lost 5 Barrels by it.

Col. Warren returnd last week to Plymouth, so that I shall not hear any thing from you till he goes back again which will not be till the last of ⟨*next*⟩ this month.

He Damp'd my Spirits greatly by telling me that the Court had prolonged your Stay an other month. I was pleasing myself with the thoughts that you would soon be upon your return. Tis in vain to repine. I hope the publick will reap what I sacrifice.

I wish I knew what mighty things were fabricating. If a form of Goverment is to be established here what one will be assumed? Will it be left to our assemblies to chuse one? and will not many men have many minds? and shall we not run into Dissentions among ourselves?

I am more and more convinced that Man is a dangerous creature, and that power whether vested in many or a few is ever grasping, and like the grave cries give, give. The great fish swallow up the small, and he who is most strenuous for the Rights of the people, when vested with power, is as eager after the perogatives of Goverment. You tell me of degrees of perfection to which Humane Nature is capable of arriving, and I believe it, but at the same time lament that our admiration should arise from the scarcity of the instances.

The Building up a Great Empire, which was only hinted at by my correspondent may now I suppose be realized even by the unbelievers. Yet will not ten thousand Difficulties arise in the formation of it? The Reigns of Goverment have been so long slakned, that I fear the people will not quietly submit to those restraints which are necessary for the peace, and security, of the community; if we seperate from Brittain, what Code of Laws will be established. How shall we be governd so as to retain our Liberties? Can any goverment be free which is not adminstred by general stated Laws? Who shall frame these Laws? Who will give them force and energy? Tis true your Resolution[s] as a Body have heithertoo had the force of Laws. But will they continue to have?

When I consider these things and the prejudices of people in favour of Ancient customs and Regulations, I feel anxious for the fate of our Monarchy or Democracy or what ever is to take place. I soon get lost in a Labyrinth of perplexities, but whatever occurs, may justice and righteousness be the Stability of our times, and order arise out of confusion. Great difficulties may be surmounted, by patience and perseverance.

I believe I have tired you with politicks. As to news we have not any at all. I shudder at the approach of winter when I think I am to remain desolate. Suppose your weather is warm yet. Mr. Mason and Thaxter live with me, and render some part of my time less disconsolate. Mr. Mason is a youth who will please you, he has Spirit, taste and Sense. His application to his Studies is constant and I am much mistaken if he does not make a very good figure in his profession.

I have with me now, the only Daughter of your Brother; I feel a tenderer affection for her as she has lost a kind parent. Though too young to be sensible of her own loss, I can pitty her. She appears to be a child of a very good Disposition—only wants to be a little used to company.

Our Little ones send Duty to pappa and want much to see him. Tom says he wont come home till the Battle is over—some strange notion he has got into his head. He has got a political cread to say to him when he returns.

I must bid you good night. Tis late for one who am much of an invalide. I was dissapointed last week in receiving a packet by the post, and upon unsealing it found only four news papers. I think you are more cautious than you need be. All Letters I believe have come safe to hand. I have Sixteen from you, and wish I had as many more. Adieu. Yours.

John Adams, tired, but determined to resolve the dilemma posed by the Massachusetts legislature's electing him Chief Justice and also reelecting him to Congress, obtained leave to return home. He arrived in Braintree on December 21 to remain a month. Having decided to retain at least for the time his place in Congress, he began his journey southward on January 24 with a stop at Cambridge that was memorable. Upon reaching neighboring Watertown, he dispatched a letter to his wife, taking care lest he repeat the transgression of his September departure.

JA to AA

My dear Nabby Watertown Jan. 24. 1776

I am determined not to commit a fault which escaped me, the last Time I sat out for the southward.

I waited on General Thomas at Roxbury this Morning, and then went to Cambridge where I dined at Coll. Mifflins with the General, and Lady, and a vast Collection of other Company, among whom were six or seven Sachems and Warriours, of the French Cagnawaga Indians, with several of their Wives and Children. A savage Feast they made of it, yet were very polite in the Indian style. One of these sachems is an Englishman a Native of this Colony whose Name was Williams, captivated in his Infancy with his Mother, and adopted by some kind Squaw—another I think is half french Blood.

I was introduced to them by the General as one of the grand Council Fire at Philadelphia which made them prick up their Ears, they came and shook Hands with me, and made me low Bows, and scrapes &c. In short I was much pleased with this Days entertainment.

The General is to make them presents in Cloaths and Trinketts, they have visited the Lines at Cambridge and are going to see those at Roxbury.

Tomorrow We mount, for the grand Council Fire—Where I shall think often of my little Brood at the Foot of Pens Hill. Remember me particularly to Nabby, Johnny, Charly and Tommy. Tell them I charge them to be good, honest, active and industrious for their own sakes, as well as ours.

In early 1776, the idea that the conflict between England and its colonies would be resolved in no way other than by independence received more widespread and public statement throughout the Colonies. The publication in Philadelphia in January of *Common Sense* by Thomas Paine was both a clear manifestation of this and of a new concern in men's minds—the nature of the governments that would be organized in the former colonies. John Adams was soon led to speculate seriously on "what is proper and necessary to be done, in order to form Constitutions for single Colonies, as well as a great Model of Union for the whole." After circulating to good effect in manuscript among the members of Congress, his essay was published anonymously in Philadelphia in April with the title *Thoughts on Government.*

The decision by Congress in January to send a special committee to Canada to persuade its people to make "a 14th colony" was as much the product of the new tendency to consider what would be the situation prevailing in America after independence had been achieved, as it was dictated by the ineffectiveness of the military invasion of Canada undertaken six months earlier.

In Massachusetts too, long committed to independence but engrossed in immediate military problems, there were new stirrings. The storming of Dorchester Heights on March 4 by the American forces and the consequent evacuation of Boston on March 17 freed minds there to reflect on the less immediate: on government and its unresolved problems—on America's relations with foreign powers, on slavery, on the status of women.

JA to AA

My dearest Friend February 18. 1776

I sent you from New York a Pamphlet intituled Common Sense, written in Vindication of Doctrines which there is Reason to expect that the further Encroachments of Tyranny and Depredations of Oppression, will soon make the common Faith: unless the cunning Ministry, by proposing Negociations and Terms of Reconciliation, should divert the present Current from its Channell.

Reconciliation if practicable and Peace if attainable, you very well know would be as agreable to my Inclinations and as advantageous to my Interest, as to any Man's. But I see no Prospect, no Probability, no Possibility. And I cannot but despise the Understanding, which sincerely expects an honourable Peace, for its Credulity, and detest the hypocritical Heart, which pretends to expect it, when in Truth it does not. The News Papers here are full of free Speculations, the Tendency of which you will easily discover. The Writers reason from Topicks which have been long in Contemplation, and fully understood by the People at large in New England, but have been attended to in the southern Colonies only by Gentlemen of free Spirits and liberal Minds, who are very few. I shall endeavour to inclose to you as many of the Papers and Pamphlets as I can, as long as I stay here. Some will go by this Conveyance.

Dr. Franklin, Mr. Chase, and Mr. Charles Carroll of Carrollton in Maryland, are chosen a Committee to go into Canada. The Characters of the two first you know. The last is not a Member of Congress, but a Gentleman of independant Fortune, perhaps the largest in America, 150 or 200, thousand Pounds sterling, educated in some University in France, tho a Native of America, of great Abilities and Learning, compleat Master of French Language and a Professor of the Roman catholic Religion, yet a warm, a firm, a zealous Supporter of the Rights of America, in whose Cause he has hazarded his all.

Mr. John Carroll of Maryland, a Roman Catholic Priest and a Jesuit, is to go with the Committee. The Priests in Canada having refused Baptism and Absolution to our Friends there.

General Lee is to command in that Country, whose Address, Experience, and Abilities added to his Fluency in the French Language, will give him great Advantages.

The Events of War are uncertain: We cannot insure Success, but We can deserve it. I am happy in this Provision for that important Department, because I think it the best that could be made in our Circumstances. Your Prudence will direct you to communicate the Circumstances of the Priest, the Jesuit and the Romish Religion only to such Persons as can judge of the Measure upon large and generous Principles, and will not indiscreetly divulge it. The Step was necessary, for the Anathema's of the Church are very terrible to our Friends in Canada.

I wish I understood French as well as you. I would have gone to Canada, if I had. I feel the Want of Education every Day—particularly of that Language. I pray My dear, that you would not suffer your Sons or your Daughter, ever to feel a similar Pain. It is in your Power to teach them French, and I every day see more and more that it will become a necessary Accomplishment of an American Gentleman and Lady. Pray write me in your next the Name of the Author of your thin French Grammar, which gives you the Pronunciation of the French Words in English Letters, i.e. which shews you, how the same Sounds would be signified by English Vowells and Consonants.

Write me as often as you can—tell me all the News. Desire the Children to write to me, and believe me to be theirs and yours.

AA to JA

B[raintr]ee March 16 1776

I last Evening Received yours of March 8. I must confess my self in fault that I did not write sooner to you, but I was in continual Expectation that some important event would take place and give me a subject worth writing upon. Before this reaches you I immagine you will have Received two Letters from me; the last I closed this Day week; since that time there has been some movements amongst the Ministerial Troops as if they meant to evacuate the Town of Boston. Between 70 and 80 vessels of various sizes are gone down and lay in a row in fair sight of this place, all of which appear to be loaded and by what can be collected from our own observations and from deserters they have been plundering the Town. I have been very faithless with regard to their quitting Boston, and know not how to account for it, nor am I yet satisfied that they will leave it—tho it seems to be the prevailing opinion of most people; we are obliged to place the Militia upon Gaurd every Night upon the shoars thro fear of an invasion. There has been no firing since Last twesday, till about 12 o clock last Night, when I was waked out of my sleep with a smart Cannonade which continued till nine o clock this morning, and prevented any further repose for me; the occasion I have not yet heard, but before I close this Letter I may be able to give you some account of it.

By the accounts in the publick papers the plot thickens; and some very important Crisis seems near at hand. Perhaps providence see's it necessary in order to answer important ends and designs that the Seat of War should be changed from this to the Southeren colonies that each may have a proper sympathy for the other, and unite in a seperation. The Refuge of the Believer amidst all the afflictive dispensations of providence, is that the Lord Reigneth, and that he can restrain the Arm of Man.

Orders are given to our Army to hold themselves in readiness to March at a moments warning. I'll meet you at Philippi said the Ghost of Caesar to Brutus.

Sunday Noon

Being quite sick with a voilent cold I have tarried at Home to day;

I find the fireing was occasiond by our peoples taking possession of Nook Hill, which they kept in spite of the Cannonade, and which has really obliged our Enemy to decamp this morning on board the Transports; as I hear by a mesenger just come from Head Quarters. Some of the Select Men have been to the lines and inform that they have carried of [every] thing they could [po]ssibly take, and what they could not they have [burnt, broke, or hove into the water. This] is I [believe fact,] many articles of good Household furniture having in the course of the week come on shore at Great Hill, both upon this and Weymouth Side, Lids of Desks, mahogona chairs, tables &c. Our People I hear will have Liberty to enter Boston, those who have had the small pox. The Enemy have not yet come under sail. I cannot help suspecting some design which we do not yet comprehend; to what quarter of the World they are bound is wholy unknown, but tis generally Thought to New york. Many people are elated with their quitting Boston. I confess I do not feel so, tis only lifting the burden from one shoulder to the other which perhaps is less able or less willing to support it.—To what a contemptable situation are the Troops of Britain reduced! I feel glad however that Boston is not distroyed. I hope it will be so secured and guarded as to baffel all future attemps against it.—I hear that General How said upon going upon some Eminence in Town to view our Troops who had taken Dorchester Hill unperceived by them till sun rise, "My God these fellows have done more work in one night than I could make my Army do in three months" and he might well say so for in one night two forts and long Breast Works were sprung up besides several Barracks. 300 & 70 teems were imployed most of which went 3 load in the night, beside 4000 men who worked with good Hearts.

From Pens Hill we have a view of the largest Fleet ever seen in America. You may count upwards of 100 & 70 Sail. They look like a Forrest. It was very lucky for us that we got possession of Nook Hill. They had placed their cannon so as to fire upon the Top of the Hill where they had observed our people marking out the Ground, but it was only to elude them for they began lower upon the Hill and nearer the Town. It was a very foggy dark evening and they had possession of the Hill six hours before a gun was fired, and when they did fire they over shot our people so that they were coverd before morning and not one man lost, which the enemy no sooner discoverd than Bunker Hill was abandoned and every Man decamp'd as soon as he could for they found they should not be able to get away if we once got our cannon mounted. Our General may say with Ceasar veni vidi et vici.

What Effect does the Expectation of commisioners have with you? Are they held in disdain as they are here. It is come to that pass now that the longest sword must deside the contest—and the sword is less dreaded here than the commisioners.

You mention Threats upon B[raintre]e. I know of none, nor ever heard of any till you mentiond them. The Tories look a little crest fallen; as for Cleverly he looks like the knight of the woful countanance. I hear all the Mongrel Breed are left in Boston—and our people who were prisoners are put into Irons and carried of.

As to all your own private affair[s] I generally avoid mentioning them to you; I take the best care I am capable of them. I have found some difficulty attending the only Man I have upon the place, being so often taking of. John and Jonathan have taken all the care in his absence, and performed very well. Bass got home very well. My Fathers horse came home in fine order and much to his satisfaction. Your own very poor.—Cannot you hire a Se[r]vant where you are. I am sorry you are put to so much difficulty for want of one.—I suppose you do not think one word about comeing home, and how you will get home I know not.

I made a mistake in the Name of the Grammer—tis Tandons, instead of Took. I wish you could purchase Lord Chesterfields Letters—I have lately heard them very highly spoken of. I smiled at your couplet of Lattin, your Daughter may be able in time to conster it as she has already made some considerable proficiency in her accidents, but her Mamma was obliged to get it translated.

Pray write Lord Sterlings character. I want to know whether you live in any harmony with ——— and how you setled matters. I think he seems in better humour.

I think I do not admire the Speach from the Rostrum, tis a heavy unelegant, verbose performance and did not strike my fancy at all. I am very sausy suppose you will say. Tis a Liberty I take with you; indulgance is apt to spoil one. Adieu—Yours most Sincerely.

PS Pray convey me a little paper. I have but enough for one Letter more.

Monday morning

A fine quiet night—no allarms no Cannon. The more I think of our Enemies quitting Boston, the more amaz'd I am, that they should leave such a harbour, such fortifications, such intrenchments, and that we should be in peaceable possession of a Town which we expected would cost us a river of Blood without one Drop shed. Shurely it is the Lords doings and it is Marvelous in our Eyes. Every foot of Ground which they obtain now they must fight for, and may [they purchase it at] a Bunker Hill price.

AA to JA

Braintree March 31 1776

I wish you would ever write me a Letter half as long as I write you; and tell me if you may where your Fleet are gone? What sort of Defence Virginia can make against our common Enemy? Whether it is so situated as to make an able Defence? Are not the Gentery Lords and the common people vassals, are they not like the uncivilized Natives Brittain represents us to be? I hope their Riffel Men who have shewen themselves very savage and even Blood thirsty; are not a specimen of the Generality of the people.

I am willing to allow the Colony great merrit for having produced a Washington but they have been shamefully duped by a Dunmore.

I have sometimes been ready to think that the passion for Liberty cannot be Eaquelly Strong in the Breasts of those who have been accustomed to deprive their fellow Creatures of theirs. Of this I am certain that it is not founded upon that generous and christian principal of doing to others as we would that others should do unto us.

Do not you want to see Boston; I am fearfull of the small pox, or I should have been in before this time. I got Mr. Crane to go to our House and see what state it was in. I find it has been occupied by one of the Doctors of a Regiment, very dirty, but no other damage has been done to it. The few things which were left in it are all gone. Cranch has the key which he never deliverd up. I have wrote to him for it and am determined to get it cleand as soon as possible and shut it up. I look upon it a new acquisition of property, a property which one month ago I did not value at a single Shilling, and could with pleasure have seen it in flames.

The Town in General is left in a better state than we expected, more oweing to a percipitate flight than any Regard to the inhabitants, tho some individuals discoverd a sense of honour and justice and have left the rent of the Houses in which they were, for the owners and the furniture unhurt, or if damaged sufficent to make it good.

Others have committed abominable Ravages. The Mansion House of your President is safe and the furniture unhurt whilst both the House and Furniture of the Solisiter General have fallen a prey to their own merciless party. Surely the very Fiends feel a Reverential awe for Virtue and patriotism, whilst they Detest the paricide and traitor.

I feel very differently at the approach of spring to what I did a month ago. We knew not then whether we could plant or sow with safety, whether when we had toild we could reap the fruits of our own industery, whether we could rest in our own Cottages, or whether we should not be driven from the sea coasts to seek shelter in the wilderness, but now we feel as if we might sit under our own vine and eat the good of the land.

I feel a gaieti de Coar to which before I was a stranger. I think the Sun looks brighter, the Birds sing more melodiously, and Nature puts on a more chearfull countanance. We feel a temporary peace, and the poor fugitives are returning to their deserted habitations.

Tho we felicitate ourselves, we sympathize with those who are trembling least the Lot of Boston should be theirs. But they cannot be in similar circumstances unless pusilanimity and cowardise should take possession of them. They have time and warning given them to see the Evil and shun it.—I long to hear that you have declared an independancy—and by the way in the new Code of Laws which I suppose it will be necessary for you to make I desire you would Remember the Ladies, and be more generous and favourable to them than your ancestors. Do not put such unlimited power into the hands of the Husbands. Remember all Men would be tyrants if they could. If perticuliar care and attention is not paid to the Laidies we are determined to foment a Rebelion, and will not hold ourselves bound by any Laws in which we have no voice, or Representation.

That your Sex are Naturally Tyrannical is a Truth so thoroughly established as to admit of no dispute, but such of you as wish to be happy willingly give up the harsh title of Master for the more tender and endearing one of Friend. Why then, not put it out of the power of the vicious and the Lawless to use us with cruelty and indignity with impunity. Men of Sense in all Ages abhor those customs which treat us only as the vassals of your Sex. Regard us then as Beings placed by providence under your protection and in immitation of the Supreem Being make use of that power only for our happiness.

JA to AA

Ap. 14. 1776

You justly complain of my short Letters, but the critical State of Things and the Multiplicity of Avocations must plead my Excuse.—You ask where the Fleet is. The inclosed Papers will inform you. You ask what Sort of Defence Virginia can make. I believe they will make an able Defence. Their Militia and minute Men have been some time employed in training them selves, and they have Nine Battallions of regulars as they call them, maintained among them, under good Officers, at the Continental Expence. They have set up a Number of Manufactories of Fire Arms, which are busily employed. They are tolerably supplied with Powder, and are successfull and assiduous, in making Salt Petre. Their neighbouring Sister or rather Daughter Colony of North Carolina, which is a warlike Colony, and has several Battallions at the Continental Expence, as well as a pretty good Militia, are ready to assist them, and they are in very good Spirits, and seem determined to make a brave Resistance.—The Gentry are very rich, and the common People very poor. This Inequality of Property, gives an Aristocratical Turn to all their Proceedings, and occasions a strong Aversion in their Patricians, to Common Sense. But the Spirit of these Barons, is coming down, and it must submit.

It is very true, as you observe they have been duped by Dunmore. But this is a Common Case. All the Colonies are duped, more or less, at one Time and another. A more egregious Bubble was never blown up, than the Story of Commissioners coming to treat with the Congress. Yet it has gained Credit like a Charm, not only without but against the clearest Evidence. I never shall forget the Delusion, which seized our best and most sagacious Friends the dear Inhabitants of Boston, the Winter before last. Credulity and the Want of Foresight, are Imperfections in the human Character, that no Politician can sufficiently guard against.

You have given me some Pleasure, by your Account of a certain House in Queen Street. I had burned it, long ago, in Imagination. It rises now to my View like a Phœnix.—What shall I say of the Solicitor General? I pity his pretty Children, I pity his Father, and his sisters. I wish I could be clear that it is no moral Evil to pity him and his Lady. Upon Repentance they will certainly have a large Share in the Compassions of many. But let Us take Warning and give it to our Children. Whenever Vanity, and Gaiety, a Love of Pomp and Dress, Furniture, Equipage, Buildings, great Company, expensive Diversions, and elegant Entertainments get the better of the Principles and Judgments of Men or Women there is no knowing where they will stop, nor into what Evils, natural, moral, or political, they will lead us.

Your Description of your own Gaiety de Coeur, charms me. Thanks be to God you have just Cause to rejoice—and may the bright Prospect be obscured by no Cloud.

As to Declarations of Independency, be patient. Read our Privateering Laws, and our Commercial Laws. What signifies a Word.

As to your extraordinary Code of Laws, I cannot but laugh. We have been told that our Struggle has loosened the bands of Government every where. That Children and Apprentices were disobedient—that schools and Colledges were grown turbulent—that Indians slighted their Guardians and Negroes grew insolent to their Masters. But your Letter was the first Intimation that another Tribe more numerous and powerfull than all the rest were grown discontented.—This is rather too coarse a Compliment but you are so saucy, I wont blot it out.

Depend upon it, We know better than to repeal our Masculine systems. Altho they are in full Force, you know they are little more than Theory. We dare not exert our Power in its full Latitude. We are obliged to go fair, and softly, and in Practice you know We are the subjects. We have only the Name of Masters, and rather than give up this, which would compleatly subject Us to the Despotism of the Peticoat, I hope General Washington, and all our brave Heroes would fight. I am sure every good Politician would plot, as long as he would against Despotism, Empire, Monarchy, Aristocracy, Oligarchy, or Ochlocracy.—A fine Story indeed. I begin to think the Ministry as deep as they are wicked. After stirring up Tories, Landjobbers, Trimmers, Bigots, Canadians, Indians, Negroes, Hanoverians, Hessians, Russians, Irish Roman Catholicks, Scotch Renegadoes, at last they have stimulated the   to demand new Priviledges and threaten to rebell.

To the Congress that was already being carried by events toward independence came word from Britain of passage, on December 22, 1775, of the American Prohibitory Act, or "restraining Act," by which all American ships and goods were in effect outlawed. Whatever its intent, its effect could only be that those advocating complete separation would soon have their way. By a resolve adopted on May 10, the Congress recommended to the legislative bodies of the several colonies that they "adopt such government as shall . . . best conduce to the happiness and safety of their constituents . . . and America." To this, five days later, was added a preamble written by John Adams calling for the total suppression "of every kind of authority" emanating from Great Britain. An end and a beginning were at hand.

JA to AA

April 28. 1776

Yesterday, I received two Letters from you from the 7th. to the 14. of April. I believe I have received all your Letters, and I am not certain I wrote one from Framingham. The one I mean contains an Account of my dining with the Indians at Mr. Mifflins.

It gives me Concern to think of the many Cares you must have upon your Mind. Am glad you have taken [Belcher] into Pay, and that Isaac is well before now I hope.

Your Reputation, as a Farmer, or any Thing else you undertake I dare answer for.... Your Partners Character as a Statesman is much more problematical.

As to my Return, I have not a Thought of it. Journeys of such a Length are tedious, and expensive both of Time and Money neither of which are my own. I hope to spend the next Christmas, where I did the last, and after that I hope to be relieved for by that Time I shall have taken a pretty good Trick att Helm whether the Vessell has been well steer'd or not. But if My Countrymen should insist upon my serving them another Year, they must let me bring my whole Family with me. Indeed I could keep House here, with my Partner, four children and two servants, as cheap as I maintain my self here with two Horses and a servant at Lodgings.

Instead of domestic Felicity, I am destined to public Contentions. Instead of rural Felicity, I must reconcile myself to the Smoke and Noise of a city. In the Place of private Peace, I must be distracted with the Vexation of developing the deep Intrigues of Politicians and must assist in conducting the arduous Operations of War. And think myself, well rewarded, if my private Pleasure and Interest are sacrificed as they ever have been and will be, to the Happiness of others.

You tell me, our Jurors refuse to serve, because the Writs are issued in the Kings Name. I am very glad to hear, that they discover so much Sense and Spirit. I learn from another Letter that the General Court have left out of their Bills the Year of his Reign, and that they are making a Law, that the same Name shall be left out of all Writs, Commissions, and all Law Proscesses. This is good News too. The same will be the Case in all the Colonies, very soon.

You ask me how I have done the Winter past. I have not enjoyed so good Health as last Fall. But I have done complaining of any Thing. Of ill Health I have no Right to complain because it is given me by Heaven. Of Meanness, of Envy, of Littleness, of—of—of—of—I have Reason and Right to complain, but I have too much Contempt, to use that Right.

There is such a Mixture of Folly, Littleness, and Knavery in this World that, I am weary of it, and altho I behold it with unutterable Contempt and Indignation, yet the public Good requires that I should take no Notice of it, by Word or by Letter. And to this public Good I will conform.

You will see an Account of the Fleet in some of the Papers I have sent you. Give you Joy of the Admirals Success. I have Vanity enough to take to myself, a share in the Merit of the American Navy. It was always a Measure that my Heart was much engaged in, and I pursued it, for a long Time, against the Wind and Tide. But at last obtained it.

Is there no Way for two friendly Souls, to converse together, altho the Bodies are 400 Miles off?—Yes by Letter.—But I want a better Communication. I want to hear you think, or to see your Thoughts.

The Conclusion of your Letter makes my Heart throb, more than a Cannonade would. You bid me burn your Letters. But I must forget you first.

In yours of April 14. you say you miss our Friend in the Conveyance of your Letters. Dont hesitate to write by the Post. Seal well. Dont miss a single Post.

You take it for granted that I have particular Intelligence of every Thing from others. But I have not. If any one wants a Vote for a Commission, he vouchsafes me a Letter, but tells me very little News. I have more particulars from you than any one else. Pray keep me constantly informed, what ships are in the Harbour and what Fortifications are going on.

I am quite impatient to hear of more vigorous Measures for fortifying Boston Harbour. Not a Moment should be neglected. Every Man ought to go down as they did after the Battle of Lexington and work untill it is done. I would willingly pay half a Dozen Hands my self, and subsist them, rather than it should not be done immediately. It is of more importance than to raise Corn.

You say inclosed is a Prologue and a Parody, but neither was inclosed. If you did not forget it, the letter has been opened and the Inclosures taken out.

If the Small Pox spreads, run me in debt. I received a Post or two past a Letter from your Unkle at Salem, containing a most friendly and obliging Invitation to you and yours to go, and have the Distemper at his House if it should spread. He has one or two in family to have it.

The Writer of Common Sense, and the Forrester, is the same Person. His Name is Payne, a Gentleman, about two Years ago from England, a Man who G[eneral] Lee says has Genius in his Eyes. The Writer of Cassandra is said to be Mr. James Cannon a Tutor, in the Philadelphia Colledge. Cato is reported here to be Dr. Smith—a Match for Brattle. The oration was an insolent Performance.... A Motion was made to Thank the orator and ask a Copy—But opposed with great Spirit, and Vivacity from every Part of the Room, and at last withdrawn, lest it should be rejected as it certainly would have been with Indignation. The orator then printed it himself, after leaving out or altering some offensive Passages.

This is one of the many irregular, and extravagant Characters of the Age. I never heard one single person speak well of any Thing about him but his Abilities, which are generally allowed to be good. The Appointment of him to make the oration, was a great oversight, and Mistake.

The late Act of Parliament, has made so deep an Impression upon Peoples Minds throughout the Colonies, it is looked upon as the last Stretch of Oppression, that We are hastening rapidly to great Events. Governments will be up every where before Midsummer, and an End to Royal style, Titles and Authority. Such mighty Revolutions make a deep Impression on the Minds of Men and sett many violent Passions at Work. Hope, Fear, Joy, Sorrow, Love, Hatred, Malice, Envy, Revenge, Jealousy, Ambition, Avarice, Resentment, Gratitude, and every other Passion, Feeling, Sentiment, Principle and Imagination, were never in more lively Exercise than they are now, from Florida to Canada inclusively. May God in his Providence overrule the whole, for the good of Mankind. It requires more Serenity of Temper, a deeper Understanding and more Courage than fell to the Lott of Marlborough, to ride in this Whirlwind.

AA to JA

B[raintre]e May 7 1776

How many are the solitary hours I spend, ruminating upon the past, and anticipating the future, whilst you overwhelmd with the cares of State, have but few moments you can devote to any individual. All domestick pleasures and injoyments are absorbed in the great and important duty you owe your Country "for our Country is as it were a secondary God, and the First and greatest parent. It is to be preferred to Parents, Wives, Children, Friends and all things the Gods only excepted. For if our Country perishes it is as imposible to save an Individual, as to preserve one of the fingers of a Mortified Hand." Thus do I supress every wish, and silence every Murmer, acquiesceing in a painfull Seperation from the companion of my youth, and the Friend of my Heart.

I believe tis near ten days since I wrote you a line. I have not felt in a humour to entertain you. If I had taken up my pen perhaps some unbecomeing invective might have fallen from it; the Eyes of our Rulers have been closed and a Lethargy has seazd almost every Member. I fear a fatal Security has taken possession of them. Whilst the Building is on flame they tremble at the expence of water to quench it, in short two months has elapsed since the evacuation of Boston, and very little has been done in that time to secure it, or the Harbour from future invasion till the people are all in a flame; and no one among us that I have heard of even mentions expence, they think universally that there has been an amaizing neglect some where. Many have turnd out as volunteers to work upon Nodles Island, and many more would go upon Nantaskit if it was once set on foot. "Tis a Maxim of state That power and Liberty are like Heat and moisture; where they are well mixt every thing prospers, where they are single, they are destructive."

A Goverment of more Stability is much wanted in this colony, and they are ready to receive it from the Hands of the Congress, and since I have begun with Maxims of State I will add an other viz. that a people may let a king fall, yet still remain a people, but if a king let his people slip from him, he is no longer a king. And as this is most certainly our case, why not proclaim to the World in decisive terms your own importance?

Shall we not be dispiced by foreign powers for hesitateing so long at a word?

I can not say that I think you very generous to the Ladies, for whilst you are proclaiming peace and good will to Men, Emancipating all Nations, you insist upon retaining an absolute power over Wives. But you must remember that Arbitary power is like most other things which are very hard, very liable to be broken—and notwithstanding all your wise Laws and Maxims we have it in our power not only to free ourselves but to subdue our Masters, and without voilence throw both your natural and legal authority at our feet—

"Charm by accepting, by submitting sway
Yet have our Humour most when we obey."

I thank you for several Letters which I have received since I wrote Last. They alleviate a tedious absence, and I long earnestly for a Saturday Evening, and experience a similar pleasure to that which I used to find in the return of my Friend upon that day after a weeks absence. The Idea of a year dissolves all my Phylosophy.

Our Little ones whom you so often recommend to my care and instruction shall not be deficient in virtue or probity if the precepts of a Mother have their desired Effect, but they would be doubly inforced could they be indulged with the example of a Father constantly before them; I often point them to their Sire

"engaged in a corrupted State
Wrestling with vice and faction."

AA to JA

May 14 1776

I set down to write you a Letter wholy Domestick without one word of politicks or any thing of the Kind, and tho you may have matters of infinately more importance before you, yet let it come as a relaxation to you. Know then that we have had a very cold backward Spring, till about ten days past when every thing looks finely. We have had fine Spring rains which makes the Husbandary promise fair—but the great difficulty has been to procure Labourers. There is such a demand of Men from the publick and such a price given that the farmer who Hires must be greatly out of pocket. A man will not talk with you who is worth hireing under 24 pounds per year. Col. Quincy and Thayer give that price, and some give more. Isaac insisted upon my giving him 20 pounds or he would leave me. He is no mower and I found very unfit to take the lead upon the Farm, having no forethought or any contrivance to plan his Buisness, tho in the Execution faithfull. I found I wanted somebody of Spirit who was wiser than myself, to conduct my Buisness. I went about and my Friends inquired but every Labourer who was active was gone and going into the Service. I asked advice of my Friends and Neighbours [and] they all adviced me to let Isaac go, rather than give that price. I setled with him and we parted. Mr. Belcher is now with me and has undertaken to conduct the Buisness, which he has hitherto done with Spirit and activity. I know his virtues I know his faults. Hithertoo I give him 2 Shillings per day, and Daniel Nightingale works with him at the same lay. I would have hired him for the season but he was engaged to look after a place or two for people who are gone into the Army. I am still in quest of a Man by the year, but whether I shall effect it, I know not. I have done the best I could. We are just now ready to plant, the barly look[s] charmingly, I shall be quite a Farmeriss an other year.

You made no perticulir agreement with Isaac so he insisted upon my paying him 13. 6 8. I paid him 12 pounds 18 & 8 pence, and thought it sufficient.

When Bass returnd he brought me some Money from you. After the deduction of his account and the horse hire there remaind 15 pounds. I have Received 12 from Mr. Thaxter which with one note of 20 pounds which I exchanged and some small matters of interest which I received and a little Hay &c. I have discharged the following debts—To my Father for his Horse twice 12 pounds (he would not have any thing for the last time). To Bracket, £13. 6s. 8d. To Isaac 12. 18. 8. To Mr. Hunt for the House 26. 15. 4. and the Rates of two years 1774, £4 14s. 8d. and for 1775: £7. 11s. 11d. Besides this have supported the family which is no small one you know and paid all little charges which have occurd in the farming way. I hardly know how I have got thro these thing's, but it gives me great pleasure to say they are done because I know it will be an Ease to your mind which amid all other cares which surround you will some times advert to your own Little Farm and to your Family. There remains due to Mr. Hunt about 42 pounds. I determine if it lays in my power to discharge the bond, and I have some prospect of it.

Our Little Flock send duty. I call[ed] them seperately and told them Pappa wanted to send them something and requested of them what they would have. A Book was the answer of them all only Tom wanted a picture Book and Charlss the History of king and Queen. It was natural for them to think of a Book as that is the only present Pappa has been used to make them.

Adieu—Yours, Hermitta

JA to AA

May 17. 1776

I have this Morning heard Mr. Duffil upon the Signs of the Times. He run a Parrallell between the Case of Israel and that of America, and between the Conduct of Pharaoh and that of George.

Jealousy that the Israelites would throw off the Government of Egypt made him issue his Edict that the Midwives should cast the Children into the River, and the other Edict that the Men should make a large Revenue of Brick without Straw. He concluded that the Course of Events, indicated strongly the Design of Providence that We should be seperated from G. Britain, &c.

Is it not a Saying of Moses, who am I, that I should go in and out before this great People? When I consider the great Events which are passed, and those greater which are rapidly advancing, and that I may have been instrumental of touching some Springs, and turning some small Wheels, which have had and will have such Effects, I feel an Awe upon my Mind, which is not easily described.

G[reat] B[ritain] has at last driven America, to the last Step, a compleat Seperation from her, a total absolute Independence, not only of her Parliament but of her Crown, for such is the Amount of the Resolve of the 15th.

Confederation among ourselves, or Alliances with foreign Nations are not necessary, to a perfect Seperation from Britain. That is effected by extinguishing all Authority, under the Crown, Parliament and Nation as the Resolution for instituting Governments, has done, to all Intents and Purposes. Confederation will be necessary for our internal Concord, and Alliances may be so for our external Defence.

I have Reasons to believe that no Colony, which shall assume a Government under the People, will give it up. There is something very unnatural and odious in a Government 1000 Leagues off. An whole Government of our own Choice, managed by Persons whom We love, revere, and can confide in, has charms in it for which Men will fight. Two young Gentlemen from South Carolina, now in this City, who were in Charlestown when their new Constitution was promulgated, and when their new Governor and Council and Assembly walked out in Procession, attended by the Guards, Company of Cadetts, Light Horse &c., told me, that they were beheld by the People with Transports and Tears of Joy. The People gazed at them, with a Kind of Rapture. They both told me, that the Reflection that these were Gentlemen whom they all loved, esteemed and revered, Gentlemen of their own Choice, whom they could trust, and whom they could displace if any of them should behave amiss, affected them so that they could not help crying.

They say their People will never give up this Government.

One of these Gentlemen is a Relation of yours, a Mr. Smith, son of Mr. Thomas Smith. I shall give him this Letter or another to you.

A Privateer fitted out here by Coll. Reberdeau [Roberdeau] and Major Bayard, since our Resolves for Privateering, I am this Moment informed, has taken a valuable Prize. This is Encouragement, at the Beginning.

In one or two of your Letters you remind me to think of you as I ought. Be assured there is not an Hour in the Day, in which I do not think of you as I ought, that is with every Sentiment of Tenderness, Esteem, and Admiration.

JA to AA

May 27. 1776

I have three of your Favours, before me—one of May 7., another of May 9. and a third of May 14th. The last has given me Relief from many Anxieties. It relates wholly to private Affairs, and contains such an Account of wise and prudent Management, as makes me very happy. I begin to be jealous, that our Neighbours will think Affairs more discreetly conducted in my Absence than at any other Time.

Whether your Suspicions concerning a Letter under a marble Cover, are just or not, it is best to say little about it. It is an hasty hurried Thing and of no great Consequence, calculated for a Meridian at a great Distance from N. England. If it has done no good, it will do no harm. It has contributed to sett People a thinking upon the subject, and in this respect has answered its End. The Manufactory of Governments having, since the Publication of that Letter, been as much talk'd of, as that of salt Petre was before.

I rejoice at your Account of the Spirit of Fortification, and the good Effects of it. I hope by this Time you are in a tolerable Posture of defence. The Inhabitants of Boston have done themselves great Honour, by their laudable Zeal, the worthy Clergymen especially.

I think you shine as a Stateswoman, of late as well as a Farmeress. Pray where do you get your Maxims of State, they are very apropos.

I am much obliged to Judge Cushing, and his Lady for their polite Visit to you: should be very happy to see him, and converse with him about many Things but cannot hope for that Pleasure, very soon. The Affairs of America, are in so critical a State, such great Events are struggling for Birth, that I must not quit this station at this Time. Yet I dread the melting Heats of a Philadelphia Summer, and know not how my frail Constitution will endure it. Such constant Care, such incessant Application of Mind, drinking up and exhausting the finer Spirits upon which Life and Health so essentially depend, will wear away a stronger Man than I am.—Yet I will not shrink from this Danger or this Toil. While my Health shall be such that I can discharge in any tolerable manner, the Duties of this important Post, I will not desert it.

Am pleased to hear that the superiour Court is to sit, at Ipswich in June. This will contribute to give Stability to the Government, I hope, in all its Branches.... But I presume other Steps will be taken for this Purpose. A Governor and Lt. Governor, I hope will be chosen, and the Constitution a little more fixed. I hope too that the Councill will this year be more full and augmented by the Addition of good Men.

I hope Mr. Bowdoin will be Governor, if his Health will permit, and Dr. Winthrop Lt. Governor. These are wise, learned, and prudent Men. The first has a great Fortune, and wealthy Connections, the other has the Advantage of a Name and Family which is much reverenced, besides his Personal Abilities and Virtues, which are very great.

Our Friend, I sincerely hope, will not refuse his Appointment, for although I have ever thought that Bench should be fill'd from the Bar, and once laboured successfully to effect it, yet as the Gentlemen have seen fit to decline, I know of no Gentleman, who would do more Honour to the Station than my Friend. None would be so agreable to me, whether I am to sit by him, or before him. I suppose it must be disagreable to him and his Lady, because he loves to be upon his Farm, and they both love to be together. But you must tell them of a Couple of their Friends who are as fond of living together, who are obliged to sacrifice their rural Amusements and domestic Happiness to the Requisitions of the public.

The Generals Washington, Gates, and Mifflin are all here, and We shall derive Spirit, Unanimity, and Vigour from their Presence and Advice. I hope you will have some General Officers at Boston soon.—I am, with constant Wishes and Prayers for your Health, and Prosperity, forever yours.

III

JUNE 1776 ~ OCTOBER 1777

The Congress have been pleased to give me more Business than I am qualified for. — John Adams

I keep up some Spirits yet, tho I would have you prepaird for any Event that may happen.
— Abigail Adams

THE DECLARATION OF INDEPENDENCE,
4 JULY 1776 AT PHILADELPHIA

Even before Congress could be brought to the decisive vote for independence, it took steps to regularize the administration of the military forces fighting for that unacknowledged object. On June 12, 1776, a Board of War was created with Adams as chairman. In this post he had ample opportunity to learn of the human frailties and professional jealousies that plagued the young army.

Morale in that army had suffered in the year since men rallied to enlist after the skirmishes at Lexington and Concord. The expedition to Canada had failed. Retreating troops were decimated by smallpox.

From this and other evidence John Adams knew that a long struggle impended. He sensed too that prolonged separation from his family would thenceforward be the pattern of his life. In early June he acted to guard the records of his correspondence with his wife—the precious letters by which he would maintain his ties with Braintree. At the shop of William Trickett, a stationer on Philadelphia's Front Street, Adams made a historic purchase—a blank folio volume. In it he began the practice of making a meticulous copy of every letter he sent home.

In the first days of July the decision, long in preparation, was reached. The Congress resolved on July 2: "That these United Colonies are, and, of right, ought to be, Free and Independent States. . . ." In two letters written a day later, Adams tried to sum up what this meant for Americans of his own time and in the future.

JA to AA

June 2. 1776

Yesterday I dined with Captain Richards, the Gentleman who made me the present of the brass Pistolls. We had Cherries, Strawberries and Green Peas in Plenty. The Fruits are three Weeks earlier here than with you, indeed they are a fortnight earlier on the East, than on the West side of Delaware River. We have had green Peas, this Week past, but they were brought over the River from New Jersey to this Markett. There are none grown in the City, or on the West side of the River yet. The Reason is, the Soil of New Jersey is a warm Sand, that of Pensilvania, a cold Clay. So much for Peas and Berries.

Now for something of more Importance. In all the Correspondencies I have maintained, during a Course of twenty Years at least that I have been a Writer of Letters, I never kept a single Copy. This Negligence and Inaccuracy, has been a great Misfortune to me, on many

Occasions.—I have now purchased a Folio Book, in the first Page of which, excepting one blank Leaff, I am writing this Letter, and intend to write all my Letters to you in it from this Time forward. This will be an Advantage to me in several Respects. In the first Place, I shall write more deliberately. In the second Place, I shall be able at all times to review what I have written. 3. I shall know how often I write. 4. I shall discover by this Means, whether any of my Letters to you, miscarry.

If it were possible for me to find a Conveyance, I would send you such another blank Book, as a Present, that you might begin the Practice at the same Time, for I really think that your Letters are much better worth preserving than mine. Your Daughter and Sons will very soon write so good Hands that they will copy the Letters for you from your Book, which will improve them at the same Time that it relieves you.

AA to JA

June 3. 1776

I received by Mr. Church a few lines from you; I wish to hear from you every opportunity tho you say no more than that you are well. I feel concernd least your cloaths should go to rags having nobody to take any care of you in your long absence, and then you have not with you a proper change for the Seasons. However you must do the best you can. I have a suit of homespun for you whenever you return. I cannot avoid sometimes repineing that the gifts of fortune were not bestowed upon us, that I might have injoyed the happiness of spending my days with my Partner. But as it is, I think it my duty to attend with frugality and oeconomy to our own private affairs, and if I cannot add to our Little Substance yet see that it is not diminished. I should enjoy but little comfort in a state of Idleness, and uselessness. Here I can serve my partner, my family and myself, and injoy the Satisfaction of your serving your Country.

I wish you would write me what I had best do with our House at Boston. I would advertise it if you think best. There are so many Houses torn to peices and so many others abused that I might stand a chance of Letting it perhaps as it is in so good repair.

My Brother is desirous of Joining the Army again, but would chuse to be a field officer. I have mentiond him to some of the House and suppose he will be recommended to congress, for a commission. I hardly know where you will find Men to form the Regiments required. I begin to think population a very important Branch in the American Manufactorys.

I enclose a List of Counsel. The House consists of more than 200 & 50 Members. Your former pupil A[ngie]r comes from Bridgwater, and 5 others. I hope they will proceed in Buisness with a little more Spirit than Heretofore. They are procuring two row Gallies, but when they will be finished I know not. I thought they were near done, but find to day they are not yet contracted for. All our Gentery are gone from Nantasket road except the commodore and one or two small craft.

Every thing bears a very great price. The Merchant complains of the Farmer and the Farmer of the Merchant. Both are extravagant. Living is double what it was one year ago.

I find you have licenced Tea but I am determined not to be a purchaser unless I can have it at Congress price, and in that article the venders pay no regard to congress, asking 10. 8. and the lowest is 7.6 per pound. I should like a little Green, but they say there is none to be had here; I only wish it for a medicine, as a relief to a nervious pain in my Head to which I am sometimes subject. Were it as plenty as ever I would not practice the use of it.

Our Family are all well. It has been reported here that congress were going to remove 40 miles beyond Philadelphia. I gave no credit to the report, I heard no reason assignd for it. I had much rather they would come a hundred miles nearer here.

Adieu—Yours.

JA to AA

June 26. 1776

I have written so seldom to you, that I am really grieved at the Recollection. I wrote you, a few Lines, June 2. and a few more June 16. These are all that I have written to you, since this Month began. It has been the busyest Month, that ever I saw. I have found Time to inclose all the News papers, which I hope you will receive in due Time.

Our Misfortunes in Canada, are enough to melt an Heart of Stone. The Small Pox is ten times more terrible than Britons, Canadians and Indians together. This was the Cause of our precipitate Retreat from Quebec, this the Cause of our Disgraces at the Cedars.—I dont mean that this was all. There has been Want, approaching to Famine, as well as Pestilence. And these Discouragements seem to have so disheartened our Officers, that none of them seem to Act with Prudence and Firmness.

But these Reverses of Fortune dont discourage me. It was natural to expect them, and We ought to be prepared in our Minds for greater Changes, and more melancholly Scenes still. It is an animating Cause, and brave Spirits are not subdued with Difficulties.

Amidst all our gloomy Prospects in Canada, We receive some Pleasure from Boston. I congratulate you on your Victory over your Enemies, in the Harbour. This has long lain near my Heart, and it gives me great Pleasure to think that what was so much wished, is accomplished.

I hope our People will now make the Lower Harbour, impregnable, and never again suffer the Flagg of a Tyrant to fly, within any Part of it.

The Congress have been pleased to give me more Business than I am qualified for, and more than I fear, I can go through, with safety to my Health. They have established a Board of War and Ordinance and made me President of it, an Honour to which I never aspired, a Trust to which I feel my self vastly unequal. But I am determined to do as well as I can and make Industry supply, in some degree the Place of Abilities and Experience. The Board sits, every Morning and every Evening. This, with Constant Attendance in Congress, will so entirely engross my Time, that I fear, I shall not be able to write you, so often as I have. But I will steal Time to write to you.

The small Pox! The small Pox! What shall We do with it? I could almost wish that an innoculating Hospital was opened, in every Town in New England. It is some small Consolation, that the Scoundrell Savages have taken a large Dose of it. They plundered the Baggage, and stripped off the Cloaths of our Men, who had the Small Pox, out full upon them at the Cedars.

JA to AA

Philadelphia July 3. 1776

Your Favour of June 17. dated at Plymouth, was handed me, by Yesterdays Post. I was much pleased to find that you had taken a Journey to Plymouth, to see your Friends in the long Absence of one whom you may wish to see. The Excursion will be an Amusement, and will serve your Health. How happy would it have made me to have taken this Journey with you?

I was informed, a day or two before the Receipt of your Letter, that you was gone to Plymouth, by Mrs. Polly Palmer, who was obliging enough in your Absence, to inform me, of the Particulars of the Expedition to the lower Harbour against the Men of War. Her Narration is executed, with a Precision and Perspicuity, which would have become the Pen of an accomplished Historian.

I am very glad you had so good an opportunity of seeing one of our little American Men of War. Many Ideas, new to you, must have presented themselves in such a Scene; and you will in future, better understand the Relations of Sea Engagements.

I rejoice extreamly at Dr. Bulfinches Petition to open an Hospital. But I hope, the Business will be done upon a larger Scale. I hope, that one Hospital will be licensed in every County, if not in every Town. I am happy to find you resolved, to be with the Children, in the first Class. Mr. Whitney and Mrs. Katy Quincy, are cleverly through Innoculation, in this City.

I have one favour to ask, and that is, that in your future Letters, you would acknowledge the Receipt of all those you may receive from me, and mention their Dates. By this Means I shall know if any of mine miscarry.

The Information you give me of our Friends refusing his Appointment, has given me much Pain, Grief and Anxiety. I believe I shall be obliged to follow his Example. I have not Fortune enough to support my Family, and what is of more Importance, to support the Dignity of that exalted Station. It is too high and lifted up, for me; who delight in nothing so much as Retreat, Solitude, Silence, and Obscurity. In private Life, no one has a Right to censure me for following my own Inclinations, in Retirement, Simplicity, and Frugality: in public Life, every Man has a Right to remark as he pleases, at least he thinks so.

Yesterday the greatest Question was decided, which ever was debated in America, and a greater perhaps, never was or will be decided among Men. A Resolution was passed without one dissenting Colony "that these united Colonies, are, and of right ought to be free and independent States, and as such, they have, and of Right ought to have full Power to make War, conclude Peace, establish Commerce, and to do all the other Acts and Things, which other States may rightfully do." You will see in a few days a Declaration setting forth the Causes, which have impell'd Us to this mighty Revolution, and the Reasons which will justify it, in the Sight of God and Man. A Plan of Confederation will be taken up in a few days.

When I look back to the Year 1761, and recollect the Argument concerning Writs of Assistance, in the Superiour Court, which I have hitherto considered as the Commencement of the Controversy, between Great Britain and America, and run through the whole Period from that Time to this, and recollect the series of political Events, the Chain of Causes and Effects, I am surprized at the Suddenness, as well as Greatness of this Revolution. Britain has been fill'd with Folly, and America with Wisdom, at least this is my Judgment.—Time must determine. It is the Will of Heaven, that the two Countries should be sundered forever. It may be the Will of Heaven that America shall suffer Calamities still more wasting and Distresses yet more dreadfull. If this is to be the Case, it will have this good Effect, at least: it will inspire Us with many Virtues, which We have not, and correct many Errors, Follies, and Vices, which threaten to disturb, dishonour, and destroy Us.—The Furnace of Affliction produces Refinement, in States as well as Individuals. And the new Governments we are assuming, in every Part, will require a Purification from our Vices, and an Augmentation of our Virtues or they will be no Blessings. The People will have unbounded Power. And the People are extreamly addicted to Corruption and Venality, as well as the Great. —I am not without Apprehensions from this Quarter. But I must submit all my Hopes and Fears, to an overruling Providence, in which, unfashionable as the Faith may be, I firmly believe.

JA to AA

Philadelphia July 3d. 1776

Had a Declaration of Independency been made seven Months ago, it would have been attended with many great and glorious Effects.... We might before this Hour, have formed Alliances with foreign States.—We should have mastered Quebec and been in Possession of Canada.... You will perhaps wonder, how such a Declaration would have influenced our Affairs, in Canada, but if I could write with Freedom I could easily convince you, that it would, and explain to you the manner how.—Many Gentlemen in high Stations and of great Influence have been duped, by the ministerial Bubble of Commissioners to treat.... And in real, sincere Expectation of this Event, which they so fondly wished, they have been slow and languid, in promoting Measures for the Reduction of that Province. Others there are in the Colonies who really wished that our Enterprise in Canada would be defeated, that the Colonies might be brought into Danger and Distress between two Fires, and be thus induced to submit. Others really wished to defeat the Expedition to Canada, lest the Conquest of it, should elevate the Minds of the People too much to hearken to those Terms of Reconciliation which they believed would be offered Us. These jarring Views, Wishes and Designs, occasioned an opposition to many salutary Measures, which were proposed for the Support of that Expedition, and caused Obstructions, Embarrassments and studied Delays, which have finally, lost Us the Province.

All these Causes however in Conjunction would not have disappointed Us, if it had not been for a Misfortune, which could not be foreseen, and perhaps could not have been prevented, I mean the

I am apt to believe that it will be celebrated, by succeeding Generations, as the great anniversary Festival. It ought to be commemorated, as the Day of Deliverance by solemn Acts of Devotion to God Almighty. It ought to be solemnized with Pomp and Parade with Shews, Games, Sports, Guns, Bells, Bonfires and Illuminations from one End of this Continent to the other from this Time forward forever more.

You will think me transported with Enthusiasm but I am not. — I am well aware of the Toil and Blood and Treasure, that it will cost Us to maintain this Declaration, and support and defend these States. — Yet through all the Gloom I can see the Rays of ravishing Light and Glory. I can see that the End is more than worth all the Means. And that Posterity will tryumph in that Days Transaction, even altho We should rue it, which I trust in God We shall not. —

"I AM APT TO BELIEVE THAT IT WILL BE CELEBRATED BY SUCCEEDING GENERATIONS, AS THE GREAT ANNIVERSARY FESTIVAL"

Prevalence of the small Pox among our Troops.... This fatal Pestilence compleated our Destruction.—It is a Frown of Providence upon Us, which We ought to lay to heart.

But on the other Hand, the Delay of this Declaration to this Time, has many great Advantages attending it.—The Hopes of Reconciliation, which were fondly entertained by Multitudes of honest and well meaning tho weak and mistaken People, have been gradually and at last totally extinguished.—Time has been given for the whole People, maturely to consider the great Question of Independence and to ripen their Judgments, dissipate their Fears, and allure their Hopes, by discussing it in News Papers and Pamphletts, by debating it, in Assemblies, Conventions, Committees of Safety and Inspection, in Town and County Meetings, as well as in private Conversations, so that the whole People in every Colony of the 13, have now adopted it, as their own Act.—This will cement the Union, and avoid those Heats and perhaps Convulsions which might have been occasioned, by such a Declaration Six Months ago.

But the Day is past. The Second Day of July 1776, will be the most memorable Epocha, in the History of America.—I am apt to believe that it will be celebrated, by succeeding Generations, as the great anniversary Festival. It ought to be commemorated, as the Day of Deliverance by solemn Acts of Devotion to God Almighty. It ought to be solemnized with Pomp and Parade, with Shews, Games, Sports, Guns, Bells, Bonfires and Illuminations from one End of this Continent to the other from this Time forward forever more.

You will think me transported with Enthusiasm but I am not.—I am well aware of the Toil and Blood and Treasure, that it will cost Us to maintain this Declaration, and support and defend these States.—Yet through all the Gloom I can see the Rays of ravishing Light and Glory. I can see that the End is more than worth all the Means. And that Posterity will tryumph in that Days Transaction, even altho We should rue it, which I trust in God We shall not.

Simultaneously with Congress' Declaration of July 4, plans of government were being adopted in the new states. Adams recorded with enthusiasm that these plans were alike in providing that in those chosen for office "Capacity, Spirit and Zeal in the Cause" would "supply the Place of Fortune, Family, and every other Consideration, which used to have Weight with Mankind." The new governments created were remarkable too in that each was conceived as having a "popular" base, even more "popular" than he had posited in his *Thoughts on Government*.

JA to AA

June [*i.e.* July] 10. 1776

You will see by the Newspapers, which I from time to time inclose, with what Rapidity, the Colonies proceed in their political Maneuvres. How many Calamities might have been avoided if these Measures had been taken twelve Months ago, or even no longer ago than last december?

The Colonies to the South, are pursuing the same Maxims, which have heretofore governed those to the North. In constituting their new Governments, their Plans are remarkably popular, more so than I could ever have imagined, even more popular than the "Thoughts on Government." And in the Choice of their Rulers, Capacity, Spirit and Zeal in the Cause, supply the Place of Fortune, Family, and every other Consideration, which used to have Weight with Mankind. My Friend Archibald Bullock Esq. is Governor of Georgia. John Rutledge Esq. is Governor of South Carolina. Patrick Henry Esq. is Governor of Virginia &c. Dr. Franklin will be Governor of Pensilvania. The new Members of this City, are all in this Taste, chosen because of their inflexible Zeal for Independence. All the old Members left out, because they opposed Independence, or at least were lukewarm about it. Dickinson, Morris, Allen, all fallen, like Grass before the Scythe notwithstanding all their vast Advantages in Point of Fortune, Family and Abilities.

I am inclined to think however, and to wish that these Gentlemen may be restored, at a fresh Election, because, altho mistaken in some Points, they are good Characters, and their great Wealth and numerous Connections, will contribute to strengthen America, and cement her Union.

I wish I were at perfect Liberty, to pourtray before you, all those Characters, in their genuine Lights, and to explain to you the Course of political Changes in this Province. It would give you a great Idea of the Spirit and Resolution of the People, and shew you, in a striking Point of View, the deep Roots of American Independence in all the Colonies. But it is not prudent, to commit to Writing such free Speculations, in the present State of Things.

Time which takes away the Veil, may lay open the secret Springs of this surprizing Revolution.... But I find, altho the Colonies have differed in Religion, Laws, Customs, and Manners, yet in the great Essentials of Society and Government, they are all alike.

Without notice to her husband, Abigail Adams undertook this summer to have herself and her children inoculated in Boston. Her uncle Isaac

Smith offered the use of his home to the augmented family group from Braintree. When a concerned John Adams learned of her venture, he hurried to his colleague Dr. Benjamin Rush for reassurance, and he entreated his wife: "Make Mr. Mason, Mr. any Body write to me, by every Post—dont miss one for any Cause whatever."

As the weeks of confinement went by and the outcome, despite serious setbacks, proved successful, the Adamses took heart. As before, when family perils had been surmounted, the range of topics evoked in their correspondence broadened. Their letters of late July and August encompassed general reflections on the New England character, education, learned societies—the last stimulated by John Adams' first acquaintance with the American Philosophical Society. But they also were filled with items more transient and homely. One such relates to the loss sustained in the lameness of their gray horse and the enlistment of family members in finding a substitute to bring Adams home. A topic that engaged both correspondents was a proper outlet for the "Lucubrations" of the inventive and talented Richard Cranch. Another was the plight of the estimable Elbridge Gerry, ensnared in a romance with a Watertown belle unable to read or answer his letters. From Philadelphia came John Adams' first comments on art, for example on Charles Willson Peale's success in recording in oil the likenesses of patriots, and on the deliberations over a design of a Great Seal for the new nation. Adams' suggestion for the Seal was a classical allegory long a favorite of his—the Choice of Hercules between Virtue's "rugged Mountain" and the "flowery Paths of Pleasure."

AA to JA

Boston July 13 1776

I must begin with apoligising to you for not writing since the 17 of June. I have really had so many cares upon my Hands and Mind, with a bad inflamation in my Eyes that I have not been able to write. I now date from Boston where I yesterday arrived and was with all 4 of our Little ones innoculated for the small pox. My unkle and Aunt were so kind as to send me an invitation with my family. Mr. Cranch and wife and family, My Sister Betsy and her Little Neice, Cotton Tufts and Mr. Thaxter, a maid who has had the Distemper and my old Nurse compose our family. A Boy too I should have added. 17 in all. My unkles maid with his Little daughter and a Negro Man are here. We had our Bedding &c. to bring. A Cow we have driven down from B[raintre]e and some Hay I have had put into the Stable, wood &c. and we have really commenced housekeepers here. The House was furnished with almost every article (except Beds) which we have free use of, and think ourselves much obliged by the fine accommodations and kind offer of our Friends. All our necessary Stores we purchase jointly. Our Little ones stood the opperation Manfully. Dr. Bulfinch is our Physician. Such a Spirit of innoculation never before took place; the Town and every House in it, are as full as they can hold. I believe there are not less than 30 persons from Braintree. Mrs. Quincy, Mrs. Lincoln, Miss Betsy and Nancy are our near Neighbours. God Grant that we may all go comfortably thro the Distemper, the phisick part is bad enough I know. I knew your mind so perfectly upon the subject that I thought nothing, but our recovery would give you eaquel pleasure, and as to safety there was none. The Soldiers innoculated privately, so did many of the inhabitants and the paper curency spread it everywhere. I immediately determined to set myself about it, and get ready with my children. I wish it was so you could have been with us, but I submit.

I received some Letters from you last Saturday Night 26 of June. You mention a Letter of the 16 which I have never received, and I suppose must relate something to private affairs which I wrote about in May and sent by Harry.

As to News we have taken several fine prizes since I wrote you as you will see by the news papers. The present Report is of Lord Hows comeing with unlimited powers. However suppose it is so, I believe he little thinks of treating with us as independant States. How can any person yet dreem of a settlement, accommodations &c. They have neither the spirit nor feeling of Men, yet I see some who never were call'd Tories, gratified with the Idea of Lord Hows being upon his passage with such powers.

Sunday july 14

By yesterdays post I received two Letters dated 3 and 4 of July and tho your Letters never fail to give me pleasure, be the subject what it will, yet it was greatly heightned by the prospect of the future happiness and glory of our Country; nor am I a little Gratified when I reflect that a person so nearly connected with me has had the Honour of being a principal actor, in laying a foundation for its future Greatness. May the foundation of our new constitution, be justice, Truth and Righteousness. Like the wise Mans house may it be founded upon those Rocks and then neither storms or temptests will overthrow it.

I cannot but feel sorry that some of the most Manly Sentiments in the Declaration are Expunged from the printed coppy. Perhaps wise reasons induced it.

Poor Canady I lament Canady but we ought to be in some measure sufferers for the past folly of our conduct. The fatal effects of the small pox there, has led almost every person to consent to Hospitals in every Town. In many Towns, already arround Boston the Selectmen have granted Liberty for innoculation. I hope the necessity is now fully seen.

I had many dissagreable Sensations at the Thoughts of comeing myself, but to see my children thro it I thought my duty, and all those feelings vanished as soon as I was innoculated and I trust a kind providence will carry me safely thro. Our Friends from Plymouth came into Town yesterday. We have enough upon our hands in the morning. The Little folks are very sick then and puke every morning but after that they are comfortable. I shall write you now very often. Pray inform me constantly of every important transaction. Every expression of tenderness is a cordial to my Heart. Unimportant as they are to the rest of the world, to me they are *every Thing.*

We have had during all the month of June a most severe Drougth which cut of all our promising hopes of english Grain and the first crop of Grass, but since july came in we have had a plenty of rain and now every thing looks well. There is one Misfortune in our family which I have never mentiond in hopes it would have been in my power to have remedied it, but all hopes of that kind are at an end. It is the loss of your Grey Horse. About 2 months ago, I had occasion to send Jonathan of an errant to my unkle Quincys (the other Horse being a plowing). Upon his return a little below the church she trod upon a rolling stone and lamed herself to that degree that it was with great difficulty that she could be got home. I immediately sent for Tirrel and every thing was done for her by Baths, ointments, polticeing, Bleeding &c. that could be done. Still she continued extreem lame tho not so bad as at first. I then got her carried to Domet but he pronounces her incurable, as a callous is grown upon her footlock joint. You can hardly tell, not even by your own feelings how much I lament her. She was not with foal, as you immagined, but I hope she is now as care has been taken in that Respect.

I suppose you have heard of a fleet which came up pretty near the Light and kept us all with our mouths open ready to catch them, but after staying near a week and makeing what observations they could set sail and went of to our great mortification who were [prepared?] for them in every respect. If our Ship of 32 Guns which [was] Built at Portsmouth and waiting only for Guns and an other of [. . .] at Plimouth in the same state, had been in readiness we should in all probability been Masters of them. Where the blame lies in that respect I know not, tis laid upon Congress, and Congress is also blamed for not appointing us a General.—But Rome was not Built in a day.

I hope the Multiplicity of cares and avocations which invellope you will not be too powerfull for you. I have many anxietyes upon that account. Nabby and Johnny send duty and desire Mamma to say that an inflamation in their Eyes which has been as much of a distemper as the small pox, has prevented their writing, but they hope soon to be able to acquaint Pappa of their happy recovery from the Distemper.—Mr. C[ranch] and wife, Sister B[etsy] and all our Friend[s] desire to be rememberd to you and foremost in that Number stands your Portia

PS A little India herb would have been mighty agreable now.

JA to AA

Philadelphia July 20. 1776

This has been a dull day to me: I waited the Arrival of the Post with much Solicitude and Impatience, but his Arrival made me more solicitous still.—"To be left at the Post Office" in your Hand Writing, on the back of a few Lines from the Dr. were all that I could learn of you, and my little Folks. If you was too busy to write, I hoped that some kind Hand would have been found to let me know something about you.

Do my Friends think that I have been a Politician so long as to have lost all feeling? Do they suppose I have forgotten my Wife and Children? Or are they so panic struck with the Loss of Canada, as to be afraid to correspond with me? Or have they forgotten that you have an Husband and your Children a Father? What have I done, or omitted to do, that I should be thus forgotten and neglected in the most tender and affecting scæne of my Life! Dont mistake me, I dont blame you. Your Time and Thoughts must have been wholly taken up, with your own and your Families situation and Necessities.—But twenty other Persons might have informed me.

I suspect, that you intended to have run slyly, through the small Pox with the family, without letting me know it, and then have sent me an Account that you were all well. This might be a kind Intention, and if the design had succeeded, would have made me very joyous. But the secret is out, and I am left to conjecture. But as the Faculty have this distemper so much under Command I will flatter myself with the Hope and Expectation of soon hearing of your Recovery.

AA to JA

July 21 1776 Boston

I have no doubt but that my dearest Friend is anxious to know how his Portia does, and his little flock of children under the opperation of a disease once so formidable.

I have the pleasure to tell him that they are all comfortable tho some of them complaining. Nabby has been very ill, but the Eruption begins to make its appearence upon her, and upon Johnny. Tommy is so well that the Dr. innoculated him again to day fearing it had not taken. Charlly has no complaints yet, tho his arm has been very soar.

I have been out to meeting this forenoon, but have so many dissagreable Sensations this afternoon that I thought it prudent to tarry at home. The Dr. says they are very good feelings. Mr. Cranch has passed thro the preparation and the Eruption is comeing out cleverly upon him without any Sickness at all. Mrs. Cranch is cleverly and so are all her children. Those who are broke out are pretty full for the new method as tis call'd, the Suttonian they profess to practice upon. I hope to give you a good account when I write next, but our Eyes are very weak and the Dr. is not fond of either writing or reading for his patients. But I must transgress a little.

I received a Letter from you by wedensday Post 7 of July and tho I think it a choise one in the Litterary Way, containing many usefull hints and judicious observations which will greatly assist me in the future instruction of our Little ones, yet it Lacked some essential engrediants to make it compleat. Not one word respecting yourself, your Health or your present Situation. My anxiety for your welfare will never leave me but with my parting Breath, tis of more importance to me than all this World contains besides. The cruel Seperation to which I am necessatated cuts of half the enjoyments of life, the other half are comprised in the hope I have that what I do and what I suffer may be serviceable to you, to our Little ones and our Country; I must beseach you therefore for the future never to omit what is so essential to my happiness.

Last Thursday after hearing a very Good Sermon I went with the Multitude into Kings Street to hear the proclamation for independance read and proclamed. Some Field peices with the Train were brought there, the troops appeard under Arms and all the inhabitants assembled there (the small pox prevented many thousand from the Country). When Col. Crafts read from the Belcona of the State House the Proclamation, great attention was given to every word. As soon as he ended, the cry from the Belcona, was God Save our American States and then 3 cheers which rended the air, the Bells rang, the privateers fired, the forts and Batteries, the cannon were discharged, the platoons followed and every face appeard joyfull. Mr. Bowdoin then gave a Sentiment, Stability and perpetuity to American independance. After dinner the kings arms were taken down from the State House and every vestage of him from every place in which it appeard and burnt in King Street. Thus ends royall Authority in this State, and all the people shall say Amen.

I have been a little surprized that we collect no better accounts with regard to the horrid conspiricy at New York, and that so little mention has been made of it here. It made a talk for a few days but now seems all hushed in Silence. The Tories say that it was not a conspiricy but an association, and pretend that there was no plot to assasinate the General. Even their hardned Hearts ⟨*Blush*⟩ feel —— the discovery. We have in Gorge a match for a Borgia and a Catiline, a Wretch Callous to every Humane feeling. Our worthy preacher told us that he believed one of our Great Sins for which a righteous God has come out in judgment against us, was our Biggoted attachment to so wicked a Man. May our repentance be sincere.

JA to AA

Aug. 4 [1776]

Went this Morning to the Baptist Meeting, in Hopes of hearing Mr. Stillman, but was dissappointed. He was there, but another Gentleman preached. His Action was violent to a degree bordering on fury. His Gestures, unnatural, and distorted. Not the least Idea of Grace in his Motions, or Elegance in his Style. His Voice was vociferous and boisterous, and his Composition almost wholly destitute of Ingenuity. I wonder extreamly at the Fondness of our People for schollars educated at the Southward and for southern Preachers. There is no one Thing, in which We excell them more, than in our University, our schollars, and Preachers. Particular Gentlemen here, who have improved upon their Education by Travel, shine. But in general, old Massachusetts outshines her younger sisters, still. In several Particulars, they have more Wit, than We. They have Societies; the philosophical Society particularly, which excites a scientific Emulation, and propagates their Fame. If ever I get through this Scene of Politicks and War, I will spend the Remainder of my days, in endeavouring to instruct my Countrymen in the Art of making the most of their Abilities and Virtues, an Art, which they have hitherto, too much neglected. A philosophical society shall be established at Boston, if I have Wit and Address enough to accomplish it, sometime or other.—Pray set Brother Cranch's Philosophical Head to plodding upon this Project. Many of his Lucubrations would have been published and preserved, for the Benefit of Mankind, and for his Honour, if such a Clubb had existed.

My Countrymen want Art and Address. They want Knowledge of the World. They want the exteriour and superficial Accomplishments of Gentlemen, upon which the World has foolishly set so high a Value. In solid Abilities and real Virtues, they vastly excell in general, any People upon this Continent. Our N. England People are Aukward and bashfull; yet they are pert, ostentatious and vain, a Mixture which excites Ridicule and gives Disgust. They have not the faculty of shewing themselves to the best Advantage, nor the Art of concealing this faculty. An Art and Faculty which some People possess in the highest degree. Our Deficiencies in these Respects, are owing wholly to the little Intercourse We have had with strangers, and to our Inexperience in the World. These Imperfections must be remedied, for New England must produce the Heroes, the statesmen, the Philosophers, or America will make no great Figure for some Time.

Our Army is rather sickly at N. York, and We live in daily Expectation of hearing of some great Event. May God almighty grant it may be prosperous for America.—Hope is an Anchor and a Cordial. Disappointment however will not disconcert me.

If you will come to Philadelphia in September, I will stay, as long as you please. I should be as proud and happy as a Bridegroom. Yours.

AA to JA

Boston August 5 1776

I this Evening Received Your two Letters of july 10 and 11, and last Evening the Post brought me yours of july 23. I am really astonished at looking over the Number I have received during this month, more I believe than for 3 months before. I hope tis your amusement and relaxation from care to be thus imployed. It has been a feast to me during my absence from Home, and cheerd me in my most painfull Moments. At Last I Hear what I have long expected, and have feard for some time. I was certain that your Nerves must bee new Braced, and your Constitution new moulded, to continue well, through such a load of Buisness. Such intense application, in such a climate through the burning Heats of the Summer, tis too much for a constitution of Steel, and ought not to be required.

I intreat you to return, and that speidily. Mr. Gerry has recoverd his Health and Spirits by his journey. He call'd upon me a few moments. I knew Him by the same instinct by which I first discoverd him, and ventured to call him by Name tho his person was never discribed to me. I cannot account for it but so it was. He appeard a modest Man, and has a fine inteligent Eye. I wanted to ask him many questions which I could not do as he was a stranger, and we had company. He has promised to call upon me again before he returns which he proposes to do in about ten Days.

I have been trying all day to get time to write to you. I am now obliged to Rob my Sleep. Mrs. Cranch, Billy and Lucy are very unwell, all of them with the Symptoms I suppose. Lucy I fear has taken the

Distemper in the natural way, as tis more than 3 weeks since she was innoculated, and her Arm being inflamed deceived us. I took the precaution of having all mine who had not the Symptoms the 9th day innoculated a second time, and I hope they have all pass'd through except Charlly, and what to do with him I know not. I cannot get the small pox to opperate upon him, his Arm both times has been very soar, and he lives freely, that is he eats a small Quantity of meat, and I have given him wine but all will not do. Tommy is cleverly, has about a dozen, and is very gay and happy.

I have abundant reason to be thankfull that we are so many of us carried comfortably through a Disease so formidable in its natural opperation, and though our Symptoms have run high, yet they have been the worst, for the Eruption has been a triffel, really should have been glad to have had them in greater plenty. I hope to be able to return to Braintree the Latter end of next week which will compleat me 5 weeks. I have been unlucky in a Maid, who has not one qualification to recommend her but that she has had the small pox. She has been twice sick since she has been with us, and put us to much difficulty. I have attended publick worship constantly, except one day and a half ever since I have been in Town. I rejoice in a preacher who has some warmth, some energy, some feeling. Deliver me from your cold phlegmatick Preachers, Politicians, Friends, Lovers and Husbands. I thank Heaven I am not so constituted my-self and so connected.

How destitute are they of all those Sensations which sweeten as well as embitter our probationary State! And How seldom do we find true Genious residing in such a constitution, but may I ask if the same temperament and the same Sensibility which constitutes a poet and a painter will not be apt to make a Lover and a Debauchee?

When I reflect upon Humane Nature, the various passions and appetites to which it is subject, I am ready to cry out with the Psalmist Lord what is Man?

You ask me How you shall get Home. I know not. Is there any assistance you can think of that I can procure for you. Pray Let me know. Our Court do not set till the 28 of this month, no delegates can be chosen to releave you till then, but if you are so low in Health do not wait for that. Mr. Bowdoin has the Gout in his Stomack, is very ill. I do not think he could by any means bear close application. Mr. Dana and Mr. Lowell are very good Men, I wish they would appoint them. Our Friend ⟨*Warren*⟩ has some family difficulties. I know not whether he could possibly leave it. A partner dear to him you know beyond description almost Heart broken, by the Situation of one very dear to *her* whose great attention and care you well know has been to Train them up in the way in which they ought to go. Would to Heaven they did not depart from it. Impaired in Health, impaird in mind, impaird in Morrals, is a Situation truly deplorable, but do not mention the Matter—not even to them by the slightest hint Tis a wound which cannot be touched.

God grant we may never mourn a similiar Situation, but I have some times the Heartake when I look upon the fire, spirit and vivacity, joind to a comely person in the Eldest, soft, tender and pathetick in the second, Manly, firm and intrepid in the third. I fear less for him, but alass we are short sighted mortals.

> O Blindness to the future kindly given
> that each may fill the circle marked by Heaven.

Adieu dearest Best of Friend[s] adieu.

AA to JA

August 14 1776

I wrote you to day by Mr. Smith but as I suppose this will reach you sooner, I omitted mentioning any thing of my family in it.

Nabby has enough of the small Pox for all the family beside. She is pretty well coverd, not a spot but what is so soar that she can neither walk sit stand or lay with any comfort. She is as patient as one can expect, but they are a very soar sort. If it was a disorder to which we could be subject more than once I would go as far as it was possible to avoid it. She is sweld a good deal. You will receive a perticuliar account before this reaches you of the uncommon manner in which the small Pox acts, it bafels the skill of the most Experience'd here. Billy Cranch is now out with about 40, and so well as not to be detaind at Home an hour for it. Charlly remains in the same state he did.

Your Letter of August 3 came by this days Post. I find it very conveniant to be so handy. I can receive a Letter at Night, sit down and reply to it, and send it of in the morning.

You remark upon the deficiency of Education in your Countrymen. It never I believe was in a worse state, at least for many years. The Colledge is not in the state one could wish, the Schollars complain that their professer in Philosophy is taken of by publick Buisness to their great detriment. In this Town I never saw so great a neglect of Education. The poorer sort of children are wholly neglected, and left to range the Streets without Schools, without Buisness, given up to all Evil. The Town is not as formerly divided into Wards. There is either too much Buisness left upon the hands of a few, or too little care to do it. We daily see the Necessity of a regular Goverment.—You speak of our Worthy Brother. I often lament it that a Man so peculiarly formed for the Education of youth, and so well qualified as he is in many Branches of Litrature, excelling in Philosiphy and the Mathematicks, should not be imployd in some publick Station. I know not the person who would make half so good a Successor to Dr. Winthrope. He has a peculiar easy manner of communicating his Ideas to Youth, and the Goodness of his Heart, and the purity of his morrals without an affected austerity must have a happy Effect upon the minds of Pupils.

If you complain of neglect of Education in sons, What shall I say with regard to daughters, who every day experience the want of it. With regard to the Education of my own children, I find myself soon out of my debth, and destitute and deficient in every part of Education.

I most sincerely wish that some more liberal plan might be laid and executed for the Benefit of the rising Generation, and that our new constitution may be distinguished for Learning and Virtue. If we mean to have Heroes, Statesmen and Philosophers, we should have learned women. The world perhaps would laugh at me, and accuse me of vanity, But you I know have a mind too enlarged and liberal to disregard the Sentiment. If much depends as is allowed upon the early Education of youth and the first principals which are instilld take the deepest root, great benifit must arise from litirary accomplishments in women.

Excuse me my pen has run away with me. I have no thoughts of comeing to P[hiladelphi]a. The length of time I have [and] shall be detaind here would have prevented me, even if you had no thoughts of returning till December, but I live in daily Expectation of seeing you here. Your Health I think requires your immediate return. I expected Mr. Gerry would have set off before now, but he finds it perhaps very hard to leave his Mistress—I wont say harder than some do to leave their wives. Mr. Gerry stood very high in my Esteem—what is meat for one is not for an other—no accounting for fancy. She is a queer dame and leads people wild dances.

But hush—Post, dont betray your trust and loose my Letter.

Nabby is poorly this morning. The pock are near the turn, 6 or 7 hundred boils are no agreable feeling. You and I know not what a feeling it is. Miss Katy can tell. I had but 3 they were very clever and fill'd nicely. The Town instead of being clear of this distemper are now in the height of it, hundreds having it in the natural way through the deceitfulness of innoculation.

Adieu ever yours. Breakfast waits. Portia

JA to AA

Philadelphia 14. August 1776

This is the Anniversary of a memorable day, in the History of America: a day when the Principle of American Resistance and Independence, was first asserted, and carried into Action. The Stamp Office fell before the rising Spirit of our Countrymen.—It is not impossible that the two *gratefull* Brothers may make their grand Attack this very day: if they should, it is possible it may be more glorious for this Country, than ever: it is certain it will become more memorable.

Your Favours of August 1. and 5. came by Yesterdays Post. I congratulate you all upon your agreable Prospects. Even my pathetic little Hero Charles, I hope will have the Distemper finely. It is very odd that the Dr. cant put Infection enough into his Veigns, nay it is unaccountable to me that he has not taken it, in the natural Way before now. I am under little Apprehension, prepared as he is, if he should. I am concerned about you, much more. So many Persons about you, sick. The Children troublesome—your Mind perplexed—yourself weak and relaxed. The Situation must be disagreable. The Country Air, and Exercise however, will refresh you.

I am put upon a Committee to prepare a Device for a Golden Medal to commemorate the Surrender of Boston to the American Arms, and upon another to prepare Devices for a Great Seal for the confederated States. There is a Gentleman here of French Extraction, whose Name is Du simitiere, a Painter by Profession whose Designs are very ingenious, and his Drawings well executed. He has been applied to for his Advice. I waited on him yesterday, and saw his Sketches. For the Medal he proposes Liberty with her Spear and Pileus, leaning on General Washington. The British Fleet in Boston Harbour, with all their Sterns towards the Town, the American Troops, marching in. For the Seal he proposes. The Arms of the several Nations from whence America has been peopled, as English, Scotch, Irish, Dutch, German &c. each in a Shield. On one side of them Liberty, with her Pileus, on the other a Rifler, in his Uniform, with his Rifled Gun in one Hand, and his Tomahauk, in the other. This Dress and these Troops with this Kind of Armour, being peculiar to America—unless the Dress was known to the Romans. Dr. F[ranklin] shewed me, yesterday, a Book, containing an Account of the Dresses of all the Roman Soldiers, one of which, appeared exactly like it.

This Mr. Du simitiere is a very curious Man. He has begun a Collection of Materials for an History of this Revolution. He begins with the first Advices of the Tea Ships. He cutts out of the News-

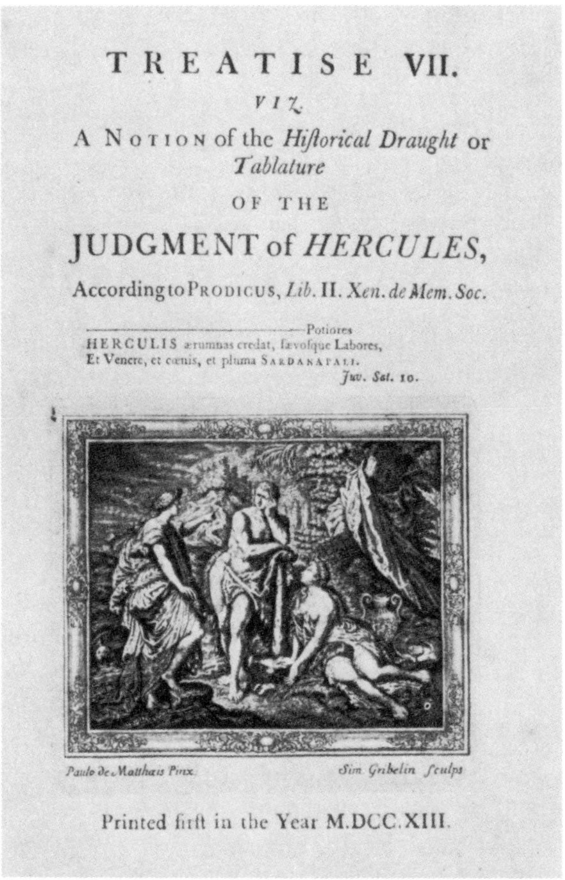

TREATISE VII.

viz.

A NOTION of the *Hiſtorical Draught* or *Tablature*

OF THE

JUDGMENT of *HERCULES*,

According to PRODICUS, *Lib.* II. *Xen. de Mem. Soc.*

———————Potiores
HERCULIS ærumnas credat, ſævoſque Labores,
Et Venere, et cœnis, et pluma SARDANAPALI.
Juv. Sat. 10.

Printed firſt in the Year M.DCC.XIII.

THE "CHOICE OF HERCULES," PROPOSED BY JOHN ADAMS FOR THE GREAT SEAL OF THE UNITED STATES

papers, every Scrap of Intelligence, and every Piece of Speculation, and pastes it upon clean Paper, arranging them under the Head of the State to which they belong and intends to bind them up in Volumes. He has a List of every Speculation and Pamphlet concerning Independence, and another of those concerning Forms of Government.

Dr. F. proposes a Device for a Seal. Moses lifting up his Wand, and dividing the Red Sea, and Pharaoh, in his Chariot overwhelmed with the Waters.—This Motto. Rebellion to Tyrants is Obedience to God.

Mr. Jefferson proposed. The Children of Israel in the Wilderness, led by a Cloud by day, and a Pillar of Fire by night, and on the other Side Hengist and Horsa, the Saxon Chiefs, from whom We claim the Honour of being descended and whose Political Principles and Form of Government We have assumed.

I proposed the Choice of Hercules, as engraved by Gribeline in some Editions of Lord Shaftsburys Works. The Hero resting on his Clubb. Virtue pointing to her rugged Mountain, on one Hand, and perswading him to ascend. Sloth, glancing at her flowery Paths of Pleasure, wantonly reclining on the Ground, displaying the Charms both of her Eloquence and Person, to seduce him into Vice. But this is too complicated a Group for a Seal or Medal, and it is not original.

I shall conclude by repeating my Request for Horses and a servant. Let the Horses be good ones. I cant ride a bad Horse, so many hundred Miles. If our Affairs had not been in so critical a state at N. York, I should have run away before now. But I am determined now to stay, untill some Gentleman is sent here in my Room, and untill my Horses come. But the Time will be very tedious.

The whole Force is arrived at Staten Island.

JA to AA

Philadelphia August 21. 1776

Yesterday Morning I took a Walk, into Arch Street, to see Mr. Peele's Painters Room. Peele is from Maryland, a tender, soft, affectionate Creature.... He shewed me a large Picture containing a Group of Figures, which upon Inquiry I found were his Family. His Mother, and his Wifes Mother, himself and his Wife, his Brothers and sisters, and his Children, Sons and Daughters all young. There was a pleasant, a happy Chearfulness in their Countenances, and a Familiarity in their Airs towards each other.

He shewed me one moving Picture. His Wife, all bathed in Tears, with a Child about six months old, laid out, upon her Lap. This Picture struck me prodigiously.

He has a Variety of Portraits—very well done. But not so well as Copeleys Portraits. Copeley is the greatest Master, that ever was in America. His Portraits far exceed Wests.

Peele has taken General Washington, Dr. Franklin, Mrs. Washington, Mrs. Rush, Mrs. Hopkinson. Mr. Blair McClenachan and his little Daughter in one Picture. His Lady and her little son, in another.

Peele shewed me some Books upon the Art of Painting, among

the rest one by Sir Joshua Reynolds, the President of the English Accademy of Painters, by whom the Pictures of General Conway and Coll. Barry [Barré] in Fanuil Hall were taken.

He shewed me too a great Number of Miniature Pictures, among the rest Mr. Hancock and his Lady—Mr. Smith, of S.C. whom you saw the other day in Boston—Mr. Custis, and many others.

He shewed me, likewise, Draughts, or rather Sketches of Gentlemen's Seats in Virginia, where he had been—Mr. Corbins, Mr. Pages, General Washingtons &c.

Also a Variety of rough Drawings, made by great Masters in Italy, which he keeps as Modells.

He shewed me, several Imitations of Heads, which he had made in Clay, as large as the Life, with his Hands only. Among the Rest one of his own Head and Face, which was a great Likeness.

He is ingenious. He has Vanity—loves Finery—Wears a sword—gold Lace—speaks French—is capable of Friendship, and strong Family Attachments and natural Affections.

At this shop I met Mr. Francis Hopkinson, late a Mandamus Councillor of New Jersey, now a Member of the Continental Congress, who it seems is a Native of Philadelphia, a son of a Prothonotary of this County who was a Person much respected. The son was liberally educated, and is a Painter and a Poet.

I have a Curiosity to penetrate a little deeper into the Bosom of this curious Gentleman, and may possibly give you some more particulars concerning him.... He is one of your pretty little, curious, ingenious Men. His Head is not bigger, than a large Apple—less than our Friend Pemberton or Dr. Simon Tufts. I have not met with any Thing in natural History much more amusing and entertaining, than his personal Appearance. Yet he is genteel and well bred, and is very social.

I wish I had Leisure, and Tranquility of Mind to amuse myself with these Elegant, and ingenious Arts of Painting, Sculpture, Statuary, Architecture, and Musick. But I have not. A Taste in all of them, is an agreable Accomplishment.

Mr. Hopkinson has taken in Crayons, with his own Hand, a Picture of Miss Keys, a famous New Jersey Beauty. He talks of bringing it to Town, and in that Case I shall see it, I hope.

AA to JA

Boston August 25 1776

I sent Johnny last Evening to the Post office for Letters. He soon returnd and pulling one from under his Gown gave it me, the young Rogue smiling and watching Mammas countanance draws out an other, and then an other, highly gratified to think he had so many presents to bestow.

Our Friends are very kind. My Father sends his Horse and Dr. Tufts has offerd me an other one he had of unkle Q[uinc]y about 5 year old. He has never been journeys, but is able enough. Mr. Bass is just come, and says he cannot sit out till tomorrow week without great damage to his Buisness. He has been a long time out of Stock, and about a week ago obtaind a Quantity and has engaged 20 pair of shooes which will be eaquel to 20 Dollors to him, which he must losse if I will not consent to his tarrying till then. Tho I urged him to sit of tomorrow, yet the Horses will be in a better State as they will not be used and more able to perform the journey. I am obliged to consent to his tarrying till then when you may certainly expect him.

Bass is affraid that the Drs. Horse will not be able to travel so fast as he must go. He will go and see him, and in case he is not your Brother has promised to let one of his go. I only have to regret that I did not sooner make trial of my Friends, and have sent for you 3 weeks ago. I fear you will think me neglegent, and inatentive. If I had been at Home, I should have been sooner in a capacity to have assisted you. I was talking of sending for you and trying to procure horses for you when little Charles who lay upon the couch coverd over with small Pox, and nobody knew that he heard or regarded any thing which was said, lifted up his head and says Mamma, take my Dollor and get a Horse for Pappa. Poor fellow has had a tedious time of it as well as I, but tis now upon the turn, and he is much easier, and better. I hope I shall be able to get out of Town a Saturday next.

Mr. and Mrs. Cranch with their children went out a fryday. I feel rather lonely. Such a change from 1 or 2 and twenty to only 5 or 6 is a great alteration. I took the Liberty of sending my complements to General Lincoln and asking him some questions which you proposed to me, but which I was really unable to answer, and he has promised me a perticuliar reply to them.

As to provisions there is no Scarcity. Tis true they are high, but that is more oweing to the advanced price of Labour than the Scarcity. English Goods of every kind are not purchasable, at least by me. They are extravagantly high, West india articles are very high all except Sugars, which have fallen half since I came into Town. Our New England Rum is 4 Shillings pr. Gallon, Molasses the same price. Loaf Sugar 2s. 4d. pr. pound, cotton wool 4 Shillings pr. pound, sheeps wool 2 Shillings, flax 1 & 6. In short one hundred pound two year ago would purchase more than two will now.

House Rent in this Town is very low. Some of the best and Genteelest houses in Town rent for 20 pounds pr. year. Ben Hollowell [Hallowell's] has been offerd for 10. and Mr. Shurdens [Chardon's] for 13 6 & 8 pence.

The privateer Independance which saild from Plymouth about 3 weeks ago has taken a jamaca man laiden with Sugars and sent her into Marblehead last Saturday. I hear the Defence has taken an other.

I think we make a fine hand at prizes.

Coll. Q[uinc]y desires me to ask you whether you have received a Letter from him, he wrote you some time ago.

I like Dr. F[ranklin's] device for a Seal. It is such a one as will please most—at least it will be most agreable to the Spirit of New england.

We have not any news here—anxiously waiting the Event, and in daily Expectation of hearing tidings from New york. Heaven Grant they may be Glorious for our Country and Country men, then will I glory in being an American. Ever ever Yours, Portia

PS We are in such want of Lead as to be obliged to take down the Leads from the windows in this Town.

AA to JA

Dearest Friend Boston August 29 1776

I have spent the 3 days past almost intirely with you. The weather has been stormy, I have had little company, and I have amused my self in my closet reading over the Letters I have received from you since I have been here.

I have possession of my Aunts chamber in which you know is a very conveniant pretty closet with a window which looks into her flower Garden. In this closet are a number of Book Shelves, which are but poorly furnished, however I have a pretty little desk or cabinet here where I write all my Letters and keep my papers unmollested by any one. I do not covet my Neighbours Goods, but I should like to be the owner of such conveniances. I always had a fancy for a closet with a window which I could more peculiarly call my own.

Here I say I have amused myself in reading and thinking of my absent Friend, sometimes with a mixture of paine, sometimes with pleasure, sometimes anticipating a joyfull and happy meeting, whilst my Heart would bound and palpitate with the pleasing Idea, and with the purest affection I have held you to my Bosom till my whole Soul has dissolved in Tenderness and my pen fallen from my Hand.

How often do I reflect with pleasure that I hold in possession a Heart Eaqually warm with my own, and full as Susceptable of the Tenderest impressions, and Who even now whilst he is reading here, feels all I discribe.

Forgive this Revere, this Delusion, and since I am debared real, suffer me, to enjoy, and indulge In Ideal pleasures—and tell me they are not inconsistant with the stern virtue of a senator and a Patriot.

I must leave my pen to recover myself and write in an other strain. I feel anxious for a post day, and am full as solicitious for two Letters a week and as uneasy if I do not get them, as I used to be when I got but one in a month or 5 weeks. Thus do I presume upon indulgance, and this is Humane Nature, and brings to my mind a sentiment of one of your correspondents viz. "That Man is the only animal who is hungery with His Belly full."

Last Evening Dr. Cooper came in and brought me your favour from the post office of August 18 and Coll. Whipple arrived yesterday morning and deliverd me the two Bundles you sent, and a Letter of the 12 of August. They have already afforded me much amusement, and I expect much more from them.

I am sorry to find from your last as well as from some others of your Letters that you feel so dissatisfied with the office to which you are chosen. Tho in your acceptance of it, I know you was actuated by the purest motives, and I know of no person here so well qualified to discharge the important Duties of it, Yet I will not urge you to it. In accepting of it you must be excluded from all other employments. There never will be a Salery addequate to the importance of the office or to support you and your family from penury. If you possess a fortune I would urge you to it, in spight of all the flears and gibes of minds who themselves are incapable of acting a disintrested part, and have no conception that others can.

I have never heard any Speaches about it, nor did I know that such insinuations had been Thrown out.

Pure and disintrested Virtue must ever be its own reward. Mankind are too selfish and too depraved to discover the pure Gold from the baser mettle.

I wish for peace and tranquility. All my desires and all my ambition is to be Esteemed and Loved by my Partner, to join with him in the Education and instruction of our Little ones, to set under our own vines in Peace, Liberty and Safety.

Adieu my Dearest Friend, soon, soon return to your most affectionate

Portia

The plans Adams had entertained of returning to Massachusetts in September were abruptly put aside. In New York the British had defeated and almost captured Washington's forces at the battle of Long Island. "Our Affairs having taken a Turn . . . so much to our Disadvantage," he wrote his wife, "I cannot see my Way clear, to return home so soon as I intended." General John Sullivan of New Hampshire, captured in that battle, was sent to Philadelphia by Admiral Lord Howe to request a private conversation on Howe's part "with some of the Members of Congress." Reluctantly, Adams accompanied Benjamin Franklin and Edward Rutledge on a bizarre and fruitless journey behind enemy lines to discuss with Howe "a bubble, an Ambuscade, a mere insidious Maneuvre, calculated only to decoy and deceive."

JA to AA

Fryday Septr. 6. 1776

This day, I think, has been the most remarkable of all. Sullivan came here from Lord Howe, five days ago with a Message that his Lordship desired a half an Hours Conversation with some of the Members of Congress, in their private Capacities. We have spent three or four days in debating whether We should take any Notice of it. I have, to the Utmost of my Abilities during the whole Time, opposed our taking any Notice of it. But at last it was determined by a Majority "that the Congress being the Representatives of the free and independent states of America, it was improper to appoint any of their Members to confer, in their private Characters with his Lordship. But they would appoint a Committee of their Body, to wait on him, to know whether he had Power, to treat with Congress upon Terms of Peace and to hear any Propositions, that his Lordship may think proper to make."

When the Committee came to be ballotted for, Dr. Franklin and your humble servant, were unanimously chosen. Coll. R. H. Lee and Mr. [Edward] Rutledge, had an equal Number: but upon a second Vote Mr. R. was chosen. I requested to be excused, but was desired to consider of it untill tomorrow. My Friends here Advise me to go. All the stanch and intrepid, are very earnest with me to go, and the timid and wavering, if any such there are, agree in the request. So I believe I shall undertake the Journey. I doubt whether his Lordship will see Us, but the same Committee will be directed to inquire into the State of the Army, at New York, so that there will be Business enough, if his Lordship makes none.—It would fill this Letter Book, to give you all the Arguments, for and against this Measure, if I had Liberty to attempt it.—His Lordship seems to have been playing off a Number of Machiavillian Maneuvres, in order to throw upon Us the Odium of continuing this War. Those who have been Advocates for the Appointment of this Committee, are for opposing Maneuvre to Maneuvre, and are confident that the Consequence will be, that the Odium will fall upon him. However this may be, my Lesson is plain, to ask a few Questions, and take his Answers.

I can think of but one Reason for their putting me upon this Embassy, and that is this. An Idea has crept into many Minds here that his Lordship is such another as Mr. Hutchinson, and they may possibly think that a Man who has been accustomed to penetrate into the mazy Windings of Hutchinsons Heart, and the serpentine Wiles of his Head, may be tolerably qualified to converse with his Lordship.

JA to AA

Philadelphia Saturday Septr. 14. 1776

Yesterday Morning I returned with Dr. F. and Mr. R. from Staten Island where We met L[ord] H[owe] and had about three Hours Conversation with him. The Result of this Interview, will do no disservice to Us. It is now plain that his L[ordshi]p has no Power, but what is given him in the Act of P[arliament]. His Commission authorises him to grant Pardons upon Submission, and to converse, confer, consult and advise with such Persons as he may think proper, upon American Grievances, upon the Instructions to Governors and the Acts of Parliament, and if any Errors should be found to have crept in, his Majesty and the Ministry were willing they should be rectified.

I found yours of 31. of Aug. and 2d. of September. I now congratulate you on your Return home with the Children. Am sorry to find you anxious on Account of idle Reports.—Dont regard them. I think our Friends are to blame to mention such silly Stories to you. What good do they expect to do by it?

My Ride has been of Service to me. We were absent but four days. It was an agreable Excursion. His L[ordshi]p is about fifty

Years of Age. He is a well bred Man, but his Address is not so irresistable, as it has been represented. I could name you many Americans, in your own Neighbourhood, whose Art, Address, and Abilities are greatly superiour. His head is rather confused, I think.

When I shall return I cant say. I expect now, every day, fresh Hands from Watertown.

AA to JA

Braintree Sepbr. 20 1777 [*i.e.* 1776]

I sit down this Evening to write you, but I hardly know what to think about your going to N.Y.—The Story has been told so many times, and with circumstances so perticuliar that I with others have given some heed [to] it tho my not hearing any thing of it from you leaves me at a loss.

Yours of Sepbr. 4 came to hand last Night, our Worthy unkle is a constant attendant upon the Post office for me and brought it me.

Yours of Sepbr. 5 came to Night to B[raintre]e and was left as directed with the Cannister. Am sorry you gave yourself so much trouble about them. I got about half you sent me by Mr. Gerry. Am much obliged to you, and hope to have the pleasure of making the greater part of it for you. Your Letter damp't my Spirits; when I had no expectation of your return till December, I endeavourd to bring my mind to acquiess in the too painfull Situation, but I have now been in a state of Hopefull expectation. I have recond the days since Bass went away a hundred times over, and every Letter expected to find the day set for your return.

But now I fear it is far distant. I have frequently been told that the communication would be cut of and that you would not be ever able to return. Sometimes I have been told so by those who really wish'd it might be so, with Malicious pleasure. Sometimes your timid folks have apprehended that it would be so. I wish any thing would bring you nearer. If there is really any danger I should think you would remove. Tis a plan your Enemies would rejoice to see accomplished, and will Effect if it lies in their power.

I am not apt to be intimidated you know. I have given as little heed to that and a thousand other Bug Bear reports as posible. I have slept as soundly since my return not withstanding all the Ghosts and hobgoblings, as ever I did in my life. Tis true I never close my Eyes at night till I have been to P[hiladelphi]a, and my first visit in the morning is there.

How unfealing are the world! They tell me they Heard you was dead with as little sensibility as a stock or a stone, and I have now got to be provoked at it, and can hardly help snubing the person who tells me so.

The Story of your being upon this conference at New york came in a Letter as I am told from R. T. P[aine] to his Brother in Law G[reenlea]fe. Many very many have been the conjectures of the Multitude upon it. Some have supposed the War concluded, the Nation setled, others an exchange of prisoners, others a reconsiliation with Brittain &c. &c.

I cannot consent to your tarrying much longer. I know your Health must greatly suffer from so constant application to Buisness and so little excercise. Besides I shall send you word by and by as Regulus'es steward did, that whilst you are engaged in the Senate your own domestick affairs require your presence at Home, and that your wife and children are in Danger of wanting Bread. If the Senate of America will take care of us, as the Senate of Rome did of the family of Regulus, you may serve them again, but unless you return what little property you possess will be lost. In the first place the House at Boston is going to ruin. When I was there I hired a Girl to clean it, it had a cart load of Dirt in it. I speak within Bounds. One of the chambers was used to keep poultry in, an other sea coal, and an other salt. You may conceive How it look'd. The House is so exceeding damp being shut up, that the floors are mildewd, the sealing falling down, and the paper mouldy and falling from the walls. I took care to have it often opened and aird whilst I tarried in Town. I put it into the best state I could.

In the next place, the Lighter of which you are or should be part owner is lying rotting at the wharf. One year more without any care and she is worth nothing. You have no Bill of Sale, no right to convey any part of her should any person appear to purchase her. The Pew I let, after having paid a tax for the repairs of the meeting House.

As to what is here under my more immediate inspection I do the best I can with it, but it will not at the high price Labour is, pay its way.

I know the weight of publick cares lye so heavey upon you that I have been loth to mention your own private ones.

The Best accounts we can collect from New York assure us that our Men fought valiantly. We are no ways dispiritted here, we possess a Spirit that will not be conquerd. If our Men are all drawn of and we should be attacked, you would find a Race of Amazons in America.

But I trust we shall yet tread down our Enemies.

I must intreat you to remember me often. I never think your Letters half long enough. I do not complain. I have no reason to, no one can boast of more Letters than Your Portia

JA to AA

Philadelphia Octr. 11. 1776

I suppose your Ladyship has been in the Twitters, for some Time past, because you have not received a Letter by every Post, as you used to do.—But I am coming to make my Apology in Person. I, Yesterday asked and obtained Leave of Absence. It will take me till next Monday, to get ready, to finish off a few Remnants of public Business, and to put my private Affairs in proper Order. On the 14th. day of October, I shall get away, perhaps. But I dont expect to reach Home, in less than a fortnight, perhaps not in three Weeks, as I shall be obliged to make stops by the Way.

Two days later John Adams set out for Braintree. In the next month he was elected to another term in Congress, but this time with six colleagues to share the delegation's duties. The Adamses' letters in early 1777 show that he had promised that this would be his last absence of this kind, but their parting on January 9 was made no easier by this vow, for Abigail had just learned that she was carrying their sixth child—a child she must bear alone, without her husband or her mother at her side. Adams' journey to Congress was no easier than his farewell to his wife. With one of his colleagues, he undertook a roundabout route south, skirting British-occupied New York City by crossing from the Hudson Highlands into New Jersey and Pennsylvania. After a brief visit to the Moravian community at Bethlehem, they continued on to Baltimore, where Congress had adjourned when General Howe's army pushed into New Jersey. "After the longest Journey, and through the worst Roads and the worst Weather, that I have ever experienced," Adams arrived in Baltimore on the first day of February.

JA to AA

Baltimore Feby. 3. 1777

This Day has been observed in this Place, with exemplary Decency and Solemnity, in Consequence of an Appointment of the Government, in Observance of a Recommendation of Congress, as a Day of Fasting. I went to the Presbyterian Meeting and heard Mr. Allison deliver a most pathetic and animating, as well as pious, patriotic and elegant Discourse. I have seldom been better pleased or more affected with a sermon.

The Presbyterian Meeting House in Baltimore stands upon an Hill just at the Back of the Town, from whence We have a very fair Prospect of the Town, and of the Water upon which it stands, and of the

Country round it. Behind this Eminence, which is the Bacon [Beacon] Hill of Baltimore, lies a beautifull Meadow, which is entirely incircled by a Stream of Water. This most beautifull Scæne must be partly natural and partly artificial. Beyond the Meadow and Canall, you have a charming View of the Country. Besides the Meeting House there is upon this Height, a large and elegant Court House, as yet unfinished within, and a small Church of England in which an old Clergyman officiates, Mr. Chase, Father of Mr. Chace one of the Delegates of Maryland, who they say is not so zealous a Whigg as the Son.

I shall take Opportunities to describe this Town and State more particularly to you hereafter. I shall inquire into their Religion, their Laws, their Customs, their Manners, their Descent and Education, their Learning, their Schools and Colledges and their Morals.—It was said of Ulysses I think that he saw the Manners of many Men and many Cities, which is like to be my Case, as far as American Men and Cities extend, provided Congress should continue in the rolling Humour, which I hope they will not. I wish however, that my Mind was more at rest than it is, that I might be able to make more exact Observations of Men and Things as far as I go.

When I reflect upon the Prospect before me of so long an Absence from all that I hold dear in this World, I mean all that contributes to my private personal Happiness, it makes me melancholly. When I think on your *Circumstances* I am more so, and yet I rejoice at them in spight of all this Melancholly.—God almightys Providence protect and bless you and yours and mine.

JA to AA

Baltimore Feb. 7. 1777

I think, in some Letter I sent you, since I left Bethlehem, I promised you a more particular Account of that curious and remarkable Town.

When We first came in sight of the Town, We found a Country better cultivated and more agreably diversified with Prospects of orchards and Fields, Groves and Meadows, Hills and Valleys, than any We had seen.

When We came into the Town We were directed to a public House kept by a Mr. Johnson, which I think was the best Inn, I ever saw. It belongs it seems to the Society, is furnished, at their Expence, and is kept for their Profit, or at their Loss. Here you might find every Accommodation that you could wish for yourself, your servants and Horses, and at no extravagant Rates neither.

The Town is regularly laid out, the Streets straight and at right Angles like those in Philadelphia. It stands upon an Eminence and has a fine large Brook flowing on one End of it, and the Lehigh a

Branch of the Delaware on the other. Between the Town and the Lehigh are beautifull public Gardens.

They have carried the mechanical Arts to greater Perfection here than in any Place which I have seen. They have a sett of Pumps which go by Water, which force the Water up through leaden Pipes, from the River to the Top of the Hill, near an hundred feet, and to the Top of a little Building, in the shape of a Pyramid, or Obelisk, which stands upon the Top of the Hill and is twenty or thirty feet high. From this Fountain Water is conveyed in Pipes to every Part of the Town.

Upon the River they have a fine Sett of Mills. The best Grist Mills and bolting Mills, that are any where to be found. The best fulling Mills, an oil Mill, a Mill to grind Bark for the Tanyard, a Dying House where all Colours are died, Machines for shearing Cloth &c.

There are three public Institutions here of a very remarkable Nature. One, a Society of the young Men, another of the young Women, and a Third of the Widows. There is a large Building, divided into many Appartments, where the young Men reside, by themselves, and carry on their several Trades. They pay a Rent to the Society for their Rooms, and they pay for their Board, and what they earn is their own.

There is another large Building, appropriated in the same Manner to the young Women. There is a Governess, a little like the Lady Abbess, in some other Institutions, who has the Superintendence of the whole, and they have elders. Each Apartment has a Number of young Women, who are vastly industrious, some Spinning, some Weaving, others employed in all the most curious Works in Linnen, Wool, Cotton, Silver and Gold, Silk and Velvet. This Institution displeased me much. Their Dress was uniform and clean, but very inelegant. Their Rooms were kept extreamly warm with Dutch Stoves: and the Heat, the Want of fresh Air and Exercise, relaxed the poor Girls in such a manner, as must I think destroy their Health. Their Countenances were languid and pale.

The Society of Widows is very similar. Industry and Æconomy are remarkable in all these Institutions.

They shewed Us their Church which is hung round with Pictures of our Saviour from his Birth to his Death, Resurrection and Ascention. It is done with very strong Colours, and very violent Passions, but not in a very elegant Taste. The Painter who is still living in Bethelehem, but very old—he has formerly been in Italy, the school of Paints. They have a very good organ in their Church of their own make. They have a public Building, on Purpose for the Reception of the dead, to which the Corps is carried as soon as it expires, where it lies untill the Time of Sepulture.

Christian Love is their professed Object, but it is said they love Money and make their public Institutions subservient to the Gratification of that Passion.

They suffer no Law suits with one another, and as few as possible with other Men. It is said that they now profess to be against War.

They have a Custom, peculiar, respecting Courtship and Marriage. The Elders pick out Pairs to be coupled together, who have no Opportunity of Conversing together, more than once or twice, before the Knot is tied. The Youth of the two sexes have very little Conversation with one another, before Marriage.

Mr. Hassey, a very agreable, sensible Gentleman, who shewed Us the Curiosities of the Place, told me, upon Inquiry that they profess the Augsburg Confession of Faith, are Lutherans rather than Calvinists, distinguish between Bishops and Presbyters, but have no Idea of the Necessity of the uninterrupted Succession, are very liberal and candid in their Notions in opposition to Bigottry, and live in Charity with all Denominations.

AA to JA

Braintree March 8 1777

We have had very severe weather almost ever since you left us. About the middle of Febry. came a snow of a foot and half deep upon a Level which made it fine going for about 10 day's when a snow storm succeeded with a High wind and banks 5 and 6 feet high. I do not remember to have seen the Roads so obstructed since my remembrance; there has been no passing since except for a Horse.

I Have wrote you 3 Letters since your absence but whether you have ever received one of them I know not. The Post office has been in such a Situation that there has been no confiding in it, but I hear Hazard is come to put it upon a better footing.

We know not what is passing with you nor with the Army, any more than if we lived with the Antipodes. I want a Bird of passage. It has given me great pleasure to find by your Letters which I have received that your Spirits are so Good, and that your Health has not sufferd by your tedious journey. Posterity who are to reap the Blessings, will scarcly be able to conceive the Hardships and Sufferings of their Ancesstors.—"But tis a day of suffering says the Author of the Crisis, and we ought to expect it. What we contend for is worthy the affliction we may go through. If we get but Bread to eat and any kind of rayment to put on, we ought not only to be contented, but thankfull. What are the inconveniencies of a few Months or years to the Tributary bondage of ages?" These are Sentiments which do Honour to Humane Nature.

We have the Debates of Parliment by which it appears there are Many who apprehend a War inevitable and foresee the precipice upon which they stand. We have a report Here that Letters are come to Congress from administration, and proposals of a treaty, and some other Stories fit to amuse children, but Experienced Birds are not to be caught with chaff. What is said of the english nation by Hume in the Reign of Harry the 8th may very aptly be applied to them now, that they are so thoroughly subdued that like Eastern Slaves they are inclined to admire even those acts of tyranny and violence which are exercised over themselves at their own expence.

Thus far I wrote when I received a Letter dated Febry. 10, favourd by —— but it was a mistake it was not favourd by any body, and not being frank'd cost me a Dollor. The Man who deliverd it to my unkle brought him a Letter at the same time for which he paid the same price. If it had containd half as much as I wanted to know I would not have grumbld, but you do not tell me How you do, nor what accommodations you have, which is of more consequence to me than all the discriptions of cities, states and kingdoms in the world. I wish the Men of War better imployd than in taking flower vessels since it creates a Temporary famine Here, if I would give a Guiney for a pound of flower I dont think I could purchase it. There is such a Cry for Bread in the Town of Boston as I suppose was never before Heard, and the Bakers deal out but a loaf a day to the largest families. There is such a demand for Indian and Rye, that a Scarcity will soon take place in the Country. Tis now next to imposible to purchase a Bushel of Rye. In short since the late act there is very little selling. The meat that is carried to market is miserabley poor, and so little of it that many people say they were as well supplied in the Seige.

I am asshamed of my Country men. The Merchant and farmer are both alike. Some there are who have virtue enough to adhere to it, but more who evade it.

Even before Abigail wrote on March 8, her husband and his brethren in Congress had moved again, returning to Philadelphia the first week of March. Adams wrote cheerfully that further moves were being discussed. "It is good to change Place—it promotes Health and Spirits. It does good many Ways—it does good to the Place We remove from as well as to that We remove to—and it does good to those who move."

Once he had settled as a lodger at the home of Captain Robert Duncan in Walnut Street, with congenial friends nearby, Adams' mood, despite his manifest desire to be with his own family, was playful and bright enough. But in little more than a month the frustrations of his situation had again taken their toll. What solace he found was in the countryside.

JA to AA

Philadelphia March 16. 1777

The Spring advances, very rapidly, and all Nature will soon be cloathed in her gayest Robes. The green Grass, which begins to shew itself, here, and there, revives in my longing Imagination my little Farm, and its dear Inhabitants. What Pleasures has not this vile War deprived me of? I want to wander, in my Meadows, to ramble over my Mountains, and to sit in Solitude, or with her who has all my Heart, by the side of the Brooks. These beautifull Scænes would contribute more to my Happiness, than the sublime ones which surround me.

I begin to suspect that I have not much of the Grand in my Composition. The Pride and Pomp of War, the continual Sound of Drums and Fifes as well played, as any in the World, the Prancings and Tramplings of the Light Horse numbers of whom are paraded in the Streets every day, have no Charms for me. I long for rural and domestic scænes, for the warbling of Birds and the Prattle of my Children.—Dont you think I am somewhat poetical this morning, for one of my Years, and considering the Gravity, and Insipidity of my Employment.—As much as I converse with Sages and Heroes, they have very little of my Love or Admiration. I should prefer the Delights of a Garden to the Dominion of a World. I have nothing of Cæsars Greatness in my soul. Power has not my Wishes in her Train. The Gods, by granting me Health, and Peace and Competence, the Society of my Family and Friends, the Perusal of my Books, and the Enjoyment of my Farm and Garden, would make me as happy as my Nature and State will bear.

Of that Ambition which has Power for its Object, I dont believe I have a Spark in my Heart. . . . There [are] other Kinds of Ambition of which I have a great deal.

I am now situated, in a pleasant Part of the Town, in Walnutt Street, in the south side of it, between second and third Streets, at the House of Mr. Duncan, a Gentleman from Boston, who has a Wife and three Children. It is an agreable Family. General Wolcott of Connecticutt, and Coll. Whipple of Portsmouth, are with me in the same House. Mr. Adams has removed to Mrs. Cheasmans [Cheesman's], in fourth Street near the Corner of Markett Street, where he has a curious Group of Company consisting of Characters as opposite, as North and South. Ingersol, the Stamp man and Judge of Admiralty, Sherman, an old Puritan, as honest as an Angell and as ⟨*stanch as a blood Hound*⟩ firm ⟨*as a Rock*⟩ in the Cause of American Independence, as Mount Atlass, and Coll. Thornton, as droll and funny as Tristram Shandy. Between the Fun of Thornton, the Gravity of Sherman, and the formal Toryism of Ingersol, Adams will have a curious Life of it.

The Landlady too who has buried four Husbands, one Tailor, two shoemakers and Gilbert Tenant [Tennent], and still is ready for a fifth, and well deserves him too, will add to the Entertainment.—Gerry and Lovell are yet at Miss Leonards, under the Auspices of Mrs. Yard.

Mr. Hancock has taken an House in Chesnutt Street, near the Corner of fourth Street near the State House.

AA to JA

April 17. 1777

Your obliging favours of March 14, 16 and 22, have received, and most sincerely thank you for them. I know not How I should support an absence already tedious, and many times attended with melancholy reflections, if it was not for so frequently hearing from you. That is a consolation to me, tho a cold comfort in a winters Night.

As the Summer advances I have many anxieties, some of which I should not feel or at least should find them greatly alleviated if you could be with me. But as that is a Satisfaction I know I must not look for, (tho I have a good mind to hold You to your promise since some perticuliar circumstances were really upon that condition) I must summon all the Phylosophy I am mistress of since what cannot be help'd must be endured.

Mrs. Howard a Lady for whom I know you had a great respect died yesterday to the inexpressible Grief of her Friends. She was deliverd of a Son or Daughter I know not which yesterday week, a mortification in her Bowels occasiond her death. Every thing of this kind naturally shocks a person in similar circumstances. How great the mind that can overcome the fear of Death! How anxious the Heart of a parent who looks round upon a family of young and helpless children and thinks of leaving them to a World full of snares and temptations which they have neither discretion to foresee, nor prudence to avoid.

But I will quit [the] Subject least it should excite painfull Sensations in a Heart that I would not willingly wound.

You give me an account in one of your Letters of the removal of your Lodgings. The extravagance of Board is greater there than here tho here every thing is at such prices as was not ever before known. Many articles are not to be had tho at ever so great a price. Sugar, Molasses, Rum, cotton wool, Coffe, chocolate, cannot all be consumed. Yet there are none, or next to none to be sold, perhaps you may procure a pound at a time, but no more. I have sometimes stoped 15 or 20 Butchers in a day with plenty of meat but not a mouthfull to be had unless I would give 4 pence per pound and 2 pence per pound for bringing. I have never yet indulged them and am determined I will not whilst I have a mouthfull of salt meat, to Eat, but the act is no more regarded now than if it had never been made and has only this Effect I think, that it makes people worse than they would have been without it. As to cloathing of any sort for myself or family I think no more of purchaseing any than if they were to live like Adam and Eve in innocence.

I seek wool and flax and can work willingly with my Hands, and tho my Household are not cloathed with fine linnen nor scarlet, they are cloathed with what is perhaps full as Honorary, the plain and decent manufactory of my own family, and tho I do not abound, I am not in want. I have neither poverty nor Riches but food which is conveniant for me and a Heart to be thankfull and content that in such perilous times so large a share of the comforts of life are allotted to me.

I have a large Share of Health to be thankfull for, not only for myself but for my family.

I have enjoyed as much Health since the small pox, as I have known in any year not with standing a paleness which has very near resembled a whited wall, but which for about 3 weeks past I have got the Better of. Coulour and a clumsy figure make their appearence in so much that Master John says, Mar, I never saw any body grow so fat as you do.

I really think this Letter would make a curious figure if it should fall into the Hands of any person but yourself—and pray if it comes safe to you, burn it.

But ever remember with the tenderest Sentiments her who knows no earthly happiness eaquel to that of being tenderly beloved by her dearest Friend.

JA to AA

Saturday Evening 26 April 1777

I have been lately more remiss, than usual in Writing to you. There has been a great Dearth of News. Nothing from England, nothing from France, Spain, or any other Part of Europe, nothing from the West Indies. Nothing from Howe, and his Banditti, nothing from General Washington.

There are various Conjectures that Lord How is dead, sick, or gone to England, as the Proclamations run in the Name of Will. Howe only, and nobody from New York can tell any Thing of his Lordship.

I am wearied out, with Expectations that the Massachusetts Troops would have arrived, e'er now, at Head Quarters.—Do our People intend to leave the Continent in the Lurch? Do they mean to submit? or what Fatality attends them? With the noblest Prize in View, that ever Mortals contended for, and with the fairest Prospect of obtaining it upon easy Terms, The People of the Massachusetts Bay, are dead.

Does our State intend to send only half, or a third of their Quota? Do they wish to see another, crippled, disastrous and disgracefull Campaign for Want of an Army?—I am more sick and more ashamed of my own Countrymen, than ever I was before. The Spleen, the Vapours, the Dismals, the Horrors, seem to have seized our whole State.

More Wrath than Terror, has seized me. I am very mad. The gloomy Cowardice of the Times, is intollerable in N. England.

Indeed I feel not a little out of Humour, from Indisposition of Body. You know, I cannot pass a Spring, or fall, without an ill Turn—and I have had one these four or five Weeks—a Cold, as usual. Warm Weather, and a little Exercise, with a little Medicine, I suppose will cure me as usual. I am not confined, but moap about and drudge as usual, like a Gally Slave. I am a Fool if ever there was one to be such a Slave. I wont be much longer. I will be more free, in some World or other.

Is it not intollerable, that the opening Spring, which I should enjoy with my Wife and Children upon my little Farm, should pass away, and laugh at me, for labouring, Day after Day, and Month after Month, in a Conclave, Where neither Taste, nor Fancy, nor Reason, nor Passion, nor Appetite can be gratified?

Posterity! You will never know, how much it cost the present Generation, to preserve your Freedom! I hope you will make a good Use of it. If you do not, I shall repent in Heaven, that I ever took half the Pains to preserve it.

JA to AA

May 22 [1777]. 4 O Clock in the Morning

After a Series of the souerest, and harshest Weather that ever I felt in this Climate, We are at last, blessed with a bright Sun and a soft Air. The Weather here has been like our old Easterly Winds to me, and southerly Winds to you.

The Charms of the Morning at this Hour, are irresistable. The Streakes of Glory dawning in the East: the freshness and Purity in the Air, the bright blue of the sky, the sweet Warblings of a great Variety of Birds intermingling with the martial Clarions of an hundred Cocks now within my Hearing, all conspire to chear the Spirits.

This kind of puerile Description is a very pretty Employment for an old Fellow whose Brow is furrowed with the Cares of Politicks and War.

I shall be on Horseback in a few Minutes, and then I shall enjoy the Morning, in more Perfection.

I spent last Evening at the War-Office, with General Arnold....

He has been basely slandered and libelled. The Regulars say, "he fought like Julius Cæsar."

I am wearied to Death with the Wrangles between military officers, high and low. They Quarrell like Cats and Dogs. They worry one another like Mastiffs. Scrambling for Rank and Pay like Apes for Nutts.

I believe there is no one Principle, which predominates in human Nature so much in every stage of Life, from the Cradle to the Grave, in Males and females, old and young, black and white, rich and poor, high and low, as this Passion for Superiority.... Every human Being compares itself in its own Imagination, with every other round about it, and will find some Superiority over every other real or imaginary, or it will die of Grief and Vexation. I have seen it among Boys and Girls at school, among Lads at Colledge, among Practicers at the Bar, among the Clergy in their Associations, among Clubbs of Friends, among the People in Town Meetings, among the Members of an House of Rep[resentative]s, among the Grave Councillors, on the more solemn Bench of Justice, and in that awfully August Body the Congress, and on many of its Committees—and among Ladies every Where—But I never saw it operate with such Keenness, Ferocity and Fury, as among military Officers. They will go terrible Lengths, in their Emulations, their Envy and Revenge, in Consequence of it.

So much for Philosophy.—I hope my five or six Babes are all well. My Duty to my Mother and your Father and Love to sisters and Brothers, Aunts and Uncles.

Pray how does your Asparagus perform? &c.

I would give Three Guineas for a Barrell of your Cyder—not one drop is to be had here for Gold. And wine is not to be had under Six or Eight Dollars a Gallon and that very bad. I would give a Guinea for a Barrell of your Beer. The small beer here is wretchedly bad. In short I can get nothing that I can drink, and I believe I shall be sick from this Cause alone. Rum at forty shillings a Gallon and bad Water, will never do, in this hot Climate in summer where Acid Liquors are necessary against Putrefaction.

JA to AA

May 25. 1777

At half past four this Morning, I mounted my Horse, and took a ride, in a Road that was new to me. I went to Kensington, and then to Point No Point, by Land, the Place where I went, once before, with a large Company in the Rowe Gallies, by Water. That Frolic was almost two Years ago. I gave you a Relation of it, in the Time, I suppose. The Road to Point No Point lies along the River Delaware, in fair

Sight of it, and its opposite shore. For near four Miles the Road is as strait as the Streets of Philadelphia. On each Side, are beautifull Rowes of Trees, Buttonwoods, Oaks, Walnutts, Cherries and Willows, especially down towards the Banks of the River. The Meadows, Pastures, and Grass Plotts, are as Green as Leeks. There are many Fruit Trees and fine orchards, set with the nicest Regularity. But the Fields of Grain, the Rye, and Wheat, exceed all Description. These Fields are all sown in Ridges; and the Furrough between each Couple of Ridges, is as plainly to be seen, as if a swarth had been mown along. Yet it is no wider than a Plough share, and it is as strait as an Arrow. It looks as if the Sower had gone along the Furrough with his Spectacles to pick up every grain that should accidentally fall into it.

The Corn is just coming out of the Ground. The Furroughs struck out for the Hills to be planted in, are each Way, as straight as mathematical right Lines; and the Squares between every four Hills, as exact as they could be done by Plumb and Line, or Scale and Compass.

I am ashamed of our Farmers. They are a lazy, ignorant sett, in Husbandry, I mean—For they know infinitely more of every Thing else, than these. But after all the Native Face of our Country, diversified as it is, with Hill and Dale, Sea and Land, is to me more agreable than this enchanting artificial scæne.

June and July 1777 were sorely trying months. There was little reassurance in reports from beyond the environs of Braintree. General Burgoyne's army was advancing from Canada, and the stronghold at Ticonderoga was imperiled. Inaction seemed to have laid hold upon the Congress. Looking inward, Abigail Adams found herself in those concluding months of her pregnancy more apprehensive than she had ever been before. "I look forward to the middle of july with more anxiety than I can describe, and the Thoughts of 3 hundreds miles distance are as Greivious as the perils I have to pass through," she wrote. "I am cut of from the privilidge which some of the Brute creation enjoy, that of having their mate sit by them with anxious care during all their Solitary confinement." Of the eleven surviving letters John Adams wrote his wife between the end of June and July 28, in which he vainly and repetitiously attempted in some measure to alleviate the loneliness of her ordeal, only one appears below. The terse intelligence he received on the latter date from the faithful John Thaxter at the farm cottage in Braintree confirmed that Abigail's apprehensions were only too well grounded.

AA to JA

June 8. 1777

I generally endeavour to write you once a week, if my Letters do not reach you, tis oweing to the neglect of the post. I generally get

Letters from you once a week, but seldom in a fortnight after they are wrote. I am sorry to find that your Health fails. I should greatly rejoice to see you, I know of no earthly blessing which would make me happier, but I cannot wish it upon the terms of ill Health. No seperation was ever more painfull to me than the last, may the joy of meeting again be eaquel to the pain of seperation; I regret that I am in a Situation to wish away one of the most precious Blessings of life, yet as the months pass of[f], I count them up with pleasure and reckon upon tomorrow as the 5th which has passd since your absence. I have some times melancholly reflections, and immagine these seperations as preparatory to a still more painfull one in which even hope the anchor of the Soul is lost, but whilst that remains no Temperary absence can ever wean or abate the ardor of my affection. Bound together by many tender ties, there scarcly wanted an addition, yet I feel that there soon will be an additionall one. Many many are the tender sentiments I have felt for the parent on this occasion. I doubt not they are reciprocal, but I often feel the want of his presence and the soothing tenderness of his affection. Is this weakness or is it not?

I am happy in a daughter who is both a companion and an assistant in my Family affairs and who I think has a prudence and steadiness beyond her years.

You express a longing after the enjoyments of your little Farm. I do not wonder at it, that also wants the care and attention of its master—all that the mistress can do is to see that it does not go to ruin. She would take pleasure in improvements, and study them with assiduity if she was possessd with a sufficency to accomplish them. The season promisses plenty at present and the english grass never lookd better.

You inquire after the Asparagrass. It performs very well this year and produces us a great plenty. I long to send you a Barrell of cider, but find it impracticable, as no vessels can pass from this State to yours. I rejoice at the good way our affairs seem to be in and Hope your Herculian Labours will be crownd with more success this year than the last. Every thing wears a better aspect, we have already taken two Transports of theirs with Hessians on board, and this week a prize was carried into Salem taken by the Tyranicide with 4000 Blankets and other valuable articles on board.

I do not feel very apprehensive of an attack upon Boston. I hope we shall be quiet. I should make a misirable hand of running now. Boston is not what it once was. It has no Head, no Men of distinguishd abilities, they behave like children.

Col. Holland the infamous Hampshire counterfeiter was taken last week in Boston and is committed to Jail in Irons. I hope they will now keep a strong guard upon him.

We are not like to get our *now* unpopular act repeald I fear. I own I was in favour of it, but I have seen it fail and the ill consequences arising from it have made me wish it had never been made. Yet the House are nearly divided about it. Genell. W[arre]n will write you I suppose. He and his Lady have spent part of the week with me.

I wish you would be so good as to mention the dates of the Letters you receive from me. The last date of yours was May 22. 5 dated in May since this day week. I wonder how you get time to write so much. I feel very thankfull to you for every line. You will I know remember me often when I cannot write to you.

Good Night tis so dark that I cannot see to add more than that I am with the utmost tenderness Yours ever Yours.

AA to JA

June 23 1777

I have just retird to my Chamber, but an impulce seazes me to write you a few lines before I close my Eye's. Here I often come and sit myself down alone to think of my absent Friend, to ruminate over past scenes, to read over Letters, journals &c.

Tis a melancholy kind of pleasure I find in this amusement, whilst the weighty cares of state scarcly leave room for a tender recollection or sentiment to steal into the Bosome of my Friend.

In my last I expressd some fears least the Enemy should soon invade us here. My apprehensions are in a great measure abated by late accounts received from the General.

We have a very fine Season here, rather cold for a fortnight, but nothing like a drought. You would smile to see what a Farmer our Brother C[ranc]h makes, his whole attention is as much engaged in it, as it ever was in Spermacity Works, Watch Work, or Prophesies. You must know he has purchased, (in spight of the C[olone]ls Threats) that Farm he talkd of. He gave a large price for it tis True, but tis a neat, profitable place, 300 sterling, but money is lookd upon of very little value, and you can scarcly purchase any article now but by Barter. You shall have wool for flax or flax for wool, you shall have veal, Beaf or pork for salt, for sugar, for Rum, &c. but mony we will not take, is the daily language. I will work for you for Corn, for flax or wool, but if I work for money you must give a cart load of it be sure.

What can be done, and which way shall we help ourselves? Every article and necessary of life is rising daily. Gold dear Gold would soon lessen the Evils. I was offerd an article the other day for two dollors in silver for which they askd me six in paper.

I have no more to purchase with than if every dollor was a silver one. Every paper dollor cost a silver one, why then cannot it be eaquelly valuable? You will refer me to Lord Kames I know, who solves the matter. I hope in favour you will not Emit any more paper, till what we have at least becomes more valuable.

Nothing remarkable has occurd since I wrote you last. You do not in your last Letters mention how you do—I will hope better. I want a companion a Nights, many of them are wakefull and Lonesome, and "tierd Natures sweet restorer, Balmy Sleep," flies me. How hard it is to reconcile myself to six months longer absence! Do you feel it urksome? Do you sigh for Home? And would you willingly share with me what I have to pass through? Perhaps before this reaches you and meets with a Return, —— I wish the day passt, yet dread its arrival.—Adieu most sincerely most affectionately Yours.

AA to JA

July 9 1777

I sit down to write you this post, and from my present feelings tis the last I shall be able to write for some time if I should do well. I have been very unwell for this week past, with some complaints that have been new to me, tho I hope not dangerous.

I was last night taken with a shaking fit, and am very apprehensive that a life was lost. As I have no reason to day to think otherways; what may be the consequences to me, Heaven only knows. I know not of any injury to myself, nor any thing which could occasion what I fear.

I would not Have you too much allarmd. I keep up some Spirits yet, tho I would have you prepaird for any Event that may happen.

I can add no more than that I am in every Situation unfeignedly Yours, Yours.

JA to AA

Philadelphia July 10. 1777. Thursday

My Mind is again Anxious, and my Heart in Pain for my dearest Friend. . . .

Three Times have I felt the most distressing Sympathy with my Partner, without being able to afford her any Kind of Solace, or Assistance.

When the Family was sick of the Dissentery, and so many of our Friends died of it.

When you all had the small Pox.

july 9 1777.

I Sit down to write you this post, and from my present feelings tis the last I Shall be able to write for some time if I Should do well, I have been very unwell for this week past, with some complaints that have been new to me tho I hope not dangerous

I was last night, taken with a shaking fit, and am very apprehensive that a life was lost, as I have no reason to day to think otherways, what may be the consequences to me, Heaven only knows. I know not of any injury to my-self, nor any thing which could occasion what I fear

I would not have you too much allarmd, I keep up some Spirits yet, tho I would have you prepaird for any Event that may happen.

I can add no more than that I am in every situation unfeignedly

Yours, Yours

"I KEEP UP SOME SPIRITS YET, THO I WOULD HAVE YOU PREPAIRD FOR ANY EVENT THAT MAY HAPPEN"

And now I think I feel as anxious as ever.—Oh that I could be near, to say a few kind Words, or shew a few Kind Looks, or do a few kind Actions. Oh that I could take from my dearest, a share of her Distress, or relieve her of the whole.

Before this shall rea[c]h you I hope you will be happy in the Embraces of a Daughter, as fair, and good, and wise, and virtuous as the Mother, or if it is a son I hope it will still resemble the Mother in Person, Mind and Heart.

AA to JA

July 10 [*1777*] 9 o clock Evening

About an Hour ago I received a Letter from my Friend dated June 21: begining in this manner "my dearest Friend." It gave me a most agreable Sensation, it was a cordial to my Heart. That one single expression dwelt upon my mind and playd about my Heart, and was more valuable to me than any part of the Letter, except the close of it. It was because my Heart was softned and my mind enervated by my sufferings, and I wanted the personal and tender soothings of my dearest Friend, that [ren]derd it so valuable to me at this time. I have [no] doubt of the tenderest affection or sincerest regard of my absent Friend, yet an expression of that kind will sooth my Heart to rest amidst a thousand anxietyes.

Tis now 48 Hours since I can say I really enjoyed any Ease, nor am I ill enough to summons any attendance unless my sisters. Slow, lingering and troublesome is the present situation. The Dr. encourages me to Hope that my apprehensions are groundless respecting what I wrote you yesterday, tho I cannot say I have had any reason to allter my mind. My spirits However are better than they were yesterday, and I almost wish I had not let that Letter go. If there should be agreable News to tell you, you shall know it as soon as the post can convey it. I pray Heaven that it may be soon or it seems to me I shall be worn out. I must lay my pen down this moment, to bear what I cannot fly from—and now I have endured it I reassume my pen and will lay by all my own feelings and thank you for your obligeing Letters.—A prize arrived this week at Marble Head with 400 Hogsheads of rum a board sent in by Manly.—Every article and necessary of life rises here daily. Sugar has got to [8 pounds?] per hundred, Lamb to 1 shilling per pound and all ot[her] things in proportion.—We have the finest Season here that I have known for many years. The fruit was injured by the cold East winds and falls of, the Corn looks well, Hay will be plenty, but your Farm wants manure. I shall endeavour to have Sea weed carted every Leasure moment that can be had. That will not be many. Help is so scarce and so expensive I can not Hire a days mowing under 6 shillings.

How has done himself no honour by his late retreat. We fear most now for Tycon[deroga.] Tis reported to day that tis taken. We have a vast many men who look like officers continually riding about. I wonder what they can be after, why they do not repair to the army.

We wonder too what Congress are a doing? We have not heard of late.

How do you do? Are you glad you are out of the way of sour faces. I could look pleasent upon you in the midst of sufferings—allmighty God carry me safely through them. There I would hope I have a Friend ever nigh and ready to assist me, unto whom I commit myself.

This is Thursday Evening. It cannot go till monday, and then I hope will be accompanied with more agreable inteligance.

Most sincerely Yours.

July 11

I got more rest last night than I expected, this morning am rather more ill than I was yesterday. This day ten years ago master John came into this world. May I have reason again to recollect it with peculiar gratitude. Adieu.

John Thaxter to John Adams

Sir Braintree July 13th. 1777

The day before Yesterday Mrs. Adams was delivered of a daughter; ⟨*but*⟩ it grieves me to add, Sir, that it was still born. It was an exceeding fine looking Child.

Mrs. Adams is as comfortable, as She has Just inform'd me, as can be expected; and has desired me to write a few lines to acquaint you that She is in a good Way, which I am very happy in doing.

Every thing in my power that respects her Comfort, or that respects the Children, shall be attended to by Sir, Your most obedient Servt.,

J. Thaxter Junr.

AA to JA July 16 1777

Join with me my dearest Friend in Gratitude to Heaven, that a life I know you value, has been spaired and carried thro Distress and danger altho the dear Infant is numberd with its ancestors.

My apprehensions with regard to it were well founded. Tho my

Friends would have fain perswaded me that the Spleen [or] the Vapours had taken hold of me I was as perfectly sensible of its discease as I ever before was of its existance. I was also aware of the danger which awaited me; and which tho my suffering[s] were great thanks be to Heaven I have been supported through, and would silently submit to its dispensations in the loss of a sweet daughter; it appeard to be a very fine Babe, and as it never opened its Eyes in this world it lookd as tho they were only closed for sleep. The circumstance which put an end to its existance, was evident upon its birth, but at this distance and in a Letter which may possibly fall into the Hands of some unfealing Ruffian I must omit particuliars. Suffice it to say that it was not oweing to any injury which I had sustaind, nor could any care of mine have prevented it.

My Heart was much set upon a Daughter. I had had a strong perswasion that my desire would be granted me. It was—but to shew me the uncertanty of all sublinary enjoyments cut of e'er I could call it mine. No one was so much affected with the loss of it as its Sister who mournd in tears for Hours. I have so much cause for thankfullness amidst my sorrow, that I would not entertain a repineing thought. So short sighted and so little a way can we look into futurity that we ought patiently to submit to the dispensation of Heaven.

I am so comfortable that I am amaizd at myself, after what I have sufferd I did not expect to rise from my Bed for many days. This is but the 5th day and I have set up some Hours.

I However feel myself weakend by this exertion, yet I could not refrain [from] the temptation of writing with my own Hand to you.

Adieu dearest of Friends adieu—Yours most affectionately.

AA to JA

My dearest Friend July 23 1777

Notwithstanding my confinement I think I have not omitted writing you by every post. I have recoverd Health and strength beyond expectation; and never was so well in so short a time before. Could I see my Friend in reality as I often do in immagination I think I should feel a happiness beyond expression; I had pleasd myself with the Idea of presenting him a fine son or daughter upon his return, and had figurd to myself the smiles of joy and pleasure with which he would receive it, but [those?] dreams are buried in the Grave, transitory as the morning Cloud, short lived as the Dew Drops.

Heaven continue to us those we already have and make them blessings. I think I feel more solicitious for their welfare than ever, and more anxious if posible for the life and Health of their parent. I fear the extreem Heat of the season, and the different temperament of the climate and the continual application to Buisness will finish a constitution naturally feeble.

I know not in what manner you will be affected at the loss, Evacuation, sale, giving up—which of the terms befits the late conduct at Tycondoroga. You may know more of the reasons for this conduct (as I hear the commanding officer went immediately to Congress) than we can devine this way; but this I can truly say no Event since the commencement of the War has appeard so allarming to me, or given me eaquel uneasiness. Had the Enemy fought and conquerd the fort, I could have borne it, but to leave it with all the stores before it was even attackd, has exited a thousand Suspicions, and gives room for more wrath than despondency.

We every day look for an attack upon us this way. The reports of this week are that a number of Transports with Troops have a[rriv]ed at Newport. Some expresses went through this Town yesterday.

Yours of June 30 reach'd me last week. I am not a little surprizd that you have not received Letters from me later than the 9 of June. I have never faild for this two months writing you once a week. Tho they contain matters of no great importance I should be glad to know when you receive them.

We have had a remarkable fine Season here, no drought this summer. The Corn looks well, and english Grain promiseing. We cannot be sufficently thankfull to a Bountifull providence that the Horrours of famine are not added to those of war, and that so much more Health prevails in our Camps than in the year past.

Many of your Friends desire to be rememberd to you. Some complain that you do not write them. Adieu. Master Tom stands by and sends duty—he often recollects How *par* used to put him to Jail as he calls it. They are all very Healthy this summer, and are in expectation of a Letter every packet that arrives. Yours, ever yours, Portia

PS Price Current!! This day I gave 4 dollors a peice for Sythes and a Guiney a Gallon for New england Rum. We come on here finely. What do you think will become of us. If you will come Home and turn Farmer, I will be dairy woman. You will make more than is allowd you, and we shall grow wealthy. Our Boys shall go into the Feild and work with you, and my Girl shall stay in the House and assist me.

JA to AA

My dearest Friend Philadelphia July 28. 1777

Never in my whole Life, was my Heart affected with such Emotions and Sensations, as were this Day occasioned by your Letters of the 9. 10. 11. and 16 of July. Devoutly do I return Thanks to God, whose kind Providence has preserved to me a Life that is dearer to me than all other Blessings in this World. Most fervently do I pray, for a Continuance of his Goodness in the compleat Restoration of my best Friend to perfect Health.

Is it not unaccountable, that one should feel so strong an Affection for an Infant, that one has never seen, nor shall see? Yet I must confess to you, the Loss of this sweet little Girl, has most tenderly and sensibly affected me. I feel a Grief and Mortification, that is heightened tho it is not wholly occasioned, by my Sympathy with the Mother. My dear little Nabbys Tears are sweetly becoming her generous Tenderness and sensibility of Nature. They are Arguments too of her good sense and Discretion.

The recovery of Abigail Adams in body and in spirit continued to be rapid and in a very short time was complete. Fortunately so, for the rumors and realities of General Howe's military strategy were to be faced. Howe sailed from New York on July 23 with 260 ships and 15,000 men. Until his fleet was sighted off the Delaware Capes a week later, ports to the north were kept in alarm that they were to be objects of invasion. Boston was panicked into premature evacuation by speculation and rumors. The actual threat, however, was to Philadelphia and the Congress. Despite the hopes raised by the brave show of the Continental troops, now "well appointed," marching through Philadelphia's streets on their way to block Howe's approach, the city soon fell and the delegates scattered to reassemble eventually at York, Pennsylvania.

AA to JA

July 31 [*1777*]

I have nothing new to entertain you with, unless it is an account of a New Set of Mobility which have lately taken the Lead in B[osto]n. You must know that there is a great Scarcity of Sugar and Coffe, articles which the Female part of the State are very loth to give up, expecially whilst they consider the Scarcity occasiond by the merchants having secreted a large Quantity. There has been much rout and Noise in the Town for several weeks. Some Stores had been opend by a number of people and the Coffe and Sugar carried into the Market and dealt out by pounds. It was rumourd that an eminent, wealthy, stingy Merchant (who is a Batchelor) had a Hogshead of Coffe in his Store which he refused to sell to the committee under 6 shillings per pound.

A Number of Females some say a hundred, some say more assembled with a cart and trucks, marchd down to the Ware House and demanded the keys, which he refused to deliver, upon which one of them seazd him by his Neck and tossd him into the cart. Upon his finding no Quarter he deliverd the keys, when they tipd up the cart and dischargd him, then opend the Warehouse, Hoisted out the Coffe themselves, put it into the trucks and drove off.

It was reported that he had a Spanking among them, but this I believe was not true. A large concourse of Men stood amazd silent Spectators of the whole transaction.

Your kind favour received dated july 11, favourd by the Hon. Mr. Hews, left at my unkles in Boston. Tis not like he will make an Excursion this way, if he should shall treat him in the best manner I am able.—What day does your post arrive, and how long are Letters travelling from me to you? I receive one from you every week, and I as regularly write one but you make no mention of receiving any, or very seldom. In your Hurry do you forget it, or do they not reach you. I am very well for the time, not yet 3 weeks since my confinement and yet I think I have wrote you a very long Letter.

Adieu, your good Mother is just come, desires to be rememberd to you. So does my Father and Sister who have just left me, and so does she whose greatest happiness consists in being tenderly beloved by her absent Friend and subscribes herself ever his Portia

AA to JA

August 5. [*1777*]

If allarming half a dozen places at the same time is an act of Generalship *How* may boast of his late conduct. We have never since the Evacuation of Boston been under apprehensions of an invasion from them eaquel to what we sufferd last week. All Boston was in confusion, packing up and carting out of Town, Household furniture, military stores, goods &c. Not less than a thousand Teams were imployd a fryday and saturday—and to their shame be it told, not a small trunk would they carry under 8 dollors and many of them I am told askd a hundred dollors a load, for carting a Hogshead of Molasses 8 miles 30 dollors.—O! Humane Nature, or rather O! inhumane nature what art thou? The report of the Fleets being seen of[f] of Cape Ann a fryday Night, gave me the allarm, and tho pretty weak, I set about packing up my things and a saturday removed a load.

When I looked around me and beheld the bounties of Heaven so liberally bestowed in fine Feilds of corn, grass, flax and english grain, and thought it might soon become a prey to these merciless ravagers, our habitations laid waste, and if our flight preserved our lives, we must return to barren Feilds, empty barns and desolated habitations if any we found, perhaps no where to lay our Heads, my Heart was too full to bear the weight of affliction which I thought just ready to overtake us, and my body too weak almost to bear the shock unsupported by my better Half.

But thanks be to Heaven we are at present releaved from our Fears, respecting ourselves. I now feel anxious for your safety but hope prudence will direct to a proper care and attention to yourselves.

May this second attempt of Hows prove his utter ruin. May destruction overtake him as a whirlwind.

We have a report of an engagement at the Northward in which our troops behaved well, drove the Enemy into their lines, killd and took 300 & 50 prisoners. The account came in last Night. I have not perticuliars. – We are under apprehensions that the Hancock is taken.

Your obligeing Letters of the 8th, 10th and 13th came to hand last week. I hope before this time you are releaved from the anxiety you express for your Bosom Friend. I feel my sufferings amply rewarded in the tenderness you express for me, but in one of your Letters you have drawn a picture which drew a flood of tears from my Eyes, and rung my Heart with anguish inexpressible. I pray Heaven I may not live to realize it.

Tis almost 14 years since we were united, but not more than half that time have we had the happiness of living together.

The unfealing world may consider it in what light they please, I consider it as a sacrifice to my Country and one of my greatest misfortunes [for my husband] to be seperated from my children at a time of life when the joint instructions and admonition of parents sink deeper than in maturer years.

The Hopes of the smiles and approbation of my Friend sweetens all my toil and Labours–

Ye pow'rs whom Men, and birds obey,
Great rulers of your creatures, say
Why mourning comes, by bliss convey'd
And ev'n the Sweets of Love allay'd?
Where grows enjoyment, tall and fair,
Around it twines entangling care
While fear for what our Souls possess
Enervates ev'ry powe'r to Bless.
Yet Friendship forms the Bliss above
And life! what art thou without love?

JA to AA Aug. 11. 1777

Your kind Favour of July 30. and 31. was handed me, just now from the Post office.

I have regularly received a Letter from you every Week excepting one, for a long Time past, and as regularly send a Line to you inclosing Papers.—My Letters are scarcely worth sending. Indeed I dont choose to indulge much Speculation, lest a Letter should miscarry, and free Sentiments upon public Affairs intercepted, from me, might do much hurt.

Where the Scourge of God, and the Plague of Mankind is gone, no one can guess. An Express from Sinnepuxent, a Place between the Capes of Delaware and the Capes of Cheasapeak, informs that a fleet of 100 sail was seen off that Place last Thursday. But whether this is Fishermens News like that from Cape Ann, I know not.

The Time spends and the Campaign wears away and Howe makes no great Figure yet.—How many Men and Horses will he cripple by this strange Coasting Vo[y]age of 5 Weeks.

We have given N. Englandmen what they will think a compleat Tryumph in the Removal of Generals from the Northward and sending Gates there. I hope every Part of New England will now exert itself, to its Utmost Efforts. Never was a more glorious Opportunity than Burgoine has given Us of destroying him, by marching down so far towards Albany. Let New England turn out and cutt off his Retreat.

Pray continue to write me every Week. You have made me merry with the female Frolic, with the Miser. But I hope the Females will leave off their Attachment to Coffee. I assure you, the best Families in this Place have left off in a great Measure the Use of West India Goods. We must bring ourselves to live upon the Produce of our own Country. What would I give for some of your Cyder?

Milk has become the Breakfast of many of the wealthiest and genteelest Families here.

Fenno put me into a Kind of Frenzy to go home, by the Description he gave me last night of the Fertility of the Season, the Plenty of Fish, &c. &c. &c. in Boston and about it.—I am condemned to this Place a miserable Exile from every Thing that is agreable to me. God will my Banishment shall not last long.

Sharing his wife's grief at the loss of their daughter, John Adams sensed more clearly than ever the weight of the burdens he had left her to bear alone in Braintree. A year earlier, Abigail had confessed that, in educating their children, she found herself "out of my debth, and destitute and deficient in every part." Her husband now did what he could to relieve her of this worry with letters like the following one to their oldest son. Guiding their children's studies at long distance was to become standard practice for Adams statesmen over several generations.

John Adams to John Quincy Adams

My dear Son Philadelphia August 11. 1777

As the War in which your Country is engaged will probably hereafter attract your Attention, more than it does at this Time, and as the future Circumstances of your Country, may require other Wars, as well as Councils and Negotiations, similar to those which are now in Agitation, I wish to turn your Thoughts early to such Studies, as will afford you the most solid Instruction and Improvement for the Part which may be allotted you to act on the Stage of Life.

There is no History, perhaps, better adapted to this usefull Purpose than that of Thucidides, an Author, of whom I hope you will make yourself perfect Master, in original Language, which is Greek, the most perfect of all human Languages. In order to understand him fully in his own Tongue, you must however take Advantage, of every Help you can procure and particularly of Translations of him into your own Mother Tongue.

You will find in your Fathers Library, the Works of Mr. Hobbes, in which among a great deal of mischievous Philosophy, you will find a learned and exact Translation of Thucidides, which will be usefull to you.

But there is another Translation of him, much more elegant, intituled "The History of the Peloponnesian War, translated from the Greek of Thucidides in two Volumes Quarto, by William Smith A.M. Rector of the Parish of the holy Trinity in Chester, and Chaplain to the Right Honourable the Earl of Derby."

If you preserve this Letter, it may hereafter remind you, to procure the Book.

You will find it full of Instruction to the Orator, the Statesman, the General, as well as to the Historian and the Philosopher. You may find Something of the Peloponnesian War, in Rollin.

I am with much Affection your Father, John Adams

JA to AA

My best Friend Aug. 19. 1777 Tuesday

Your obliging Favour of the 5th. came by Yesterdays Post, and I intended to have answered it by this Mornings Post, but was delayed by many Matters, untill he gave me the slip.

I am sorry that you and the People of Boston were put to so much Trouble, but glad to hear that such Numbers determined to fly. The Prices for Carting which were demanded, were detestable. I wish your Fatigue and Anxiety may not have injured your Health.

Dont be anxious, for my Safety. If Howe comes here I shall run away, I suppose with the rest. We are too brittle ware you know to stand the Dashing of Balls and Bombs. I wonder upon what Principle the Roman Senators refused to fly from the Gauls and determined to sit, with their Ivory Staves and hoary Beards in the Porticoes of their Houses untill the Enemy entered the City, and altho they confessed they resembled the Gods, put them to the Sword.

I should not choose to indulge this sort of Dignity, but I confess I feel myself so much injured by these barbarean Britains, that I have a strong Inclination to meet them in the Field. This is not Revenge I believe, but there is something sweet and delicious in the Contemplation of it. There is in our Hearts, an Indignation against Wrong, that is righteous and benevolent, and he who is destitute of it, is defective in the Ballance of his Affections and in his moral Character.

As long as there is a Conscience in our Breasts, a moral Sense which distinguishes between Right and Wrong, approving, esteeming, loving the former, and condemning and detesting the other, We must feel a Pleasure in the Punishment, of so eminent a Contemner of all that is Right and good and just, as Howe is. They are virtuous and pious Passions that prompt Us to desire his Destruction, and to lament and deplore his success and Prosperity.

The Desire of assisting towards his Disgrace, is an honest Wish.

It is too late in Life, my Constitution is too much debilitated by Speculation, and indeed it is too late a Period in the War, for me to think of girding on a sword: But if I had the last four Years to run over again, I certainly would.

AA to JA

My dearest Friend — Boston August 22 1777

I came yesterday to this Town for a ride after my confinement, and to see my Friends. I have not been into it since I had the happiness of spending a week here with you. I am feeble and faint with the Heat of the weather, but otherways very well. I feel very anxious for your Health and almost fear to hear from you least I should hear you were sick; but hope your temperance and caution will preserve your Health. I hope, if you can get any way through these Hot months you will recruit. Tis very Healthy throughout Town and Country for the Season, the chin cough prevails in Town among children but has not yet reachd the Country.

Your Letters of August 1, 3 and 4th came by last nights post, and I have to acknowledge the recept of yours of july 27, 28 and 30th by last wedensdays post. I acknowledge my self greatly indebted to you for so frequently writing amidst all your other cares and attentions. I would fain believe that tis a releafe to you after the cares of the day, to converse with your Friend. I most sincerely wish your situation was such that the amusements your family could afford you, might have been intermixed with the weighty cares that oppress you.—

"My Bosome is thy dearest home;
I'd lull you there to rest."

As to *How* I wish we could know what he means that we might be able to gaurd against him. I hope however that he will not come this way, and I believe the Season is so far advanced, that he will not venture.

At the Northward our affairs look more favorable. We have been successfull in several of our late engagements. Heaven preserve our dear Countrymen who behave worthy of us and reward them both here and hereafter. Our Militia are chiefly raisd, and will I hope be marchd of immediately. There has been a most shamefull neglect some where. This continent has paid thousands to officers and Men who have been loitering about playing foot-Ball and nine pins, and doing their own private buisness whilst they ought to have been defending our forts and we are now suffering for the neglect.

The late call of Men from us will distress us in our Husbandry. I am a great sufferer as the High Bounty one hundred dollors, has tempted of my Negro Head, and left me just in the midst of our Hay. The english and fresh indeed we have finishd, but the salt is just comeing on, and How to turn my self, or what to do I know not. His going away would not worry me so much if it was not for the rapid depretiation of our money. We can scarcly get a days work done for money and if money is paid tis at such a rate that tis almost imposible to live. I live as I never did before, but I am not agoing to complain. Heaven has blessd us with fine crops. I hope to have 200 hundred Bushels of corn and a hundred & 50 weight of flax. English Hay we have more than we had last year, notwithstanding your ground wants manure. We are like to have a plenty of sause. I shall fat Beaf and pork enough, make butter and cheesse enough. If I have neither Sugar, molasses, coffe nor Tea I have no right to complain. I can live without any of them and if what I enjoy I can share with my partner and with Liberty, I can sing o be joyfull and sit down content—

"Man wants but little here below
Nor wants that little long."

As to cloathing I have heithertoo procured materials sufficent to cloath my children and servants which I have done wholy in Home Spun. I have contracted no debts that I have not discharg'd, and one of our Labourers Prince I have paid seven months wages to since you left me. Besides that I have paid Bracket near all we owed him which was to the amount of 15 pounds lawfull money, set up a cider press &c., besides procuring and repairing many other articles in the Husbandery way, which you know are constantly wanted. I should do exceeding well if we could but keep the money good, but at the rate we go on I know not what will become of us.

But I must bid you adieu or the post will go of without my Letter.—Dearest Friend, adieu. Words cannot convey to you the tenderness of my affection. Portia

JA to AA

My dearest Friend Philadelphia August 24. 1777

We had last Evening a Thunder Gust, very sharp and violent, attended with plentifull Rain. The Lightning struck in several Places. It struck the Quaker Alms House in Walnut Street, between third and fourth Streets, not far from Captn. Duncans, where I lodge. They had been wise enough to place an Iron Rod upon the Top of the Steeple, for a Vane to turn on, and had provided no Conductor to the Ground. It also struck in fourth Street, near Mrs. Cheesmans. No Person was hurt.

This Morning was fair, but now it is overcast and rains very hard which will spoil our Show, and wett the Army.

12. O Clock. The Rain ceased and the Army marched through the Town, between Seven and Ten O Clock. The Waggons went another Road. Four Regiments of Light Horse—Blands, Bailers [Baylor's], Sheldons, and Moylands [Moylan's]. Four Grand Divisions of the Army—and the Artillery with the Matrosses. They marched Twelve deep, and yet took up above two Hours in passing by.

General Washington and the other General Officers, with their Aids on Horse back. The Colonels and other Field Officers on Horse back.

We have now an Army, well appointed between Us and Mr. Howe, and this Army will be immediately joined, by ten Thousand Militia. So that I feel as secure here, as if I was at Braintree, but not so happy. My Happiness is no where to be found, but there.

After viewing this fine Spectacle and firm Defence I went to Mr. Duffields Meeting, to hear him pray, as he did most fervently, and I believe he was very sincerely joined by all present, for its success.

The Army, upon an accurate Inspection of it, I find to be extreamly well armed, pretty well cloathed, and tolerably disciplined. ⟨*Edes*⟩ Gill and Town by the Mottoes to their Newspapers, will bring Discipline into Vogue, in Time.—There is such a Mixture of the Sublime, and the Beautifull, together with the Usefull, in military Discipline, that I wonder, every Officer We have is not charmed with it.—Much remains yet to be done. Our soldiers have not yet, quite the Air of Soldiers. They dont step exactly in Time. They dont hold up their Heads, quite erect, nor turn out their Toes, so exactly as they ought. They dont all of them cock their Hats—and such as do, dont all wear them the same Way.

A Disciplinarian has affixed to him commonly the Ideas of Cruelty, severity, Tyranny &c. But if I were an Officer I am convinced I should be the most decisive Disciplinarian in the Army. I am convinced their is no other effectual Way of indulging Benevolence, Humanity, and the tender Social Passions, in an Army. There is no other Way of preserving the Health and Spirits of the Men. There is no other Way of making them active, and skillfull, in War—no other Method of guarding an Army against Destruction by surprizes, and no other Method of giving them Confidence in one another, or making them stand by one another, in the Hour of Battle.

Discipline in an Army, is like the Laws, in civil Society.

There can be no Liberty, in a Commonwealth, where the Laws are not revered, and most sacredly observed, nor can there be Happiness or Safety in an Army, for a single Hour, where the Discipline is not observed.

Obedience is the only Thing wanting now for our Salvation—Obedience to the Laws, in the States, and Obedience to Officers, in the Army.

12 O Clock. No Express, nor accidental News from Maryland to day, as yet.

AA to JA

Best of Friends Sep 17. [1777]

I have to acknowlidge a feast of Letters from you since I wrote last, their dates from August 19 to Sepbr. 1. It is a very great satisfaction to me to know from day to day the Movements of How, and his Bantitti. We live in hourly expectation of important inteligance from both armies. Heaven Grant us victory and peace, two Blessing[s] I fear we are very undeserving of.

Enclosed you will find a Letter to Mr. L[ovel]l who was so obliging as to send me a plan of that part of the Country which is like to be the present seat of war. He accompanied it with a very polite Letter, and I esteem myself much obliged to him, but there is no reward this side the grave that would be a temptation to me to undergo the agitation and distress I was thrown into by receiving a Letter in his Handwriting franked by him. It seems almost imposible that the Humane mind could take in, in so small a space of time, so many Ideas as rushd upon mine in the space of a moment, I cannot describe to you what I felt.

The sickness or death of the dearest of Friends with ten thousand horrours seazd my immagination. I took up the Letter, then laid it down, then gave it out of my Hand unable to open it, then collected resolution enough to unseal it, but dared not read it, begun at the bottom, read a line, then attempted to begin it, but could not. A paper was enclosed, I venturd upon that, and finding it a plan, recoverd enough to read the Letter——but I pray Heaven I may never realize such a nother moment of distress.

I designd to have wrote you a long Letter for really I owe you one, but have been prevented by our worthy P[lymout]h Friends who are Here upon a visit in their way Home and tis now so late at Night just struck 12 that I will defer any thing further till the next post. Good Night Friend of my Heart, companion of my youth–Husband and Lover–Angles watch thy Repose.

JA to AA

York Town Pensylvania,
Septr. 30. 1777 Tuesday

My best Friend

It is now a long Time, since I had an Opportunity of writing to you, and I fear you have suffered unnecessary Anxiety on my Account.–In the Morning of the 19th. Inst., the Congress were allarmed, in their Beds, by a Letter from Mr. Hamilton one of General Washingtons Family, that the Enemy were in Possession of the Ford over the Schuylkill, and the Boats, so that they had it in their Power to be in Philadelphia, before Morning. The Papers of Congress, belonging to the Secretary's Office, the War Office, the Treasury Office, &c. were before sent to Bristol. The President, and all the other Gentlemen were gone that Road, so I followed, with my Friend Mr. Merchant [Marchant] of Rhode Island, to Trenton in the Jersies. We stayed at Trenton, untill the 21. when We set off, to Easton upon the Forks of Delaware. From Easton We went to Bethlehem, from thence to Reading, from thence to Lancaster, and from thence to this Town, which is about a dozen Miles over the Susquehannah River.—Here Congress is to sit.

In order to convey the Papers, with safety, which are of more Importance than all the Members, We were induced to take this Circuit, which is near 180 Miles, whereas this Town by the directest Road is not more than 88 Miles from Philadelphia. This Tour has given me an Opportunity of seeing many Parts of this Country, which I never saw before.

This Morning Major Throop arrived here with a large Packett from General Gates, containing very agreable Intelligence, which I need not repeat, as you have much earlier Intelligence from that Part than We have.

I wish Affairs here wore as pleasing an Aspect.—But alass they do not.

I shall avoid every Thing like History, and make no Reflections.

However, General Washington is in a Condition tolerably respectable, and the Militia are now turning out, from Virginia, Maryland and Pensilvania, in small Numbers. All the Apology that can be made, for this Part of the World is that Mr. Howes march from Elke to Philadelphia, was thro the very Regions of Passive obedience. The whole Country thro which he passed, is inhabited by Quakers. There is not such another Body of Quakers in all America, perhaps not in all the World.

I am still of Opinion that Philadelphia will be no Loss to Us.

I am very comfortably situated, here, in the House of General Roberdeau, whose Hospitality has taken in Mr. S[amuel] A[dams], Mr. G[erry] and me. My Health is as good as common, and I assure you my Spirits not the worse for the Loss of Philadelphia.

Biddle in the Continental Frigate at S. Carolina has made a noble Cruise and taken four very valuable W.I. Prizes.

Continue to write me by the Post, and I shall pay my Debts.

AA to JA

Dearest Friend October 6 [*i.e.* 5]. 1777. Sunday

I know not where to direct to you, but hope you are secure. Tis said in some part of the Jersies, but I know this only from report. I sent to Town yesterday (saturday) but the Post did not get in till the person by whom I sent came out of Town. I could not rest but sent again this morning. The Post came but brought no Letters for me, and but two for any person that I could learn, and no late intelligence.

To the removal of congress I attribute my not hearing, but I never was more anxious to hear. I want to know every movement of the Armies. Mr. Niles by whom I send this sets of tomorrow and promisses to find you and deliver this into your Hand. I doubt not you will let me hear from you by the first conveyance. Tell me where you are, how you are situated and how you do? Whether your spirits are good, and what you think of the present state of our Arms. Will Mr. How get possession of the city? Tis a day of doubtfull expectation, Heaven only knows our destiny. I observe often in the account of actions that our Men are sometimes obliged to retreat for want of ammunition, their cartridges are spent. How is this? Is it good Generalship. We never hear of that complaint in the regular Army.—There is a private expedition tis said. The Troops have all marched last monday. I own I have no great faith in it. I wish it may succeed better than I apprehend.

No News of any importance from the Northward; I long for spirited exertions every where. I want some grand important actions to take place. We have both armies from their Shipping. Tis what we have long sought for, now is the important Day; Heaven seems to have granted us our desire, may it also direct us to improve it aright.

We are all well. I write nothing of any importance, till I know where you are, and how to convey to you. Believe me at all times unalterably yours—yours.

Even with the loss of Philadelphia, Americans could face the autumn and winter with optimism. General Horatio Gates had captured Burgoyne's army at Saratoga. The British general, his staff, and the officers of his German mercenary troops were to come to Cambridge as captives—symbols of the failure of the British plan to cut the new nation in two. Continental troops had thrown back enemy attacks on key forts on the Delaware River under circumstances particularly satisfying to John Adams. And Abigail Adams, expecting her husband's early return to resume his law practice, could write on her wedding anniversary with confidence that it would be the last time that they would have to celebrate the occasion separately.

AA to JA

Boston October 25 1777 Saturday Evening

The joyfull News of the Surrender of General Burgoin and all his Army to our Victorious Troops prompted me to take a ride this afternoon with my daughter to Town to join to morrow with my Friends in thanksgiving and praise to the Supreem Being who hath so remarkably deliverd our Enimies into our Hands.

And hearing that an express is to go of tomorrow morning, I have retired to write you a few line's. I have received no letters from you since you left P[hiladelphi]a by the post, and but one by any private Hand. I have wrote you once before this. Do not fail writing by the return of this express and direct your Letters to the care of my unkle who has been a kind and faithfull hand to me through the whole Season and a constant attendant upon the post office.

Burgoine is expected in by the middle of the week. I have read many Articles of Capitulation, but none which ever containd so generous Terms before. Many people find fault with them but perhaps do not consider sufficently the circumstances of General Gates, who ⟨*perhaps*⟩ by delaying and exacting more might have lost all. This must be said of him that he has followed the golden rule and done as he would wish himself in like circumstances to be dealt with.—Must not the vapouring Burgoine who tis said possesses great Sensibility, be humbled to the dust. He may now write the Blocade of Saratago. I have heard it proposed that he should take up his quarters in the old South, but believe he will not be permitted to come to this Town.—Heaven grant us success at the Southard. That saying of king Richard often occurs to my mind "God helps those who help themselves" but if Men turn their backs and run from an Enemy they cannot surely expect to conquer them.

This day dearest of Friends compleats 13 years since we were solemly united in wedlock; 3 years of the time we have been cruelly seperated. I have patiently as I could endured it with the Belief that you were serving your Country, and rendering your fellow creatures essential Benefits. May future Generations rise up and call you Blessed, and the present behave worthy of the blessings you are Labouring to secure to them, and I shall have less reason to regreat the deprivation of my own perticuliar felicity.

Adieu dearest of Friends adieu.

JA to AA

My dearest Friend York Town Octr. 26. 1777

Mr. Colman goes off for Boston Tomorrow.

I have seized a Moment, to congratulate you on the great and glorious Success of our Arms at the Northward, and in Delaware River. The Forts at Province Island and Red Bank have been defended, with a Magnanimity, which will give our Country a Reputation in Europe.

Coll. Green repulsed the Enemy from Red bank and took Count Donop and his Aid Prisoners. Coll. Smith repulsed a bold Attack upon Fort Mifflin, and our Gallies disabled two Men of War a 64 and 20

Gun ship in such a Manner, that the Enemy blew them up. This comes confirmed this Evening, in Letters from Gen. Washington inclosing Original Letters from Officers in the Forts.

Congress will appoint a Thanksgiving, and one Cause of it ought to be that the Glory of turning the Tide of Arms, is not immediately due to the Commander in Chief, nor to southern Troops. If it had been, Idolatry, and Adulation would have been unbounded, so excessive as to endanger our Liberties for what I know.

Now We can allow a certain Citizen to be wise, virtuous, and good, without thinking him a Deity or a saviour.

IV

NOVEMBER 1777 ~ JULY 1780

I must request you always to be minute and to write me by every conveyance. — Abigail Adams

The Character and Situation in which I am here, and the Situation of public Affairs absolutely forbid my Writing, freely. — John Adams

On November 7, 1777, Congress at York voted "That Mr. Samuel Adams, and Mr. J. Adams, have leave of absence to visit their families." It had been a year of wracking labor for John Adams because of his added responsibilities, now that several military campaigns were being carried on simultaneously, as chairman of the Board of War and Ordnance. He had complained of drooping health and weakened eyesight since spring, but he stayed on in the hope of voting for the final version of the Articles of Confederation. He did not quite succeed; the Articles were adopted by Congress on the fifteenth, but he and his cousin Sam had set out on the eleventh and arrived home before the end of the month.

In his Autobiography, Adams tells how he immediately started to regain his law practice and restore his depressed finances by taking an important admiralty case about to be tried in Portsmouth, New Hampshire. The "Cause" was that of the brig *Lusanna*, a Massachusetts-owned vessel captured by a New Hampshire privateer and claimed by the captor on the ground that the *Lusanna* was trading with the enemy. Adams' defense of the owners, unsuccessful before the jury, was based mainly upon a view, then new, that in a conflict between state law and the resolves of Congress, the federal power should prevail. Adams' public duties did not permit his participation in the appeals which culminated in a Supreme Court decision in 1795 sustaining his position.

JA to AA

My dear — Portsmouth Decr. 15. 1777

I arrived here, last Evening, in good Health. This Morning, General Whipple made me a Visit, at the Tavern, Tiltons, and insists upon my taking a Bed at his House, in so very affectionate, and urgent a Manner, that I believe I shall go to his House.

The Cause comes on Tomorrow, before my old Friend Dr. Joshua Brackett, as Judge of Admiralty. How it will go I know not. The Captors are a numerous Company, and are said to be very tenacious, and have many Connections; so that We have Prejudice, and Influence to fear: Justice, Policy and Law, are, I am very sure, on our Side.

I have had many Opportunities, in the Course of this Journey, to observe, how deeply rooted, our righteous Cause is in the Minds of the People—and could write you many Anecdotes in Proof of it. But I will reserve them for private Conversation. But on 2d Thoughts why should I?

One Evening, as I satt in one Room, I overheard Company of the Common sort of People in another, conversing upon serious subjects. One of them, whom I afterwards found upon Enquiry to be a reputable, religious Man, was more eloquent than the rest—he was upon the Danger of despizing and neglecting serious Things. Said whatever Person or People made light of them would soon find themselves terribly mistaken. At length I heard these Words—"it appears to me the eternal son of God is opperating Powerfully against the British Nation for their treating lightly serious Things."

One Morning, I asked my Landlady what I had to pay? Nothing she said—"I was welcome, and she hoped I would always make her House my Home, and she should be happy to entertain all those Gentlemen who had been raised up by Providence to be the Saviours of their Country." This was flattering enough to my vain Heart. But it made a greater Impression on me, as a Proof, how deeply this Cause had sunk into the Minds and Hearts of the People.—In short every Thing I see and hear, indicates the same Thing.

Adams' good spirits in Portsmouth mirrored his satisfaction in being again in legal harness and reunited with his family. He was not aware that his appearance in the *Lusanna* case would be his last in a courtroom as a practicing attorney. But an official dispatch from Henry Laurens, the president of Congress, and a letter from James Lovell, a Massachusetts delegate and active member of the Committee for Foreign Affairs, had brought portentous news to Braintree in Adams' absence.

Laurens' dispatch enclosed the following extract from the Journal of Congress of November 28: "Congress proceeded to the election of a commissioner at the court of France in the room of S. Deane esqr. and the ballots being taken John Adams esqr. was elected." Back of this action lay growing dissatisfaction over the free-wheeling conduct of Silas Deane, joint American commissioner with Benjamin Franklin and Arthur Lee in Paris since late in 1776. Lovell's letter pressed for Adams' compliance with Congress' wish: "Doctor Franklin's Age allarms us. We want one man of inflexible Integrity on that Embassy. . . . You see I am ripe in hope about your acceptance, however your dear amiable Partner may be tempted to condemn my Persuasions of you to distance yourself from her farther than Baltimore or York Town."

Abigail Adams to James Lovell

Dear Sir [*Braintree, ca. 15 December 1777*]

Your Letters arrived in the absence of Mr. Adams who is gone as far as Portsmouth, little thinking of your plot against him.

O Sir you who are possessd of Sensibility, and a tender Heart, how could you contrive to rob me of all my happiness?

I can forgive Mr. Geary because he is a Stranger to domestick felicity and knows no tenderer attachment than that which he feel[s] for his Country, tho I think the Stoickism which every Batchelor discovers ought to be attributed to him as a fault.

He may retort upon me and ask if in such an Instance as this he is not the happier Man of the two, for tho destitute of the highest felicity in life he is not exposed to the keen pangs which attend a Seperation from our dear connexions. This is reasoning like a Batchelor still.

Desire him from me to make trial of a different Situation and then tell me his Sentiments.

But you Sir I can hardly be reconciled to you, you who so lately experienced what it was to be restored to your family after a painfull absence from it, and then in a few weeks torn from it by a call from your Country. You disinterestedly obeyed the Summons. But how could you so soon forget your sufferings and place your Friend in a more painfull situation considering the Risk and hazard of a foreign voyage. I pittied the conflict I saw in your mind, and tho a Stranger to your worthy partner sympathized with her and thought it cruel in your Friends to insist upon such a Sacrifice.

I know Sir by this appointment you mean the publick good, or you would not thus call upon me to sacrifice my tranquility and happiness.

The deputing my Friend upon so important an Embassy is a gratefull proof to me of the esteem of his Country. Tho I would not wish him to be less deserving I am sometimes almost selfish enough to wish his abilities confind to private life, and the more so for that wish is according with his own inclinations.

I have often experienced the want of his aid and assistance in the last 3 years of his absence and that Demand increases as our little ones grow up 3 of whom are sons and at this time of life stand most in need of the joint force of his example and precepts.

And can I Sir consent to be seperated from him whom my Heart esteems above all earthly things, and for an unlimited time? My life will be one continued scene of anxiety and apprehension, and must I cheerfully comply with the Demand of my Country?

I know you think I ought, or you [would] not have been accessary to the Call.

I have improved this absence to bring my mind to bear the Event with fortitude and resignation, tho I own it has been at the expence both of food and rest.

I beg your Excuse Sir for writing thus freely, it has been a relief to my mind to drop some of my sorrows through my pen, which had your Friend been present would have been poured only into his bosome.

Accept my sincere wishes for your welfare and happiness and Rank among the Number of your Friend[s], Your Humble Servant,

AA

From John Adams' Autobiography

[DECEMBER 1777]

When the Dispatches from Congress were read, the first question was whether I should accept the Commission or return it to Congress. The dangers of the Seas and the Sufferings of a Winter passage, although I had no experience of either, had little Weight with me. The British Men of War, were a more serious Consideration. The News of my Appointment, I had no doubt were known in Rhode Island, where a part of the British Navy and Army then lay, as soon as they were to me, and transmitted to England as soon as possible. I had every reason to expect, that Ships would be ordered to intercept the Boston from Rhode Island and from Hallifax, and that Intelligence would be secretly sent them, as accurately as possible of the time when she was to sail. For there always have been and still are Spies in America as well as in France, England and other Countries. The Consequence of a Capture would be a Lodging in New Gate. For the Spirit of Contempt as well as indignation and vindictive rage, with which the British Government had to that time conducted both the Controversy and the War forbade me to hope for the honor of an Appartment in the Tower as a State Prisoner. As their Act of Parliament would authorise them to try me in England for Treason, and proceed to execution too, I had no doubt they would go to the extent of their power, and practice upon me all the Cruelties of their punishment of Treason. My Family consisting of a dearly beloved Wife and four young Children, excited Sentiments of tenderness, which a Father and a Lover only can conceive, and which no language can express. And my Want of qualifications for the Office was by no means forgotten.

On the other hand my Country was in deep distress and in great danger. Her dearest Interest would be involved in the relations she might form with foreign nations. My own plan of these relations had been deliberately formed and fully communicated to Congress, nearly two Years before. The Confidence of my Country was committed to me, without my Solicitation. My Wife who had always encouraged and animated me, in all antecedent dangers and perplexities, did not fail me on this Occasion: But she discovered an inclination to bear me Company with all our Children. This proposal however, she was soon convinced, was too hazardous and imprudent.

The *Boston*, a 24-gun Continental frigate, Captain Samuel Tucker, was ordered to convey the new plenipotentiary and his ten-year-old son, John Quincy, to France from a secret point of embarkation. The stores put aboard for the passengers included a bushel of Indian meal, a case of rum, a quire of paper, two account books (now in the Adams Papers), "1/4 hundred Quills," wax wafers and ink, pipes and tobacco, mustard, tea, and "A Matross & Bolster."

On a blustery day in mid-February, Captain Tucker came in his barge from the *Boston* to Hough's Neck, near the house of Adams' uncle Norton Quincy, where the Adamses had taken shelter, and on the morning of the fifteenth the party sailed away from Nantasket Roads.

Uncle Quincys half after 11. O Clock
Feby. 13. 1778

JA to AA

Dearest of Friends

I had not been 20 Minutes in this House before I had the Happiness to see Captn. Tucker, and a Midshipman, coming for me. We shall be soon on Board, and may God prosper our Voyage, in every Stage of it, as much as at the Beginning, and send to you, my dear Children and all my Friends, the choisest of Blessings—so Wishes and prays yours, with an Ardour, that neither Absence, nor any other Event can abate,

John Adams

Johnny sends his Duty to his Mamma and his Love to his sister and Brothers. He behaves like a Man.

On Board the Frigate Boston
5 O Clock in the Afternoon
Feb. 13. 1778

JA to AA

Dearest of Friends

I am favoured with an unexpected Opportunity, by Mr. Woodward the lame Man who once lived at Mr. Belchers, and who promises in a very kind manner to take great Care of the Letter, to inform you of our Safe Passage from the Moon head, on Board the ship.—

The seas ran very high, and the Spray of the seas would have wet Us, but Captn. Tucker kindly brought great Coats on Purpose with which he covered Up me and John so that We came very dry.—To-morrow Morning We sail.—God bless you, and my Nabby, my Charley, my Tommy and all my Friends.

Yours, ever, ever, ever yours, John Adams

The very full record of the voyage in John Adams' Diary contains enough naval encounters, accidents, and storms to have more than satisfied a first-time transatlantic passenger. In the last days of March the *Boston* entered the Gironde and ran up to Bordeaux. The man from Braintree marveled at the elegance of the "Churches, Convents, Gentlemens seats" and most of all at the high cultivation of the land on both sides of the river. Before landing he penned a little prayer: "Europe thou great Theatre of Arts, Sciences, Commerce, War, am I at last permitted to visit thy Territories—May the Design of my Voyage be answered."

From John Adams' Diary and Autobiography

1778 APRIL 1. WEDNESDAY.

This Morning Mr. J. C. Champagne, negociant and Courtier de Marine, at Blaye, came on board, to make a Visit and pay his Compliments.

He says, that of the first Grouths of Wine, in the Province of Guienne, there are four Sorts, Chateau Margeaux, Hautbrion, La Fitte, and Latour.

This Morning I took Leave of the Ship, and went up to Town with my Son, and servant, Mr. Vernon, Mr. Jesse, and Dr. Noel, in the Pinnace. When We came up to the Town We had the Luck to see Mr. McClary, and Major Fraser [Frazer], on the Shore. Mr. McClary came on board our Boat, and conducted Us up to his Lodgings. Mr. Pringle was there. We dined there, in the Fashion of the Country. We had fish and Beans, and Salad, and Claret, Champain and Mountain Wine. After Dinner Mr. Bondfield, who is Agent here, invited me to take a Walk, which We did to his Lodgings, where We drank Tea. Then We walked about the Town, and to see the new Comedie. After this We went to the Opera, where the Scenery, the Dancing, the Music, afforded to me a very chearfull, sprightly Amusement, having never seen any Thing of the Kind before. After this We returned to Mr. McClarys Lodgings, where We supped.

1778 APRIL 2. THURSDAY.

Walked round the Town, to see the Chamber and Council of Commerce, the Parliament which was sitting, where We heard the Council. Then We went round to the Ship Yards &c. Made many Visits—dined at the Hotel D'Angleterre. Visited the Customhouse, the Post office—visited the Commandant of the Chateau Trompette, a Work of Vaubans—visited the Premiere President of the Parliament of Bourdeaux. Went to the Coffee house. Went to the Commedie—saw Les deux Avares. Supped at Messrs. Reuiles De Basmarein and Raimbaux.

One of the most elegant Ladies at Table, young and handsome, tho married to a Gentleman in the Company, was pleased to Address her discourse to me. Mr. Bondfield must interpret the Speech which he did in these Words "Mr. Adams, by your Name I conclude you are descended from the first Man and Woman, and probably in your family may be preserved the tradition which may resolve a difficulty which I could never explain. I never could understand how the first Couple found out the Art of lying together?" Whether her phrase was L'Art de se coucher ensemble, or any other more energetic, I know not, but Mr. Bondfield rendered it by that I have mentioned. To me, whose Acquaintance with Women had been confined to America, where the manners of the Ladies were universally characterised at that time by Modesty, Delicacy and Dignity, this question was surprizing and shocking: but although I believe at first I blushed, I was determined not to be disconcerted. I thought it would be as well for once to set a brazen face against a brazen face and answer a fool according to her folly, and accordingly composing my countenance into an Ironical Gravity I answered her "Madame My Family resembles the first Couple both in the name and in their frailties so much that I have no doubt We are descended from that in Paradise. But the Subject was perfectly understood by Us, whether by tradition I could not tell: I rather thought it was by Instinct, for there was a Physical quality in Us resembling the Power of Electricity or of the Magnet, by which when a Pair approached within a striking distance they flew together like the Needle to the Pole or like two Objects in electric Experiments." When this Answer was explained to her, she replied "Well I know not how it was, but this I know it is a very happy Shock." I should have added "in a lawfull Way" after "a striking distance," but if I had her Ladyship and all the Company would only have thought it Pedantry and Bigottry. This is a decent Story in comparison with many which I heard in Bourdeaux, in the short time I remained there, concerning married Ladies of Fashion and reputation.

HOTEL DE VALENTINOIS, RESIDENCE OF THE AMERICAN COMMISSIONERS AT PASSY

April 8th. Wednesday 1778. We rode through Orleans, and arrived at Paris about nine O Clock. For thirty miles from Paris the Road was paved and the Scænes were delightfull.

On our Arrival at a certain Barrier We were stopped and searched and paid the Duties for about twenty five Bottles, of Wine which were left, of the generous present of Mr. Delap at Bourdeaux. We passed the Bridge over the River Seine, and went through the Louvre. The Streets crouded with Carriages with a multitude of Servants in Liveries.

At Paris We went to several Hotells which were full; particularly the Hotel D'Artois, and the Hotel Bayonne. We were then advised to the Hotel de Valois, Rue de Richelieu, where We found Entertainment, but We could not have it, without taking all Chambers upon the Floor, which were four in number, very elegant and richly furnished, at the small price of two Crowns and an half a day without any thing to eat or drink. I took the Apartments only for two or three days, and sent for Provisions to the Cooks. Immediately on our Arrival We were called upon for our Names, as We had been at Mrs. Rives's at Bourdeaux. My little Son had sustained this long Journey of nearly five hundred miles, at the rate of an hundred miles a day, with the utmost firmness, as he did our fatiguing and dangerous Voyage.

April 9. Thursday. 1778. Though the City was very silent and still in the latter part of the night, the Bells, Carriages and Cries in the Street, were noisy enough in the morning.

Went in a Coach to Passy with Dr. Noel and my Son. [We visited] Dr. Franklin with whom I had served the best part of two Years in Congress in great Harmony and Civility, and there had grown up between Us that kind of Friendship, which is commonly felt between two members of the same public Assembly, who meet each other every day not only in public deliberations, but at private Breakfasts, dinners and Suppers, and especially in secret confidential Consultations, and who always agreed in their Opinions and Sentiments of public affairs. This had been the History of my Acquaintance with Franklin and he received me accordingly with great apparent Cordiality. Mr. Deane was gone to Marseilles to embark with D'Estaing for America. Franklin undertook the care of Jesse Deane, as I suppose had been agreed between him and the Childs Father before his departure. And he was soon sent, with my Son and Dr. Franklins Grandson Benjamin Franklin Bache, whom as well as William Franklin whom he called his Grandson, the Dr. had brought with him from America, to the Pension of Mr. Le Cœur at Passy.

Although he must have conveyed some word of his safe arrival, here follows Adams' first surviving letter to his wife from France, written four days after he reached Paris.

JA to AA

My dearest Friend — Passy April 12. 1778

I am so sensible of the Difficulty of conveying Letters safe, to you, that I am afraid to write, any Thing more than to tell you that after all the Fatigues and Dangers of my Voyage, and Journey, I am here in Health....

The Reception I have met, in this Kingdom, has been as friendly, as polite, and as respectfull as was possible. It is the universal Opinion of the People here, of all Ranks, that a Friendship between France and America, is the Interest of both Countries, and the late Alliance, so happily formed, is universally popular: so much so that I have been told by Persons of good Judgment, that the Government here, would have been under a Sort of Necessity of agreeing to it even if it had not been agreable to themselves.

The Delights of France are innumerable. The Politeness, the Elegance, the Softness, the Delicacy, is extreme.

In short stern and hauty Republican as I am, I cannot help loving these People, for their earnest Desire, and Assiduity to please.

It would be futile to attempt Descriptions of this Country especially of Paris and Versailles. The public Buildings and Gardens, the Paintings, Sculpture, Architecture, Musick, &c. of these Cities have already filled many Volumes. The Richness, the Magnificence, and Splendor, is beyond all Description.

This Magnificence is not confined to public Buildings such as Churches, Hospitals, Schools &c., but extends to private Houses, to Furniture, Equipage, Dress, and especially to Entertainments.—But what is all this to me? I receive but little Pleasure in beholding all these Things, because I cannot but consider them as Bagatelles, introduced, by Time and Luxury in Exchange for the great Qualities and hardy manly Virtues of the human Heart. I cannot help suspecting that the more Elegance, the less Virtue in all Times and Countries.—Yet I fear that even my own dear Country wants the Power and Opportunity more than the Inclination, to be elegant, soft, and luxurious.

All the Luxury I desire in this World is the Company of my dearest Friend, and my Children, and such Friends as they delight in, which I have sanguine Hopes, I shall, after a few Years enjoy in Peace.—I am with inexpressible Affection Yours, yours, John Adams

JA to AA

My dearest Friend — Passi Ap. 25. 1778

Monsieur Chaumont has just informed me of a Vessell bound to Boston: but I am reduced to such a Moment of Time, that I can only inform you that I am well, and inclose a few Lines from Johnny, to let you know that he is so. I have ordered the Things you desired, to be sent you, but I will not yet say by what Conveyance, for fear of Accidents.

If human Nature could be made happy by any Thing that can please the Eye, the Ear, the Taste or any other sense, or Passion or Fancy, this Country would be the Region for Happiness:—But, if my

Country were at Peace, I should be happier, among the Rocks and shades of Pens hill: and would chearfully exchange, all the Elegance, Magnificence and sublimity of Europe, for the Simplicity of Braintree and Weymouth.

To tell you the Truth, I admire the Ladies here. Dont be jealous. They are handsome, and very well educated. Their Accomplishments are exceedingly brilliant. And their Knowledge of Letters and Arts, exceeds that of the English Ladies much, I believe.

Tell Mrs. W[arren] that I shall write her a Letter, as she desired, and let her know some of my Reflections in this Country.

My venerable Colleague enjoys a Priviledge here, that is much to be envyd. Being seventy Years of Age, the Ladies not only allow him to ⟨*buss them as often as he p*⟩ embrace them as often as he pleases, but they are perpetually embracing him.—I told him Yesterday, I would write this to America.

AA to JA

May 18 1778

I have waited with great patience, restraining as much as posible every anxious Idea for 3 Months. But now every Vessel which arrives sits my expectation upon the wing, and I pray my Gaurdian Genious to waft me the happy tidings of your Safety and Welfare. Heitherto my wandering Ideas Rove like the Son of Ulissis from Sea to Sea, and from Shore to Shore, not knowing where to find you. Sometimes I fancy'd you upon the Mighty Waters, sometimes at your desired Haven; sometimes upon the ungratefull and Hostile Shore of Britain, but at all times and in all places under the protecting care and Guardianship of that Being who not only cloathes the lilies of the Feild and hears the young Ravens when they cry, but hath said of how much more worth are ye than many Sparrows, and this confidence which the world cannot deprive me of, is my food by day and my Rest by Night, and was all my consolation under the Horrid Ideas of assassination, the only Event of which I had not thought, and in some measure prepaird my mind.

When my Imagination sits you down upon the Gallick Shore, a Land to which Americans are now bound to transfer their affections, and to eradicate all those national prejudices which the Proud and Haughty Nations whom we once revered, craftily instilld into us whom they once stiled their children; I anticipate the pleasure you must feel, and tho so many leagus distant share in the joy of finding the great Interest of our Country so generously espoused, and nobly aided by so powerfull a Monarck. Your prospe[cts] must be much brightned, for when you left your Native Land they were rather Gloomy. If an unwearied Zeal and persevering attachment to the cause of truth and justice, regardless of the allurements of ambition on the one Hand or the threats of calamity on the other, can intitle any one to the Reward of peace, Liberty and Safety, a large portion of those Blessings are reserved for my Friend, in His Native Land.

> O Would'st thou keep thy Country's loud Applause
> Lov'd as her Father, as her God ado'rd
> Be still the bold assertor of her cause
> Her Voice, in Council; (in the Fight her Sword)
> In peace, in War persue thy Countrys Good
> For her, bare thy bold Breast, and pour thy Gen'rous Blood.

Difficult as the Day is, cruel as this War has been, seperated as I am on account of it from the dearest connextion in life, I would not exchange my Country for the Wealth of the Indies, or be any other than an American tho I might be Queen or Empress of any Nation upon the Globe. My Soul is unambitious of pomp or power. Beneath my Humble roof, Bless'd with the Society and tenderest affection of my dear partner, I have enjoyed as much felicity, and as exquisite happiness as falls to the share of mortals; and tho I have been calld to sacrifice to my Country, I can glory in my Sacrifice, and derive pleasure from my intimate connextion with one who is esteemed worthy of the important trust devolved upon him.

Britain as usual has added insult to injustice and cruelty, by what she calls a concilitary plan. From my Soul I dispice her meaness, but she has long ago lost that treasure which a great authority tell[s] us exalteth a Nation, and is receiving the reproaches due to her crimes.

I have been much gratified with the perusal of the Duke of Richmonds Speach. Were there ten such Men to be found, I should still have some hopes that a revolution would take place in favour of the virtuous few; "and the Laws, the Rights, the Generous plan of power deliverd down, From age to age by our renown'd forefathers" be again restored to that unhappy Island.

I hope by the close of this month to receive from you a large packet. I have wrote twice before this, some opportunities I may miss of, by my distance from the Capital. I have enjoyed a good share of Health since you left me. I have not mentiond my dear son tho I have often thought of him since I began this Letter, becaus I propose writing to him by this opportunity. I omit many domestick matters becaus I will not risk their comeing to the publick Eye. I shall have a small Bill to

BENJAMIN FRANKLIN.
Né à Boston, dans la nouvelle Angleterre le 17 Janvier 1706.

BENJAMIN FRANKLIN IN 1777

draw upon you in the month of june. I think to send it to Mr. MacCrery who by a Letter received since you went away I find is Setled in Bordeaux in the mercantile way, and I dare say will procure for me any thing I may have occasion for. I wish you would be so good as to write him a line requesting the favour of him to procure me such things as I may have occasion for, and in addition to the Bills which may be drawn Let him add ten pounds Sterling at a time, if I desire it. The Bills will be at 3 different times in a year. If they should arrive safe they would render me essential service. Our Publick finnances are upon no better footing than they were when you left us. 500 Dollors is now offerd by this Town per Man for 9 Months to recruit the Army, 12 pounds a Month for Farming Labour is the price, and not to be procured under. Our Friends are all well and desire to be rememberd to you. So many tender sentiments rush upon my mind when about to close this Letter to you, that I can only ask you to measure them by those which you find in your own Bosome for your affectionate Portia

Before John Adams had left Braintree, the capitulation at Saratoga had effected what the most brilliant diplomacy could never have done by itself: an alliance with France, signed at Versailles on February 6. There was now both less and more for Adams to do in Paris than anyone could have supposed before. The daily business of the joint commission—in negotiations and correspondence with manufacturers and merchants of arms and military stores, with ship captains, and with government and private agents and hangers-on of all descriptions—was staggering. Adams' experience on the Board of War had prepared him well for such tasks.

But he was not prepared, and was temperamentally unsuited, for the role of mediator between two such colleagues as Arthur Lee and Benjamin Franklin—the one morbidly irritable and suspicious, and the other almost maddeningly casual and devoted to intellectual and other pleasures. Surviving letterbooks and account books of the joint commission bear out Adams' assertion that for long periods he carried the chief burden of its paperwork.

The description that follows of Franklin's mode of life at Passy, written long after the event, is to be sure colored by later incidents in their relationship and also by a jealousy Adams never overcame. It is not wholly invented; but when he wrote it, Adams had forgotten, if he ever knew, how sorely he had tried the patience of a very patient man.

From John Adams' Autobiography

[MAY 27TH 1778]

I found that the Business of our Commission would never be done, unless I did it. My two Colleagues would agree in nothing. The Life of Dr. Franklin was a Scene of continual discipation. I could never obtain the favour of his Company in a Morning before Breakfast which would have been the most convenient time to read over the Letters and papers, deliberate on their contents, and decide upon the Substance of the Answers. It was late when he breakfasted, and as soon as Breakfast was over, a crowd of Carriges came to his Levee or if you like the term better to his Lodgings, with all Sorts of People; some Phylosophers, Accademicians and Economists; some of his small tribe of humble friends in the litterary Way whom he employed to translate some of his ancient Compositions, such as his Bonhomme Richard and for what I know his Polly Baker &c.; but by far the greater part were Women and Children, come to have the honour to see the great Franklin, and to have the pleasure of telling Stories about his Simplicity, his bald head and scattering strait hairs, among their Acquaintances. These Visitors occupied all the time, commonly, till it was time to dress to go to Dinner. He was invited to dine abroad every day and never declined unless when We had invited Company to dine with Us. I was always invited with him, till I found it necessary to send Apologies, that I might have some time to study the french Language and do the Business of the mission. Mr. Franklin kept a horn book always in his Pockett in which he minuted all his invitations to dinner, and Mr. Lee said it was the only thing in which he was punctual. It was the Custom in France to dine between one and two O Clock: so that when the time came to dress, it was time for the Voiture to be ready to carry him to dinner. Mr. Lee came daily to my Appartment to attend to Business, but we could rarely obtain the Company of Dr. Franklin for a few minutes, and often when I had drawn the Papers and had them fairly copied for Signature, and Mr. Lee and I had signed them, I was frequently obliged to wait several days, before I could procure the Signature of Dr. Franklin to them. He went according to his Invitation to his Dinner and after that went sometimes to the Play, sometimes to the Philosophers but most commonly to visit those Ladies who were complaisant enough to depart from the custom of France so far as to procure Setts of Tea Geer as it is called and make Tea for him. Some of these Ladies I knew as Madam Hellvetius, Madam Brillon, Madam Chaumont, Madam Le Roy &c. and others whom I never knew and never enquired for. After Tea the Evening was spent, in hearing the Ladies sing and play upon their Piano Fortes and other instruments of Musick, and in various Games as Cards, Chess, Backgammon, &c. &c. Mr. Franklin I believe however never play'd at any Thing but Chess or Checquers. In these Agreable and important Occupations and Amusements, The Afternoon and Evening was spent, and he came home at all hours from Nine to twelve O Clock at night. This Course of Life contributed to his Pleasure and I believe to his health and Longevity. He was now between Seventy and Eighty and I had so much respect and compassion for his Age, that I should have been happy to have done all the Business or rather all the Drudgery, if I could have been favoured with a few moments in a day to receive his Advice concerning the manner in which it ought to be done. But this condescention was not attainable. All that could be had was his Signature, after it was done, and this it is true he very rarely refused though he sometimes delayed.

JA to AA

My dearest Friend — Passi June 3 1778

On the 13 of Feb. I left you. It is now the 3d. of June, and I have not received a Line, nor heard a Word, directly nor indirectly, concerning you since my departure. This is a Situation of Mind, in which I never was before, and I assure you I feel a great deal of Anxiety at it: yet I do not wonder at it, because I suppose few Vessels have sailed from Boston since ours.

I have shipped for you, the Articles you requested, and the black Cloth for your Father, to whom present my most affectionate and dutiful Respects. C[aptain] Tucker, if he should not be unlucky, will give you an Account of your Things.

It would be endless to attempt a Description of this Country. It is one great Garden. Nature and Art have conspired to render every Thing here delightful. Religion and Government, you will say ought to be excepted.—With all my Heart.—But these are no Afflictions to me, because I have well fixed it in my Mind as a Principle, that every Nation has a Right to that Religion and Government, which it chooses, and as long as any People please themselves in these great Points, I am determined they shall not displease me.

There is so much danger that my Letter may fall into malicious Hands, that I should not choose to be too free in my Observations upon the Customs and Manners of this People. But thus much I may say with Truth and without offence, that there is no People in the World, who take so much Pains to please, nor any whose Endeavours in this Way, have more success. Their Arts, Manners, Taste and Language are more respected in Europe than those of any other Nation. Luxury, dissipation, and Effeminacy, are pretty nearly at the same degree of Excess here, and in every other Part of Europe. The great Cardinal Virtue of Temperance, however, I believe flourishes here more than in any other Part of Europe.

My dear Country men! how shall I perswade you, to avoid the Plague of Europe? Luxury has as many and as bewitching Charms, on your Side of the Ocean as on this—and Luxury, wherever she goes, effaces from human Nature the Image of the Divinity. If I had Power I would forever banish and exclude from America, all Gold, silver, precious stones, Alabaster, Marble, Silk, Velvet and Lace.

Oh the Tyrant! the American Ladies would say! What!—Ay, my dear Girls, these Passions of yours, which are so easily allarmed, and others of my own sex which are exactly like them, have done and will do the Work of Tyrants in all Ages. Tyrants different from me, whose Power has banished, not Gold indeed, but other Things of greater Value, Wisdom, Virtue and Liberty. My Son and Servant are well. I am, with an Ardour that Words have not Power to express, yours,

John Adams

John Adams' observations on the accomplishments of French women evoked from his wife a just and recurrent complaint—the "contracted Education of the Females of my own country."

AA to JA

Dearest of Friends June 30 [*1778*]

Shall I tell my dearest that tears of joy filld my Eyes this morning at the sight of his well known hand, the first line which has bless[ed] my Sight since his four months absence during which time I have never been able to learn a word from him, or my dear son till about ten days ago an english paper taken in a prize and brought into Salem containd an account under the Paris News of your arrival at the abode of Dr. Franklin, and last week a Carteel from Halifax brought Capt. Welch of the Boston who informd that he left you well the Eleventh of March, that he had Letters for me but distroyed them, when he was taken, and this is all the information I have ever been able to obtain. Our Enemies have told us the vessel was taken and named the frigate which took her and that she was carried into Plimouth. I have lived a life of fear and anxiety ever since you left me, not more than a week after your absence the Horrid Story of Doctor Franklins assassination was received from France and sent by Mr. Purveyance of Baltimore to Congress and to Boston. Near two months before that was contradicted, then we could not hear a word from the Boston, and most people gave her up as taken or lost, thus has my mind been agitated like a troubled sea. You will easily Conceive how gratefull to me your favour of April 25 and those of our Son were to me and mine, tho I regret your short warning and the little time you had to write, by which means I know not how you fared upon your Voiage, what reception you have met with, (not even from the Ladies, tho you profess yourself an admirer of them,) and a thousand circumstances which I wish to know, and which are always perticuliarly interesting to [a] near connextion. I must request you always to be minute and to write me by every conveyance. Some perhaps which may appear unlikely to reach [me] will be the first to arrive. I own I was mortified at so Short a Letter, but I quiet my Heart with thinking there are many more upon their passage to me. I have wrote Seven before this and some of them very long. Now I know you are Safe I wish myself with you. Whenever you entertain such a wish recollect that I would have willingly hazarded all dangers to have been your companion, but as that was not permitted you must console me in your absence by a Recital of all your adventures, tho methinks I would not have them in all respects too similar to those related of your venerable Colleigue, Whose Mentor like appearence, age and philosiphy must certainly lead the polite scientifick Ladies of France to suppose they are embraceing the God of Wisdom, in a Humane Form, but I who own that I never yet wish'd an Angle whom I loved a Man, shall be full as content if those divine Honours are omitted. The whole Heart of my Friend is in the Bosom of his partner, more than half a score of years has so riveted [it] there that the fabrick which contains it must crumble into Dust e'er the particles can be seperated. I can hear of the Brilliant accomplishment[s] of any of my Sex with pleasure and rejoice in that Liberality of Sentiment which acknowledges them. At the same time I regret the trifling narrow contracted Education of the Females of my own country. I have entertaind a superiour opinion of the accomplishments of the French Ladies ever since I read the Letters of Dr. Sherbear, who professes that he had rather take the opinion of an accomplished Lady in matters of polite writing than the first wits of Itally and should think himself safer with her approbation than of a long List of Literati, and he give[s] this reason for it that Women have in general more delicate Sensations than Men, what touches them is for the most part true in Nature, whereas men warpt by Education, judge amiss from previous prejudice and refering all things to the model of the ancients, condemn that by comparison where no true Similitud ought to be expected.

But in this country you need not be told how much female Education is neglected, nor how fashonable it has been to ridicule Female learning, tho I acknowled[ge] it my happiness to be connected with a person of a more generous mind and liberal Sentiments. I cannot forbear transcribing a few Generous Sentiments which I lately met with upon this Subject. If women says the writer are to be esteemed our Enemies, methinks it is an Ignoble Cowardice thus to disarm them and not allow them the same weapons we use ourselves, but if they deserve the title of our Friends tis an inhumane Tyranny to debar them of priviliges of ingenious Education which would also render their Friendship so much the more delightfull to themselves and us. Nature is seldom observed to be niggardly of her choisest Gifts to the Sex, their Senses are generally as quick as ours, their Reason as nervious, their judgment as mature and solid. Add but to these natural perfections the advantages of acquired learning what polite and charming creatures would they prove whilst their external Beauty does the office of a Crystal to the Lamp not shrowding but discloseing their Brighter intellects. Nor need we fear to loose our Empire over them by thus improveing their native abilities since where there is most Learning, Sence and knowledge there is always observed to be the most modesty and Rectitude of manners.

AA to JA

Dearest of Friends [*Braintree, ca. 15 July 1778*]

By Mr. Tailor, who has promised me to deliver this with his own hand to you, or distroy it if necessary, I take the liberty of writing rather more freely than I should otherways venture to do. I cannot think but with pain of being debared this privilidge, the only one left me for my consolation in the many solitary and I may add melancholy hours which pass. I promissed myself a negative kind of happiness whenever I could hear of your safe arrival but alass I find a craveing void left akeing in my Breast, and I find myself some days especially more unhappy than I would even wish an Enemy to be. In vain do I strive to divert my attention, my Heart, like a poor bird hunted from her nest, is still returning to the place of its affections, and fastens upon the object where all its cares and tenderness are centered. I must not expect, I ought not indeed for the sake of your repose to wish to be thus frequently, and thus fondly the subject of your meditation, but may I not believe that you employ a few moments every day from the Buisness and pleasures which surround you in thinking of her who wishes not her existance to survive your affection, who never recollects the cruel hour of seperation but with tears. From whence shall I gather firmness of mind bereft of the amicable prop upon which it used to rest and acquire fortitude? The subject is too tender to persue. I see it touches your Heart. I will quit it at the midnight hour, and rise in the morning suppressing these too tender sensibilities.

Tis 5 month since the Boston sailed during all which time I have only received two very short Letters. That you have wrote more I know tho you do not mention them. Cautious as tis necessary you should be, methinks you need not be so parsimonious. Friendship and affection will suggest a thousand things to say to an intimate Friend which if ridiculed by an Enemy will only be an other proof among the thousands we already have of a savage barbarity. A variety of new scenes must arise the discription of which would afford ample amusement to your domestick Friend.

I had the pleasure of drinking tea a few days ago with Sir James Jay and Mr. Diggs. It was a pleasure to hear so directly from you and my dear Jack. The Gentlemen were very social and communicative. I found they had throughly enterd into the character of my Friend, who they represented as rather relucttantly entering into the modes and customs of --- and rather conforming from necessity than inclination. They diverted me with an account of the Freedoms and fondness of the ...... for the venerable Doctor. At the same time I could not refrain figuring to myself a grave American republican starting at the sight unaccustomed to such freedoms even from the partner of his youth. After 13 years intimate connexion, who can recollect the time when had she laid her hand upon his—a universal Blush would have coverd her.—Much however must be allowed for Forms and Customs which render even dissagreable practise'es familiar. I can even consent that they should practise their *Forms* upon your Lordship considering your natural fondness for the practise whilst I hold possession of what I think they cannot rob me of. Tis mine by a free gift, mine by exchange, mine by a long possession, mine by merrit and mine by every law humane and divine.

If I was sure this would reach you I should say many things which I dare not venture to. I stand corrected if I have said any thing already which I ought not to. I feel myself embaresse'd whilst my Heart overflows, and longs to give utterance to my pen. Many domestick affairs I wish to consult upon. I have studied for a method of defraying the necessary expences of my family. In no one Instance is a hundred pound L M better than thirteen pounds Six and Eight pence used to be, in foreign Articles no ways eaquel, in taxes but a fourth part as good. Day Labour at 24 shillings per day. What then can you think my situation must be? I will tell you after much embaresment in endeavouring to procure faithfull hands I concluded to put out the Farm and reduce my family as much as posible. I sit about removeing the Tenants from the House, which with much difficulty I effected, but not till I had paid a Quarters Rent in an other House for them. I then with the kind assistance of Dr. T[uft]s procured two young Men Brothers newly married and placed them as Tenants to the halves retaining in my own Hands only one Horse and two Cows with pasturage for my Horse in summer, and Q[uinc]y medow for fodder in winter. At present I have no reason to repent of my situation, my family consists at present of only myself, two children and two Domesticks. Our daughter is at School in Boston, and I wait only to know how I shall be able to discharge my schooling for Master Charles to place him at Haverhill. Debts are my abhorrance. I never will borrow if any other method can be devised. I have thought of this which I wish you to assent to, to order some saleable articles which I will mention to be sent to the care of my unkle S[mit]h a small trunk at a time, containing ten or 15 pounds Sterling, from which I may supply my family with such things as I need, and the rest place in the hands of Dr. T[uft]s Son who has lately come into Trade, and would sell them for me, by which means if I must pay extravagant prices I shall be more upon an eaquel footing with my Neighbours.

I have been obliged to make fence this year to the amount of 100 & 50 Dollors. I have occasion for only a pair of cart wheels for which I must give 60 pounds Lawfull money. I mention these few articles to serve as a specimen of the rest. I inquired the price of a new carrage the other day and found it to be no *more* than 300 pounds Lawfull money —at this rate I never will ask for a supply of this *light commodity* from any Body let my situation be what it will. The Season has been fine for grass but for about 3 weeks past we have had a sharp and severe Drouth which has greatly injured our grain and a blast upon english grain with a scarcity for flower so that a loaf which once sold for 4 pence is 4 shillings. Tis rumourd that the French fleet to the amount of 18ten have arrived of Chesepeak. The Enemy have left Philidelphia, but for politicks I refer you to the publick Letters which will accompany this.—Mr. Tailor promisses to bring Letters from you whenever he returns. I am in daily expectation of hearing from you. I lament that you lay so far from the sea ports that you must omit some opportunities of writing. I will not suppose that with more leisure you have less inclination to write to your affectionate and Lonely Friend

Portia

JA to AA

My dearest Friend Passi July 26. 1778

Yours of the Tenth of June by Captain Barnes was brought to me Yesterday, which is only the second that I have yet received from you. The other is of 25 March. I have written to you, several Times, as often as I could, and hope they will arrive. I have put on board one ship, all the Articles in your Minute. By Captain Niles I have sent you a smal Present of Tea. By Captain Barnes, I will send some few Things.

You enquire how you shall pay Taxes?—I will tell you.—Ask the favour of your Uncle Smith or Some other Friend to let you have Silver, and draw your Bills upon me. The Money shall be paid, in the instant of the sight of your Bill, but let it be drawn in your own Hand Writing. Any body who wants to remit Cash to France, Spain, Holland or England, will let you have the Money. You may draw with Confidence, for the Cash shall be paid here. I suppose however, that one hundred Pounds, a Year, sterling will be as much as you will have Occasion for. With silver, you may get your Father, or your Uncle or Brother Cranch to pay your Taxes.

You have made your Son very happy by your Letter to him—he is writing a long Answer. He begins to read and speak French, pretty well. He behaves well, and is much esteemed here, which gives me constant Pleasure.—His Sister is to blame for not writing to him as well as to me.—He has been very good, is almost constantly writing to her, and his Brothers, and to his Cousins and his Friend Joshua Green, and many other Correspondents. He wrote a french Letter the other Day to his Grand Pa. He will write to his Grand ma, to whom present his and my most affectionate and dutiful Respects.

As to Politicks, The Emperor and K[ing] of Prussia are at War. France and England are the same altho there is yet no formal Manifesto. America, I think has nothing to fear from Europe. Let her chase away the broken Remnants of her Ennemies, now within her Limits, and lay on Taxes, with a manly Resolution, in order to raise the Credit of her Currency and she will do very well.

This is a delicious Country. Every Thing that can sooth, charm and bewitch is here. But these are no Enchantments for me. My Time is employed in the public Business, in studying French like a school Boy, and in fervent Wishes, that the happy Time may arrive soon, when I may exchange the Elegances and Magnificence of Europe for the Simplicity of Pens Hill, and the Glory of War, for the Obscurity of private Contemplation. Farewell.

Soon after the Adamses arrived in France and joined Franklin's extensive household in Passy, John Quincy was placed in M. Le Coeur's pension school in Passy, where there were several other young Americans. With his father so close by and with periodic letters from his mother, not to mention his inbred urge toward self-improvement, there was never any danger of his falling into idle habits. His earliest letterbook begins at about this time, although his first extant diary does not begin until November 1779.

John Quincy Adams to Abigail Adams

Honoured Mamma Passy september the 27th 1778

My Pappa enjoins it upon me to keep a journal, or a diary, of the Events that happen to me, and of objects that I See, and of Characters that I converse with from day, to day, and altho I am Convinced of the utility, importance, & necessity, of this Exercise, yet I have not patience, & perseverance, enough to do it so Constantly as I ought. My Pappa who takes a great deal of Pains to put me in the right way, has also advised me to Preserve Copies of all my letters, & has given me a Convenient Blank Book for this end; and altho I shall have the mortification a few years hence, to read a great deal of my Childish nonsense, yet I shall have the Pleasure, & advantage, of Remarking the several steps, by which I shall have advanced, in taste, judgment, & knowledge. a journal Book & a letter Book of a Lad of Eleven years old, Cannot be expected to Contain much of Science, Litterature, arts, wisdom, or wit, yet it may Serve to perpetuate many observations that I may make, & may hereafter help me to recolect both persons, & things, that would other ways escape my memory. I have been to see the Palace & gardens of Versailles, the Military scholl at Paris, the hospital of Invalids, the hospital of Foundling Children, the Church of Notre Dame, the Heights of Calvare, of Montmartre, of Minemontan, & other scenes of Magnificense, in & about Paris, which if I had written down in a diary, or a Letter Book, would give me at this time much Pleasure to revise, & would enable me hereafter to Entertain my Freinds, but I have neglected it & therefore, can now only resolve to be more thoughtful, & Industrious, for the Future & to encourage me in this resolution & enable me to keep it with more ease & advantage my father has given me hopes of a Present of a Pencil & Pencil Book in which I can make notes upon the spot to be Transfered afterwards in my Diary & my Letters this will give me great Pleasure both because it will be a sure means of improvement to myself & enable me to be more entertain[in]g to you.

I am my ever honoured & revered Mamma your Dutiful & affectionate Son John Quincy Adams

There are few parallels elsewhere in the correspondence of Abigail and John Adams to their occasional unhappiness springing from Abigail's resentment that her husband's letters were so infrequent and brief and from John Adams' inability to endure the pain of her reproaches. The frequent loss of mail in transit, the months that often elapsed before a letter's delivery, his guardedness of utterance from fear of spies and the like, all contributed to the mutual frustration. But she was right in her complaint at this time. His claim that he had written her "not much less I believe than fifty Letters" during the first nine months of his absence in Europe was an exaggeration made under momentary stress.

AA to JA

[*Braintree, 21 October 1778*]

How dear to me was the Signature of my Friend this Evening received by the Boston a ship more valued to me than all the American Navy besides, valuable for conveying safely my choisest comfort, my dearest Blessings. "I Love the place where Helen was but born."

You write me that you have by several vessels convey'd me tokens of your Friendship. The only Letters I have received from you or my dear Son were dated last April and containd only a few lines—judge then what my Heart has sufferd. You could not have sufferd more upon your Voyage than I have felt cut of from all communication with you. My Harp has been hung upon the willows, and I have scarcly ever taken my pen to write but the tears have flowed faster than the Ink. I have wrote often to you but was unfortunate enough to have my last and largest packets distroyd the vessel being taken and carried into Halifax. Mr. Ingraham of Boston will convey this to you with his own hand. You will I know rejoice to see him as a Bostonian, an American and a Man of Merit, I need not ask you to notice him. I apprehend that this will never reach you yet this apprehension shall not prevent my writing by every opportunity. The French Ships are still in the Harbour of Boston. I have received great civility and every mark of Respect that it has been in the power of their officers to shew me.

Count dEstaing has been exceeding polite to me, he took perticulir care to see me, sending an officer to request I would meet him at Col. Q[uinc]ys as it was inconvenient to be at a greater Distance from his ship. I according waited upon his Excellency who very politely received me, insisted upon my Dineing on board his Ship, appointed his day and sent his Barge, requested I would bring any of my Friends with me. We made up a company of 13 and waited upon him. An entertainment fit for a princiss was prepared, we spent a most agreable day. The Count is a most agreable Man, Sedate, polite, affible with a dignity that is lost in Ease yet his brow at times would be overclouded with cares and anxieties so like a dear absent Friends that I was pained for him. But I determine to write you more perticuliarly by an other opportunity. I lament the loss of my last packet. I hate to write duplicates. Our Friend[s] here are all well. Let me intreat you to write me more Letters at a time, sure you cannot want subjects. They are my food by day and my rest by night. Do not deal them so spairingly to your own Portia

AA to JA

[*Braintree, 25 October 1778*]

The Morning after I received your very short Letter I determined to have devoted the day in writing to my Friend but I had only just Breakfasted when I had a visit from Monsieur Rivers an officer on board the Langudock who speaks English well, the Captain of the Zara and 6 or 8 other officers from on Board an other ship. The first Gentlemen dined with me and spent the day so that I had no opportunity of writing that day. The Gentlemen officers have made me several visits and I have dined twice on board at very Elegant entertainments. Count dEstaing has been exceeding polite to me. Soon after he arrived here I received a Message from him requesting that I would meet him at Col. Q[uinc]y['s] as it was inconvenient leaving his ship for any long time. I waited upon him and was very politely received. Upon parting he requested that the family would accompany me on board his Ship and dine with him the next thursday with any Friends we chose to bring and his Barge should come for us. We went according to the invitation and were sumptuously entertaind with every delicacy that this country produces and the addition of every foreign article that could render our feast Splendid. Musick and dancing for the young folks closed the day.

The temperance of these Gentlemen, the peaceable quiet disposition both of officers and men joined to many other virtues which they have exibeted dur[ing] their continuance with us, is sufficent to make Europe[ans] and American[s] too blush at their own degeneracy of manners. Not one officer has been seen the least disguised with Liquour since their arrival. Most that I have seen appear to be gentlemen of family and Education. I have been the mo[re] desirous to take notice of them as I cannot help saying that they have been neglected in the town of Boston. Generals Heath and Hancock have done their part, but very few if any private families have any acquaintance with them.

Perhaps I feel more anxious to have them distinguished on account of the near and dear connextion I have among them. It would gratify me much if I had it in my power to entertain every officer in the Fleet.

In the very few lines I have received from you not the least mention is made that you have ever received a line from me. I have not been so parsimonious as my Friend, perhaps I am not so prudent but I cannot take my pen with my Heart overflowing and not give utterance to some of the abundance which is in it. Could you after a thousand fears and anxieties, long expectation and painfull suspences be satisfied with my telling you that I was well, that I wished you were with me, that my daughter sent her duty, that I had orderd some articles for you which I hoped would arrive &c. &c.—By Heaven if you could you have changed Hearts with some frozen Laplander or made a voyage to a region that has chilld every Drop of your Blood.—But I will restrain a pen already I fear too rash, nor shall it tell you how much I have sufferd from this appearance of——inattention.

The articles sent by Capt. Tucker have arrived safe and will be of great service to me. Our Money is very little better than blank paper, it takes 40 dollors to purchase a Barrel of cider, 50 pounds Lawfull for a 100 of Sugar and 50 dollors for a hundred of flower, 4 dollors per day for a Labourer and find him which will amount to 4 more. You will find by Bills drawn before the date of this that I had taken the method which I was happy in finding you had directed me to. I shall draw for the rest as I find my situation requires. No article that can be named foreign or domestick but what costs more than double in hard money what it once sold for. In one Letter I have given you an account of our Local Situation, and of *every thing* I thought you might wish to know. 4 or 5 sheets of paper wrote to you by the last Mail were distroyd when she was taken. Duplicates are my Aversion tho I believe I should set a value upon them if I was to receive them from a certain Friend, ⟨*since so little*⟩ a Friend who never was deficient, in testifying his regard and affection to his

Portia

JA to AA

My dearest Friend — Passy Novr. 6 1778

We have received Information that so many of our Letters have been thrown overboard, that I fear you will not have heard so often from me, as both of us wish.

I have written often. But my Letters have not been worth so much as other Things which I have sent you. I sent you a small Present by Captain Niles. But he is taken by a Jersey Privateer. I sent you also, some other Things by Captain Barnes, and what affects me quite as much, I sent the Things that my dear Brother Cranch requested me to send, by the same Vessells. These Vessells were chosen because they were fast Sailers, and so small as to be able to see Danger before they could be seen, but all is taken and sent into Guernsy and Jersy.

By Captain Tucker I sent you the whole of the List you gave me of

Articles for the Family. These I hope have arrived safe. But I have been so unlucky, that I feel averse to meddling in this Way. The whole Loss is a Trifle it is true: but to you, in the Convenience of the Family, and to Mr. Cranch in his Business they would have been of Value. If the Boston arrives, the little Chest she carries to you will be of service.

My Anxiety for you and for the public is not diminished by Time or Distance. The great Number of accidental Dissappointments in the Course of the last summer are afflicting. But We hope for better Luck another Year.

It seems to be the Intention of Heaven, that We should be taught the full Value of our Liberty by the dearness of the Purchase, and the Importance of public Virtue by the Necessity of it. There seems to be also a further Design, that of eradicating forever from the Heart of every American, every tender Sentiment towards Great Britain, that We may sometime or other know how to make the full Advantage of our Independence by more extensive Connections with other Countries.

Whatever Syren songs of Peace may be sung in your Ears, you may depend upon it from me, (who unhappily have been seldom mistaken in my Guesses of the Intentions of the British Government for fourteen Years,) that every malevolent Passion, and every insidious Art, will predominate in the British Cabinet against Us.

Their Threats of Russians, and of great Reinforcements, are false and impracticable and they know them to be so: But their Threats of doing Mischief with the Forces they have, will be verified as far as their Power.

It is by no means pleasant to me, to be forever imputing malicious Policy to a Nation, that I have ever wished and still wish I could esteem: But Truth must be attended to: and almost all Europe, the Dutch especially, are at this day talking of G. Britain in the style of American sons of Liberty.

I hope the unfortunate Events at Rhode Island will produce no Heart Burnings, between our Countrymen and the Comte D'Estaing, who is allowed by all Europe to be a great and worthy Officer, and by all that know him to be a zealous friend of America.

I have enjoyed uncommon Health, since my Arrival in this Country and if it was Peace, and my family here, I could be happy. But never never shall I enjoy happy days, without either.

My little son gives me great Pleasure, both by his Assiduity to his Books and his discreet Behaviour. The Lessons of his Mamma are a constant Law to him, and the Reflexion that they are so to his sister and Brothers, are a never failing Consolation to me at Times when I feel more tenderness for them, than Words can express, or than I should choose to express if I had Power.

Remember me, in the most affectionate Manner to our Parents, Brothers, Sisters, Unkles, Aunts, and what shall I say—Children.

My Respects where they are due, which is in so many Places that I cannot name them.

With Regard to my Connections with the Public Business here, which you will be naturally inquisitive to know something of, I can only say that We have many Disagreable Circumstances here, many Difficulties to accomplish the Wishes of our Constituents, and to give Satisfaction to certain half anglified Americains, and what is more serious and affecting to real and deserving Americans who are suffering in England and escaping from thence: But from this Court, this City, and Nation I have experienced nothing, but uninterupted Politeness.

It is not possible for me to express more Tenderness and Affection to you than will be suggested by the Name of John Adams

AA to JA

[*Braintree, 12–23 November 1778*]

I have taken up my pen again to relieve the anxiety of a Heart too susceptable for its own repose, nor can I help complaining to my Dearest Friend that his painfull absence is not as formerly alleiviated by the tender tokens of his Friendship, 3 very short Letters only have reachd my Hands during 9 months absence.

I cannot be so unjust to his affection as to suppose he has not wrote much oftener and more perticularly, but must sit down to the Score of misfortune that so few have reachd me.

I cannot charge myself with any deficiency in this perticular as I have never let an opportunity slip without writing to you since we parted, tho you make no mention of having received a line from me; if they are become of so little importance as not to be worth noticeing with your own Hand, be so kind as to direct your Secretary

I will not finish the sentance, my Heart denies the justice of the acqusation, nor does it believe your affection in the least diminished by distance or absence, but my Soul is wounded at a Seperation from you, and my fortitude all dissolved in frailty and weakness. When I cast my ⟨*Eye*⟩ thoughts across the Atlantick and view the distance, the dangers and Hazards which you have already passd through, and to which you must probably be again exposed, e'er we shall meet, the Time of your absence unlimitted, all all conspire to cast a Gloom over my solitary hours, and bereave me of all domestick felicity. In vain do I strive to through of [throw off] in the company of my Friends some of the anxiety of my Heart, it increases in proportion to my endeavours to conceal it; the only alleiviation I know of would be a frequent intercourse by Letters unrestrained by the apprehension of their becomeing food for our Enemies. The affection I feel for my Friend is of the tenderest kind, matured by years, [sanctified?] by choise and approved by Heaven. Angles can witness to its purity, what care I then for the Ridicule of Britains should this testimony of it fall into their Hands, nor can I endure that so much caution and circumspection on your part should deprive me of the only consolor of your absence—a consolation that our Enemies enjoy in a much higher degree than I do, Many of them having received 3 or 4 Letters from their Friend[s] in England to one that I have received from France.

Thus far I wrote more than ten day[s] ago, my mind as you will easily see far from tranquil, and my Heart so wounded by the Idea of inattention that the very Name of my Dearest Friend would draw tears from me. Forgive me for harbouring an Idea so unjust, to your affection. Were you not dearer to me than all this universe contains beside, I could not have sufferd as I have done, But your Letters of April 12, of June 3 and June 16 calmd my Soul to peace. I cannot discribe the Effect they had upon me, cheerfullness and tranquility took place of greif and anxiety. I placed them Next my Heart and soothed myself to rest with the tender assurences of a Heart all my own.

I was not a little mortified to find that the few Lin[e]s wrote by way of Holland were the only ones you had received from me, when I had wrote many sheets of paper long before that time and sent by so many different hands that I thought you must have heard often from me, ⟨*and led me to suppose that many of your Letters to me must have shared the same fate*⟩.

But this circumstance will make me more cautious how I suffer such cruel Ideas to [haunt? hound?] me again. Tis the 23 of November now. Count Estaing has saild near a fortnight, Biron with 15 sail lay upon the watch for him, but a very terrible Storm prevented the Count from sailing, and shatterd Birons Fleet. 11 Sail only have arrived at Newport, the Somerset was lost upon Nantucket Shoals. I fed many of the prisoners upon their march to Boston. About 40 were drowned, the rest deliverd themselves as prisoners. The two other ships which are missing were supposed to be lost there, as the Hulks appear and a 50 gun ship which came out with Biron from England has not been heard of since. Thus they have made a fine voyage of watching dEstaing, lost 3 capital ships, never saw the French Fleet, returnd into port with one Ship dismasted and the rest much damaged.

Heaven continue to be propitious to our Friends and allies for whom I have contracted a most sincere regard. If chastity, temperance, industery, frugality, sobriety and purity of morals, added to politeness and complasance can entitle any people to Friendship and respect, the Behaviour of this whole Fleet whilst they lay in this harbour which was more than two months, demand from every unprejudiced person an acknowledgment of their merrit. If I ever had any national prejudices they are done away and I am ashamed to own I was ever possessd of so narrow a spirit—and I blush to find so many of my country men possessd with such low vulgar prejudices and capable of such mean reflections as I have heard thrown out against the Nation of our allies though the unblamable conduct of this Fleet left them not one personal reflexion to cast.

Let me Imitate and instill it into my children the Liberal Spirit of that great Man who declared he had no Local attachments. It is indifferent to me say[s] he whether a man is rocked in his cradle on this Side of the Tweed, or on that, I seek for merrit whereever it is to be found. Detested be national reflexions, they are unjust.

JA to AA

My dearest Friend — Passy Decr. 2 1778

Last Night an Express from M. De Sartine, whose Politeness upon this Occasion, was very obliging, brought me your Letters of September 29 and Octr. 10.

The Joy which the Receipt of these Packets afforded me, was damped, by the disagreable Articles of Intelligence, but still more so by the Symptoms of Grief and Complaint, which appeared in the Letters. For Heavens Sake, my dear dont indulge a Thought that it is possible for me to neglect, or forget all that is dear to me in this World.

It is impossible for me to write as I did in America. What should I write? It is not safe to write any Thing, that one is not willing should go into all the Newspapers of the World.—I know not by whom to write. I never know what Conveyance is safe.—Vessells may have arrived without Letters from me. I am 500 Miles from Bourdeaux and not much less distant from Nantes. I know nothing of many Vessells that go from the Seaports, and if I knew of all there are some that I should not trust. Notwithstanding this, I have written to you, not much less I believe than fifty Letters. I am astonished that you have received no more. But almost every Vessell has been taken. Two Vessells by which I sent Goods to you for the Use of your Family and one by which I sent Mr. Cranches Things, We know have been taken, in every one of these I sent large Packetts of Letters and Papers for Congress, for you and for many Friends. God knows I dont spend my Time, in Idleness, nor in gazing at Curiosities. I never wrote more Letters, however empty they may have been. But by what I hear they have been all or nearly all taken or sunk.

My Friends complain that they have not received Letters from me. I may as well complain. I have received scarcely any Letters, from America. I have written three, where I have received one. From my Friend Mr. A. I have received only one short Card—from Mr. Gerry not a syllable—from Mr. Lovell only two or three very short.—What shall I say? I doubt not they have written oftener—but Letters miscarry. Drs. Cooper and Gordon write to Dr. F. not to me.

My Friend Warren has been good as usual, I have received several fine long Letters full of Sound sense, Usefull Intelligence and Reflexions as virtuous as wise, as usual, from him. I have answered them and written more, but whether they arrive I know not.

I approve very much of your draught upon me, in favour of your Cousin. The Moment it arrives it shall be paid. Draw for more as you may have Occasion. But make them give you Silver for your Bills.

Your Son is the Joy of my Heart, without abating in the least degree of my Affection for the young Rogue that did not seem as if he had a Father, or his Brother or sister. Tell Nabby, her Pappa likes her the better for what she tells her Brother, vizt. that she dont talk much, because I know she thinks and feels the more.—I hope the Boston has arrived—she carried many Things for you.

Last Night a Friend from England brought me the Kings Speech. Their Delirium continues, and they go on with the War, but the Speech betrays a manifest Expectation that Spain will join against them, and the Debates betray a dread of Holland. They have Reason for both.

They have not, and cannot get an Ally. They cannot send any considerable Reinforcement to America.

Your Reflections upon the Rewards of the Virtuous Friends of the public are very just. But if Virtue was to be rewarded with Wealth it would not be Virtue. If Virtue was to be rewarded with Fame, it would not be Virtue of the sublimest Kind. Who would not rather be Fabricius than Cæsar? Who would not rather be Aristides, than even W[illiam] the 3d? Who? Nobody would be of this Mind but Aristides and Fabricius.

These Characters are very rare, but the more prescious. Nature has made more Insects than Birds, more Butterflys than Eagles, more Foxes than Lyons, more Pebbles than Diamonds. The most excellent of her Productions, both in the physical, intellectual and moral World, are the most rare.—I would not be a Butterfly because Children run after them, nor because the dull Phylosophers boast of them in their Cabinets.

Have you ever read J. J. Rousseau. If not, read him—your Cousin Smith has him. What a Difference between him and Chesterfield, and even Voltaire? But he was too virtuous for the Age, and for Europe—I wish I could not say for another Country.

I am much dissappointed in not receiving Dispatches from Congress by this Opportunity. We expect Alterations in the Plan here. What will be done with me I cant conjecture. If I am recalled, I will endeavour to get a safe Opportunity, home. I will watch the proper Season and look out for a good Vessell. And if I can get safe to Penns Hill, shall never repent of my Voyage to Europe, because I have gained an Insight into several Things that I never should have understood without it.

I pray you to remember me with every Sentiment of Tenderness, Duty and Affection, to your Father and my Mother, Your and my Brothers and Sisters, Uncles, Aunts, Cousins and every Body else that you know deserves it. What shall I say too and of my dear young Friends by your Fireside, may God almighty bless them, and make them wise.

JA to AA

Passy Decr. 18 1778

This Moment I had, what shall I say? the Pleasure or the pain of your Letter of 25 of Octr. As a Letter from my dearest Freind it gave me a pleasure that it would be in vain to attempt to describe: but the Complaints in it gave me more pain than I can express—this is the third Letter I have recd. in this complaining style. the former two I have not answer'd.—I had Endeavour'd to answer them.—I have wrote several answers, but upon a review, they appear'd to be such I could not send. One was angry, another was full of Greif, and the third with Melancholy, so that I burnt them all. —if you write me in this style I shall leave of writing intirely, it kills me. Can Professions of Esteem be Wanting from me to you? Can Protestation of affection be necessary? can tokens of Remembrance be desir'd? The very Idea of this sickens me. Am I not wretched Enough, in this Banishment, without this. What Course shall I take to convince you that my Heart is warm? you doubt, it seems.—shall I declare it? shall I swear to it?—Would you doubt it the less?—And is it possible you should doubt it? I know it is not?—If I could once believe it possible, I cannot answer for the Consequences.—But I beg you would never more write to me in such a strain for it really makes me unhappy.

Be assured that no time nor place, can change my heart: but that I think so often & so much, of the Blessings from which I am seperated as to be too unmindful of those who accompany me, & that I write to you so often as my Duty will permit.

I am extremely obliged to the Comte D'Estaing and his officers for their Politeness to you, and am very Glad you have had an opportunity, of seing so much of the french Nation. The accounts from all hands agree that there was an agreable intercourse, & happy harmony upon the whole between the inhabitants and the Fleet, the more this Nation is known, & the more their Language is understood, the more narrow Prejudices will wear away. British Fleet and Armys, are very different from theirs. in Point of Temperance and Politeness there is no Comparison.

This is not a correct Copy, but you will pardon it, because it is done by an Hand as dear to you as to your John Adams

AA to JA

Sunday Evening December 27 1778

How lonely are my days? How solitary are my Nights? Secluded from all Society but my two Little Boys, and my domesticks, by the Mountains of snow which surround me I could almost fancy myself in Greenland. We have had four of the coldest Days I ever knew, and they were followed by the severest snow storm I ever remember, the wind blowing like a Hurricane for 15 or 20 hours renderd it imposible for Man or Beast to live abroad, and has blocked up the roads so that they are impassible.

A week ago I parted with my Daughter at the request of our P[lymout]h Friends to spend a month with them, so that I am solitary indeed.

Can the best of Friends recollect that for 14 years past, I have not spent a whole winter alone. Some part of the Dismal Season has heretofore been Mitigated and Softned by the Social converse and participation of the Friend of my youth.

How insupportable the Idea that 3000 leigues, and the vast ocean now devide us—but devide only our persons for the Heart of my Friend is in the Bosom of his partner. More than half a score years has so rivetted it there, that the Fabrick which contains it must crumble into Dust, e'er the particles can be seperated.

"For in one fate, our Hearts our fortunes
And our Beings blend."

I cannot discribe to you How much I was affected the other day with a Scotch song which was sung to me by a young Lady in order to divert a Melancholy hour, but it had a quite different Effect, and the Native Simplicity of it, had all the power of a well wrought Tradidy [tragedy]. When I could conquer my Sensibility I beg'd the song, and Master Charles has learnt it and consoles his Mamma by singing it to her. I will enclose it to you. It has Beauties in it to me, which an indifferent person would not feel perhaps—

His very foot has Musick in't,
As he comes up the stairs.

How oft has my Heart danced to the sound of that Musick?

And shall I see his face again?
And shall I hear him speak?

Gracious Heaven hear and answer my daily petition, "by banishing all my Grief."

I am sometimes quite discouraged from writing. So many vessels are taken, that there is Little chance of a Letters reaching your Hands. That I meet with so few returns is a circumstance that lies heavy at my Heart. If this finds its way to you, it will go by the Alliance. By her I have wrote before, she has not yet saild, and I love to amuse myself with my pen, and pour out some of the tender sentiments of a Heart over flowing with affection, not for the Eye of a cruel Enemy who no doubt would ridicule every Humane and Social Sentiment long ago grown Callous to the finer sensibilities—but for the sympathetick Heart that Beats in unison with Portias

Late in November, John Adams had heard rumors that Congress was adopting a suggestion that he himself had first made: to save money at home and wrangles among Americans abroad, the joint commission was to be dissolved and a single minister would represent the United States in France. But feelings were heating up at home over foreign policy. Angered by his treatment at the hands of Congress, Silas Deane published in December a bitter public attack on Arthur Lee and his supporters in Congress. When John Adams read it early in February, he declared "That there appeared to me no Alternative left but the Ruin of Mr. Deane, or the Ruin of his Country." He predicted accurately that it would open an irreparable division of Congress and "the States" into parties. The debate that followed and that continued through most of 1779 has been called the first chapter of national party history in the United States. The issue, which was whether the interests of America should be subordinated to the world strategy of her indispensable ally France, was to keep Adams dangling in suspense for months and to impede all his future diplomatic negotiations.

JA to AA

My dearest Friend Passy Feb 9. 1779

It is now a Year within a Day or two of my Departure from home. It is in vain for me to think of writing of what is passed.

The Character and Situation in which I am here, and the Situation of public Affairs absolutely forbid my Writing, freely.

I must be excused.—So many Vessells are taken, and there are so many Persons indiscreet, and so many others inquisitive, that I may not write. God knows how much I suffer for Want of Writing to you. It used to be a cordial to my Spirits.

Thus much I can say with perfect sincerity, that I have found nothing to disgust me, discontent me, or in any manner disturb me, in the French Nation. My Evils here arise altogether from Americans.

If I would have inlisted myself under the Banners of Either Party, I might have filled America I doubt not with Panegyricks of me, from one Party and Curses and Slanders from another. I have endeavoured to be hitherto impartial, to search for nothing but the Truth and to love nobody and nothing but the public Good, at least not more than the public Good. I have hoped that Animosities might be softened, and the still small Voice of Reason heard more, and the boisterous Roar of Passions and Prejudices less.—But the Publication of a certain Address to the People, has destroyed all such Hopes.

Nothing remains now but the fearfull Looking for of the fiery Indignation of the Monster Party, here.

My Consolation is, that the Partisans are no more than Bubbles on the Sea of Matter born—they rise—they break and to that Sea return.

The People of America, I know stand like Mount Atlass, but these Altercations occasion a great deal of Unhappiness for the present, and they prolong the War.

Those must answer for it who are guilty. I am not.

AA to JA

My Dearest Friend *Febry.* 13. 1779

This is the Anniversary of a very melancholy Day to me, it rose upon me this morning with the recollection of Scenes too tender to Name.—Your own Sensibility will supply your Memory and dictate to your pen a kind remembrance of those dear connections to whom you waved an adeiu, whilst the full Heart and weeping Eye followed your foot steps till intervening objects obstructed the Sight.

This Anniversary shall ever be more particularly Devoted to my Friend till the happy Day arrives that shall give him back to me again. Heaven grant that it may not be far distant, and that the blessings which he has so unweariedly and constantly sought after may crown his Labours and bless his country.

It is with double pleasure that I hold my pen this day to acquaint my Friend that I have had a rich feast indeed, by the Miflin privateer, which arrived here the 8th of this month and brought his Letters of 9 of Sepbr., 23 of october, 2d of November, 2d of December all together making more than I have received since your absence at one time. The Hankerchiefs in which the[y] were tied felt to me like the return of an absent Friend—tis Natural to feel an affection for every thing which belongs to those we love, and most so when the object is far—far distant from us.

You chide me for my complaints, when in reality I had so little occasion for them. I must intreat you to attribute it to the real cause—an over anxious Solicitude to hear of your welfare, and an ill grounded fear least multiplicity of publick cares, and avocations might render you less attentive to your pen than I could wish. But bury my dear Sir, in oblivion every expression of complaint—erase them from the Letters which contain them, as I have from my mind every Idea so contrary to that regard and affection you have ever manifested towards me.—Have you a coppy of your Letter December the 2d. Some diss-agreable circumstances had agitated your mind News from Rhoad Island—or what? Why was I not by to sooth my Friend to placidness—but I unhappily had contributed to it. With this consideration I read those passages, which would have been omited had the Letter been coppied.

And does my Friend think that there are no hopes of peace? Must we still endure the Desolations of war with all the direfull consequences attending it.—I fear we must and that America is less and less worthy of the blessings of peace.

Luxery that bainfull poison has unstrung and enfeabled her sons. The soft penetrating plague has insinuated itself into the freeborn mind, blasting that noble ardor, that impatient Scorn of base subjection which formerly distinguished your Native Land, and the Benevolent wish of general good is swallowed up by a Narrow selfish Spirit, by a spirit of oppression and extortion.

Nourished and supported by the flood of paper which has nearly overwhelmed us, and which depreciates in proportion to the exertions to save it, and tho so necessary to us is of less value than any commodity whatever, yet the demand for it is beyond conception, and those to whom great sums of it have fallen, or been acquired, vest it in Luxurys, dissapate it in Extravagance, realize it at any rate. But I hope the time is not far distant when we shall in some measure be extricated from our present difficulties and a more virtuous spirit succeed the unfealing dissapation which at present prevails, And America shine with virtuous citizens as much as she now deplores her degenerate sons.

Enclosed you will find a Letter wrote at your request, and if rewarded by your approbation it will abundantly gratify your

Portia

The "Marquiss" in the following letter was Lafayette, who had sailed for France from Boston in January bearing, among other things, new instructions from Congress to Franklin, now appointed sole minister. The British "Proclamation" mentioned was circulated in America by the Carlisle conciliatory commission, whose purpose had been to offset the effects of the capitulation at Saratoga. It had failed completely.

JA to AA

My dearest Friend — Passy Feb. 13 1779

Yours of 15 Decr. was sent me Yesterday by the Marquiss whose Praises are celebrated in all the Letters from America. You must be content to receive a short Letter, because I have not Time now to write a long one.—I have lost many of your Letters, which are invaluable to me, and you have lost a vast Number of mine. Barns, Niles, and many other Vessells are lost.

I have received Intelligence much more agreable, than that of a removal to Holland, I mean that of being reduced to a private Citizen which gives me more Pleasure, than you can imagine. I shall therefore soon present before you, your own good Man. Happy—happy indeed shall I be, once more to see our Fireside.

I have written before to Mrs. Warren and shall write again now.

Dr. J. is transcribing your scotch song, which is a charming one. Oh my leaping Heart.

I must not write a Word to you about Politicks, because you are a Woman.

What an offence have I committed?—a Woman!

I shall soon make it up. I think Women better than Men in General, and I know that you can keep a Secret as well as any Man whatever. But the World dont know this. Therefore if I were to write any Secrets to you and the letter should be caught, and hitched into a Newspaper, the World would say, I was not to be trusted with a Secret.

I never had so much Trouble in my Life, as here, yet I grow fat. The Climate and soil agree with me—so do the Cookery and even the Manners of the People, of those of them at least that I converse with, Churlish Republican, as some of you, on your side the Water call me. The English have got at me in their News Papers. They make fine Work of me—fanatic—Bigot—perfect Cypher—not one Word of the Language—aukward Figure—uncouth dress—no Address—No Character—cunning hard headed Attorney. But the falsest of it all is, that I am disgusted with the Parisians—Whereas I declare I admire the Parisians prodigiously. They are the happiest People in the World, I believe, and have the best Disposition to make others so.

If I had your Ladyship and our little folks here, and no Politicks to plague me and an hundred Thousand Livres a Year Rent, I should be the happiest Being on Earth—nay I believe I could make it do with twenty Thousand.

One word of Politicks—The English reproach the French with Gasconade, but I dont believe their whole History could produce so much of it as the English have practised this War.

The Commissioners Proclamation, with its sanction from the Ministry and Ratification by both Houses, I suppose is hereafter to be interpreted like Burgoines—Speaking Daggers, but using none. They cannot send any considerable Reinforcement, nor get an Ally in Europe—this I think you may depend upon. Their Artifice in throwing out such extravagant Threats, was so gross, that I presume it has not imposed on any. Yet a Nation that regarded its Character never could have threatned in that manner.

Adieu.

News that he had been "reduced to a private Citizen" did not seem all that "agreable" to John Adams as he reflected on it. On the one hand, he was ostensibly free to return to his own fireside. On the other, Congress might have some other European mission in mind for him. But Congress appeared to ignore him, and as the weeks and months of early 1779 went by he felt he had been "left kicking and sprawling in the Mire." Mocking both himself and Abigail, Adams in late February wrote his wife a series of sightseeing letters. Then, on March 3, he took formal leave of the French ministry, and on the eighth set out with John Quincy for Nantes, expecting to sail promptly for home on the new American frigate *Alliance*.

JA to AA

My dear Passy Feb. 21. 1779

Yours by Mr. Williams have received. The little Bill must be paid, but I confess it allarms me a little. The Expence of my Son here is greater than I ever imagined. Altho his Company is almost all the Pleasure I have, in Life, yet I should not have brought him, if I had known the Expence. His Expences, together with what you have drawn for, and a little Collection of Books I have bought, will amount to more than will ever be allowed me. My Accounts must not be drawn into Intricacy nor Obscurity. I must not be involved in Suspicions of medling in Trade, nor any Thing else but my proper Business.

You complain that I dont write often enough, and that when I do, my Letters are too short. If I were to tell you all the Tenderness of my Heart, I should do nothing but write to you. I beg of you not to be uneasy. I write you as often and as much as I ought.

If I had an Heart at Ease and Leisure enough, I could write you, several sheets a day, of the Curiosities of this Country. But it is as much impossible for me to think of such subjects as to work Miracles.

Let me entreat you to consider, if some of your Letters had by any Accident been taken, what a figure would they have made in a Newspaper to be read by the whole World. Some of them it is true would have done Honour to the most virtuous and most accomplished Roman Matron: but others of them, would have made you and me, very ridiculous.

In one of yours you hint that I am to go to Holland. But I think you must be misinformed. By all that I can learn, some Gentlemen intend to vote for me to H[olland] vs. Mr. D[eane], others to Spain vs. Mr. Lee. Neither I think will succeed, and therefore I think I have but one Course to steer, and that is homewards. But I can determine nothing absolutely. I must govern myself, according to the Intelligence, which may hereafter arise, the orders of Congress, and the best Judgment I can form of my own Duty and the Public Good.

I am advised to take a ride to Geneva, or to Amsterdam: and I have been so confined from Exercise, having never been farther from Paris than Versailles since my arrival here, that some such Excursion seems necessary for my Health, yet I cannot well bear the Thought of putting the public to an Expence merely for the Sake of my Pleasure, Health or Convenience.

Yet my situation here is painfull. I never was in such a situation before as I am now, and my present Feelings are new to me. If I should return, and in my Absence, any orders should arrive here for me to execute, in that Case nobody would be here to execute them, and they might possibly fail of success for Want of Somebody with

Power to perform them. At least this may be suspected and said and believed.—However, upon the whole, as Congress have said nothing to me good or bad, I have no right to presume that they mean to say any Thing and therefore, on the whole it is my duty to return, by the first good Opportunity, unless I should receive counter orders, before that occurs.

If ever the Time should occur, when I could have a little Leisure and a quiet Mind, I could entertain you with Accounts of Things, which would amuse you and your Children. There are an Infinity of Curiosities here, but so far from having Leisure to describe them I have found none even to see them, except a very few.

The Clymate here is charming. The Weather is every day, pleasant as the Month of May—soft mild Air,—some foggy days, and about 10 or twelve days in January, were cold and icy. But we have had scarce 3 Inches of snow the whole Winter. The Climate is more favourable to my Constitution than ours. The Cookery, and manner of living here, which you know, Americans were taught by their former absurd Masters to dislike is more agreable to me, than you can imagine. The Manners of the People have an Affection in them that is very amiable. Their is such a Choice of elegant Entertainments in the theatric Way, of good Company and excellent Books, that nothing would be wanting to me in this Country, but my family and Peace to my Country, to make me, one of the happyest of Men.—John Bull would growl and bellow at this Description—let him bellow if he will, for he is but a Brute.

JA to AA Feb. 26. 1779

I have this day taken a long Ramble, with my son. The Weather is as delightfull as you can imagine. There is not in the Month of May, a softer Air, a warmer sun, or a more delicious Appearance of Things about Boston.

We walked all over the Gardens of the Royal Castle of Muet, at Passy. The Gardens are very spacious, on one Quarter looking to Mount Calvare, on another to the famous Castle of Madrid, built by Francis the 1st, whose History you will see in Robertson, C[harles] 5., on another looking over the Plain de sablon, or sandy Plain to the Gate of Maillot.—The Rowes of Trees, and gravel Walks are very pretty, and the orangerie are very grand. But the whole is much neglected—the Trees are all mossy, and have a distempered Look.

We then walked in the Bois du Boulogne, rambling about in by Paths, a long Time, till we came to a Gate which We presumed to open and found ourselves in a noble Garden, the salads green and flourishing ready for the Table, long Rows of Wall Fruits, Trees of every species, Apples, Peaches, Appricots, Plumbs &c. and next to the Garden a fine extensive Farm, the Fields and Pastures already shining with Verdure. Upon Enquiry of the Gardiners I was told it belonged to Madame Le Comtess de Boufleure. We passed by the Castle, after having viewed all the Farm and Gardens, into the street of Auteuil, the Village where Boileau was born, lived and died – it is the next Village to Passy. We then walked through the fields along the Castle and Seignoury of Passy which belongs to the Comte De Boulainvilliers and returned home, much pleased with our Walk and better for the Air and Exercise.

Now Madam dont you think I have spent my Time very wisely in writing all this important History to your Ladyship. Would it not have been as well spent in conjugating two or three french Verbs, which I could have done through all the Moods, Tenses and Persons, of the Active and passive Voice in this Time.

We expect the Honour of Mr. Turgot, the famous Financier, as well as learned and virtuous Man, to dine with Us. And if there should be some Ladies, at the feast, it will not be at my Invitation and therefore you need not be uneasy.

Suppose I should undertake to write the Description of every Castle and Garden I see as Richardson did in his Tour through Great Britain, would not you blush at such a Waste of my time.

Suppose I should describe the Persons and Manners of all the Company I see, and the fashions, the Plays, the Games, the sports, the spectacles, the Churches and religious Ceremonies—and all that—should not you think me turned fool in my old Age—have I not other Things to do of more importance?

Let me alone, and have my own Way. You know that I shall not injure you and you ought to believe that I have good Reasons, for what I do, and not treat me so roughly, as you have done.

Adieu.

JA to AA

Feb. 28. 1779

I suppose I must write every day, in order to keep or rather to restore good Humour, whether I have any thing to say or not.

The Scaffold is cutt away, and I am left kicking and sprawling in the Mire, I think. It is hardly a state of Disgrace that I am in but rather of total Neglect and Contempt. The humane People about me, feel for my situation they say: But I feel for my Countrys situation. If I had deserved such Treatment, I should have deserved to be told so at least, and then I should have known my Duty.

After sending orders to me at five hundred Miles distance which I neither solicited, nor expected nor desired, to go to Europe through the Gulf Stream, through Thunder and Lightning, through three successive storms, and three successive Squadrons of British Men of War, if I had committed any Crime which deserved to hang me up in a Gibet in the Face of all Europe, I think I ought to have been told what it was—or if I had proved myself totally insignificant, I think I ought to have been called away at least from a Place, where I might remain a Monument of the Want of Discernment in sending me here.

I have given Notice here and written to Congress, of my Intentions to return, by the first good Opportunity, unless I should receive other orders before my Embarkation, orders that I can execute with Honour and some Prospect of Advantage to the Public.—You know probably before now what orders if any are sent me. If none or such as I cannot observe you may expect to see me in June or July. If otherwise I know not when.

In the first letter he had written to Abigail in more than two months, John Adams did not begin to recite all the "Embarrassements and Disappointments" he had met with in the ports of western France. There were to be still more before he and his son finally sailed from Lorient aboard His Most Christian Majesty's frigate *La Sensible* on June 17. They reached Boston Harbor on August 2.

JA to AA

My dearest Friend — L'orient May 14. 1779

When I left Paris, the 8 March, I expected to have been at Home before this Day and have done my Utmost to get to sea, but the Embarrassements and Disappointments I have met with, have been many, very many. I have however in the Course of them had a fine Opportunity of seeing Nantes, L'orient and Brest, as well as the intermediate Country.

By the gracious Invitation of the King, I am now to take Passage in his Frigate the Sensible, with his new Ambassador to America the Chevalier De la Luzerne.

I hope to see you in six or seven Weeks. Never was any Man in such a state of Uncertainty and suspense as I have been from last October, entirely uninformed of the Intentions of Congress concerning me.

This would not have been very painfull to me if I could have got home, for Your Conversation is a Compensation to me, for all other Things.

My Son has had a great Opportunity to see this Country: but this has unavoidably retarded his Education in some other Things.

He has enjoyed perfect Health from first to last and is respected wherever he goes for his Vigour and Vivacity both of Mind and Body, for his constant good Humour and for his rapid Progress in French, as well as his general Knowledge which for his Age is uncommon.—I long to see his Sister and Brothers—I need not Add—

JA to AA

My dearest Friend L'Orient June 14. 1779

I have been often disappointed, and therefore cannot be perfectly sure now: but my Baggage is all on Board a Frigate of the Kings, and I am to take Passage in her, with the Chevalier de la Luzerne the new Ambassador to the united States, and Monsieur Marbois, the Secretary to the Commission, two Gentlemen of the most amiable Characters. Their will be Eighteen or twenty Persons in their Train. We expect to go to Boston, but may possibly go to Philadelphia.

I ought not to give you an History of my Adventures for Four Months past, untill I see you. This goes by another Vessell: but I hope you will see me before it.

The French Fleet is out from Brest, and the French look up now with a good Countenance.—England is torn with Distractions, and Spain is expected soon to declare. Holland and the Northern Powers have made Declarations which sufficiently indicate their Determination, which is favourable to Us. Britannia, in short must soon hearken to Reason.

My dear Fellow Traveller is very well, and is the Comfort of my Life. He is much caressed, wherever he goes.—Remember me to the rest. What can I say more? No Words, no Actions can express the Ardour of Affection with which I am theirs & yours.

John Adams

Not one Line from America since yours by the Alliance, nor any from Congress since October or the Beg[inning] of Novr.—a Pause that has consumed a great deal of my Patience, but I have Bags and Boxes of it yet left, in Abundance.

At home, John Adams put his papers in order. In the time-honored style of retiring diplomats, he formally reported to the President of Congress his views on the status and policies of the European powers, especially as they affected American interests. He also compiled his accounts for submission to Congress, but was interrupted by his election to represent Braintree in a convention to prepare a constitution for Massachusetts. The

Convention began its sittings on the first day of September, and Adams soon found himself chosen "a Sub Sub Committee" of one to draft what became, after ratification by the people in 1780, a new frame of government. Still in force today as the organic law of the Commonwealth, it proved to be Adams' most enduring, or at any rate his most visible, legacy as a statesman.

He was deep in this congenial labor when he learned that after "a great deal of disagreeable altercation and debate" Congress had finally made a new arrangement of its foreign service, and that he had been elected sole minister plenipotentiary to negotiate treaties of peace and commerce with Great Britain. Although the French government and its representatives in Philadelphia would have much preferred the accommodating Franklin to the unbending Adams, the amenities were observed, and *La Sensible*, still lying in Boston Harbor, was made ready to convey the new minister to France in proper style. He had been at home little more than three months.

Once again, Adams found the challenges presented by public service irresistible. According to his code, the highest duty entailed the greatest labor, difficulties, and privation. The fewer the chances of success, the higher the honor of the enterprise. His wife would not have dreamt of questioning his decision, for she subscribed to the same stern code.

This time Adams took, along with John Quincy, his second son, Charles, who at nine and a half was three years younger. In the party also were Francis Dana as secretary of legation and young John Thaxter as private secretary to the minister and tutor to the boys. Their voyage nearly ended in disaster before the leaky *Sensible* crept into port at the northwestern tip of Spain with "seven feet of Water in her Hold." Adams now faced the unpleasant alternatives of an indefinite wait for a vessel sailing to a French port or a winter's journey across northern Spain and over the Pyrenees. He chose the latter but many times in the course of the trip regretted the ordeal the choice imposed on them all. The travelers finally reached Paris on February 9.

JA to AA

My dearest Friend — Boston Novr. 13. 1779

I have just sent Mr. Thaxter, Johnny and Stephens with the Things on Board. I shall go with Charles at four O Clock. It is now three. Have seen the Captain, and the Navy Board &c.

It is proposed to sail tomorrow. Perhaps however, it may not be till next day. Mr. Dana will come on board at Nine tomorrow.

Mr. Hancock has sent me a Card, to invite me to go on board with him in the Castle Barge.—Dont make many Words of this.

Your Aunt has given me a Barrell of Cramberries. I shall make a good Use of them, I hope.

Let me intreat you, to keep up your Spirits and throw off Cares as much as possible. Love to Nabby and Thommy. We shall yet be happy, I hope and pray, and I dont doubt it. I shall have Vexations enough, as usual. You will have Anxiety and Tenderness enough as usual. Pray strive, not to have too much. I will write, by every Opportunity I can get.

Yours, ever, ever yours, John Adams

AA to JA

Dearest of Friends November 14 1779

My habitation, how disconsolate it looks! My table I set down to it but cannot swallow my food. O Why was I born with so much Sensibility and why possessing it have I so often been call'd to struggle with it? I wish to see you again, was I sure you would not be gone, I could not withstand the temptation of comeing to town, tho my Heart would suffer over again the cruel torture of Seperation.

What a cordial to my dejected Spirits were the few lines last night received. And does your Heart forebode that we shall again be happy. My hopes and fears rise alternately. I cannot resign more than I do, unless life itself was called for.—My dear sons I can not think of them without a tear, little do they know the feelings of a Mothers Heart! May they be good and usefull as their Father then will they in some measure reward the anxiety of a Mother. My tenderest Love to them. Remember me also to Mr. Thaxter whose civilities and kindness I shall miss.

God almighty bless and protect my dearest Friend and in his own time restore him to the affectionate Bosom of Portia

JA to AA

My dearest Friend Ferrol December 11th. 1779

We have had an Escape again: but are arrived safely in Spain. As the Frigate will probably not get from this place these two Months, I must go by Land to Paris, which I suppose is a Journey of between three and four hundred Leagues. That part of it, which is in Spain is very mountainous. No Post—bad Roads—bad Taverns and very dear. We must ride Mules, Horses not being to be had. I must get some kind of Carriage for the Children, if possible. They are very well. Charles has sustained the Voyage and behaves as well as ever his Brother did. He is much pleased with what he sees. Sammy Cooper too is very well. These young Gentry will give me a vast deal of Trouble, in this unexpected Journey. I have bought a Dictionary and Grammar and they are learning the Spanish Language as fast as possible. What could We do, if You and all the family had been with me?

Ferrol is a magnificent Port and Harbour. It is fortified by Nature, by Rows of lofty rocky Mountains on each Side the narrow Entrance of it, and the public Works, the Fortifications, Barracks, Arsenals &c. which are of Stone very like Braintree Stone, exceed any thing I have seen.

I dined the day before Yesterday with Don Joseph Saint Vincent, the Lieutenant General of the Marine, who is the Commandant in this Port, with four and twenty French and Spanish Officers. The Difference between Gravity and Gaiety was an amusing Speculation.

Yesterday I dined on Board the Triumphant, an Eighty Gun French Ship commanded by the Chef D'Escadre Mr. Sade, and have engagements for every day for a much longer Time than I shall stay.

The French Consul and Vice Consul have been particularly polite and obliging to me. In short I never was better pleased with a Reception at any place.

There is no News. Nothing has been done in Europe. England is as insolent in Language as ever, but this is only ridiculous as it is apparently impotent. My Love to Nabby and Tommy. Adieu.

John Adams

John Adams to Abigail Adams 2d

My dear Daughter — Ferrol Decr. 12. 1779

If I could send you some of the Lemons, Oranges, or Water Melons of this Place, it would give me more Pleasure than you. But there are very seldom merchant Vessells at this Place from America.

We are here in the Latitude of 43, which is better than half a degree farther north than Boston, yet there has not yet been the slightest frost. The Verdure on the Fields and in the Gardens is as fresh as ever. We see large Quantities of Indian Corn, hanging up in Bunches of Ears, about the higher Parts of the Houses, which shews Us that that Species of Grain grows and is cultivated here, altho the Ears and the Kernel is much smaller than with Us.

I have much Curiosity to see Madrid and a strong Inclination to go that Way: but it is a great Way farther and I have some doubts for several other Reasons whether I ought to go there. But I shall go through Bilboa from whence I shall again write to you if I can.

I have met with few Things more remarkable than the Chocolate which is the finest I ever saw. I will enquire whether it is the Superiour Quality of the Cocoa Nut, or any other Ingredient which they intermix with it, or a better Art of making it, which renders it so much superiour to any other.

I see very little, which would be entertaining to a young Lady of your Turn of thinking, in this Place, which seems to be wholly devoted to military Affairs. There is what they call, an Italien Opera: but neither the Theaters, nor the Actors, nor the Pieces, nor the Musick are very pleasing. I have been once there, but not understanding the Italien Language, and seeing very little Company, and scarcely any Ladies who are always to me the most pleasing ornaments of such Spectacles, I don't think it worth while for me to go again: but the Gentlemen, and your Brothers with them are about going this Evening. They may possibly learn a little of the Spanish Language, as the Piece tonight is to be in that Tongue.

In the Course of my Journeys, I shall embrace any Moments of Leisure, to inform you of any Thing that I observe which may contribute to your Improvement or Entertainment: But you must remember that my Voyages and Journeys are not for my private Information, Instruction, Improvement, Entertainment or Pleasure; but laborious and hazardous Enterprizes of Business. I shall never be much polished, by Travel, whatever your Brothers may be. I hope they will be improved. I hope they will increase in Knowledge as they go: but I am not anxious about their being very much polished.

Gold is very little more prescious for being burnished. Silver and Steel are as usefull without polishing as with it.

I dont mean by this however to suggest, that Arts and Accomplishments which are merely ornamental, should be wholly avoided or neglected especially by your Sex: but that they ought to be slighted when in Comparison or Competition, with those which are useful and essential.

I hope your Attention will be fixed chiefly upon those Virtues and Accomplishments, which contribute the most to qualify Women to act their Parts well in the various Relations of Life, those of Daughter, Sister, Wife, Mother, Friend.—Yours Affectionately,

John Adams

JA to AA

My dearest Friend — Corunna December 16. 1779

Last night We all arrived in this Place from Ferrol. The Distance is about twenty miles by Land over high Mountains and bad Roads. You would have been diverted to have seen Us all mounted upon our Mules and marching in Train. From the Mountains We had all along the Prospect of a rich fertile Country, cultivated up to the Tops of the highest Hills and down to the very edge of Water all along the shore.

I made my Visits last night to the Governor of the Province, who resides here and to the Governor of the Town, and was politely received by both. I have a long Journey before me of a thousand miles I suppose at least to Paris. Through this Kingdom We shall have bad roads and worse Accommodations, I dont expect to be able to get to Paris in less than thirty days. I shall have an Opportunity of seeing Spain, but it will be at a great Expence. I am advised by every Body to go by Land. The Frigate the Sensible is in so bad Condition as to make it probable she will not be fit to put to Sea in less than three or four Weeks perhaps five or six, and then We should have the storms and Enemies of the Bay of Biscay, to escape, or encounter.

After this wandering Way of Life is passed I hope to return, to my best friend and pass the Remainder of our Days in Quiet.

I cannot learn that G[reat] B[ritain] is yet in Temper to listen to Propositions of Peace, and I dont expect before another Winter to have much to do in my present Capacity.

My tenderest affection to our dear Children, and believe me, ever yours,

John Adams

From John Adams' Diary

1779. DECR. 28. TUESDAY.

Went from Castillan to Baamonde. The first Part of the Road, very bad, the latter Part tolerable.

The whole Country We have passed, is very mountainous and rocky. There is here and there a Vally, and here and there a Farm that looks beautifully cultivated. But in general the Mountains are covered with Furze, and are not well cultivated. I am astonished to see so few Trees. Scarce an Elm, Oak, or any other Tree to be seen. A very few Walnut Trees, and a very few fruit Trees.

At Baamonde, We stop untill Tomorrow to get a new Axletree to one of our Calashes.

The House where We now are is better, than our last nights Lodgings. We have a Chamber, for seven of Us to lodge in. We shall lay our Beds upon Tables, Seats and Chairs, or the floor as last night. We have no Smoke and less dirt, but the floor was never washed I believe. The Kitchen and Stable are below as usual, but in better order. The Fire in the Middle of the Kitchen, but the Air holes pierced thro the Tiles of the Roof draw up the smoke, so that one may set at the fire without Inconvenience. The Mules, Hogs, fowls, and human Inhabitants live however all together below, and Cleanliness seems never to be tho't of.—Our Calashes and Mules are worth describing. We have three Calashes in Company. In one of them I ride with my two Children John and Charles. In another goes Mr. Dana and Mr. Thaxter.

In a third Mr. Allen and Sam. Cooper Johonnot. Our three servants ride on Mules. Sometimes the Gentlemen mount the servants mules—sometimes the Children—sometimes all walk.

The Calashes are like those in Use in Boston fifty Years ago. There is finery about them in Brass nails and Paint, but the Leather is very old and never felt Oil, since it was made. The Tackling is broken and tied with twine and Cords &c. but these merit a more particular Description. The Furniture of the Mules is equally curious. This Country is an hundred Years behind the Massachusetts Bay, in the Repair of Roads and in all Conveniences for travelling.

The natural Description of a Mule may be spared. Their Ears are shorn close to the skin, so are their Necks, Backs, Rumps and Tails at least half Way to the End. They are lean, but very strong and sure footed, and seem to be well shod. The Saddles have large Ears, and large Rims or Ridges round behind. They have a Breast Plate before, and a Breech Band behind. They have large Wooden Stirrips made like Boxes in a semicircular Form, close at one End, open at the other, in which you insert your foot, which is well defended by them against rain and Sloughs. The wooden Boxes are bound round with Iron.

We have magnificent Curb Bridles to two or three. The rest are guided by Halters. And there is an Halter as well as a Curb Bridle to each of the others.

There are Walletts, or Saddle bags, on each made with Canvas, in which We carry Bread and Cheese, Meat, Knives and forks, Spoons, Apples and Nutts.

6 [JANUARY 1780] THURSDAY.

Went to view the Cathedral Church which is magnificent, but not equal to that at Astorga if to that at Lugo. It was the day of the Feast of the King, and We happened to be at the Celebration of high Mass. We saw the Procession, of the Bishop and of all the Canons, in rich Habits of Silk, Velvet, Silver and Gold. The Bishop, as he turned the Corners of the Church, spread out his Hand to the People, who all prostrated themselves on their Knees as he passed. Our Guide told Us, We must do the same, but I contented myself with a Bow.

Went to see the Council Chamber of the Bishop and Chapter—hung with crimson Damask, the Seats all round crimson Velvet. This Room and a smaller, where the Bishop sometimes took aside some of the Cannons, were very elegant.

Saw the Casa del Ciudad, and the old Castle of King Alphonsus, which is said to be 1936 Years old. It is of Stone, and the Work very neat.

But there is no Appearance of Commerce, Manufactures or Industry. The Houses are low, built of brick and Mud and Pebble stones from the fields. No Market worth notice. Nothing looks either rich or chearfull but the Churches and Churchmen. There is a Statue of Charles 5 in this Church, but very badly done.

There is a School of Saint Mark here as it is called, an Institution for the Education of noble Youths here in Mathematicks and Philosophy.

Dined in Leon, got into our Carriages and upon our Mules about one O Clock, to proceed on our Journey, passed the new Bridge of Leon, which is a beautiful new Piece of Work. It is all of Stone. The River, which comes down from the Mountains of Asturias, is not now very large, but in the Spring when the Snows melt upon the Mountains it is swelled by the freshes to a very great Size. This River also runs down into the Kingdom of Portugal. Not long after We passed another Bridge and River, which the Peasants told me to call Rio y Puente de Biliarente. This River also comes down from the Asturias and flows down into Portugal. We passed thro several, very little Villages, in every one of which We saw the young People Men and Women dancing, a Dance that they call Fandango. One of the young Women beats a Machine, somewhat like a section of a Drum. It is covered with Parchment. She sings and beats on her drum, and the Company dance, with Each a Pair of Clackers in his and her Hand. The Clackers are two Pieces of Wood, cut handsomely enough, which they have the Art to rattle in their Hands to the Time of the Drum. They had all, Males and Females, wooden shoes, in the Spanish fashion, which is mounted on stilts. We stopped once to look and a Man came out with a Bottle of Wine and a glass to treat Us. We drank his Wine in Complaisance to his Urbanity, tho it was very Sour, and I ordered our Guide to give him somewhat.

JA to AA

My dearest Friend — Bilbao January 16. 1780

We arrived here, last night, all alive, but all very near sick with violent Colds taken on the Road for Want of comfortable Accommodations.

I was advised, on all Hands to come by Land rather than wait an uncertain Time for a passage by sea. But if I had known the Difficulties of travelling, in that part of Spain which I have passed through I think I should not have ventured upon the Journey.

It is vain to attempt a Description of our Passage. Through the Province of Gallicia, and again when We came to that of Biscay, We had an uninterupted succession of Mountains; thro that of Leon and the old Castile, constant Plains. A Country, tolerably good, by Nature, but not well cultivated.

Through the whole of the Journey the Taverns were inconvenient to Us, because there are no Chimneys in their Houses and We had cold Weather. A great Part of the Way, the Wretchedness of our Accommodation exceeds all Description.

At Bilbao, We fare very well, and have received much Civility from Mr. Gardoqui and sons as We did at Ferrol and Corunna from Mr. Detournelle and Mr. Lagoanere.

I wish I could send you, some few Things for the Use of the Family from hence, but the Risque is such that I believe, I had better wait untill We get to France.

I have undergone the greatest Anxiety for the Children, thro a tedious Journey and Voyage. I hope their Travels will be of Service to them, but those at home are best off. My Love to them.

Adieu, Adieu, John Adams

AA to JA

My Dearest Friend Janry. 18 1780

It is now a little more than two months since you left me. I have many hopes that you had a prosperous voyage and that you were some weeks ago safely landed in France.

I have been so happy as to hear from you twice upon your passage. Capt. Carr arrived safe and carefully deliverd your Letters. You left this coast in the best time that could have been chosen. Winter set in with all its horrors in a week after you saild, and has continued with all its rigours ever since. Such mountains of snow have not been known for 60 years. No passing for this fortnight, only for foot travellers, [and] no prospect of any as one Storm succeeds another so soon that the roads are filld before a path can be made.

I hope you are in a climate more Friendly to Health and more condusive of pleasure than the unsocial Gloom and chill which presents itself to my view.

The Blocade of the roads has been a sad hinderance to the meeting of the convention, a few only of the near Members could get together, so few that they were obliged to adjourn. Many of them mourn the absence of one whom water, not snow seperates from them. They are pleased to say that he was more attended to than any other member, and had more weight and influence upon the minds of the convention.

This Town have received an invitation to elect an other member in the room of your *Excellency*, but do not appear to consider the importance of it, since the fear of expence overpowers every other consideration. Indeed their is but one person who could do them any Essential Service were they to elect a member and they might consider his being their representitive as an objection, tho that rule has been broken over in many places.

It is a pitty that so noble a structure should undergo such a mutilation as to make it limp and totter all the rest of its life, yet I fear this will be its fate. Enclosed to you are the journals and News papers which Mr. Lovell has forwarded to me with directions to enclose them to you. Generall Warren has just acquainted me that a packquet will sail for Spain in a day or two, that Mr. Austin goes in her in a publick character with dispatches for you, and that you may have the opportunity of conveying whatever you please in a State Frigate.

You will learn from Mr. Austin the state of our currency and the rate of exchange which renders it needless for me to say any thing upon the subject.

John Paul Jones is at present the subject of conversation and admiration. I wish to know the History of this adventurous Hero, his Letter to Lady Selkirk fixed him in my memory.

I need not add how much I wish to hear of your safety and happiness, as well as the success of your Embassy. Of the latter I can form no very flattering expectation at present.

Present my respectfull complements to Mr. Dana. The inclement Season has prevented all communication between his good Lady and your Portia, but when ever the Season will permit shall not fail visiting a sister in seperation, and hope by that time to rejoice with her in the assurance of the safety and happiness of our partners.

Believe me dear sir with the tenderest sentiments of regard affectionately yours.

Abigail Adams to John Quincy Adams

My dear Son — Janry. 19 1780

I hope you have had no occasion either from Enemies or the Dangers of the Sea to repent your second voyage to France. If I had thought your reluctance arose from proper deliberation, or that you was capable of judgeing what was most for your own benifit, I should not have urged you to have accompanied your Father and Brother when you appeared so averse to the voyage.

You however readily submitted to my advice, and I hope will never have occasion yourself, nor give me reason to Lament it. Your knowledge of the Language must give you greater advantages now, than you could possibly have reaped whilst Ignorant of it, and as you increase in years you will find your understanding opening and daily improveing.

Some Author that I have met with compares a judicious traveller, to a river that increases its stream the farther it flows from its source, or to certain springs which running through rich veins of minerals improve their qualities as they pass along. It will be expected of you my son that as you are favourd with superiour advantages under the instructive Eye of a tender parent, that your improvements should bear some proportion to your advantages. Nothing is wanting with you, but attention, dilligence and steady application, Nature has not been deficient.

These are times in which a Genious would wish to live. It is not in the still calm of life, or the repose of a pacific station, that great characters are formed. Would Cicero have shone so distinguished an orater, if he had not been roused, kindled and enflamed by the Tyranny of Catiline, Millo, Verres and Mark Anthony. The Habits of a vigorous mind are formed in contending with difficulties. All History will convince you of this, and that wisdom and penetration are the fruits of experience, not the Lessons of retirement and leisure.

Great necessities call out great virtues. When a mind is raised, and animated by scenes that engage the Heart, then those qualities which would otherways lay dormant, wake into Life, and form the Character of the Hero and the Statesman.

War, Tyrrany and Desolation are the Scourges of the Almighty, and ought no doubt to be deprecated. Yet it is your Lot my Son to be an Eye witness of these Calimities in your own Native land, and at the same time to owe your existance among a people who have made a glorious defence of their invaded Liberties, and who, aided by a generous and powerfull Ally, with the blessing of heaven will transmit this inheritance to ages yet unborn.

Nor ought it to be one of the least of your excitements towards exerting every power and faculty of your mind, that you have a parent who has taken so large and active a share in this contest, and discharged the trust reposed in him with so much satisfaction as to be honourd with the important Embassy, which at present calls him abroad.

I cannot fulfill the whole of my duty towards you, if I close this Letter, without reminding you of a failing which calls for a strict attention and watchfull care to correct. You must do it for yourself. You must curb that impetuosity of temper, for which I have frequently chid you, but which properly directed may be productive of great good.

VERGENNES, FRENCH MINISTER OF FOREIGN AFFAIRS

I know you capable of these exertions, with pleasure I observed my advice was not lost upon you. If you indulge yourself in the practise of any foible or vice in youth, it will gain strength with your years and become your conquerer.

The strict and invoilable regard you have ever paid to truth, gives me pleasing hopes that you will not swerve from her dictates, but add justice, fortitude, and every Manly Virtue which can adorn a good citizen, do Honour to your Country, and render your parents supreemly happy, particuliarly your ever affectionate Mother,

AA

Adams had seen as much as he wanted, or more, of Franklin's household at Passy during his earlier tour of duty in France. Besides, his peace mission was designedly separate from Franklin's continuing role as American minister to the Court of Versailles. So the Adamses stayed in a Paris hotel. The boys were placed in M. Pechigny's school; their father kept close track of their studies and sometimes took them sightseeing. Adams' letters show a continuously sharp conflict in his mind between the appeal of the elegant arts of Europe and his conviction that, as the product of a luxury-loving and corrupt society, they should not be cultivated in America. If they were, he was convinced, his country would not long remain a free and virtuous republic.

The aims of his mission were blunted from the start by the unwillingness of the Comte de Vergennes, the French foreign minister, to make it officially known. Adams remained patient for some time, but he refused to be ignored indefinitely. He entered into correspondence with the foreign minister on other matters as well, but what he had to say was soon found distasteful.

JA to AA

My dear Portia [*Paris, April–May 1780*]

Yesterday We went to see the Garden of the King, Jardin du Roi, and his Cabinet of natural History, Cabinet d'Histoire naturell.

The Cabinet of natural History is a great Collection, of Metals, Mineral[s], shells, Insects, Birds, Beasts, Fishes, and presscious stones. They are arranged in good order, and preserved in good condition, with the name of every thing beautifully written on a piece of paper annexed to it. There is also a Collection of Woods and marbles.

The garden is large and airy, affording fine Walks between Rows of Trees. Here is a Collection from all Parts of the World, of all the plants, Roots and Vegetables that are used in medicine, and indeed of all the Plants and trees in the World.

A fine Scæne for the studious youth in Physick or Philosophy. It was a public day. There was a great deal of Company, and I had opportunity only to take a cursory view. The whole is very curious. There is an handsome statue of Mr. Buffon, the great natural Historian whose Works you have, whose labours have given fame to this Cabinet and Garden. When shall We have in America, such Collections? The Collection of American Curiosities that I saw at Norwalk in Connecticutt made by Mr. Arnold, which he afterwards to my great mortification sold to Gov. Tryon, convinces me, that our Country affords as ample materials, for Collections of this nature as any part of the World.

Five midshipmen of the Alliance, came here last night, Marston, Hogan, Fitzgerald and two others, from Norway, where they were sent with Prizes, which the Court of Denmark were absurd and unjust enough, to restore to the English. They however treated the Officers and People well, and defrayed their Expences. They say the Norwegians were very angry, with the Court of Copenhagen, for delivering up these Vessells. It was the Blunder of Ignorance, I believe, rather than any ill Will.

Every day when I ride out, without any particular Business to do, or Visit to make, I order my servant to carry me to some place where I never was before, so that at last I believe I have seen all Paris, and all the fields and scenes about it, that are near it. It is very pleasant.

Charles is as well beloved here as at home. Wherever he goes, every body loves him. Mr. D[ana] is as fond of him, I think as I am. He learns very well.

There is a Volume in folio just published here, which I Yesterday, run over at a Booksellers shop. It is a description and a copper Plate of all the Engravings upon precious stones in the Collection of the Duke of Orleans. The stamps are extreamly beautiful, and are representations of the Gods and Heroes of Antiquity, with most of the fables of their Mithology. Such a Book would be very usefull to the Children in studiing the Classicks, but it is too dear—3 Guineas, unbound.

There is every Thing here that can inform the Understanding, or refine the Taste, and indeed one would think that could purify the Heart. Yet it must be remembered there is every thing here too, which can seduce, betray, deceive, deprave, corrupt and debauch it. Hercules marches here in full View of the Steeps of Virtue on one hand, and the flowery Paths of Pleasure on the other—and there are few who make the Choice of Hercules. That my Children may follow his Example, is my earnest Prayer: but I sometimes tremble, when I hear the syren songs of sloth, least they should be captivated with her bewitching Charms and her soft, insinuating Musick.

AA to JA

My Dearest Friend May 1 1780

Last week arrived at Boston the Marquis de la Fayette to the universal joy of all who know the Merit and Worth of that Nobleman. He was received with the ringing of Bells, fireing of cannon, bon fires &c.

He was so kind as to forward my Letters immediately, but his haste to set of for Philadelphia deprived me of the Honour of a visit from him at Braintree which I had hoped for, and but just gave me the opportunity of writing him a Billet.

I am just informed that the General Pickering is to sail from Salem in a day or two, and that my Letters must be instantly ready. I was in hopes that the new State Frigate call'd the *Protector* would have gone, but find it otherways determined. I have written to you by Mr. Guile, who goes first to Amsterdam. I could have wished that those Letters had gone by this vessel as it is the first direct conveyance I have had since you left me.

You will be so good as to notice the dates of Letters which you receive from time to time. I shall then be able to judge what is necessary to repeat if any should be lost. I will however mention again that Capt. Babson arrived and that I received the articles you ordered for me to the amount of 40 pounds sterling.

All your Letters have come safe to hand that you have written since you left me, except what may be on Board the Alliance who is not yet arrived by which I hope the tide of fortune is turned in my favour.

I enclose a set of Bills. I have been particuliar in my Letters by Mr. Guile, but as I wish a return by this vessel, and least he should not arrive I will repeat that I requested you to send me 12 Ells of black and white striped Lutestring or changeable, Mr. Bondfeild sent a peice to Mr. Warren, the same kind I want, would send a pattern, but have none, and 12 Ells of Led coulourd proper for mourning. The first I want for Nabby, the other for myself, as I greatly fear I shall soon have a call for it. Your Brother will soon be a widower we all apprehend, his wife is in the last stages of a consumption, has been confined to her room for more than two months, and in circumstances too, otherways allarming.

I added to those a peice of black Ribbon common width and a peice of Narrow about 4 or 5 sols per yard, 3 yard of black plain gauze and 6 figured, 2 black fans, 3 black gauze hankerchiefs. I also mentioned that what remained of the Bills you might if you pleased order remitted in common calico low priced hankerchiefs and fans which are articles that turn to the best account here. I have enclosed a list of some articles for Cotton Tufts for which he paid me 7 Louis d'oers to be deducted from the Bills in lieu of the calico, and other articles provided you find yourself in the least straitned which I fear you will. The remittance from Bilboa will render me very comfortable for this 12 month, even tho I should purchase the land which belonged to Nate'll Belcher, which I have written to you about. I have drawn one Bill of an hundred dollors in favour of Bomstead for you know what. He used formerly to have 50 pounds for the best Sort, I could not get it so low now, but have paid the rest myself by turning my hankerchiefs (a part of them) to very good account. I would not have drawn at all; but hoped to make a purchase of the land.

Received the present by the Marquis. You desire to know what I want that may be sent in the same manner—a peice or two of Holland Apron tape, a pair of silk mitts or Gloves, an Ell or two of Muslin or figured Lawn, and as a little of what you call frippery is very necessary towards looking like the rest of the world, Nabby would have me add, a few yard of Black or White Gauze, low priced black or white lace or a few yards of Ribbon but would have Mamma write to Pappa at the same time that she has no passion for dress further than he would approve of or to appear when she goes from home a little like those of her own age. But I must add that I do not wish you to send much of any of these articles in this way as I find by compareing the articles you was so kind as to send me, with those put up, both by Mr. Bondfeild, and the other Gentleman, whose Name I cannot undertake to spell, that they turn out much Dearer by retail. The hankerchiefs were exceeding nice, but being Linnen they will not last like the India Silk which are hardly so high priced, and which here will fetch double.

Crosby has had his medow measured again and makes 6 acres and a quarter. French measured it and has given a plan of it. It will not do to call for an other measure, it will multiply to 7, so I must settle in the best manner I can. I have a Castle in the air which I shall write to you upon by the next opportunity, either for you to laugh at and reject, or to think of if practicable.

I wrote to Mr. L[ovel]l two months ago that I feard you would be embarrassed if he did not supply you. I shall as you desire repeat it to him.

I have written to my dear sons by Mr. Guile. Your daughter too, has written to you. If I have time I shall not fail writing to Mr. Thaxter who is very good to remember me so often. I highly esteem both him and his Letters. I found him to be all you discribe him, and knew you could not be better suited. I am happy however in finding that my loss is your gain, I really miss his services and attentions.

Our Friends are in pretty good health excepting Sister A[dam]s. Your worthy parent is much broken by the severity of the winter—mine stood the winter well but fails much more than I have known him this spring.

So many others will write you the state of politicks that I believe I shall not touch upon them. I have enclosed Philadelphia papers and journals. Our currency too is a Subject which you must learn from others; if I can procure sufficient to pay my taxes I shall be content, I want no more. I will just mention that the last years tax upon only two acres and half of Medow in Milton was 60 dollors and a parish tax for the land you own in the next parish 50 dollors. This year tis impossible to say to what amount they will rise. The tenants are all scared and declare they will quit Farms as tis impossible for them to pay half the taxes. Mine talked in the same strain but finally concluded to tarry an other year.

This Letter wholy upon Buisness must conclude with an assurance of the most affectionate regard of your Portia

JA to AA

My dear Portia [*Paris, post 12 May 1780*]

The inclosed Dialogue in the Shades was written by Mr. Edmund Jennings now residing at Brussells, a Native of Maryland. I will send you the Rest when I can get it.

How I lament the Loss of my Packets by Austin! There were I suppose Letters from Congress of great Importance to me. I know not what I shall do without them. I suppose there was Authority to draw &c. Mr. T[haxter]'s Letter from his father, hints that Mr. L. is coming here. This will be excellent.

Since my Arrival this time I have driven about Paris, more than I did before. The rural Scenes around this Town are charming. The public Walks, Gardens, &c. are extreamly beautifull. The Gardens of the Palais Royal, the Gardens of the Tuilleries, are very fine. The Place de Louis 15, the Place Vendome or Place de Louis 14, the Place victoire, the Place royal, are fine Squares, ornamented with very magnificent statues. I wish I had time to describe these objects to you in a manner, that I should have done, 25 Years ago, but my Head is too full of Schemes and my Heart of Anxiety to use Expressions borrowed from you know whom.

To take a Walk in the Gardens of the Palace of the Tuilleries, and describe the Statues there, all in marble, in which the ancient Divinities and Heroes are represented with exquisite Art, would be a very pleasant Amusement, and instructive Entertainment, improving in History, Mythology, Poetry, as well as in Statuary. Another Walk in the Gardens of Versailles, would be usefull and agreable.—But to observe these Objects with Taste and describe them so as to be understood, would require more time and thought than I can possibly Spare. It is not indeed the fine Arts, which our Country requires. The Usefull, the mechanic Arts, are those which We have occasion for in a young Country, as yet simple and not far advanced in Luxury, altho perhaps much too far for her Age and Character.

I could fill Volumes with Descriptions of Temples and Palaces, Paintings, Sculptures, Tapestry, Porcelaine, &c. &c. &c.—if I could have time. But I could not do this without neglecting my duty.—The Science of Government it is my Duty to study, more than all other Sciences: the Art of Legislation and Administration and Negotiation, ought to take Place, indeed to exclude in a manner all other Arts.—I must study Politicks and War that my sons may have liberty to study Mathematicks and Philosophy. My sons ought to study Mathematicks and Philosophy, Geography, natural History, Naval Architecture, navigation, Commerce and Agriculture, in order to give their Children a right to study Painting, Poetry, Musick, Architecture, Statuary, Tapestry and Porcelaine.

Adieu.

John Adams' allusion to "small Presents . . . in the family Way," together with many other allusions of the same sort, not to mention his wife's acknowledgments and further requests, indicates one means by which the family's affairs were kept afloat in the sea of wartime inflation. Though some were lost and others arrived in damaged condition, these imports were good for cash in Massachusetts, where not too many other things were during hard times.

"The Machine" which was so "horribly dear" reflects a feminine whim not very consonant with Abigail Adams' usual and strongly professed Puritan ethic. Before his second voyage to Europe, her husband had promised she could have a chaise or carriage made that would be fit for the wife of a minister plenipotentiary to ride in. It is amusing to find that in writing about it both husband and wife avoided the name of this "you know what."

JA to AA

My dear Portia — June 17. 1780

I yesterday received a Letter of 26 April from Brother Cranch, for which I thank him and will answer as soon as possible. He tells me you have drawn a little Bill upon me. I am sorry for it, because I have sent and should continue to send you, small Presents by which you would be enabled to do better than by drawing Bills. I would not have you draw any more. I will send you Things in the family Way which will defray your Expences better. The Machine is horribly dear. Mr. C. desires to know if he may draw on me. I wish it was in my power to oblige him but it is not. I have no Remittances nor any Thing to depend on, not a Line from Congress nor any member since I left you. My Expences thro Spain, were beyond all Imagination, and my Expences here are so exorbitant, that I cant answer any Bill from any body not even from you, excepting the one you have drawn. I must beg you, to be as prudent as possible. Depend upon it, your Children will have Occasion for all your Œconomy. Mr. Johonnot must send me some Bills. Every farthing is expended and more. You can have no Idea of my unavoidable Expences. I know not what to do.

Your little affairs and those of all our Friends, Mr. Wibert &c. are on Board the Alliance and have been so these 4 months, or ready to be.—Pray write me by the Way of Spain and Holland as well as France. We are all well.—My Duty to your father, my Mother, and affections and Respects where due.

My affections I fear got the better of my Judgment in bringing my Boys. They behave very well however.

London is in the Horrors.—Governor Hutchinson fell down dead at the first appearance of Mobs. They have been terrible. A Spirit of Bigotry and Fanaticism mixing with the universal discontents of the nation, has broke out into Violences of the most dreadful Nature—burnt Lord Mansfields House, Books, Manuscripts—burnd the Kings Bench Prison, and all the other Prisons—let loose all the Debtors and Criminals. Tore to Pieces Sir G. Savilles House—insulted all the Lords of Parliament &c. &c. Many have been killed—martial Law proclaimed—many hanged—Lord George Gordon committed to the Tower for high Treason—and where it will end God only knows.—The Mobs all cryd Peace with America, and War with France—poor Wretches! as if this were possible.

In the English Papers they have inserted the Death of Mr. Hutchinson with severity, in these Words—Governor Hutchinson is no more. On Saturday last he dropped down dead. It is charity to hope that his sins will be buried with him in the Tomb, but they must be recorded in his Epitaph. His Misrepresentations have contributed to the Continuance of the War with America. Examples are necessary. It is to be hoped that all will not escape into the Grave, without a previous Appearance, either on a Gibbet or a scaffold.

Govr. Bernard I am told died last fall. I wish, that with these primary Instruments of the Calamities that now distress almost all the

World the Evils themselves may come to an End. For although they will undoubtedly End, in the Welfare of Mankind, and accomplish the Benevolent designs of Providence, towards the two Worlds; Yet for the present they are not joyous but grievous.

May Heaven permit you and me to enjoy the cool Evening of Life, in Tranquility, undisturbed by the Cares of Politicks or War—and above all with the sweetest of all Reflections, that neither Ambition, nor Vanity, nor Avarice, nor Malice, nor Envy, nor Revenge, nor Fear, nor any base Motive, or sordid Passion through the whole Course of this mighty Revolution, and the rapid impetuous Course of great and terrible Events that have attended it, have drawn Us aside from the Line of our Duty and the Dictates of our Consciences!—Let Us have Ambition enough to keep our Simplicity, or Frugality and our Integrity, and transmit these Virtues as the fairest of Inheritances to our Children.

"The Man who . . . ought to be our *Chief*," mentioned near the end of the letter that follows, was James Bowdoin. The "tinkleling cymball" was John Hancock. Mrs. Adams was correct in her prediction: in the first election under the new Constitution, held in September, Hancock defeated Bowdoin for governor.

AA to JA

My Dearest Friend July 5 1780

Your favour of April 6th reachd me to day per favour Mr. Williams, and is the only one I have had the pleasure of receiving since the arrival of the Marquiss.

I wish you would be so particular in yours as to notice any you may receive from me, for to this day I am at a loss to know whether you have yet received a line. Mrs. D[an]a told me that Mr. D—a had mentiond hearing twice from her. I never omitted an opportunity which she improved, if I knew of it, so imagine you must have received some.

I wish I had agreable intelligence to communicate to you, I should certainly write you with more pleasure. Our present situation is very dissagreable, it is Alarming, but perhaps not more so than you have heretofore been witness to; who ever takes a retrospective view of the war in which we are engaged, will find that Providence has so intermixed our successes, and our defeats, that on the one hand we have not been left to despond, nor on the other, to be unduely elated. We have been taught to sing both of Mercies and of judgements—and when our Enimies have supposed us subdued, we have rise[n] the conquerors. That Charlestown is taken is a Truth—yet it excites not the Rage which our Road Island or Penobscot dissapointments did. They stung as Disgraces, this after a Gallant Defence yealded to superiour force, and is considerd as a misfortune, and each one is reanimated with spirit to remedy the Evil. The 3 years Men all disbanded, a large victorious Army in persuit of a small brave, but unfortunate one—a currency in which there is no Stability or Faith—are circumstances to puzzel wise Heads and to distress Benevolent Hearts. But as "affliction is the good mans shining time" so does America give proof of her Virtue when distressd. This State have raised, and are procuring their Men with vigor to act in concert with the Fleet and Army of our Generous Ally which we are impatiently looking for. The importance of immediately recruiting our Army is known to be such, that the Demands of pay are exorbitent, yet we fill up at any rate. We pay any price. "To spare now would be the height of extravagance and to consult present ease would be to sacrifice it perhaps forever," says C[ommon] S[ense].

Goverment now see to their sorrow their deplorable mistake in not inlisting their Army during the war. Thousands of Lives might have been saved and a million of treasure. We now only patch and patch, find a temporary relief at an immence expence and by this false step give our Enemies advantages they could never have obtained if we had possessd a Regular Army.

Nothing could have been more fortunate for me than the arrival of the few articles you orderd for me from Bilboa, just as the time when the calls for large sums of money took place. (The Quarterly tax for the state and continent amounts to 7 hundred pounds Lawfull, my part.) Mr. Tracy kindly forwarded them to me, with this complement, that he wished there had been ten times as much.

Enclosed is a Resolve of Congress with regard to your sallery and a coppy of their Resolve with regard to your accounts. Mr. L[ovel]l wrote me that the Treasurer would draw a Bill for the Balance, which shall enclose as soon as I receive. From Spain there are ten opportunities of getting merchandize to one from France. If you should think proper to make further remittances from Bilboa, be so kind as to send the following list, in lieu of Barcelona hankerchiefs with which the Market is at present Glutted. Order 15 yards of thin black mode, ditto white, ditto red, ditto blew, some black sattin proper for cloaks and low priced black lace, calico and Irish linnen, which is not higher priced than dutch, but sells much better, the best Hyson tea, the first I had was of the best sort, the last very ordinary.

Enclosed is a set of Bills. The other sent by Mr. Guile who I hope is safely arrived, but least he should not I will enclose a list of some things which I wrote for by him and some patterns of silk which I want for mourning for myself and Nabby – 15 yards of each kind which will be about four Livers per yard. If any thing of the wollen kind could be had which would answer for winter wear, be so kind as to order enough for two Gowns. 2 or 3 pair of black silk Gloves, if they were not in a former list which you carried. I have forgot. 3 black fans, a peice of black ribbon, half a peice of Narrow, 6 yard of plain black Gauze, 6 figured, four yard of plain Muslin. If I omitted in a former list a pound of white thread, (none to be coarse) we can make that; please to add it now and half a dozen peices of Quality binding different colours, ditto shoe binding. Calico can never come amiss, nothing in greater demand here. With Linnen am well supplied. Spain the best port to send that from. Some figured Lawn like the pattern enclosed about 2 Livers per yard, 6 or 8 yard –of Cap wire, a dozen peices.–The Alliance not yet arrived, a speady passage to her, I want my trunk.

No intrigues, no machinations that I hear of. There are some Great Folks here who I believe are sincerely glad that you do not stand in *their way* which from all Quarters is said would have been the case had you been here. I had rather distant as it is that you abide where you are for the present. The Man who from Merrit, fortune and abilities ought to be our *Chief* is not *popular*, and tho he will have the votes of the sensible judicious part of the State, he will be more than out Numberd by the Lovers of the tinkleling cymball.

What a politician you have made me? If I cannot be a voter upon this occasion, I will be a writer of votes. I can do some thing in that way but fear I shall have the mortification of a defeat.

Adieu. How many pages does it take to pay the debt of one? How do my dear sons. Well I hope. Charley, the darling of the Neighbourhood is more deared over than all the rest, he possessd the faculty of fastning every body to him. Thommy sends duty to pappa, respects [to] Mr. T[haxte]r and Loves his Brothers. I will not add any thing for their Sister, but that She does not write half so often as I urge her to. My paper warns me to close, yet gives me room to add the Signature of your ever affectionate Portia

AA to JA

My dearest Love July 24 1780

Your affectionate Letter by the Count de Noailles reachd me but yesterday, together with your present by Col. Fleury which was very nice and Good. Should you send any thing of the kind in the same way, be so good as to let it be blew, white or red. Silk Gloves or mittins, black or white lace, Muslin or a Bandano hankerchief, and *even a few yard of Ribbon* might be conveyed in the same manner. I mention these things as they are small articles, and easily contained in a Letter, all of which by Resolve of congress are orderd to come Free. The Articles you orderd me from Bilboa are of great service to me. The great plenty of Barcelona hankerchiefs make them unsaleable at present, but Linnens are an article in great demand, and will exchange for any family necessary to good account, or sell for money, which is in greater demand at present than I have known it since paper was first Emitted. High prices, high taxes, high bounties render such a Quantity of it necessary, that few people can procure sufficient to answer necessary demands. The usual Estimation is a Dollor at a copper, yet exchange at the highest has been at 75 for one. Country produce exceeds foreign articles, Lamb at 10 Dollors per pound, veal at 7, flower a hundred and 60 pound per hundred, Rye 100 & 10 Dollors per Bushel. I had determined not to have written you the account of prices &c., have avoided it all along, chose you should learn it from inquiry of others but insensibly fell into it.

I have a request to you which I hope you will not dissapoint me of, a minature of Him I best Love. Indulge me the pleasing melancholy of contemplating a likeness. The attempt here faild, and was more the resemblance of a cloisterd Monk, than the Smileing Image of my Friend. I could not endure the sight of it.—By Sampson will be a Good opportunity. Should he be taken none but a Savage would rob a Lady, of what could be of no value, but to her. Let him put it into his chest and it will come safe I dare say. Let it be set, it will be better done with you than here.

I mentioned sending Bills by this opportunity but as I have already sent 3 sets was advised to defer the others till I knew whether they had faild. If I have not been too extravagant already, I would mention one article more, as I do not expect an other opportunity from France for a twelve month. It is a Green umbrella.

You think you run great risks in taking our two Sons. What then was mine? I could have accompanied you through any Dangers and fatigues, but whether I could have sustaind them I know not. An intimation that I could have renderd you more comfortable and happy, would have outweighd all my timidity. I should have had no other consideration. Yet the dangers of the sea, of Enimies and the fatigues of a long journey are not objects that I wish to encounter. A small portion of my own Country will be all I shall ever visit, nor should I carry my wishes further, if they would not seperate what God joined together. Ever remember with tenderness and affection yours & yours only, Portia

V

AUGUST 1780 ~ SEPTEMBER 1782

Mars, Belona and old Neptune are in league against me.
— Abigail Adams

I am keeping House, but I want an Housekeeper.
— John Adams

TRUCE CHAMBER AT THE HAGUE WHERE JOHN ADAMS SIGNED THE DUTCH-AMERICAN TREATY OF 1782

On July 27, 1780, John Adams, accompanied by his sons, left Paris on a trip to the Low Countries, apparently intending to return to Paris in a matter of weeks. Although the trip was partly a sightseeing venture, its immediate impulsion was a break in the already strained relations of Adams and the Comte de Vergennes. In the preceding month Adams had addressed strongly worded letters to the Foreign Minister on two subjects. In one series he urged a greater concentration of French naval power on the North American coast if France did indeed desire to bring the war to an early conclusion. In the other, he again objected to Vergennes' ban on announcing Adams' missions to the British government as a denial of the opportunity to stir up British popular sentiment in favor of peace. In his replies Vergennes attempted refutations and at the same time icily told Adams he was in no need of further advice from him.

If Adams' departure from Paris seemed abrupt, his going to the Netherlands was predicated on his knowledge of Congress' long-standing interest in negotiating a Dutch loan. Congress acted in October 1779 in issuing a commission to that end to Henry Laurens. But Laurens did not depart for months. In Europe, the likelihood of a favorable response to an American initiative increased markedly with the deterioration of relations between Britain and the Netherlands. Adams proposed to test the waters or to conduct, as those who disapproved termed it, "a fishing expedition," in anticipation of the arrival of the appointed emissary. In the letter that follows, the first that survives addressed to Abigail after he left Paris and written a month after his arrival in Amsterdam, there is a casual tone that suggests that he still retained the view that the trip would be of short duration and perhaps of not much import.

However, in June the Congress had dispatched Colonel James Searle to Europe with a letter empowering Adams, pending Laurens' arrival, to act in his stead. On receipt of this word, brought by Francis Dana on September 16, he made arrangements for an extended stay in the Netherlands. He ordered Thaxter to join him, bringing from Paris all the papers Adams had left there. He also entered John Quincy and Charles in the Latin School on the Singel in Amsterdam.

In October, when he heard of Laurens' capture at sea, Adams knew his residence would be further prolonged. He realized that the effort would fall to him alone to win recognition from the Dutch Republic, to secure a loan for the prosecution of the war, and to make the Netherlands a center from which to disseminate information useful to the American cause.

JA to AA

My dear Portia Amsterdam septr. 4. 1780

I have ordered the Things you desired for yourself and Mr. Tufts by Captain Edward Davis in the Brig Dolphin. They are very dear, as you will see. I insured them at 25 per Cent.

The French and Spaniards have at length, made a Hall as the saying is of 40 or 50 ships at once from the English. A few more such strokes will answer a very good End. But not make Peace. This will never be while the English have one soldier in the United States.

We are all well—thank Nabby for her Letter, and tell Master T. that I should have been obliged to him for one.

We are all Impatience to hear from N[orth] A[merica] and the W. Indies. Proportional good News from thence would make Us very happy.

I have been here three or four Weeks, and have spent my time very agreably here. I am very much pleased with Holland. It is a singular Country. It is like no other. It is all the Effect of Industry, and the Work of Art.

The Frugality, Industry, Cleanliness, &c. here, deserve the Imitation of my Countrymen. The Fruit of these Virtues has been immense Wealth, and great Prosperity. They are not Ambitious, and therefore happy. They are very sociable, however, in their peculiar Fashion.

Adieu, yours forever.

JA to AA

My dear Portia Amsterdam Septr. 15. 1780

I wish you to write me, by every Opportunity to this Place, as well as to France. It seems as if I never should get any more Letters from America. I have sent you some Things by Captn. Davis, but he has no Arms, and I fear they will be lost, by Capture.—I sent Things by the Alliance.

The Country where I am is the greatest Curiosity in the World. This Nation is not known any where, not even by its Neighbours. The Dutch Language is spoken by none but themselves. Therefore They converse with nobody and nobody converses with them. The English are a great nation, and they despize the Dutch because they are smaller. The French are a greater Nation still, and therefore they despize the Dutch because they are still smaller in comparison to them.

But I doubt much whether there is any Nation of Europe more estimable than the Dutch, in Proportion.

Their Industry and Œconomy ought to be Examples to the World. They have less Ambition, I mean that of Conquest and military Glory, than their Neighbours, but I dont perceive that they have more

Avarice. And they carry Learning and Arts I think to greater Extent.

The Collections of Curiosities public and private are innumerable.

I am told that Mr. Searle is arrived at Brest: but I have learned nothing from him as yet—nor do I know his Destination.

The French and Spanish Fleets have made a sweep of Sixty upon the English E. and W. India Fleets. This must have great Effects.

We are all well.—Dont expect Peace. The English have not yet forgot the Acquisition of Charlestown, for which they are still making the most childish Exultations. The new Parliament will give Ministry a Run. Mark my Words, You will have no Peace, but what you give yourselves, by destroying Root and Branch all the British Force in America.

The English cannot bear the Thought that France should dictate the Terms of Peace, as they call it. They say they must make a dishonourable Peace now—a shameful Peace, a degrading Peace. This is worse than death to them, and thus they will go on, untill they are forced to sue for a Peace, still more shamefull and humiliating.

JA to AA

My dear Portia Amsterdam Septr. 25. 1780

The new Orders I have received from your side the Water, have determined me to stay here untill further Orders. Write to me, by every Vessell this Way, or to France or Spain. The Air of Amsterdam is not so clear and pure as that of France, but I hope to preserve my Health. My two Boys are at an excellent Latin School, or in the Language of this Country, Den de Latÿnche School op de Cingel by de Munt. The Scholars here all speak French.

John has seen one of the Commencements when the young Gentlemen delivered their Orations and received their Premiums, and Promotions which set his Ambition all afire. Charles is the same amiable insinuating Creature. Wherever he goes he gets the Hearts of every Body especially the Ladies. One of these Boys is the Sublime and the other the Beautifull.

You promised me a Description of the Castle you were building in the Air, but I have not received it.

The English are revenging the Loss of their Power upon those who have uniformly endeavoured to save it. They are totally abandoned and lost. There is no Hope for them but in a civil War nor in that neither. Burke, Keppell, Sawbridge, Hartley are thrown out.

We are anxiously waiting for News from America and the Islands; but my Expectations are not very high. The Fleet is not strong enough in N. America.—I sent the Things you wrote for by Captain Davis, Son of Solomon, but they cost very dear.

I have written to Mr. Thaxter to come here—Mr. Dana is already here. I want to know how the season has been, with you, and who are your Governor and Lt. Governor &c. &c. &c.

I shall loose all Opportunity of being a man of Importance in the World by being away from home, as well as all the Pleasures of Life: for I never shall enjoy any, any where except at the Foot of Pens hill—When Oh When shall I see the Beauties of that rugged Mountain!

By your last Letters I fear my Brother is in Affliction. My Love to him and his family—and Duty & affection where due.

AA to JA

My Dearest Friend October 8 1780

My unkle who is very attentive to acquaint me with every opportunity of conveyance, last Evening let me know of a vessel going to Spain, and tho my Letters cost you much more than they are worth; I am bound as well by inclination, as your repeated injunctions to omit no opportunity of writeing.

My last to you was by way of Bilboa. A vessel will soon sail for Amsterdam, by which I shall write largely to you, to my dear Boys, and to my agreable correspondent.

I am not without some prospect that the Letters may find you at that very port. I not long ago learnt that a commission for Holland was forwarded to you.

I was much surprized to find that you had not heard from C[ongre]ss by the date of your last, the 17 of June. The communication from that Quarter is worse than it is from here, bad enough from both, for an anxious wife and an affectionate Mother.

I know not how to enter into a detail of our publick affairs—they are not what I wish them to be. The successes of the Enemy at Charlestown are mortifying. General Gates misfortune will be anounced to you before this reaches you, and the enclosed Gazet will give you all the information of the treachery of Arnold which has yet come to hand.

How ineffectual is the tye of Honour to bind the Humane Mind, unless accompanied by more permanent and Efficacious principals? Will he who laughs at a future state of Retribution, and holds himself accountable only to his fellow Mortals disdain the venal Bribe, or spurn the Ignoble hand that proffers it.

Yet such is the unhappy lot of our native land, too, too many of our chief Actors *have been and are unprincipled wretches*, or we could not have sufferd as we have done. It is Righteousness, not Iniquity, that exalteth a Nation. There are so many and so loud complaints against some persons in office that I am apt to think neither *age* nor *Fame* will screen them. All hopes that I had entertained of a vigorous campaign, have been obstructed by a superiour British naval force, and the daily Rumours of a reinforcement from France, rise and vanish with the day. The season is now so far advanced, that little or no benifit would accrue from their arrival, yet with all the force of Graves and Rodny nothing has yet been attempted, they content themselves with the conquests of Clinton, and give out that the Northern States are not worth possessing.

Peace, Peace my beloved object is farther and farther from my Embraces I fear, yet I have never asked you a Question which from the Nature of your Embassy I knew you could not determine. It is however an object so near my Heart, that it lies down and rises with me. Yet could you bring the olive Branch, even at the expiration of an *other year*, my present sacrifices should be my future triumph, and I would then try if the Honour, as I am sometimes told, could then compensate for the substantial Blessings I resign. But my dear Friend well knows that the Honour does not consist so much in the Trust reposed, as in the able, the Honest, the upright and faithfull discharge of it. From these sources I can derive a pleasure, which neither accumulated Honours, wealth, or power, could bestow without them.

But whether does my pen lead me? I meant only to write you a short Letter, if writing to you I could do so. Some months ago I wrote you an account of the death of sister A[dam]s and of her leaving a poor Babe, only 3 days old. The death of Mr. H[al]l, who full of years, was last week gatherd to the great congregation, will be no matter of surprize to you. Your M[othe]r is gone to your B[rothe]r, till a change in his condition may render her services unnecessary, which with a young family of 5 children, is not likely to be very soon. Whatever she call[s] upon me for shall endeavour to supply her with. She would have been more comfortable with me, but her compassion lead her to him. She desires me to remember, ever her tenderest affection to you. I always make her a sharer with me in whatever I receive from you, but some small present from your own Hand to her, would I know be particularly gratefull to her, half a dozen yards of dark chints, if you are at a loss to know what, or any thing—it is not the value but the notice which would be pleasing. Excuse my mentioning it, I know you burdend with matters of more importance, yet these attentions are the more gratefull on that very account.

Pray make my Respectfull complements to Mr. D[an]a and tell him that his Lady made me a Friendly visit last week, and we talked as much as we pleased of our dear *Absents*, compared Notes, Sympathized, Responded to each other, and mingled with our sacrifices some *little pride* that no Country could boast two worthyer Hearts than *we* had *permitted* to go abroad—and then they were such honest souls too, and so intirely satisfied with their American dames, that we had not an apprehension of their roveing. We mean not however to defy the Charmes of the Parissian Ladies, but to admire the constancy and fidelity with which they are resisted—but enough of Romance.

Be so good as to let Mr. T[haxte]r know that his Friends are all well, and will write by the Amsterdam vessel. This will be so expensive a conveyance that I send only a single Letter.

I have been very sick for a month past with a slow fever, but hope it is leaving me. For many years I have not escaped a sickness in the Fall.—I hope you enjoy Health, Dr. L[e]e says you grow very fat. My poor unfortunate trunk has not yet reachd America, that was forced to share the Fate of party and caballs, was detaind by Dr. W[indshi]p. I wish it in other Hands, do not let it go for Philadelphia if you can prevent it. Mr. L[ovel]l has sent me a set of Bills, which I enclose, but is much short of the balance reported in your favour. I take the remainder to be included with the other gentlemens accounts. After having stated the balance they say thus—"we beg leave to remark, that the examination of the coppy of an account marked A, which they received with Mr. A's other accounts and is for joint expences of himself Doctr. F[rankli]n and Mr. D[ean]e, cannot be gone into at present, the monies credited therein having been received, and the vouchers to said account remaining with them."

Our dear daughter is in B[osto]n but would send her duty and Love by all opportunities tho I cannot prevail with her to write so often as I wish.

Little Tom sends his Duty, learns fast now he has got a school master. My tenderest regard to my two dear Sons. The account of their good conduct is a gratefull Balm to the Heart of their & your ever affectionate

A A

AA to JA

My dearest Friend November 13th 1780

How long is the space since I heard from my dear absent Friends? Most feelingly do I experience that sentiment of Rousseaus' "that one of the greatest evils of absence, and the only one which reason cannot alleviate, is the inquietude we are under concerning the actual state of those we love, their health, their life, their repose, their affections.

JOHN ADAMS, Schildknaap,
Minister Plenipotentiaris der
XIII Vereenigde Staaten van
Noord-Amerika, bij de Republijk
der VII Vereenigde Nederlanden.
W. Holtrop, excud.

JOHN ADAMS IN 1782 BY REINIER VINKELES

Nothing escapes the apprehension of those who have every thing to lose." Nor are we more certain of the present condition than of the future. How tormenting is absence! How fatally capricious is that Situation in which we can only enjoy the past Moment, for the present is not yet arrived. Stern Winter is making hasty Strides towards me, and chills the warm fountain of my Blood by the Gloomy prospect of passing it *alone*, for what is the rest of the World to me?

"Its pomp, its pleasures and its nonesence all?"

The fond endearments of social and domestick life, is the happiness I sigh for, of that I am in a great measure deprived by a seperation from my dear partner and children, at the only season in life when it is probable we might have enjoyed them all together. In a year or two, the sons will be so far advanced in life, as to make it necessary for their Benifit, to place them at the Seats of Learning and Science, indeed the period has already arrived, and whilst I still fondle over one, it is no small relief to my anxious mind, that those, who are seperated from me, are under your care and inspection. They have arrived at an age, when a Mothers care becomes less necessary and a Fathers more important. I long to embrace them. The Tears my dear Charles shed at parting, have melted my Heart a thousand times. Why does the mind Love to turn to those painfull scenes and to recollect them with pleasure?

I last week only received a Letter written last March, and sent by Monseiur John Baptiste Petry. Where he is I know not. After nameing a Number of persons of whom I might apply for conveyance of Letters, you were pleased to add, they were your great delight when they did not censure, or complain, when they did they were your greatest punishment.

I am wholy unconscious of giving you pain in this way since your late absence. If any thing of the kind formerly escaped my pen, had I not ample retaliation, and did we not Balance accounts tho the sum was rather in your favour even after having distroyed some of the proof. In the most Intimate of Friendships, there must not be any recrimination. If I complaind, it was from the ardour of affection which could not endure the least apprehension of neglect, and you who was conscious that I had no cause would not endure the supposition. We however wanted no mediating power to adjust the difference, we no sooner understood each other properly, but as the poet says, "The falling out of Lovers is the renewal of Love."

Be to my faults a little Blind
Be to my virtues ever kind

and you are sure of a Heart all your own, which no other Earthly object ever possessd. Sure I am that not a syllable of complaint has ever stained my paper, in any Letter I have ever written since you left me. I should have been ungratefull indeed, when I have not had the shadow of a cause; but on the contrary, continual proofs of your attention to me. You well know I never doubted your Honour. Virtue and principal confirm the indissoluable Bond which affection first began and my security depends not upon your passion, which other objects might more easily excite, but upon the sober and setled dictates of Religion and Honour. It is these that cement, at the same time that they ensure the affections.

> "Here Love his golden shafts employs; here lights
> His *constant* Lamp, and waves his purple wings."

November 24.

I had written thus far when Capt. Davis arrived. The News of your being in Amsterdam soon reachd me, but judge of my dissapointment when I learnt that he had thrown over all his Letters, being chased by an American privateer, who foolishly kept up British coulours till she came along side of him. One only was saved by some accident and reachd me after hearing that the whole were lost. This tho short was a cordial to my Heart, not having received a line of a later date than 15 [*i.e.* 17] of June. This was the fourth of Sepbr., and just informd me of your Health and that you had been in Amsterdam a few weeks. My dear sons were not mentiond, and it was only by a *very* polite Letter from Mr. de Neufville that I learnt they were with you, and well. He is pleased to speak in high terms of them, I hope they deserve it.

A week after a Brig arrived at Providence and brought me your favour of Sepbr. 15 and Mr. Thaxters of August and Sepbr. from Paris. You do not mention in either of your Letters which were saved, how long you expect to reside in Holland. I fancy longer than you then Imagined, as Capt. Davis informs that you had not heard of the Capture of Mr. Lawrence. This event will make your stay there necessary. I fear for your Health in a Country so damp, abounding in stagnant water, the air of which is said to be very unfriendly to Foreigners. Otherways if I was to consult my own feelings I should wish your continuance there, as I could hear more frequently from you. If it is not really nearer, its being a sea port, gives me that Idea, and I fancy the pains of absence increase in proportion to distance, as the power of attraction encreases as the distance diminishes. Magnets are said to have the same motion tho in different places. Why may not we have the same sensations tho the wide Atlantick roll between us? I recollect your story to Madam Le Texel upon the Nature and power of Attraction and think it much more probable to unite Souls than Bodies.

You write me in yours of Sepbr. 15 that you sent my things in the Alliance. This I was sorry to see, as I hoped Mr. Moylan had informd you before that time, that Dr. Winship to whom he deliverd them neither came in the vessel or sent the things. I am not without fears that they will be embezzled. I have taken every opportunity to let you know of it, but whether you have got my Letters is uncertain. The cabals on Board the Ship threw the officers into parties, and Winship chose to involve my trunk in them. He certainly sent goods by the same vessel to other persons. General W[arre]n, my unkle and others examined and went on Board, but could find no Trunk for me. The Articles sent by private hands I believe I have got, except you sent more than one packet by Col. Flury who arrived at Newport [and] sent forward a package containing a few yards of Black Silk. A month afterwards, received a Letter from him desireing to know if I received two packages and some Letters which he brought. I received no Letter, and but one package by him. I have been endeavouring to find out the mistery, but have not yet develloped it.—The Articles you sent me from Bilboa have been of vast service to me, and greatly assisted me in dischargeing the load of Taxes which it would have otherways been impossible for me to have paid; I will enclose you a list of what I have paid, and yet remains due from july to this day. The Season has been so unfortunate in this state, that our produce is greatly diminished. There never was known so severe and so long a drought, the crops of corn and grass were cut of. Each Town in this State is called upon to furnish a suffering Army with provision. This Towns supply is 40 thousand weight of Beaf or money to purchase it. This has already been collected. Our next tax is for Grain to pay our six months and our 3 Months militia, to whom we wisely voted half a Bushel per day, the state pay, and a Bounty of a Thousand dollors each or money Equivalent to purchase the Grain. This is now collecting and our Town tax only is four times larger than our continential. You hear no such sound now, as that money is good for nothing. Hard money from 70 to 75 is made the standard, that or exchange is the way of dealing, everything is high, but more steady than for two years before. My Tenants say they must leave the Farm, that they cannot live. I am sure I cannot pay more than my proportion yet I am loth they should quit. They say two Cows would formerly pay the taxes upon this place, and that it would now take ten.

They are not alone in their complaints. The burden is greater I fear than the people will bear—and whilst the New England states are crushed by this weight, others are lagging behind, without any exertions, which has produced a convention from the New England States. A motion has been made, but which I sincerely hope will not be adopted by our Goverment, I mean to vest General Washington with the power of marching his Army into the state that refuses supplies and exacting it by Martial Law. Is not this a most dangerous step, fraught with Evils of many kinds. I tremble at the Idea. I hope Congress will never adopt such a measure, tho our delegates should receive such Instructions.

Our publick affair[s] wear a more pleasing aspect, as you will see by the inclosed Gazet yet are we very far from extirpating the British force. If we are not to look for peace till that event takes place, I fear it is very far distant. Small as our Navy is, it has captured near all the Quebeck Fleet, 19 have arrived safe in port, and fill'd Salem and Cape Ann with Goods of all kinds. Besides not a week passes but gives us a prize from some Quarter.

As to the affairs of our common wealth, you will see who is Govenour. Two good Men have been chosen as Leiut. Governour, both of whom have refused. The late judge of probate is now Elected, and tis thought will accept. Last week his Excellency gave a very Grand Ball, to introduce our Republican form of Goverment properly upon the Stage.

It was a maxim of Edward king of Portugal, that what ever was amiss in the manners of a people, either proceeds from the bad example of the Great, or may be cured by the Good. He is the patriot who when his Country is overwhelmed by Luxery, by his example stems the Torrent and delivers it from that which threatens its ruin. A writer observes with Regard to the Romans, that there must have been a considerable falling off, when Sylla won that popular favour by a shew of Lions, which in better times he could only have obtained by substantial services.

I have twice before enclosed a set of Bills, received from Mr. Lovell for you. I ventured to detain one hopeing for an opportunity to send to Holland. I enclose it now together with a list of the Articles if you think you can afford them to me. If not I shall be better satisfied in a refusal than in a compliance. The Articles you were so kind as to send me were not all to my mind. The Led coulourd Silk was clay coulour, not proper for the use I wanted it for, it was good however. A large Quantity of ordinary black ribbon, which may possibly sell for double what it cost, if it had been coulourd there would have

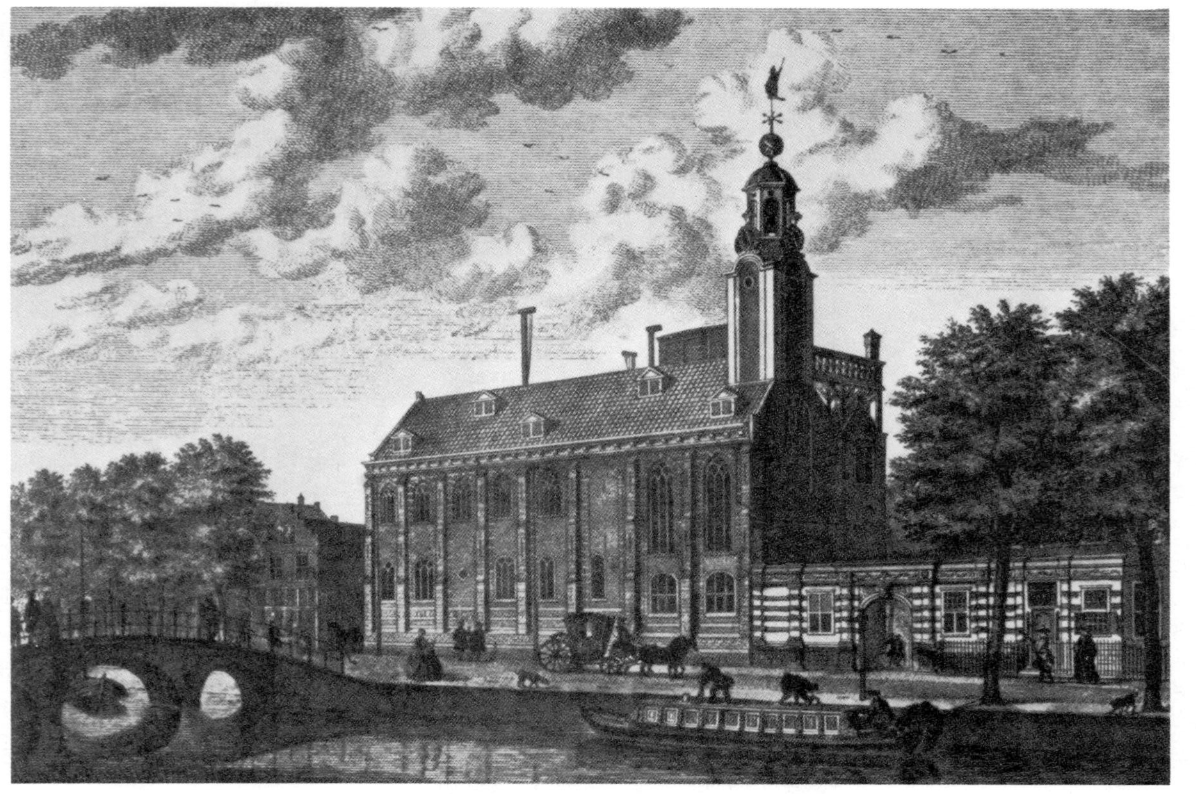

LEYDEN: VIEW ACROSS THE RAPENBURG TO THE UNIVERSITY

been no difficulty with it. The tape is of the coarsest kind, I shall not lose by it, but as I wanted it for family use, it was not the thing. The Tea was Excellent, the very best I ever had and not so high priced as from other places. All the rest of the articles were agreable.—I have written to Mr. de Neufville encloseing a duplicate Bill, and a list of the same articles, but directed him to take your orders and govern himself by them. When ever you send me any thing for sale, Linnens especially Irish, are always saleable. Common calico, that comes cheep from Holland, any thing of the wollen kind such as Tamies, Durants or caliminco with ordinary linnen hankerchiefs answer well.

I have written a very long letter. To what port it will go first [I] know not; it is too late for any vessel to go to Holland this winter from hence.—Our Friends all well. Your Brother has lost his youngest daughter. I will write to my dear John and Charles and hope [my?] Letters will not meet the fate of theirs.

Ever & at all time yours, Portia

The experience of Charles and John Quincy Adams in the Latin School at Amsterdam was not happy. The school authorities assigned John Quincy to classes at a lower scholastic level than he and his father thought proper. Their decision was based on the boy's lack of knowledge in the Dutch language; father and son relied upon John Quincy's proficiency in Greek and Latin. After a letter of protest from the father and what Rector Verheyk considered impertinence and disruptiveness on the part of the son, both boys were withdrawn.

Shortly thereafter, John Adams asked information and help from Dr. Benjamin Waterhouse of Newport, then pursuing further studies at the University of Leyden. On Waterhouse's advice, he sent the boys, accompanied by John Thaxter, to study there. They were permitted to enter classes and, when both had satisfied their professors, to matriculate in the University, even though Charles was under age.

The satisfaction that came to Adams from seeing his sons so well placed was enhanced by the special regard New Englanders had for Leyden as the home of the self-exiled company of English Separatists—or "Brownists" —before a detachment of them later known as Pilgrims embarked for America and settled in Plymouth in 1620.

JA to AA

My dearest Portia Amsterdam Decr. 18. 1780

I have this morning sent Mr. Thaxter, with my two Sons to Leyden, there to take up their Residence for some time, and there to pursue their Studies of Latin and Greek under the excellent Masters, and there to attend Lectures of the celebrated Professors in that University. It is much cheaper there than here: the Air is infinitely purer; and the Company and Conversation is better.

It is perhaps as learned an University as any in Europe.

I should not wish to have Children, educated in the common Schools in this Country, where a littleness of Soul is notorious. The Masters are mean Spirited Writches, pinching, kicking, and boxing the Children, upon every Turn.

Their is besides a general Littleness arising from the incessant Contemplation of Stivers and Doits, which pervades the whole People.

Frugality and Industry are virtues every where, but Avarice, and Stingyness are not Frugality.

The Dutch say that without an habit of thinking of every doit, before you spend it, no Man can be a good Merchant, or conduct Trade with Success. This I believe is a just Maxim in general. But I would never wish to see a Son of Mine govern himself by it. It is the sure and certain Way for an industrious Man to be rich. It is the only possible Way for a Merchant to become the first Merchant, or the richest Man in the Place. But this is an Object that I hope none of my Children will ever aim at.

It is indeed true, every where, that those who attend to small Expences are always rich.

I would have my Children attend to Doits and Farthings as devoutly as the meerest Dutchman upon Earth, if such Attention was necessary to support their Independence.

A Man who discovers a Disposition and a design to be independent seldom succeeds—a Jealousy arises against him. The Tyrants are alarmed on one side least he should oppose them. The slaves are allarmed on the other least he should expose their Servility. The Cry from all Quarters is, "He is the proudest Man in the World. He cant bear to be under Obligation."

I never in my Life observed any one endeavouring to lay me under particular Obligations to him, but I suspected he had a design to make me his dependant, and to have claims upon my Gratitude. This I should have no objection to—Because Gratitude is always in ones Power. But the Danger is that Men will expect and require more of Us, than Honour and Innocence and Rectitude will permit Us to perform.

In our Country however any Man with common Industry and Prudence may be independant.

But to put an End to this stuff Adieu, most affectionately Adieu.

John Adams to John Quincy Adams

My Son — Amsterdam Decr. 20. 1780

You are now at an University, where many of the greatest Men have received their Education.

Many of the most famous Characters, which England has produced, have pursued their Studies for some time at Leyden. Some, tho not many of the Sons of America, have studied there.

I would have you attend all the Lectures in which Experiments are made whether in Philosophy, Medicine or Chimistry, because these will open your mind for Inquiries into Nature: but by no means neglect the Languages.

I wish you to write me, an Account of all the Professorships, and the names of the Professors. I should also be obliged to you for as good an Account of the Constitution of the University as you can obtain. Let me know what degrees are conferred there; by whom; and what Examination the Candidates undergo, in order to be admitted to them.

I am your affectionate Father, John Adams

John Quincy Adams to John Adams

Honoured Sir — Leyden December 21st 1780

Mr. Thaxter and brother Charles wrote both to you the day before yesterday and as I had no subject to write upon, I did not write But I can now give you an account of our journey.

We dined on Monday at Haerlem and arrived at Leyden at Six oclock. We lodged at the Cour de Hollande and saw Mr. Waterhouse that evening. The next day we went to hear a Medicinal lecture by Professor *Horn*, we saw several experiments there. In the afternoon we went to Hear a Law lecture by Professor *Pessel*. Each lecture lasts an hour.

Yesterday Afternoon we moved from the Cour de Hollande to private lodgings in the same house in which Mr. Waterhouse boards our address is Mr. &c. by de Heer Welters, op de lange Burg, tegen over t Mantel Huis. Leyden.

I was to day in company with the parson of the brownist Church Who seems to be a clever man, he is a scotch-man but does not pray for the king of England.

I should be glad to have a pair of Scates they are of various prices from 3 Guilders to 3 Ducats those of a Ducat are as good as need to be but I should like to know whether you would chuse to have me give so much.

Mr. Waterhouse says that for riding I must have a pair leather breeches and a pair of boots. I should be glad if you would answer me upon that as soon as you receive this for there is a vacancy here which begins to morrow and in the vacancy is the best time to begin to learn to ride.

In the vacancy there will be no lectures at all but our Master will attend us all the while as much as when there is no vacancy.

I continue writing in Homer, the Greek Grammar and Greek testament every day.

I am your most dutiful Son, John Quincy Adams

John Adams to John Quincy Adams

My Son Amsterdam Dec. 28. 1780

The Ice is so universal now that I suppose you spend some Time in Skaiting every day. It is a fine Exercise for young Persons, and therefore I am willing to indulge you in it, provided you confine yourself to proper Hours, and to strict Moderation. Skaiting is a fine Art. It is not Simple Velocity or Agility that constitutes the Perfection of it but Grace. There is an Elegance of Motion, which is charming to the sight, and is useful to acquire, because it obliges you to restrain that impetuous Ardour and violent Activity, into which the Agitation of Spirits occasioned by this Exercise is apt to hurry you, and which is inconsistent both with your Health and Pleasure.

At Leyden, I suppose you may see many Gentlemen, who are perfect in the Art.—I have walked, several Times round this City from the Gate of Utrecht to that of Harlem, and seen some thousands Skaiting upon the Cingel, since the Frost set in. I have seen many skait with great Spirit, some with prodigious Swiftness, a few with a tolerably genteel Air, but none with that inimitable Grace and Beauty which I have seen some Examples of, in other Countries, even in our own.

I have seen some Officers of the British Army, at Boston, and some of our Army at Cambridge, skait with as perfect Elegance, as if they had spent their whole Lives in the study of Hogarths Principles of Beauty, and in reducing them to Practice.

I would advise you, my Son, in Skaiting, Dancing and Riding, to be always attentive to this Grace, which is founded in natural Principles, and is therefore as much for your Ease and Use, as for your Pleasure.

Do not conclude from this, that I advise you to spend much of your Time or Thoughts upon these Exercises and Diversions. In Truth I care very little about any of them. They should never be taken but as Exercise and Relaxation of Business and study. But as your Constitution requires vigorous Exercise, it will not be amiss, to spend some of your Time, in swimming, Riding, Dancing, Fencing and Skaiting, which are all manly Amusements, and it is as easy to learn by a little Attention, to perform them all with Taste, as it is to execute them in a slovenly, Awkward and ridiculous Manner.

Every Thing in Life should be done with Reflection, and Judgment, even the most insignificant Amusements. They should all be arranged in subordination, to the great Plan of Happiness, and Utility. That you may attend early to this Maxim is the Wish of your affectionate Father, John Adams

From John Adams' Diary

1781 JANUARY 11. THURSDAY.

Returned from the Hague to Leyden. Was present from 12. to one O Clock, when the Præceptor gave his Lessons in Latin and Greek to my Sons. His Name is Wenshing. He is apparently a great Master of the two Languages, besides which he speaks French and Dutch very well, understands little English, but is desirous of learning it. He obliges his Pupills to be industrious, and they have both made a great Progress for the Time. He is pleased with them and they with him. John is transcribing a Greek Grammar of his Masters Composition and Charles a Latin one. John is also transcribing a Treatise on Roman Antiquities, of his masters writing. The Master gives his Lessons in French.

This Day Dr. Waterhouse, Mr. Thaxter and my two Sons dined with me at the Cour de Hollande, and after Dinner, went to the Rector Magnificus, to be matriculated into the University. Charles was found to be too young, none under twelve Years of Age being admitted. John was admitted, after making a Declaration that he would do nothing against the Laws of the University, City or Land.

I wish to be informed concerning the Constitution and Regulations of this University. The Number of Professors, their Characters. The Government of the Students both in Morals and Studies. Their Manner of Living–their Priviledges &c. &c.

During the first six months of 1781 John Adams absorbed himself in resolving the complexities of America's interests and his own in the Netherlands. In February he received dispatches from Congress commissioning him minister plenipotentiary to the States General in succession to Laurens and instructing him to negotiate a treaty of amity and commerce with the Netherlands. Thereafter, through agents, he rented, furnished, and staffed a residence in Amsterdam judged suitable for the American minister. His own efforts toward obtaining recognition of American sovereignty were made more difficult by the devastating loss suffered by the Dutch in the surrender to the British of the commercially important port of St. Eustatius in the West Indies. This first taste of war with Great Britain left most of the Dutch leadership with little enthusiasm for its prosecution and with no inclination to extend aid to America.

Nevertheless, Adams prosecuted with zeal his attempts to gain recognition preliminary to negotiating a treaty and loan. He directed his efforts toward the effective utilization of the press both in the Netherlands and, through intermediaries, in England. One such venture saw the republication in 1782 in London of the *Dissertation on the Canon and the Feudal Law*, his earlier argument for the necessity of resistance to tyranny. His major effort in political propaganda, however, was *A Memorial to Their High Mightinesses*, which he signed and dated on April 19, 1781. In it he drew parallels between the successful struggle of the people of the Low Countries for independence and America's current struggle, and urged the immediate and future advantages to the Dutch of closer commercial relations with the United States. The *Memorial* was formally presented to officials of the government in May and subsequently circulated in Dutch, French, and English. Its impact would be evident in the next year. The comparison that Abigail Adams made between her husband's diplomacy and the remarkable negotiation of Sir William Temple in the Netherlands in 1668 was highly apposite.

JOHN ADAMS' RESIDENCE IN AMSTERDAM, 1781–1782,
"ON THE KEYSERSGRAGT NEAR THE SPIEGEL STRAAT"

JA to AA

My dearest Friend Amsterdam April 28. 1781

Congress have been pleased to give me so much other Business to do, that I have not Time to write either to Congress, or to private Friends so often as I used.

Having lately received Letters of Credence to their High mightinesses the states General of the United Provinces of the Low Countries and to his most serene Highness the Prince of Orange, I am now fixed to this Country, untill I shall be called away to Conferences for Peace, or recalled by Congress. I have accordingly taken a House in Amsterdam upon the Keysers Gragt i.e. the Emperors Canal, near the Spiegel Straat i.e. the Looking Glass street, so you may Address your Letters to me, there.

I have hitherto preserved my Health in this damp Air better than I expected. So have all of us, but Charles who has had a tertian fever but is better.

I hope this People will be in earnest, after the twentyeth of June. Americans are more Attended to and our Cause gains ground here every day. But all Motions are slow here, and much Patience is necessary. I shall now however be more settled in my own Mind having something like a Home. Alass how little like my real home.—What would I give for my dear House keeper. But this is too great a felicity for me.

I dont expect to stay long in Europe.—I really hope I shall not.—Things dont go to my Mind.

Pray get the Dissertation on the Cannon and feudal Law printed in a Pamphlet or in the Newspapers and send them to me by every Opportunity untill you know that one has arrived. I have particular Reasons for this.—My Nabby and Tommy, how do they do.

John Adams to John Quincy Adams

My dear Son Amsterdam, May 14. 1781

I received yours of 13 this morning.

If you have not found a convenient Place to remove into, you may continue in your present Lodgings another Month.

I am glad you have finished Phædrus, and made Such Progress in Nepos, and in Greek.

Amidst your Ardour for Greek and Latin I hope you will not forget your mother Tongue. Read Somewhat in the English Poets every day. You will find them elegant, entertaining and instructive Companions, through your whole Life. In all the Disquisitions you have heard concerning the Happiness of Life, has it ever been recommended to you to read Poetry?

To one who has a Taste, the Poets serve to fill up Time which would otherwise pass in Idleness, Languor, or Vice. You will never be alone, with a Poet in your Poket. You will never have an idle Hour.

How many weary hours have been made alert, how many melancholly ones gay, how many vacant ones useful, to me, in the course of my Life, by this means?

Your Brother grows dayly better but is still weak and pale. He shall write to you, Soon.

Your affectionate Father, J. Adams

AA to JA

May 25 1781

In this Beautifull month when Nature wears her gayest garb, and animal and vegetable life is diffused on every side, when the Chearfull hand of industery is laying a foundation for a plentifull Harvest who can forbear to rejoice in the Season, or refrain looking "through Nature up to Nature's God?"

"To feel the present Deity and taste
The joy of God, to see a happy World."

While my Heart expands, it sighing seeks its associate and joins its first parent in that Beautifull Discriptive passage of Milton

Sweet is the Breath of morn, her rising sweet,
With charm of earliest Bird; pleasent the Sun,
When first on this delightfull land he spreads
His orient beams, on herb, tree, fruit and flower
Glist'ring with dew; fragrant the fertile earth
After soft showers, and sweet the comeing on
of Gratefull Evening mild; then Silent Night
with this her solemn Bird, and this fair Moon
And these the Gems of heaven, her starry train;
But neither Breath of Morn when she assends
With charm of earliest Birds nor rising Sun
on this delightfull land: nor herb, fruit, flower
Glist'ring with dew; nor fragrance after showers
nor Gratefull Evening mild, nor Silent Night
with this her Solemn Bird, nor Walk by moon
or Glitt'ring Star light, "*without thee is sweet.*"

This passage has double charms for me painted by the hand of Truth, and for the same reason that a dear Friend of mine after having viewed a profusion of Beautifull pictures pronounced that which represented the parting of Hector and Andromaque to be worth them all. The journal in which this is mentiond does not add any reason why it was so, but Portia felt its full force, and paid a gratefull tear to the acknowledgment.

This day my dear Friend compleats 8 months since the date of your last Letter, and 5 since it was received. You may judge of my anxiety. I doubt not but you have written many times since but Mars, Belona and old Neptune are in league against me. I think you must still be in Holland from whence no vessels have arrived since the Declaration of War. Their are some late arrivals from France, but no private Letters. I have had the pleasure of hearing of the Safety of several vessels which went from hence, by which I wrote to you, so that I have reason to think I have communicated pleasure tho I have not been a partaker in the same way. I have just written to you by a vessel of Mr. Tracys, Capt. Brown bound for Amsterdam which I hope will reach you. If you made use of Bilboa your Friends there could forward ten Letters from thence, for one opportunity else where. Many vessels from Boston and Newbury are now bound there.

This will be deliverd to you by Mr. Storer, who is going first to Denmark and who designs to tarry abroad some time. If you had been a resident in your own country it would have been needless for me to have told you that Mr. Storer is a young Gentleman of a Fair character, I need not add amiable manners as those are so discoverable in him upon the slightest acquaintance. You will not fail to notice and patronize him according to his merrit.

We are anxiously waiting for intelligence from abroad. We shall have in the Feild a more respectable army than has appeard there since the commencement of the War and all raised for 3 years or during the war, most of them Men who have served before. The Towns have excerted themselves upon this occasion with a spirit becomeing patriots. We wish for a Naval force superiour to what we have yet had, to act in concert with our Army. We have been flattered from day to day, yet none has arrived, the Enemy exult in the Delay, and are improveing the time to ravage Carolina and Virginia.

We hardly know what to expect from the united Provinces, because we are not fully informd of their Disposition. Britain has struck a blow by the Capture of Eustatia sufficent to arouse and unite them against her, if there still exists that Spirit of Liberty which shone so conspicuous in their Ancestors and which under much greater difficulties led their hardy fore Fathers to reject the tyranny of Philip.

I wish your powers may extend to an Alliance with them, and that you may be as successful against the Artifices of Britain as a former

Ambassador was against those of an other Nation when he negotiated a triple Alliance in the course of 5 days with an address which has ever done Honour to his memory. If I was not so nearly connected, I should add, that there is no small similarity in the character of my Friend, and the Gentleman whose memoirs I have read with great pleasure.

Our state affairs I will write you if the vessel does not sail till after Election. Our Friend Mr. C[ranc]h goes from hence rep' by a *unanimous vote*. Dr. T[uft]s of W[eymout]h is chosen Senator, our Govenour and Lieut. Govenour, *as at the begining*. Our poor old currency is Breathing its last gasp. It received a most fatal wound from a collection of near the whole Bodys entering here from the Southward. Having been informed that it was treated here with more respect, and that it could purchase a solid and durable Dress here for 75 paper Dollors, but half the expence it must be at there, [it] traveld here with its whole train, and being much debauched in its manners communicated the contagion all of a sudden and is universally rejected. It has given us a great Shock. Mr. Storer can give you more information.

I have by two or 3 opportunities acquainted you that I received the calicos you orderd for me by Sampson, tho many of them were much injured by being wet. I have not got my things yet from Philadelphia. I have acquainted you with my misfortune there, oweing to the bad package. I have no invoice from Mr. Moylan or Letter, tho I have reason to think many things have been stolen out as all Dr. T[uft]s are missing, and several of mine according to Mr. L[ovel]ls invoice who was obliged to unpack what remaind and dry them by a fire, most of them much damaged. I have been more particular in other Letters.

Our Friends in general are well, your M[othe]r in a declining way. I rather think the Good Lady will not continue many years, unless Her health mends. I fear not the present. She is anxious to hear from you whilst she lives, but bids me tell you not to expect to see her again. To my dear sons I shall write by this opportunity. I have not received a line from them for this twelvemonth. I hope they continue to behave worthy the Esteem of every body, which will never fail to communicate the greatest pleasure to their affectionate parents. I inclosed an invoice of a few articles by Capt. Brown. I will repeat it here. Any thing in the goods way will be an acceptable remittance to your ever affectionate

Portia

Vergennes, on receiving a proposal from the Russian and Austrian courts for a mediation at Vienna between the warring powers, had had to summon Adams, the sole American representative in Europe empowered to discuss terms of peace, to Paris for consultation. Adams soon saw that the proposed mediation had for its purpose, "chicaning the United States out of their independence." His rejection of the terms on the part of those United States ended the matter. He returned to Amsterdam at the end of July.

Before Adams learned that a journey to Paris impended, he had been led by concern over the lingering illness of his son Charles to bring him, in May, to Amsterdam. A plan for Charles' return to America evolved in the next weeks. At about the same time, Adams was persuaded by Francis Dana to permit John Quincy to accompany him on his ministry to St. Petersburg as companion, French interpreter, and private secretary. They set out just after John Adams departed for Paris.

JA to AA

My dear Portia Paris July 11. 1781

I am called to this Place, in the Course of my Duty: but dont conceive from it any hopes of Peace. This desireable object is yet unhappily at a Distance, a long distance I fear.

My dear Charles will go home with Maj. Jackson. Put him to school and keep him steady.—He is a delightfull Child, but has too exquisite sensibility for Europe.

John is gone, a long Journey with Mr. Dana:—he will serve as an Interpreter, ⟨*if not a Clerk,*⟩ and the Expence will be little more than at Leyden. He will be satiated with travel in his Childhood, and care nothing about it, I hope in his riper Years.

I am distracted with more cares than ever, yet I grow fat. Anxiety is good for my Health I believe.

Oh that I had Wings, that I might fly and bury all my Cares at the Foot of Pens Hill.

While John Adams schemed and wrote in the Netherlands during the early part of 1781, the reverberations of his quarrel with the Comte de Vergennes in June–July 1780 were being felt in America.

Vergennes, meanwhile, had tried to make certain that Congress should hear of his displeasure with the stiff-necked American emissary who insisted on behaving as if the Franco-American alliance were a partnership of equals. He transmitted the entire correspondence that had passed between him and Adams to Benjamin Franklin, along with a letter to Franklin differentiating sharply the confidence he had in Franklin from his want of it in Adams. What he sought was at least a reprimand to Adams and, if possible, a reduction of his powers.

In reply, Franklin disingenuously denied knowledge of the positions taken by Adams, acquiesced in the charge of "Indiscretion," and expressed confidence that Adams' conduct would not be approved by Congress. On August 9, 1780, Franklin had forwarded the papers to Congress with a letter of his own in which he spoke again of "the Inconveniencies, that attend the having more than one Minister at the same Court." Adams, he continued, "seems to have endeavoured to supply what he may suppose my Negociations defective in." He thinks a "greater air of Independence and Boldness in our Demands will procure us more ample assistance. . . . He is gone to Holland to try, as he told me, whether something might not be done to render us less dependent on France."

The French minister in Philadelphia, the Chevalier de La Luzerne, exerted his considerable influence in Congress to such effect that in June 1781 Adams was deprived of his exclusive powers as peace minister by being joined in a commission of which the other members were Franklin, John Jay, Henry Laurens, and Thomas Jefferson. Further, these commissioners were ordered "ultimately to govern" themselves in everything by the "advice and opinion" of the French court. A month later, Congress revoked Adams' commission to negotiate a commercial treaty with Britain. In Adams' mind, Congress' actions remained personally and nationally humiliating.

In accounts to Mrs. Adams and to others in Boston from correspondents in Philadelphia, the significant role of Franklin's "most unkind and stabbing" letter was emphasized. Abigail Adams' resentment was deep and prolonged.

Abigail Adams to Elbridge Gerry

Sir — Braintree july 20. 1781

When I looked for your Name among those who form the Representative Body of the people this year I could not find it. I sought for it with the Senate, but was still more dissapointed. I however had the pleasure of finding it amongst the delegates of this Commonwealth to Congress, where I flatter myself you will still do us Honour which posterity will gratefully acknowledge; and the virtuous few now confess. But as you are no worshiper of the rising Sun, or Adulator at the shrine of power, you must expect with others, who possess an Independant Spirit, to be viewed in the shade, to be eyed askance, to be malign'ed and to have your Good evil spoken of. But let not this Sir discourage you in the arduous Buisness. I hope America has not yet arrived at so great a pitch of degeneracy as to be given up by those alone who can save her; I mean the disinterested patriot—who possessing an unconfined Benevolence will persevere in the path of his duty. Tho the Ingratitude of his constituents and the Malevolence of his Enemies should conspire against him, he will feel within himself the best Intimations of his duty, and he will look for no external Motive.

History informs us that the single virtue of Cato, upheld the Roman Empire for a time, and a Righteous few might have saved from the impending Wrath of an offended deity the Ancient cities of Sodom and Gomorah. Why then my dear Sir, may I ask you, do you wish to withdraw yourself from publick Life?

You have supported the cause of America with zeal with ardour and fidelity, but you have not met even with the gratitude of your fellow citizens—in that you do not stand alone.

You have a mind too Liberal to consider yourself only as an Individual, and not to regard both your Country and posterity—and in that view I know you must be anxiously concerned when you consider the undue Influence excercised in her Supreme Counsels. You can be no stranger I dare say Sir, to matters of the Highest importance to the future welfare of America as a Nation; being now before her Representitives—and that she stands in need of the collected wisdom of the United States, and the Integrity of her most virtuous members.

I will not deny Sir, that personally I feel myself much Interested in your attendance there. I fear there is a spirit prevailing, too powerfull for those who wish our prosperity; and would seek our best Interests. Mr. L⟨*ove*⟩ll and Mr. A⟨*dam*⟩s have informed you I suppose of the Intrigues and malicious aspersions of my absent Friends character, if they have not, I will forward to you a coppy of a Letter which will not want any comment of mine.

The plan which appears to be adopted both at Home and abroad, is a servile adulation and complasance to the Court of our Allies, even to the giving up some of our most valuable privileges. The Independant Spirit of your Friend, abroad, does not coinside with the selfish views and inordinate ambition of your Minister, who in consequence of it, is determined upon his distruction. Stung with envy at a merit he cannot emulate, he is allarmed with the apprehension of losing the Honour of some Brilliant action; and is useing his endeavours that every enterprize shall miscarry, in which he has not the command. To Effect this purpose he has insinuated into the minds of those in power the falsest prejudices against your Friend, and they have so far influenced the united Counsels of these States, as to induce them to join this unprincipled Man, in Commission with him for future Negotiations. If Congress had thought proper to have joined any Gentleman of real abilities and integrity with our Friend, who could have acted in concert with him; he would have gratefully received his assistance—but to clog him with a Man, who has shewn himself so Enimical to him, who has discovered the marks of a little and narrow Spirit by his malicious aspersions, and ungenerous insinuations, and whose measures for a long time they have had no reason to be gratified with, is such a proof to me of what my absent Friend has reason to expect, and what you know Sir, I very early feared; that I can see nothing but dishonour, and disgrace attending his most faithfull, and zealous exertions for the welfare of his Country.

These Ideas fill me with the deepest concern. Will you suffer Female influence so far to operate upon you; as to step forth and lend your aid to rescue your Country and your Friend, without inquiring

> "What can Cato do
> Against a World, a base degenerate World
> which courts a yoke and bows its Neck to Bondage."

There is a very serious Light in which this matter is to be viewed; the serious light in which a late distinguished Modern writer expresses it—"that we are all embarked on the same Bottom, and if our Country sinks, we must Sink with it."

Your acknowledged Friendship and former politeness has led me to the freedom of this address, and prevents my asking an excuse which I should otherways think necessary for her who has the Honour to subscribe herself your Friend and Humble Servant, Portia

PS The communication of the minister at Versails being joined with my Friend was made in confidence—I wish it may not be mentiond at present.

AA to JA

August 1 1781

O that I could realize the agreable reverie of the last Night when my dear Friend presented himself and two Son[s] safely returnd to the Arms of the affectionate wife and Mother. Cruel that I should wake only to experience a renual of my daily solicitude. The next month will compleat a whole year since a single Line from your Hand has reachd the longing Eyes of Portia. No vessels have arrived here since the declaration of war from Holland. Congress have no dispatches later than october from you. I hope and hope till hope is swallowed up in the victory of Dispair. I then consider all my anxiety as vain since I cannot benifit any one by it, or alter the established order of things. I cannot relieve your mind from the burden of publick cares, or at this distance alleviate the anxiety of your Heart, tho ever so much distressed for the welfare of your Native land or protect you from the Slanderous arrow that flieth in Secret, a Specimin of which you will find inclosed in a Letter from Mr. C[ranc]h but which you must I think have received before as many coppies have been sent. My Indig[nation] is too big for utterance.

> Falsehood and fraud shoot up in ev'ry soil
> The product of all climes—Rome had its Cea[sar.]

I will not comment upon this low this dirty this Infamous t[his] diabolical peice of envy and malice as I have already do[ne] it where I thought I might be of service—to your two Friends L[ovell] and G[err]y.

> True consious Honour is to know no Sin—

and the firm patriot whose views extend to the welfare of Mankind tho obstructed by faction and vice, tho crossed by fortune, tho wounded by calumny and reproach, shall find in the end that his generous Labour is not lost—even tho he meets with no other reward than that self approveing hour, which the poet tells us [outweighs?] whole years of stupid starers and of loud Huz[zas.]

When ever any opportunity occurs write, and write me a volume to amuse, to comfort and inform me. I turn to the loved pages of former days and read them with delight. They are all my comfort, all my consolation in the long long [in]terval of time that I have not received a line. Should I name my dear Boys a tear will flow with the Ink—not a line have I received from them for more than a Year. May they be their Fathers comfort and their Mothers delight.

No very important military events have taken place since I wrote you last which was by Capt. Young to Bilboa. Green is driving Cornwallis acting with much Spirit and viggour. We are here looking upon each other in a mere maze. Our old currency died suddenly, the carkases remain in the hands of individuals, no Burial having been yet provided for it. The New was in Good repute for a time, but all of a Sudden and in one day followed [its] Elder Brother—so that with old and New in my hand, I can not purchase a single Sixpence worth of any thing yet taxes must be paid, men must be raised for Road Island and West Point and paid too, yet the profits of what each one has sold for paper avails them not. This was a stroke of our Enemies by employing Emissaries to depreciate it who were detected and put into jail. Barter and hard money is now the only trade. The strugle will be to supply our army. How after having sold our commodities for paper we can raise hard money to pay the next demand which must be speedy, I know not. I had collected a sufficient Sum of paper to pay a very large tax which the last Session of the court levied. It now will avail me not a groat. I mentioned in a former Letter that

[I] wished you to send me a chest of Bohea tea by any vessel of Mr. Tracys or Smiths. It would turn into money quicker [*remainder missing*]

AA to JA

My dearest Friend

Sepbr. 29 1781

Three days only did it want of a year from the date of your last Letter, when I received by Capt. Newman in the Brig Gates your welcome favour of May 22d.

By various ways I had collected some little intelligence of you, but for six months past my Heart had known but little ease—not a line had reachd me from you, not a syllable from my children—and whether living or dead I could not hear. That you have written many times, I doubted not, but such is the chance of War; and such the misfortune attending a communication between absent Friends.

I learn by Mr. Brush, that Mr. Dana is gone to Petersburgh, and with him Master John. For this I am not sorry. Mr. Danas care and attention to him, I shall be well satisfied in—and Russia is an Empire I should be very fond of his visiting. My dear Charles I hear is comeing home with Gillion.

I know not your motives for sending him but dare say you have weighty reasons. That of his Health is alone sufficient, if the low countries are as prejudicial to him, as I fear they are—and will be to his Father too. Why did you not write me about it? At first I learnt it, only by hearing of a list of passengers who were to come in the Indian, amongst which was a son of Mr. A—s. This made me very uneasy—I had a thousand fears and apprehensions. Nor shall I be much at ease, you may well suppose, untill I hear of her arrival. I fear she will be an object, for the British to persue. The Event I must commit to the Supreme Ruler of the universe.—Our Friends here are all well, your Mother has recoverd beyond my expectation, my Father too is in good Health for his years. Both our parents remember you with affection.

General Green, is making the Requisition you require, and setling the preliminarys for a Peace, by extirpating the British force from Carolina. We are from the present prospect of affairs in daily expectation that Cornwallis will meet the Fate of Burgoine. God Grant it—and that this winter may produce to America an *honorable Peace*. But my fears are well grounded when I add, that some of your Colleagues are unfit for the Buisness and I really am in suspence whether you will hold your Garbled commission, for reasons to which you will be no stranger before this reaches you. But if you resign, I am not the only person by hundreds who dread the consequences, as it is probable you will find, from instructions which I hear are to be sent, from several States to their delegates in Congress. You have a delicate part to act. You will do what you esteem to be your duty, I doubt not; fearless of consequences, and futurity will discriminate the Honest Man from the knave tho the present Generation seem little disposed to.

I cannot write so freely as I wish. Your Memorial is in high estimation here.

So you have set down at Amsterdam in the House keeping way. What if I should take a trip across the Atlantick? I tell Mrs. Dana we should pass very well for Natives.—I have received a very polite Letter from Mr. DeNeufvilla. How did this Man discover, that extolling my Husband was the sweetest Musick in my ears? He has certainly touched the key which vibrates Harmony to me!

I think I have requested you to send me a chest of Bohea Tea, by any vessel of Mr. Tracys. Do not think me extravagant—I economize with the utmost Frugality I am capable of, but our Taxes are so high, and so numerous, that I know not which way to turn. I paied 60 hard dollars this week for a State and county Rate. I have 30 more to pay immediately for hireing a Man for 6 months in the Service, and a very large town tax, now comeing out. Hard Money is our only currency. I have a sum of old and new paper which lies by me useless at present. Goods of the West India kind are low as ever they were—Bills Sell greatly below par. Hard money is very scarce, but I hope never to see an other paper Medium. Difficult as the times are, and dull as Buisness is, we are in a better situation than we were before.

Where is my Friend Mr. Thaxter? that not a line has reachd me from him? His Friends are all well, but longing and impatient to hear from him. We see by the paper that he was well enough to celebrate independence on the fourth of july.—The Robinhood had Letters to all my Friends which I hope you have received. I send many to Bilboa, do you get any from thence, pray write to me by way of France and Bilboa.

This is to go by a Brig to France which I heard of but yesterday. You have I suppose received a commission for forming a Quadrupple alliance—such an one is made out.

O my dear Friend, how far distant is the day when I may expect to receive you in your Native Land?

Haughty Britain sheath your sword in pitty to yourselves. Let not an other village be added to the long list of your depredations. The Nations around you shudder at your crimes. Unhappy New London Named after your capital—may she close the devastation.

How many tender Sentiments rise to mind when about to bid you adieu. Shall I express them or comprise them all in the assurence of being ever Ever Yours, Portia

Whether the result can be attributed to receipt of word of the actions taken by Congress in regard to Adams or to the unhealthiness of the Dutch summer climate or to overwork or to a combination of all these, John Adams was brought down by a severe and protracted "nervous Fever."

Almost simultaneously with its onset in August, Adams had seen his son Charles, recently recuperated, embarked on the newly renamed frigate *South Carolina*, Captain Alexander Gillon, in the care of Major William Jackson. But Gillon was an adventurer. He chose a highly circuitous route; quarrels broke out between him and some of his passengers, including Major Jackson; and the vessel at length put in at La Coruña in Spain for repairs and for want of water and provisions. After considerable delay, Jackson, his charge, and some others took passage on the privateer *Cicero*, Captain Hill. The *Cicero* was beset by further adventures and delays on the way to and in Bilbao. Charles finally reached Beverly, Massachusetts, on January 21, 1782, more than five months after his departure from the Texel in the Netherlands.

JA to AA My dearest Friend Amsterdam October 9. 1781

This is the first Time, I have been able to write you, since my Sickness.—Soon after my Return from Paris, I was seized with a Fever, of which, as the Weather was and had long been uncommonly warm, I took little notice, but it increased very slowly, and regularly, untill it was found to be a nervous Fever, of a dangerous kind, bordering upon putrid. It seized upon my head, in such a manner that for five or six days I was lost, and so insensible to the Operations of the Physicians and surgeons, as to have lost the memory of them. My Friends were so good as to send me an excellent Physician and Surgeon, whose Skill and faithfull Attention with the Blessing of Heaven, have saved my Life. The Physicians Name is Osterdike. The surgeon the same, who cured Charles, of his Wound. I am, however still weak, and whether I shall be able to recover my Health among the pestilential Vapours from these stagnant Waters, I know not.

I hope Charles is well and happy with you, by this Time. He sailed with Commodore Gillon seven Weeks ago. We have no News from Mr. Dana and his young Fellow Traveller, since they left Berlin.

The Pamphlet inclosed, is a Dutch Translation of the Abby Raynals History of the American Revolution. It is a Curiosity for you to lay up.

With Sentiments and Affections that I cannot express, Yours.

JA to AA

My dearest Friend Amsterdam Decr. 2 1781

Your favours of September 29 and Oct. 21. are before me. I avoided saying any Thing about Charles, to save you the Anxiety, which I fear you will now feel in its greatest severity a long time. I thought he would go directly home, in a short Passage, in the best Opportunity which would probably ever present. But I am diss-appointed. Charles is at Bilbao with Major Jackson and Coll. Trumbull who take the best care of his Education as well as his Health and Behaviour. They are to go home in Captain Hill in a good Vessell of 20 Guns. Charles's health was so much affected by this tainted Atmosphere, and he had set his heart so much upon going home in Gillon that it would have broken it, to have refused him.—I desire I may never again have the Weakness to bring a Child to Europe. They are infinitely better at home.—We have all been sick here, myself, Mr. Thaxter, Stephens and another servant, but are all better. Mr. Thaxters Indisposition has been slight and short, mine and Stevens's long and severe.

I beg you would not flatter yourself with hopes of Peace. There will be no such Thing for several years.

Dont distress yourself neither about any malicious Attempts to injure me in the Estimation of my Countrymen. Let them take their Course and go the Length of their Tether. They will never hurt your Husband, whose Character is fortified with a shield of Innocence and Honour ten thousandfold stronger than brass or Iron. The contemptible Essays made by you know whom, will only tend to their own Confusion. My Letters have shewn them their own Ignorance ⟨*and Folly*⟩, a sight they could not bear. Say as little about it as I do. It has already brought them into the true system and that system is tryumphant. I laugh, and will laugh before all Posterity at their impotent ⟨, *despicable, ridiculous folly*⟩ Rage and Envy. They could not help blushing themselves if they were to review their Conduct.

Dear Tom thy Letter does thee much honour. Thy Brother Charles shall teach thee french and Dutch, at home. I wish I could get time to correspond with thee and thy sister, more regularly, but I cannot. I must trust Providence and thine excellent Mamma for the Education of my Children.

Mr. Dana and our son are well, at P[etersburg].

Hayden has some things for you. Hope he is arrived. I am sorry to learn you have a sum of Paper—how could you be so imprudent? You must be frugal, I assure you. Your Children will be poorly off. I can but barely live in the manner that is indispensibly demanded of me by every Body. Living is dear indeed here.

My Children will not be so well left by their father as he was by his. They will be infected with the Examples and Habits and Taste for Expensive Living, without the means. He was not.

My Children, shall never have the smallest soil of dishonour or disgrace brought upon them by their father, no not to please Ministers, Kings, or Nations.

At the Expence of a little of this my Children might perhaps ride at their Ease through Life, but dearly as I love them they shall live in the service of their Country, in her Navy, her Army, or even out of either in the extreamest Degree of Poverty before I will depart in the smallest Iota from my Sentiments of Honour and Delicacy, for I, even I, have sentiments of Delicacy, as exquisite as the proudest Minister that ever served a Monarch. They may not be exactly like those of some Ministers.

I beg you would excuse me to my dear Friends, to whom I cannot write so often as I wish. I have indispensible Duties which take up all my time, and require more than I have.

General Washington has done me great Honour, and much public service by sending me, authentic Accounts of his own and Gen. Greens last great Actions. They are in the Way to negotiate Peace, it lies wholly with them. No other Ministers but they and their Colleagues in the Army can accomplish the great Event.

I am keeping House, but I want an Housekeeper. What a fine Affair it would be if We could flit across the Atlantic as they say the Angels do from Planet to Planet. I would dart to Pens hill and bring you over on my Wings. But alass We must keep house seperately for some time.

But one thing I am determined on. If God should please to restore me once more to your fireside, I will never again leave it without your Ladyships Company. No not even to go to Congress at Philadelphia, and there I am determined to go if I can make Interest enough to get chosen, whenever I return.

I would give a Million sterling that you were here—and could Afford it as well as G. Britain can the thirty Millions she must spend the ensuing Year to compleat her own Ruin.

Farewell. Farewell.

The uncertainties and loneliness of her situation all but overwhelmed Abigail Adams in late 1781. Not given to resting long in lamentation, she turned to the woes of others and to planning for a time of peace when her family would be reunited.

The woe that was most evident around her and that to which she responded with feeling was occasioned by the capture and imprisonment in England of twelve young Braintree sailors. In reciting their plight and the distress of their families, she sought to enlist her husband's assistance to them. His response was to have his correspondents in England make payments to the prisoners from his own funds, no public money being available for such use. Word of Adams' benevolences reached Braintree in July and August, and the boys themselves, released by an exchange of prisoners, soon followed.

The dream which Abigail Adams long entertained of a time when she and her husband would find refuge from public controversies in a sylvan retreat in Vermont did not meet the same ready response from her husband. To her repeated sallies, he offered no comment until long after she had acted to give reality to the dream. In July 1782 she did carry out the purchase of 1,620 acres of wild land in Vermont, a project she had fancied for more than a year both as a refuge and a speculation. In October, John Adams wrote laconically: "Dont meddle any more with Vermont."

AA to JA

My Dearest Friend December 9 1781

I hear the Alliance is again going to France with the Marquis Fayett and the Count de Noiales. I will not envy the Marquis the pleasure of Annually visiting his family, considering the risk he runs in doing it. Besides he deserves the good wishes of every American and a large portion of the Honours and applause of his own Country.

He returns with the additional Merrit of Laurels won at York Town by the Capture of a whole British Army. America may boast that she has accomplished what no power before her ever did, contending with Britain—Captured two of their celebrated Generals and each [with] an Army of thousands of veteran Troops to support them. This Event whilst it must fill Britain with despondency, will draw the union already formed still closer and give us additional Allies; if properly improved must render a negotiation easier and more advantageous to America.

But I cannot reflect much upon publick affairs; untill I have unburthend the load of my own Heart. Where shall I begin my list of Grievences? Not by accusations, but lamentations. My first is that I do not hear from you. A few lines only dated in April and May, have come to hand for 15 Months. You do not mention receiving any from me, except by Capt. Caznew, tho I wrote by Col. Laurence, by Capt. Brown, by Mr. Storer, Dexter and many others. By Babson to Bilboa by Trash, and several times by way of France. You will refer me to Gillion I suppose. Gillion has acted a base part, of which no doubt you are long e'er now apprized. You had great reason to suppose that he would reach America, as soon or sooner than the Merchant vessels and placed much confidence in him, by the treasure you permited to go on Board of him. Ah! how great has my anxiety been, what have I not sufferd since I heard my dear Charles was on Board and no intelligence to be procured of the vessel for 4 months after she saild. Most people concluded that she was founderd at Sea, as she sailed before a voilent Storm. Only 3 weeks ago did I hear the contrary. My unkle dispatchd a Messenger the Moment a vessel from Bilboa arrived with the happy tidings that She was safe at Corruna, that the passenger[s] had all left the Ship in consequence of Gillions conduct, and were arrived at Bilboa. The vessel saild the day that the passengers arrived at Bilboa so that no Letters came by Capt. Lovett but a Dr. Sands reports that he saw a child whom they told him was yours and that he was well. This was a cordil to my dejected Spirits. I know not what to wish for. Should he attempt to come at this Season upon this coast, it has more Horrours than I have fortitude. I am still distresst. I must resign him to the kind protecting Hand of that Being who hath heitherto preserved him, and submit to what ever dispensation is alloted me.

What is the matter with Mr. T[haxte]r, has he forgotten all his American Friends, that out of four vessels which have arrived, not a line is to be found on Board of one of them from him?

I could Quarrell with the climate, but surely if it is subject to the Ague, there is a fever fit as well as the cold one. Mr. Guile tells me he was charged with Letters, but left them with his other things on Board the frigate, She gave him the Slip, he stept on Board Capt. Brown and happily arrived safe. From him I have learnt many things respecting my dear connextions, but still I long for that free communication which I see but little prospect of obtaining. Let me again intreat you to write by way of Guardoca, Bilboa is as safe a conveyance as any I know of.—Ah my dear John, where are you—in so remote a part of the Globe that I fear I shall not hear a Syllable from you.—Pray write me all the intelligence you get from him, send me his Letters to you. Do you know I have not a line from him for a year and half.—Alass my dear I am much afflicted with a disorder call'd the *Heartach*, nor can any remedy be found in America, it must be collected from Holland, Petersburgh and Bilboa.—And now having recited my Greifs and complaints, the next in place are those of my Neighbours. I have been applied to by the parents of several Braintree youth to write to you in their behalf, requesting your aid and assistance if it is in your power to afford it. Capt. Cathcart in the privateer Essex from Salem, went out on a cruise last April into the Channel of England, and was on the 10 of June So unfortunate as to be taken and carried into Ireland, the officers were confined there, but the Sailors were sent prisoners to Plimouth jail 12 of whom are from this Town, a list of whom I inclose. The Friends of these people have received Intelligence by way of an officer who belonged to the *Protector*, and who escaped from the jail; that in August last they were all alive, several of them very destitute of cloathing, having taken but a few with them, and those for the Summer, particularly Ned Savils and Jobe Feild. There request is that if you can, you would render them some assistance, if not by procuring an exchange, that you would get them supplied with necessary cloathing.

I have told them that you would do all in your power for them, but what that would be I could not say. Their Friends here are all well, many of them greatly distresst for their Children, and in a particular manner the Mother of Jeriah Bass.

I wish you to be very particular in letting me know by various opportunities and ways, after the recept of this, whether you have been able to do any thing for them, that I may relieve the minds of these distresst parents. The Capt. got home about 3 months ago, by escapeing to France, but could give no account of his Men after they were taken.

Two years my dearest Friend have passd away since you left your Native land. Will you not return e'er the close of an other year? I will purchase you a retreat in the woods of Virmont and retire with you from the vexations, toils and hazards of publick Life. Do you not sometimes sigh for such a Seclusion—publick peace and domestick happiness,

> "an elegant Sufficency, content
> Retirement, Rural quiet, Friendship, Books
> Ease and alternate Labour, usefull Life
> progressive Virtue and approveing Heaven."

May the time, the happy time soon arrive when we may realize these blessings so elegantly discribed by Thomson, for tho many of your country Men talk in a different Stile with regard to their intentions, and express their wishes to see you in a conspicuous point of view in your own State, I feel no ambition for a share of it. I know the voice of Fame to be a mere weathercock, unstable as Water and fleeting as a Shadow. Yet I have pride, I know I have a large portion of it.

I very fortunately received by the Apollo, by the Juno and by the Minerva the things you sent me, all in good order.

They will enable me to do I hope without drawing upon you, provided I can part with them, but Money is so scarce and taxes so high, that few purchasers are found. Goods will not double, yet they are better than drawing Bills, as they cannot be sold but with a large discount. I could not get more than 90 for a hundred Dollers, should I attempt it.

I shall inclose an invoice to the House of Ingraham Bromfild, and one to de Neufvilla. There is nothing from Bilboa that can be imported with advantage, hankerchiefs are sold here at 7 dollers & half per dozen. There are some articles which would be advantageous from Holland, but Goods there run high, and the retailing vendues which are tolerated here ruin the Shopkeepers. The articles put up, by the American House were better in Quality, for the price than those by the House of de Neufvilla. Small articles have the best profit, Gauze, ribbons, feathers and flowers to make the Ladies Gay, have the best advance. There are some articles which come from India I should suppose would be lower priced than many others—bengalls, Nankeens, persian Silk and Bandano hankerchiefs, but the House of Bromfeild & C[o]. know best what articles will suit here.

I have been fortunate and unfortunate. The things which came in Jones remain at Philadelphia yet.

Our Friends here are all well. Your Mother is rather in better Health, and my Father is yet sprightly. Believe me with more affection than Words can express ever Ever Yours, Portia

JA to AA

My dearest friend Amsterdam Decr. 18 1781

I have Letters from Mr. Dana and his young Attendant, at St. Petersbourg. Both well and in good Spirits. Letters to Mrs. D. and to you go by Captn. Troubridge and by Dr. Dexter.

I have no certain News, as yet of Charles's Sailing from Bilbao, but I presume he is sailed. You will have suffered great Anxiety on his Account, but I pray he may arrive safe. I acted for the best when I consented he should go in Gillon, little expecting that he would be landed in Spain again. Keep him to his studies and send him to Colledge, where I wish his Brother John was.

My Health is feeble, but better than it was. I am busy, enough, yet not to much perceptible Purpose as yet. There is no Prospect at all of Peace. Let our People take Care of their Trade and Privateers, next year. They have not much of a Land War to fear.

General Washington, has struck the most sublime stroke of all in that Article of the Capitulation, which reserves the Tories for Tryal by their Peers. This has struck Toryism dumb and dead. I expect that all the Rancour of the Refugees will be poured out upon Cornwallis for it.

Our Ennemies now really stand in a ridiculous Light. They feel it but cannot take the Resolution to be wise.

The Romans never saw but one caudine Forks in their whole History. Americans have shewn the Britains two, in one War.—But they must do more. Remember, you never will have Peace, while the Britains have a Company of Soldiers at Liberty, within the United States. New York must be taken, or you will never have Peace.—All in good time.

The British Army Estimates are the same as last Year, the Navy less by several ships of the Line. What can these People hope for.

I fancy the southern states will hold their Heads very high. They have a right. They will scarcely be overrun again I believe, even in the hasty manner of Cornwallis. Burgoine dont seem to be affronted that his Nose is out of Joint. He is in good Spirits. Experience has convinced him.—So I hope it has Cornwallis, that the American War is impracticable. The flour, the Choice of the British Army was with him.

The K[ing] of Eng[land] consoles his People under all their Disgraces, Disasters, and dismal Prospects, by telling them that they are brave and free. It is a pity for him that he did not allow the Americans to be so Seven Years ago. But the great designs of Providence must be accomplished. Great Indeed! The Progres of Society, will be accellerated by Centuries by this Rev[olution]. The Emperor of Germany is adopting as fast as he can American Ideas of Toleration and religious Liberty, and it will become the fashionable system of all Europe very soon. Light Spreads from the day Spring in the West, and may it shine more and more until the perfect day.

Duty to Parents, Love to Brothers, sisters and Children. It is not in the Power of Worlds to express the Tenderness with which I bid you farewell.

AA to JA

My Dearest Friend March 17th 1782

Altho I know not of a single opportunity by which I can convey to You my constant anxiety and solicitude for your Health; or obtain from you any knowledge of your present situation, yet I cannot refrain writing my sentiments upon the knowledge I have been able to obtain concerning you here. There has been a motion in C[ongre]ss to recall all their M[inisters] and s[ecretaries] except at V[ersaille]s but it did not obtain.

I have been in daily expectation for months past, that Letters would arrive from you requesting leave to resign your employments; and return again to your Native Land, assured at least of finding one Friend in the Bosom of *Portia*, who is sick, sick of a world in which selfishness predominates, who is sick of counsels unstable as the wind, and of a servility to which she hopes your mind, will never bend.

Most sincerely can she unite with you in the wish of a sequestered Life, the shades of Virmont, the uncultivated Heath are preferable in her mind to the servility of a court.

Some writer observes "that censure is a tax that a Man pays the publick for being eminent." It is in the power of every Man to preserve his probity; but no man living has it in his power to say that he can preserve his reputation. Is it not in your power to withdraw yourself from a situation in which you are certain, no honour can be obtained to yourself or Country? Why Letters have not reached America from you as well as from the minister at Versails, and Madrid since the extrodonary revocation of former powers, I cannot devine—unless purposely stoped by Intrigues and Cabals. The minister at Madrid has done himself and country Honour by refuseing to take a part in the New instructions.

What changes may have taken place in the cabinets abroad since the Capture of Cornwallis, we have not yet learnt. If America does not improve it to her own advantage, she is deficient in that Spirit of Independance which has on former occasions distinguished her.

It is true that her Finances are rather in an unpleasent state. Her Faith has been so often pledged, and having no stable funds, it has been so often forfeited to the undoing of those who confided most, that their is a distrust amongst her best Friends; C[ongres]s have not been able to obtain an impost of 5 per cent which was recommended to be laid upon the importation of all Foreign articles, salt and military stores excepted, for the purpose of raising a revenue to be at the sole disposal of C[ongre]ss.

March 25th

Thus far I wrote and laid by my pen untill I could hear of an opportunity of conveyance. By a Letter last evening received from my unkle I was informed of a vessel soon to sail for France. I reasume my pen, but my trembling anxious Heart scarcly knows what to dictate to it. Should I discribe all that has passd within it, since I heard of your illness, you would pitty its distresses. I fear the anxiety you have felt for the disgracefull concequences which your [country] was about to involve itself in, have affected your Health and impaired, your constitution. I well know how Essential the Honour and dignity of your country, its Independance and safety is, to your peace of mind and your happiness; if that cannot be promoted under present circumstances, let me intreat you to withdraw. Let me beg of you to resign; your Health suffers; my Health suffers from a dejection of Spirits which I cannot overcome—

> "O thou whose Friendship is my joy and pride
> Whose Virtues warm me; and whose precepts guide
> Say A. amidst the toils of anxious State
> does not thy secreet soul desire retreat?
> dost thou not wish the task, the duty done
> Thy Busy life at length might be thy own
> that to thy Loved philosophy resign'd
> No care might ruffle thy unbended mind?"

It is this hope, this distant Idea that cheers my languid spirits and supports me through domestick perplexities. I mentioned to you that I had received no Letters from you of a later date than July, and in a former Letter I acquainted you that our dear Charles arrived here in January in good Health, and by him I first learnt that you had been sick. My Friends were not Ignorant of it, having some months before been made acquainted with it; by Letters from Mr. Ingraham to Mr. Daws, but they had carefully concealed it from me, knowing the distress it would give me, and supposeing it would be long before I should hear again from you. Your Letter to Charles in Bilboa greatly alarmed me. God Grant that you may have recoverd your Health, and preserve a Life essential to the happiness of Portia. What a cordial, what a comfort would a Letter, with the happy tidings of your returned Health prove to the distressed Bosom of Portia. Heaven grant it speedily.

Charles is perfectly happy in his safe return, to his dear Native

Land, to which he appears the more attached from having visited foreign climes. May the promiseing dawn of future usefullness grow with his Growth and strengthen with his Strength whilst it sweetens the declining Life of those to whom he is most dear.

Major Jackson to whose care you intrusted him, was high in his praises'es and commendations. As I did not know in what situation he was placed, I inquired of Major Jackson. He informd me that when he arrived at Bilboa he drew a Bill upon you for money to answer his expences, that he had kept an account of Charles's which together with a small Balance he would leave at Col. Crafts where he lodged in Boston for me; he was a second time at Braintree, but said he had forgot his papers. Soon after he went for Philadelphia, and I heard no more of him; or his papers—which after a reasonable time I thought proper to inquire for, at his Lodgings, but was assured nothing was ever left for me. With regard to Charles passage the Captain and owners demand 25 guineys for it, which my unkle thinks very extravagent as he is well acquainted with passages, having both paid and received them from Bilboa, 80 dollors being the extent, he ever gave or received even when the Captain found stores, which was not now the case, but the Capt[ain] says the other passengers gave that, and he expects the same for him. I must therefore be under the necessity of drawing upon you for it, as I cannot answer it without dissapointing myself of a favorite object; I mean a Lot of Land of 300 acers for each of our children in the New State of Virmont, for which I have been very assidiously collecting all I could spair from taxes. They sell only 300 acers in a share and will not admit of one persons purchaseing more, so that the deeds must be made out in each childs or persons Name who is the purchaser. Several of our Friends have been purchaseing in the same Township, which is well situated upon two Rivers. I wish it was in my power to purchase 12 hundred for each instead of 3, but I dare not run ventures. The Goverment is like to be amicably setled and in a few years it will become a flourishing place.—Land here is so high taxed that people are for selling their Farms and retireing back. I can Instance to you one tax Bill which will shew you the difference of the present with the former. There are two acers and half of salt medow which you know you own in Milton, it formerly paid 3 shillings tax, and this year 36.—Mr. Alleyne has Burried his Mother and sister. He now wishes to sell his Farm and has accordingly put it upon sale. It is a place I should be fond of, but know it must still be my castle in the air.

You are loosing all opportunities for helping yourself, for those

HUIS TEN BOSCH, THE STADHOLDER'S RESIDENCE NEAR THE HAGUE

who are daily becomeing more and more unworthy of your Labours and who will neither care for you or your family when their own turn is served—so selfish are mankind. I know this is a language you are unwilling to hear. I wish it was not a truth which I daily experience.

I do not recollect through all your absence that I have ever found the person who has been inclined to consider me or my situation either on account of my being destitute of your assistance or that you are devoteing your time and talents to the publick Service (Mr. Tracy excepted who has twice refused the freight of a few articles from Bilboa). It is true my spirit is too independant to ask favours. I would fain believe you have Friends who would assist me if I really stood in need, but whilst I can help myself I will not try them. I will not ask a person to lend me money who would demand 30 per cent for it. I never yet borrowed for my expences, nor do I mean to do it. Charles passage I must draw upon you for, if they will not take a Bill. They may wait your return for borrow I will not. I shall add a list of a few articles which I wish you to send me, or rather Bring—as you will I hope whatever you have in the House keeping way, when ever you return.

I should be glad the List may be given to the House of Ingraham

&c. They best know what will suit here and do Buisness with more judgement and exactness as I found by what they once put up before. I shall depend wholy upon the remittances you may make me from time to time in the same way you have done. As to draughts I can make none but with loss. Goods are dull, but do better than Bills. Not a word from John since he went to Russia, not a Line from Mr. Thaxter. If I have not time to write to him, let him know that his Friends are well and his Sister Loring has a daughter.

Mrs. Dana was well this week. Her Brother and sister dined here to day. So did our Milton Friends who desired to be rememberd to you. Mrs. Gray is this week to be married to Mr. S.A. Otis. Are you not too old to wonder? Mr. Cranch is recovering from a very dangerous Sickness in which his Friends all dispaired of his Life. My regards to all my Friends abroad. Nabby, Charles, Tom send duty to Pappa and long again to see him.

When o when will the happy day arrive that shall restore him to the affectionate Bosom of Portia

Events elsewhere than in the Netherlands during the first half of 1782 were not particularly propitious for an early and favorable end to the conflict with Great Britain. This period encompassed the serious defeat inflicted by Admiral Rodney on de Grasse's French fleet at the battle of the Saints Passage in April, and the succession of ministries that followed the fall of Lord North's ministry and that were not strong enough to move toward serious peace negotiations.

But beginning in January 1782, an end to John Adams' long and frustrating period of waiting for a Dutch response to his efforts became visible. His diplomatic campaigning and his journalistic efforts to bring pressure "by appealing to the Nation, and arrousing their long dormant Bravery and love of Liberty" were bearing fruit. In February the first of the seven United Provinces of the Netherlands officially declared for recognition. The States General completed the lengthy process on April 19, a year to the day after Adams had submitted his *Memorial*. On April 22 the American minister was received in audience by the Stadholder, and on the next day proposed that the two countries enter into a treaty of amity and commerce. That treaty would be signed on October 8, just before Adams' departure for the peace negotiations at Paris.

The reflection of these events was many-faceted. The tenor of Adams' letters as he awaited final success was happier than for many months. In early March he purchased, and in May moved into, "an house at the Hague, fit for the Hotel des Etats Unis"—the first American-owned legation building in Europe. Public recognition was followed by numerous ceremonial and social events in which Mynheer Adams played a central part. He clearly enjoyed these attentions and his novel role as a courtier. With the satisfaction that came from his conviction that "The American Cause has obtained a Tryumph in this Country more signal, than it ever obtained before in Europe," Adams was ready to enter upon what proved an extended correspondence with Abigail touching his return to America or her journeying to Europe.

JA to AA

My dearest Friend Amsterdam March 22. 1782

Your humble Servant has lately grown much into Fashion in this Country. Nobody scarcely of so much importance, as Mynheer Adams. Every City, and Province rings with De Heer Adams &c. &c. &c. and if I were to judge of things here as We do in other Countries, I should think I was going to be received, at the Hague in awfull Pomp in a few Weeks. But I never can foresee one hour what will happen.

I have had however, great Pleasure to see, that there is a national Attachment to America, in the Body of this nation that is well worth cultivating, for there are no Allies more faithfull than they, as has abundantly appeared by their long Suffering with England.

Our Friends at Petersbourg are well. Pray God Charles may be with you.

I cant conceive what the English will do. They are in a strange Position at present. They cannot do much against America. But I hope, America will take their remaining Armies Prisoners in N.Y. and Charlestown. We must not relax, but pursue our Advantages.

The Proceedings of Rotterdam, will shew you, in the inclosed Paper, the Substance of what all the great Cities in this Republick are doing. Let Mr. Cranch translate it, and print it in the News papers. It is good News. You will have an Abundance of more, which will shew you, that We have not been idle here, but have sown Seeds for a plentifull Harvest. Some Folks will think your Husband, a Negotiator, but it is not he, it is General Washington at York Town who did the substance of the Work, the form only belongs to me.

Oh When shall I see my dearest Friend.—All in good Time. My dear blue Hills, ye are the most sublime object in my Imagination. At your reverend Foot, will I spend my old Age, if any, in a calm philosophical Retrospect upon the turbulent scænes of Politicks and War. I shall recollect Amsterdam, Leyden and the Hague with more Emotion than Philadelphia or Paris.

Adieu Adieu.

AA to JA

My dearest Friend April 10th. 1782

How great was my joy to see the well known Signature of my Friend after a Melancholy Solicitude of many months in which my hopes and fears alternately preponderated.

It was January when Charles arrived. By him I expected Letters, but found not a line; instead of which the heavy tidings of your illness reachd me. I then found my Friends had been no strangers of what they carefully conceald from me. Your Letter to Charles dated in November was the only consolation I had; by that I found that the most dangerous period of your illness was pass'd, and that you considerd yourself as recovering tho feeble. My anxiety and apprehensions from that day untill your Letters arrived, which was near 3 months, conspired to render me unhappy. Capt. Trowbridge in the Fire Brand arrived with your favours of October and December and in some measure dispeld the Gloom which hung heavy at my heart. How did it leap for joy to find I was not the misirable Being I sometimes feared I was. I felt that Gratitude to Heaven which great deliverences both demand and inspire. I will not distrust the providential Care of the supreem disposer of events, from whose Hand I have so frequently received distinguished favours. Such I call the preservation of my dear Friend and children from the uncertain Element upon which they have frequently embarked; their preservation from the hands of their enimies I have reason to consider in the same view, especially when I reflect upon the cruel and inhumane treatment experienced by a Gentleman of Mr. Laurences age and respectable character.

The restoration of my dearest Friend from so dangerous a Sickness, demands all my gratitude, whilst I fail not to supplicate Heaven for the continuance of a Life upon which my temporal happiness rests, and deprived of which my own existance would become a burden. Often has the Question which you say staggerd your philosophy occured to me, nor have I felt so misirable upon account of my own personal Situation, when I considerd that according to the common course of Nature, more than half my days were allready passt, as for those in whom our days are renewed. Their hopes and prospects would vanish, their best prospects, those of Education, would be greatly diminished—but I will not anticipate those miseries which I would shun. Hope is my best Friend and kindest comforter; she assures me that the pure unabated affection, which neither time or absence can allay or abate, shall e'er long be crowned with the completion of its fondest wishes, in the safe return of the beloved object; the age of romance has long ago past, but the affection of almost Infant years has matured and strengthend untill it has become a vital principle, nor has the world any thing to bestow which could in the smallest degree compensate for the loss. Desire and Sorrow were denounced upon our Sex; as a punishment for the transgression of Eve. I have sometimes thought that we are formed to experience more exquisite Sensations than is the Lot of your Sex. More tender and susceptable by Nature of those impression[s] which create happiness or misiry, we Suffer and enjoy in a higher degree. I never wonderd at the philosopher who thanked the Gods that he was created a Man rather than a Woman.

I cannot say, but that I was dissapointed when I found that your return to your native land was a still distant Idea. I think your Situation cannot be so dissagreable as I feared it was, yet that dreadfull climate is my terror.—You mortify me indeed when you talk of sending Charles to Colledge, who it is not probable will be fit under three or four years. Surely my dear Friend fleeting as time is I cannot reconcile myself to the Idea of living in this cruel State of Seperation for [4?] or even three years to come. Eight years have already past, since you could call yourself an Inhabitant of this State. I shall assume the Signature of Penelope, for my dear Ulysses has already been a wanderer from me near half the term of years that, that Hero was encountering Neptune, Calipso, the Circes and Syrens. In the poetical Language of Penelope I shall address you

> "Oh! haste to me! A Little longer Stay
> Will ev'ry grace, each fancy'd charm decay:
> Increasing cares, and times resistless rage
> Will waste my bloom, and wither it to age."

You will ask me I suppose what is become of my patriotick virtue? It is that which most ardently calls for your return. I greatly fear that the climate in which you now reside will prove fatal to your Life, whilst your Life and usefullness might be many years of Service to your Country in a more Healthy climate. If the Essentials of her political system are safe, as I would fain hope they are, yet the impositions and injuries, to which she is hourly liable, and daily suffering, call for the exertions of her wisest and ablest citizens. You know by many years experience what it is to struggle with difficulties —with wickedness in high places—from thence you are led to covet a private Station as the post of Honour, but should such an Idea generally prevail, who would be left to stem the torrent?

Should we at this day possess those invaluable Blessings transmitted us by our venerable Ancestors, if they had not inforced by their example, what they taught by their precepts?

> "While pride, oppression and injustice reign
> the World will still demand her Catos presence."

Why should I indulge an Idea, that whilst the active powers of my Friend remain, they will not be devoted to the Service of his country?

Can I believe that the Man who fears neither poverty or dangers, who sees not charms sufficient either in Riches, power or places to tempt him in the least to swerve from the purest Sentiments of Honour and Delicacy; will retire, unnoticed, Fameless to a Rustick cottage there by dint of Labour to earn his Bread. I need not much examination of my Heart to say I would not willing[ly] consent to it.

Have not Cincinnatus and Regulus been handed down to posterity, with immortal honour?

Without fortune it is more than probable we shall end our days, but let the well earned Fame of having Sacrificed those prospects, from a principal of universal Benevolence and good will to Man, descend as an inheritance to our ofspring. The Luxery of Foreign Nations may possibly infect them but they have not before them an example of it, so far as respects their domestick life. They are not Bred up with an Idea of possessing Hereditary Riches or Grandeur. Retired from the Capital, they see little of the extravagance or dissipation, which prevails there, and at the close of day, in lieu of the Card table, some usefull Book employs their leisure hours. These habits early fixed, and daily inculcated, will I hope render them usefull and ornamental Members of Society.—But we cannot see into futurity. —With Regard to politicks, it is rather a dull season for them, we are recruiting for the Army.

The Enemy make sad Havock with our Navigation. Mr. Lovell is appointed continential Receiver of taxes and is on his way to this State.

It is difficult to get Gentlemen of abilities and Integrity to serve in congress, few very few are willing to Sacrifice their Interest as others have done before them.

Your favour of december 18th came by way of Philadelphia, but all those Letters sent by Capt. Reeler were lost, thrown over Board. Our Friends are well and desire to be rememberd to you. Charles will write if he is able to, before the vessel sails, but he is sick at present, threatned I fear with a fever. I received one Letter from my young Russian to whom I shall write—and 2 from Mr. Thaxter. If the vessel gives me time I shall write. We wait impatiently for the result of your demand. These slow slugish wheels move not in unison with our feelings.

Adieu my dear Friend. How gladly would I visit you and partake of your Labours and cares, sooth you to rest, and alleviate your anxieties were it given me to visit you even by moon Light, as the faries are fabled to do.

I cheer my Heart with the distant prospect. All that I can hope for at present, is to hear of your welfare which of all things lies nearest the Heart of Your ever affectionate Portia

JA to AA

My dearest Friend The Hague May 14 1782

On the Twelfth, I removed into this House which I have purchased for the United States of America. But, it will be my Residence but a little while.

I must go to you or you must come to me. I cannot live, in this horrid Solitude, which it is to me, amidst Courts, Camps and Crowds. If you were to come here, such is the Unsteadiness of the Foundation that very probably We should have to return home again in a Month or six Weeks and the Atlantick is not so easily passed as Pens hill. I envy you, your Nabby, Charly and Tommy, and Mr. Dana his Johnny who are very well. A Child was never more weary of a Whistle, than I am of Embassies. The Embassy here however has done great Things. It has not merely tempted a natural Rival, and an imbittered, inveterate, hereditary Ennemy, to assist a little against G[reat] B[ritain] but it has torn from her Bosom, a constant faithfull Friend and Ally of an hundred Years duration.

It has not only prevailed with a Minister or an absolute Court to fall in with the national Prejudice: but without Money, without Friends, and in Opposition to mean Intrigue it has carried its Cause, by the still small Voice of Reason, and Perswasion, tryumphantly against the uninterrupted Opposition of Family Connections, Court Influence, and Aristocratical Despotism.

It is not a Temple forming a Triple Alliance, with a Nation whose Ruling Family was animated as well as the whole Nation, at that time, with even more Zeal than De Witt in the same Cause.

But you will hear all this represented as a Thing of Course, and of little Consequence—easily done and not worth much.—Very well! Thank God it is done, and that is what I wanted.

Jealousy is as cruel as the Grave, and Envy as spightfull as Hell—and neither have any regard to Veracity or Honour.

JA to AA

Hotel des Etats Unis a la Haye
June 16. 1782

My dearest Friend

I find that the Air of the Hague, and the Return of warm Weather, tho later than was ever known, is of great Service to my Health. I mount on Horseback every Morning, and riding is of Use to me.

I have not escaped the "Influenza," as they call it, which began in Russia and has been epidemical, in all Europe. Mr. Thaxter too has at last submitted to this all subduing Climate and had a Fever, such as Charles had, but is growing well.

You can scarcely imagine a more beautifull Place than the Hague. Yet no Place has any Charms for me but the Blue Hills. My Heart will have in it forever, an acking Void, in any other Place. If you and your Daughter were here! But I must turn my Thoughts from such Objects, which always too tenderly affect me, for my repose or Peace of Mind. I am so wedged in with the Publick Affairs that it is impossible to get away at present. I would transmit a Resignation of all my Employments but this would occasion much Puzzle and be attended with disagreable Consequences. If I thought it probable I should stay in Europe two or three Years, I would certainly request you to come here, but this is opening a scæne of Risque and Trouble for you that I shudder at.—But all is uncertain. I am not properly informed of what passes in Congress, and I know not their Designs. If they would send out another in my Room it would be the most happy News to me, that ever I heard.

The American Cause has obtained a Tryumph in this Country more signal, than it ever obtained before in Europe. It was attended with Circumstances, more glorious than could have been foreseen. A Temple, a D'Avaux, a D'Estrates, had more masterly Pens to celebrate their own Negotiations, and Hearts more at Ease, to do it with Care. Your Friend will never have Leisure, he will never have the Patience to describe the Dangers, the Mortifications, the Distresses he has undergone in Accomplishing this great Work. It is better that some of the Opposition and Intrigues he has had to encounter should be buried in Oblivion.

After all, it will be represented in America as a Thing of Course and of no Consequence. Be it so. It is done—and it is worth as much as it is.

My dear Nabby and Tommy how do ye? Charles you young Rogue! You had more Wit than all of Us. You have returned to a happy Spot. Study earnestly, go to Colledge and be an Ornament to your Country. Education is better at Cambridge, than in Europe. Besides every Child ought to be educated in his own Country. I regret extreamly that his elder Brother is not to have his Education at home. He is well [and] so is his Patron.

Adieu, Adieu, Adieu.

JA to AA

My dearest Friend The Hague July 1. 1782

Your charming Letters of April 10 and 22d were brought me, Yesterday. That of 22d is upon Business. Mr. Hill is paid I hope. I will honour your Bill if you draw. But be cautious—dont trust Money to any Body. You will never have any to lose or to spare. Your Children will want more than you and I shall have for them.

The Letter of the 10 I read over and over without End—and ardently long to be at the blue Hills, there to pass the Remainder of my feeble days. You would be surprised to see your Friend—he is much altered. He is half a Century older and feebler than ever you knew him. The Horse that he mounts every day is of service to his Health and the Air of the Hague is much better than that of Amsterdam, and besides he begins to be a Courtier, and Sups and Visits at Court among Princesses and Princes, Lords and Ladies of various Nations. I assure you it is much wholesomer to be a complaisant, good humoured, contented Courtier, than a Grumbletonian Patriot, always whining and snarling.

However I believe my Courtierism will never go any great Lengths. I must be an independent Man, and how to reconcile this to the Character of Courtier is the Question.

A Line from Unkle Smith of 6. of May makes me tremble for my Friend and Brother Cranch! I must hope he is recoverd.

I can tell you no News about Peace. There will be no Seperate Peaces made, not even by Holland—and I cannot think that the present English Ministry are firm enough in their Seats to make a general Peace, as yet.

When shall I go home? If a Peace should be made, you would soon see me.—I have had strong Conflicts within, about resigning all my Employments, as soon as I can send home a Treaty. But I know not what is duty as our Saints say. It is not that my Pride or my Vanity is piqued by the Revocation of my envied Commission. But in such Cases, a Man knows not what Construction to put. Whether it is not intended to make him resign. Heaven knows I never solicited to come to Europe. Heaven knows too what Motive I can have, to banish my self from a Country, which has given me, unequivocal Marks of its Affection, Confidence and Esteem, to encounter every Hardship and every danger by Sea and by Land, to ruin my Health, and to suffer every Humiliation and Mortification that human Nature can endure.

What affects me most is the Tryumph given to Wrong against Right, to Vice against Virtue, to Folly vs. Wisdom, to Servility against Independance, to base and vile Intrigue against inflexible Honour and Integrity. This is saying a great deal, but it is saying little more than Congress have said upon their Records, in approving that very Conduct for which I was sacrificed.—I am sometimes afraid that it is betraying the Cause of Independence and Integrity or at least the Dignity, which they ought to maintain, to continue in the service. But on the other Hand I have thought, whether it was not more dangerously betraying this Dignity, to give its Ennemies, perhaps the compleat Tryumph which they wished for and sought but could not obtain.

You will see, the American Cause has had a signal Tryumph in this Country. If this had been the only Action of my Life, it would have been a Life well spent. I see with Smiles and Scorn, little despicable Efforts to deprive me of the Honour of any Merit, in this Negotiation, but I thank God, I have enough to shew. No Negotiation to this or any other Country was every recorded in greater detail, as the World will one day see. The Letters I have written in this Country, are carefully preserved. The Conversations I have had are remembered. The Pamphlets, the Gazettes, in Dutch and French, will shew to Posterity, when it comes to be known what share I have had in them as it will be, it will be seen that the Spanish Ambassador expressed but the litteral Truth, when He said

"Monsieur a frappé la plus grand Coup de tout L'Europe.—Cette Reconnaisance fait un honneur infinie a Monsieur.—C'est lui qui a effrayée et terrassee les Anglomanes. C'est lui qui a rempli cet nation d'Enthusiasm."—&c.

Pardon a Vanity, which however is conscious of the Truth, and which has a right to boast, since the most Sordid Arts and the grossest Lies, are invented and propagated, by Means that would disgrace the Devil, to disguise the Truth from the sight of the World. I laugh at this, because I know it to be impossible. Silence!

AA to JA

My dearest Friend July 17 1782

I have delayed writing till the vessel is near ready to Sail, that my Letters may not lay 3 weeks or a month after they are written, as is commonly the case. Mr. Rogers and Lady are going passengers in this vessel; and tho I have only a slight knowledge of them I shall commit my Letters to their care. I have not heard from you since the arrival of Capt. Deshon. Your last Letters were dated in March. I replied to them by the last vessel which saild for France dated about a month ago tho she has not sailed more than a fortnight. I again grow impatient for intelligence. From the last accounts which reachd us by way of Nantys we learn that the Dutch are acquiring a firmness of conduct, that they have acknowledged the independance of America, and are determined to turn a deaf Ear to that prostituted Island of Britain. If this is true, and I sincerely hope it is, I congratulate you upon the Success of your negotiations, and hope your Situation is more eligible than for the time past. If I know you are happy, it will tend to alleiviate the pains of absence.

The Count de Grasse misfortune in the West Indias, we sensibly feel. The British will feed upon it for ages, but it will not save their Nation from the destruction which awaits them.

The Season has advanced thus far without any military Exploit on either Side. We want the one thing necessary for persueing the War with Vigor. Were we less Luxurious we should be better able to support our Independance with becomeing dignity, but having habituated ourselves to the delicacies of Life, we consider them as necessary, and are unwilling to tread back the path of Simplicity, or reflect that

"Man wants but little here below
Nor wants that little long."

By the Enterprize I gave you a particular account of the dangerous Situation our dear Brother Cranch is in. He still continues, but we have little to build our hopes upon of his long continuance with us. Heaven be better to us than our fears. The rest of our Friends are well. Charles has been to see a publick Commencement; and has returned to night much gratified with the exhibitions. He has followed his Studies with attention, since his return, under the care of a Mr. Thomas of Bridgwater; who appears well calculated for the instruction of youth; and is said by good judges, to be an admirable proficient in the Languages. But with him we are obliged to part immediately, as he is going into Buisness. I know not what to do with my Children. We have no Grammer School in the Town, nor have we had for 5 years. I give this Gentleman 2s. 6 pr week a peice, for my two. I must (could I find a School abroad to my mind) Board them at 18 Shillings pr week which is the lowest. In Boston 6 and 8 dollers is given by Gentlemen there for Board, formerly a Gentleman Boarded as well for 12 Shillings, but such is the difference. I know not how to think of their leaving Home. I could not live in the House were it so deserted. If they are gone only for a day, it is as silent as a Tomb.

What think you of your daughters comeing to keep House for you? She proposes it. Could you make a Bridge she would certainly present herself to you, nor would she make an ungracefull appearence at the Head of your table. She is rather too silent. She would please you the better. She frequently mourns the long absence of her Father, but she knows not all she suffers in consequence of it. He would prudently introduce her to the world, which her Mamma thinks proper in a great measure to seclude herself from, and the daughter is too attentive to the happiness of her Mamma to leave her much alone, nor could repeated invitations nor the solicitation of Friends joined to the consent of her Mamma, prevail with her to appear at commencement this year. But much rather would the Mamma and daughter embrace the Husband and Father in his Native Land than think of visiting foreign climes. Will the cottage be sweet? Will Retirement be desirable? Does your Heart pant for domestick tranquility, and for that reciprocation of happiness you was once no stranger to. Is there ought in Courts, in Theaters or Assemblies that can fill the void? Will Ambition, will Fame, will honour do it. Will you not reply—all, all are inadequate, but whether am I led? I cannot assume an other Subject—the Heart is softned. Good night.

JA to AA My dearest Friend — Hague 25 July 1782

In this Country, as in all others, Men are much Addicted to "Hobby Horses." These Nags are called in the Language of the Dutch "Liefhebbery," as they are called in French "Marotte." I had rather ride a Dutch Hobby Horse than an English one or a French. It is the wholesomest Exercise in the World. They live to great Ages by the Strength of it.

My Meaning is this. They pitch in early Life upon some domestick Amusement, which they follow all their days at Leisure hours. I shall give you the History of several.

I Yesterday made a Visit to one, a Mr. Lionet, a venerable old Man of 75, in full Health, Strength and Vivacity, respectable for several Offices which he holds, but more so for vast learning in various Kinds, and great Ingenuity. His Hobby Horse has been natural Knowledge. We went to see a Collection of marine Shells. We were two hours, and had not got half through. The infinite Variety of Figures and Coulours, is astonishing.

But his Curiosity has not been confined to Shells. It has extended to Insects, and he has had it in Contemplation to write as full an Account of these as Buffon has written of Birds, Beasts and Fishes. But beginning with Caterpillars, he has filled a Folio upon that Species—and drew, and engraved the Plates himself.

Thus he rode his Hobby Horse and lived. Without it, he would have died fifty Years ago.

Have you an Inclination to read and inspect Cutts of the Anatomy of Caterpillars—their Nerves, Blood, Juices, Bones, Hair, Senses,

Intellects &c. &c.—Their moral Sense, their Laws, Government, Manners and Customs.

I dont know whether he teaches the manner of destroying them, and Saving the Apple tree.

I doubt not the Book is worth studying. All Nature is so.—But I have too much to do, to Study Men, and their mischievous Designs upon Apple Trees and other Things, ever to be very intimate with Mr. Lionet, (whom I respect very much however) or his Book. Adieu.

JA to AA

My dearest Friend [*The Hague, ca. 15 August 1782*]

Mr. Thaxter is getting better and Mr. Charles Storer is now with me, and We may be all now said to be pretty well. Our northern Friends are well too.

You will hear a great deal about Peace, but dont trust to it. Remember what I have often said "We shall not be able to obtain Peace, while our Ennemies have New York and Charlestown or either of them." I know the Character and Sentiments of the King of England, and while he can hold a Post in the United States, he will have it in his Power to make the People of England believe that the People of America love him and them, and keep up their hopes of some turn of Affairs in their favour.

Lord Shelburnes System is equivocal. Fox has seized the right Idea. But the former will run down the latter for sometime. Yet the Plan of the latter must finally prevail. It is deeply laid and well digested. If he has Perseverance he will be the Man to make Peace.

By frequent Exercise on Horseback and great Care, I seem to have recovered my Health, strength and Spirits beyond my Expectations. And if the Company of Princes and Princesses, Dukes and Dutchesses, Comtes and Comptesses could make me happy, I might easily be so—but my Admired Princess is at the blue Hills, where all my Ambition and all my Wishes tend.

I know not the Reason but there is some Strange Attraction between the North Parish in Braintree and my Heart. It is a remarkable Spot. It has vomited Forth more Fire than Mount Etna. It has produced three mortals, Hancock and two Adams's, who have, with the best Intentions in the World, set the World in a blaze. I say two Adams's because the Head of the Senate sprung from thence as his father was born there.—Glorious however as the flame is, I wish I could put it out.—Some People say I was born for such Times. It is true I was born to be in such times but was not made for them. They affect too tenderly my Heart.

I love the People where I am. They have Faults but they have deep Wisdom and great Virtues—and they love America, and will be her everlasting Friend, I think. I would do a great deal to serve this nation, I own.

If Spain should acknowledge Us as I think she will soon, the two great Branches of the House of Bourbon, Holland and America, will form a PHALANX which will not easily be shaken. I hope and believe We shall continue Friends. If We do, whenever England makes Peace She will be afraid to quarrell with Us, how much soever she may hate Us. And I think the other Powers of Europe too will prefer our Friendship to our Enmity, and will choose to excuse Us from meddling in future Wars. This is the Object of all my Wishes and the End of all my Politicks. To this End and for this Reason I look upon my success in Holland as the happiest Event, and the greatest Action of my Life past or future. I think that no Opportunity will present itself for a Century to come, for Striking a Stroke so critical and of so extensive Importance, in the political system of America. How critical it has been few Persons know. It has hung upon a Thread, a Hair, a silken Fibre. Its Consequences will not be all developed for Centuries. I know there are [those] who represent it a Thing of Course and of trifling moment. But they have not seen the Diary of Mr. Van be[r]ckel, nor mine, nor the Minutes of the Cabinets of Orange and Brunswick. Nor have they seen the History of future Wars in Europe. A future War in Europe will shew the Importance, of the American Negotiation in Holland.—Be discreet in the Use you make of this. Be cautious. I want to know how our Success here is relished with you.

Adieu, tenderly Adieu.

JA to AA

Aug. 31. 1782

All well.—You will send these Papers to some Printer when you have done with them.

We have found that the only Way of guarding against Fevers is to ride. We accordingly mount our Horses every day. But the Weather through the whole Spring and most of the Summer has been very dull, damp, cold, very disagreable and dangerous. But shaking on Horseback guards pretty well against it.

I am going to Dinner with a Duke and a Dutchess and a Number [of] Ambassadors and Senators, in all the Luxury of this luxurious World: but how much more luxurious it would be to me, to dine upon roast Beef with Parson Smith, Dr. Tufts or Norton Quincy—or upon rusticrat Potatoes with Portia—Oh! Oh! hi ho hum!—and her Daughter and sons.

The "Mr. Smith" who, Mrs. Adams says in the following letter, "would adjust his affairs and come with me" if she decided to join her husband in Europe, was her cousin William Smith, a young Boston merchant.

AA to JA

My dearest Friend Sepbr. 5 1782

Your kind favours of May 14th and June 16th came to Hand last Evening; and tho I have only just time to acknowledge them, I would not omit a few lines; I have written before by this vessel; which is Bound to France. Mr. Allen your old fellow traveller is a passenger on Board, and promises to be attentive to the Letters. In my other Letter I mention a serious proposal made in a former; but do not inform you of the Nature of it, fearing a rejection of my proposal and it is of so tender a Nature I could scarcly bear a refusal; yet should a refusal take place, I know it will be upon the best grounds and reasons. But your mention in your two kind favours, your wishes with more seariousness than you have ever before exprest them, leads me again to repeat my request; it is that I may come to you, with our daughter, in the Spring, provided You are like to continue abroad. In my other Letter I have stated to you an arrangement of my affairs, and the person with whom I would chuse to come; I have slightly mentiond it to him; and he says he should like it exceedingly and I believe would adjust his affairs and come with me. Mr. Smith is the person I mean, I mention him least my other Letter should fail.

I am the more desirious to come now I learn Mr. Thaxter is comeing home. I am sure you must feel a still greater want of my attention to you. I will endeavour to find out the disposition of Congress, but I have lost my intelligence from that Quarter by Mr. Lovels return to this State. I have very little acquaintance with any Gentleman there. Mr. Jackson and Mr. Osgood are the only two Members there from this State. Mr. Lovell has lately returnd. I will see him and make some inquiry; as to peace you have my opinion in the Letter referd to by this vessel.

The acknowledgment of our Independance by the United provinces is considerd here as a most important Event, but the Newspapers do not anounce it to the world with that Eclat, which would have been rung from all Quarters had this Event been accomplished by a certain character. Indeed we have never received an official account of it untill now. Let me ask you Dear Friend, have you not been rather neglegent in writing to your Friends? Many difficulties you have had to encounter might have been laid open to them, and your character might have had justice done it. But Modest Merrit must be its own Reward. Bolingbrook in his political tracts observes, rather Ironically (but it is a certain fact,) that Ministers stand in as much need of publick writers, as they do of him. He adds, "in their prosperity they can no more subsist without daily praise, than the writers without daily Bread, and the further the Minister extends his views the more necessary are they to his Support. Let him speak as contemptuously of them as he pleases, yet it will fare with his ambition, as with a lofty Tree, which cannot shoot its Branches into the Clouds unless its Root work into the dirt."

You make no mention of receiving Letters from me, you certainly must have had some by a vessel which arrived in France some time before the Fire Brand reachd Holland. She too had Letters for you.

Accept my acknowledgement for the articles sent. As the other arrived safe, I could have wished my little memorandom by the Fire Brand had reachd you before this vessel saild; but no Matter, I can dispose of them. My Luck is great I think. I know not that I have lost any adventure you have ever sent me. Nabby requests in one of her Letters a pair of paste Buckles. When your hand is in you may send a pair for me if you please.

Adieu my dearest Friend. Remember that to render your situation more agreable I fear neither the Enemy or old Neptune, but then you must give me full assureance of your intire approbation of my request. I cannot accept a half way invitation. To say I am happy here, I cannot, but it is not an idle curiosity that make me wish to hazard the Watery Element. I much more sincerely wish your return. Could I hope for that during an other year I would endeavour to wait patiently the Event.

Once more adieu. The Messenger waits and hurrys me.—Ever Ever yours,

Portia

VI

OCTOBER 1782 ~ AUGUST 1784

My Children will have nothing but their Liberty and the Right to catch Fish, on the Banks of Newfoundland. — John Adams

I had to act my little part alone. — Abigail Adams

AMERICAN COMMISSIONERS AT THE PRELIMINARY PEACE NEGOTIATION WITH GREAT BRITAIN, PARIS, 1782

John Adams' journey to Paris in October 1782 opened the final, and perhaps most frustrating, period of his family's separation. The preliminary articles of peace with Great Britain signed by the American Commissioners on November 30 were only the first step in the diplomatic process which eventually led to the ratification of definitive treaties of peace among all the belligerents. While the preliminary articles and the armistice which accompanied them removed some of the hazards of ocean travel, the Adamses were denied a reunion for more than eighteen months by the hesitant and confusing measures taken by Congress to organize a peacetime diplomatic establishment.

Adams described the peace talks of October and November as "a constant Scuffle Morning, noon and night about Cod and Haddock on the Grand Bank, Deer skins on the Ohio and Pine Trees at Penobscat, and what were worse than all the Refugees." On the American side, the burden of the negotiations was borne by Adams and the austere John Jay of New York, with Franklin entering the scene in his masterly way at difficult and strategic moments.

Allied with Jay, of whom Adams wrote, "I love him so well that I know not what I should do in Europe without him," Adams found the experience an invigorating challenge. The end of his work was in sight, and he begged his wife to rely on the advice of Congressman Jonathan Jackson in making her plans for the spring.

Within a month, Adams' mood had changed. On December 4 he submitted his resignation to Congress and wrote Abigail: "I think it will be most *for the Happiness of my Family, and most for the Honour of our Country that I should come home.*" Although the peace he had helped win guaranteed America's boundaries and fishing rights, he could not be sure that it would be altogether popular. The commissioners had concluded and signed the articles without prior notice to the French—a clear violation of their instructions. Criticism would come, as well, for the provisions they had accepted for the protection of loyalists.

For her part, Mrs. Adams had news that made her husband even more restive. Their daughter Nabby, now seventeen, had an admirer, Royall Tyler, recently established in Braintree. The mother, though clearly taken with the young lawyer, was honest in listing his flaws. But Adams, absorbed in his duties and concerned for the safety of John Quincy in his return journey from St. Petersburg, was in no mood to listen charitably to her description of the talented and charming youth who had dissipated half a fortune and now sought the hand of the Adamses' only daughter.

AA to JA

My dearest Friend October 8th 1782

Your favour of August 17th is just put into my hands with word that Capt. Grinnel is to sail tomorrow, all of a sudden without having been to see me, or warning me of his going. I made a little excursion to Haverhill with our daughter and son Charles which prevented my getting my Letters ready. However I am determined not to close my eyes to Night untill I have written to you, and will send Charles of tomorrow morning by Sun rise. Mr. Guile is come safe and sends me word he will see me tomorrow or next day. I shall be impatient untill he comes. I want to know all about my dear Friend—O! that I could add Companion. Permit me my Dearest Friend to renew that Companionship. My Heart sighs for it. I cannot O! I cannot be reconcild to living as I have done for 3 years past. I am searious. I could be importunate with you. May I? Will you let me try to soften, if I cannot wholy releave you, from your Burden of Cares and perplexities? Shall others for their pleasure hazard, what I cannot have courage to incounter from an affection pure as ever burned in a vestal Heart—Warm and permanant as that which glows in your own dear Bosom. I Hardly think of Enemies, of terrors and storms. But I resolve with myself—to do as you wish. If I can add to your Happiness, is it not my duty? If I can soften your Cares, is it not my duty? If I can by a tender attention and assiduity prolong your most valuable Life, is it not my duty? And shall I from Female apprehensions of storms of winds, forego all these Calls? Sacrifice them to my personal ease? Alass I have not even that, for wakeing or sleeping I am ever with you. Yet if you do not consent so much is my Heart intent upon it, that your refusal must be couched in very soft terms, and you must pledge yourself to return speedily to me.

Yet my dear Sir when I can conquer the too soft sensibility of my Heart, I feel loth you should quit your station untill an Honorable peace is established, and you have added that to your other Labours. Tis no small Satisfaction to me that my country is like to profit so largely by my sacrifices.

I doubt not of your Numerous avocations. Yet when you can get time to write to your Friends here, it is of vast service to you. It sets tongues and pens at work. It informs the people of your attention to their Interests, and our negotiations are extolled and our Services are held up to view. I am unfortunate in not having in my possession a News paper to inclose, in which some person has done justice to your patience, to your perseverance, and held up as far as was prudent the difficulties you have had to encounter.

I hope you are releaved by my last Letters in some measure from your anxiety about our dear Friend and Brother Cranch. He is recoverd far beyond our expectations; he is for the first time this week attending Court. I am of opinion that his Lungs are affected, and am in terrors for him least he should have a relapse. He owes his Life the doctors say under providence, to the incessant, unwearied, indefatigable, watchfull care of his wife; who has almost sacrificed her own, to save his Life.—O! my dear Friend, how often is my Heart torn with the Idea, that I have it not in my power, let sickness or misfortune assail you thus to watch round your Bed and soften your repose.

To the Care of a gracious providence I commit you.

Your good Mother went from here this afternoon, and desires her kind Regards to you. Uncle Q[uinc]y sends his Love, is always attentive to hear from you. He applied to me a little while ago, to send for 2 yd. of green velvet proper for a pulpit cushing with fring and tossels for it or half a pd. of Green Sewing Silk. He would have sent the Money, but I refused it, because I knew it would give you pleasure to make this little present to our Church. You will be so good as to order it put up by the next conveyance. The Fire Brand is not yet arrived. We are under apprehension for her. We have a large French Fleet in our Harbour, yet are daily insulted by British cruizers. There are several officers who belong to the Fleet who hire rooms in the Town, some of them Men of learning and Character. Several of them have got introduced to me. I treat them with civility, but rather avoid a large acquaintance. I have been on Board one 84 Gun ship by the particular invitation of the Captain. Col. Quincy and family accompanied me. This afternoon a Sweed in the French service made me a second visit. He speaks english, is a Man of learning and is second in command of the America; which is given by Congress in lieu of the Ship which was lost in comeing into the Harbour. These Gentry take a good deal of pains to get an introduction here; seem to consider an acquaintance of much more importance to them, than the people who call themselves geenteel, and who compose our Beau Mond, but who have chiefly risen into Notice since you left the Country. As I have not sought their acquaintance, nor ever appeard in publick since your absence, I have not the *Honour* to be known to many of them—concequently am forgotten or unnoticed by them in all their publick entertainments. Our Allies however recollect that the only Gentleman who is employed abroad in publick service from this state May probably have a Lady and daughter, and it may be proper to notice them out of Regard to the Gentlemans publick Character; and accordingly send out their invitations which I decline and send the daughter. This has been repeatedly the case. I care not a stiver as it respects my own country. Mrs. D[an]a is treated in the same Manner, but people who are accustomed to politeness and good manners notice it. The Manners of our Country are so intirely changed from what they were in those days of simplicity when you knew it, that it has nothing of a Republick but the Name—unless you can keep a publick table and Equipage you are but of very small consideration.

What would You have thought 15 years ago, for young practicioners at the Bar to be setting up their Chariots, to be purchasing—not paying for—their country seats. P. M——n, B——n, H——n, riding in their Chariots who were clerks in offices when we removed from Town. Hogarth may exhibit his world topsa turva. I am sure I have seen it realized.

Your daughter has been writing to you. Indeed my dear Sir you would be proud of her. Not [that] she is like her *Mamma.* She has a Stat[l]iness in her manners which some misconstrue into pride and haughtyness, but which rather results from a too great reserve; she wants more affability, but she has prudence and discretion beyond her years. She is in her person tall, large and Majestick, Mammas partialiaty allows her to be a good figure. Her sensibility is not yet sufficiently a wakend to give her Manners that pleasing softness which attracts whilst it is attracted. Her Manners rather forbid all kinds of Intimacy; and awe whilst they command.

Indeed she is not like her Mamma. Had not her Mamma at her age too much sensibility, to be *very prudent.* It however won a Heart of as much sensibility—but how my pen runs. I never can write you a short Letter.—My Charles and Tommy are fine Boys. My absent one is not forgotten. How does he. I do not hear from him.—Adieu my dear Friend. How much happier should I be to fold you to my Bosom, than to bid you this Languid adieu, with a whole ocean between us. Yet whilst I recall to your mind tender Scenes of happier days, I would add a supplication that the day May not be far distant, that shall again renew them to your Ever Ever affectionate Portia

12 Oct. 1782 at the Hague
Saturday

JA to AA

My dearest Friend

I believe I shall set off for Paris next Fryday. Mr. Thaxter and Mr. Storer will go with me.

The Treaty of Commerce and the Convention respecting recaptures were signed on the 8 of this Month, and they go by this and several other Opportunities. I hope they will give Satisfaction.

Mr. Jay writes me on the 28 of Septr. that the Day before Mr.

Oswald received a Commission to treat with the United States of America—and writes pressingly for me to come but I have not been able to dispatch the Treaty and the Loan before.—I know not what to say about Peace. It will be a troublesome Business.

Dr. Franklin has been a long time much indisposed as I lately learn with the Gout and Strangury.

Mr. Dana is well and so is our son, who may perhaps return to me this Fall.

Charles minds his Book I hope. I wish John was with him, and his Father too.

I dont know whether in future Job should be reckoned "The patient Man." It seems to me, that I have had rather more Tryals than he, and have got thro them. I am now going to Paris, to another Furnace of Affliction. Yet I am very gay, more so than usual. I fear nothing. Why should I. I had like to have said nothing worse can happen. But this is too much. Heaven has hitherto preserved my Country and my Family.

I have Sent you an whole Piece of most excellent and beautiful Scarlet Cloth—it is very Saucy. 9 florins almost a Guinea a Dutch ell, much less than an English Yard. I have sent some blue too very good. Give your Boys a suit of Cloths if you Will (or keep enough for it some Years hence) and yourself and Daughter a Ridinghood in honour of the Manufactures of Haerlem. The Scarlet is "croisée" as they call it. You never saw such a Cloth. I send also a Suit of Curtains for Miss Nabby. As to her request it will be long Ad referendum. There is also a Remnant of Silk, Green. Make the best of all—but dont meddle any more with Vermont.

If We make Peace, you will see me next summer. But I have very little faith as yet. I am most inclined to think there will be another Campaign.

I am exceedingly honoured of late by the French and Spanish Ambassadors.

I never know how to close, because I can never express the Tenderness I feel.

JA to AA

My dearest Friend Paris November 8. 1782

The King of Great Britain, by a Commission under the great Seal of his Kingdom, has constituted Richard Oswald Esqr. his Commissioner to treat with the Ministers Plenipotentiary of the United States of America, and has given him full Powers which have been mutually exchanged. Thus G[reat] B[ritain] has shifted suddenly about, and from persecuting Us with unrelenting Bowells, has unconditionally and unequivocally acknowledged Us a Sovereign State and independant Nation. It is surprizing that she should be the third Power to make this Acknowledgment. She has been negotiated into it, for Jay and I peremptorily refused to speak or hear, before We were put upon an equal Foot. Franklin as usual would have taken the Advice of the C[omte] de V[ergennes] and treated, without, but nobody would join him.

As to your coming to Europe with Miss Nabby, I know not what to say. I am obliged to differ in Opinion so often from Dr. Franklin and the C. de Vergennes, in Points that essentially affect the Honour, Dignity and most prescious Interests of my Country, and these Personages are so little disposed to bear Contradiction, and Congress have gone so near enjoining upon me passive Obedience to them, that I do not expect to hold any Place in Europe longer than next Spring. Mr. Jay is in the same Predicament, and so will every honest Man be, that Congress can send.

Write however to Mr. Jackson in Congress and desire him candidly to tell you, whether he thinks Congress will continue me in Europe, upon Terms which I can submitt to with honour, another year. If he tells you as a Friend that I must stay another Year, come to me in the Spring with your Daughter. Leave the Boys in good Hands and a good school. A Trip to Europe, for one Year may do no harm to you or your Daughter. The Artifices of the Devil will be used to get me out of the Commission for Peace. If they succeed I abandon Europe for ever, for the Blue Hills without one Instants Loss of Time or even waiting for Leave to return.

For whoever is Horse Jockeyed, I will not be. Congress means well, but is egregiously imposed upon and deceived.

Mrs. Jay and Mrs. Izard will be excellent Companions for you and the Miss Izards for Miss Nabby.

AA to JA

My dearest Friend December 23. 1782

I have omited writing by the last opportunity to Holland; because I had but small Faith in the designs of the owners or passengers. The vessel sails from Nantucket, Dr. Winship is a passenger, a Mr. Gray and some others, and I had just written you so largely by a vessel bound to France, the General Galvaye that I had nothing New to say. There are few occurences in this Northen climate at this Season of the year to divert or entertain you—and in the domestick way, should I draw you the picture of my Heart, it would be what I hope you still would Love; tho it containd nothing New; the early possession you obtained there, and the absolute power you have ever maintaind over it, leaves not the smallest space unoccupied. I look back to the early days of our acquaintance, and Friendship, as to the days of Love and Innocence; and with an undiscribable pleasure I have seen near a score of years roll over our Heads, with an affection heightned and improved by time—nor have the dreary years of absence in the smallest degree effaced from my mind the Image of the dear untittled Man to whom I gave my Heart. I cannot sometimes refrain considering the Honours with which he is invested as badges of my unhappiness. The unbounded confidence I have in your attachment to me, and the dear pledges of our affection, has soothed the solitary hour, and renderd your absence more supportable; for had I [not] loved you with the same affection it must have been misiry to have doubted. Yet a cruel world too often injures my feelings, by wondering how a person possesst of domestick attachments can sacrifice them by absenting himself *for years.*

If you had known said a person to me the other day, that Mr. A[dam]s would have remained so long abroad, would you have consented that he should have gone? I recollected myself a moment, and then spoke the real dictates of my Heart. If I had known Sir that Mr. A. could have affected what he has done, I would not only have submitted to the absence I have endured, painfull as it has been; but I would not have opposed it, even tho 3 years more should be added to the Number, which Heaven avert! I feel a pleasure in being able to sacrifice my selfish passions to the general good, and in imitating the example which has taught me to consider myself and family, but as the small dust of the balance when compaired with the great community.

Your Daughter most sincerely regreets your absence, she sees me support it, yet thinks she could not imitate either parent in the disinterested motives which actuate them. She has had a strong desire to encounter the dangers of the Sea to visit you. I however am not without a suspicion that she may loose her realish for a voyage by Spring. The tranquility of mine and my dear sisters family is in a great measure restored to us, since the recovery of our worthy Friend and Brother. We had a most melancholy Summer. The young folks of the two families together with those of Col. Q[uinc]ys and General W[arre]n preserve a great Intimacy, and as they wish for but few connections in the Beau Mond, it is not to be wonderd at that they are fond of each others company. We have an agreable young Gentleman by the Name of Robbins who keeps our little School, Son to the Revd. Mr. Robbins of Plimouth, and we have in the little circle an other gentleman who has opend an office in Town, for about nine months past, and boarded in Mr. Cranch['s] family. His Father you knew. His Name is Tyler, he studied Law upon his comeing out of colledge with Mr. Dana, but when Mr. Dana went to Congress he finished his studies with Mr. Ang[i]er. Loosing his Father young and having a very pretty patrimony left him, possessing a sprightly fancy, a warm imagination and an agreable person, he was rather negligent in persueing his buisness in the way of his profession; and dissipated two or 3 years of his Life and too much of his fortune for to reflect upon with pleasure; all of which he now laments but cannot recall. At 23 the time when he took the resolution of comeing to B[osto]n and withdrawing from a too numerous acquaintance, he resolved to persue his studies, and his Buisness, and save his remaining fortune which sufferd much more from the paper currency than any other cause; so that out of 17 thousand pounds which fell to his share, he cannot now realize more than half that sum, as he told me a few days past. His Mamma is in possession of a large Estate and he is a very favorite child. When he proposed comeing to settle here he met with but little encouragement, but he was determined upon the trial. He has succeeded beyond expectation, he has popular talants, and as his behaviour has been unexceptionable since his residence in Town, in concequence of which his Buisness daily increases, he cannot fail making a distinguished figure in his profession if he steadily persues it. I am not acquainted with any young Gentleman whose attainments in literature are equal to his, who judges with greater accuracy or discovers a more delicate and refined taste. I have frequently looked upon him with the Idea that you would have taken much pleasure in such a pupil. I wish I was as well assured that you would be equally pleased with him in an other character, for such I apprehend are his distant hopes. I early saw that he was possest with powerfull attractions, and as he obtaind and deserved, I believe the character of a gay, tho not a criminal youth, I thought it prudent to keep as great a reserve as possible. In this I was seconded by the discreet conduct of a daughter, who is happy in not possessing all her Mothers Sensibility. Yet I see a growing attachment in him stimulated by that very reserve. I feel the want of your presence and advise. I think I know your Sentiments so well that the merit of a Gentleman will be your first consideration, and I have made every inquiry which I could with decency, and without discloseing my motives. Even in his most dissipated state he always applied his mornings to study, by which means he has stored his mind with a fund of usefull knowledge. I know not a young fellow upon the stage whose language is so pure, or whose natural disposition is more agreable. His days are devoted to his office, his Evenings of late to my fire side. His attachment is too obvious to escape notice. I do not think the Lady wholy indifferent; yet her reserve and apparent coldness is such that I know he is in misirable doubt. Some conversation one Evening of late took place which led me to write him a Billet and tell him, that at least it admitted a possibility that I might quit this country in the Spring; that I never would go abroad without my daughter, and if I did go, I wished to carry her with a mind unattached, besides I could have but one voice; and for that I held myself accountable to you; that he was not yet Established in Buisness sufficient to think of a connection with any one;—to which I received this answer—

Madam

I have made an exertion to answer your Billet. I can only say that the second impulse in my Breast is my Love and respect for you; and it is the foible of my nature to be the machine of those I Love and venerate. Do with me as seemeth good unto thee. I can safely trust my dearest fondest wishes and persuits in the hands of a Friend that can feel, that knows my situation and her designs. If reason pleads against me, you will do well to hestitate. If Friendship and reason unite I shall be happy. Only say I shall be happy when *I deserve*; and it shall be my every exertion to augment my merit, and this you may be assured of, whether I am blessed in my wishes or not, I will endeavour to be a character that you shall not Blush once to have entertaind an Esteem for. Yours respectfully &c.

What ought I to say? I feel too powerful a pleader within my own heart and too well recollect the Love I bore to the object of my early affections to forbid him to hope. I feel a regard for him upon an account you will smile at, I fancy I see in him Sentiments, opinions and actions which endeared to me the best of Friends. Suffer me to draw you from the depths of politicks to endearing family Scenes. I know you cannot fail being peculiarly interested in the present. I inclose you a little paper which tho trifling in itself, may serve to shew you the truth of my observations. The other day the gentleman I have been speaking of, had a difficult writ to draw. He requested the favour of looking into your Book of forms, which I readily granted; in the Evening when he returned me the key he put in to my hands a paper which I could not tell what to make of, untill he exclamed "O! Madam Madam, I have now hopes that I shall one day become worthy your regard. What a picture have I caught of my own Heart, my resolutions, my designs! I could not refrain breaking out into a Rhapsody. I found this coppy of a Letter in a pamphlet with observations upon the Study of the Law and many excellent remarks; you will I hope forgive the theft, when I deliver the paper to you, and you find how much benifit I shall derive from it."

I daily see that he will win the affections of a fine majestick Girl who has as much dignity as a princess. She is handsome, but not Beautifull. No air of levity ever accompanies either her words or actions. Should she be caught by a tender passion, sufficient to remove a little of her natural reserve and soften her form and manners, she will be a still more pleasing character. Her mind is daily improveing, and she gathers new taste for literature perhaps for its appearing in a more pleasing form to her.—If I can procure a little ode which accompanied an ice Heart I will inclose it to you.

It is now my dear Friend a long long time since I had a line from you, the Fate of Gibralter leads me to fear that a peace is far distant, and that I shall not see you—God only knows when. I shall say little about my former request, not that my desire is less, but before this can reach you tis probable I may receive your opinion. If in favour of my comeing to you, I shall have no occasion to urge it further—if against it, I would not embarrass you, by again requesting it. I will endeavour to set down, and consider it as the portion alloted me. My dear Sons are well, their application and improvements go hand in hand. Our Friends all desire to be rememberd. The Fleet of our allies expect to sail daily but where destined we know not; a great harmony has subsisted between them and the Americans ever since their residence here. I wish to write to Mr. T[haxte]r but fear I shall not have time. Mrs. D[an]a and children are well. The judge has been very sick of a fever but I believe is better. This Letter is to go by the Iris which sails with the Fleet. I hope it will reach you in safety. If it should fall into the hands of an Enemy, I hope they will be kind enough to distroy it; as I would not wish to see such a family picture in print; adieu my dear Friend. Why is it that I hear so seldom from my dear John; but one Letter have I ever received from him since he arrived in Petersburgh? I wrote him by the last opportunity. Ever remember me as I do you; with all the tenderness which it is possible for one object to feel for an other; which no time can obliterate, no distance alter, but which is always the same in the Bosom of

Portia

JA to AA

My dearest Friend — Paris Jan. 22. 1783

The Preliminaries of Peace and an Armistice, were signed at Versailles on the 20 and on the 21. We went again to pay our Respects to the King and Royal Family upon the Occasion. Mr. Jay was gone

ABIGAIL ADAMS, THE YOUNGER, IN 1785 BY MATHER BROWN

upon a little Excursion to Normandie and Mr. Laurens was gone to Bath, both for their health, so that the signature was made by Mr. Franklin and me.—I want an Excursion too.

Thus drops the Curtain upon this mighty Trajedy, it has unravelled itself happily for Us—and Heaven be praised. Some of our dearest Interests have been saved, thro many dangers. I have no News from my son, since the 8th. December, when he was at Stockholm, but hope every hour to hear of his Arrival at the Hague.

I hope to receive the Acceptance of my Resignation so as to come home in the Spring Ships.

I had written thus far when yours of 23 decr. was brought in. Its Contents have awakened all my sensibility, and shew in a stronger Light than ever the Necessity of my coming home. I confess I dont like the Subject at all. My Child is too young for such Thoughts, and

I dont like your Word "Dissipation" at all. I dont know what it means—it may mean every Thing. There is not Modesty and Diffidence enough in the Traits you send me. My Child is a Model, as you represent her and as I know her, and is not to be the Prize, I hope of any, even reformed Rake. A Lawyer would be my Choice, but it must be a Lawyer who spends his Midnights as well as Evenings at his Age over his Books not at any Ladys Fire Side. I should have thought you had seen enough to be more upon your Guard than to write Billets upon such a subject to such a youth. A Youth who has been giddy enough to spend his Fortune or half his Fortune in Gaieties, is not the Youth for me, Let his Person, Family, Connections and Taste for Poetry be what they will. I am not looking out for a Poet, nor a Professor of belle Letters.

In the Name of all that is tender dont criticise Your Daughter for those qualities which are her greatest Glory, her Reserve, and her Prudence which I am amazed to hear you call Want of Sensibility. The more Silent She is in Company, the better for me in exact Proportion and I would have this observed as a Rule by the Mother as well as the Daughter.

You know moreover or ought to know my utter Inability to do any Thing for my Children, and you know the long dependence of young Gentlemen of the most promising Talents and obstinate Industry, at the Bar. My Children will have nothing but their Liberty and the Right to catch Fish, on the Banks of Newfoundland. This is all the Fortune that I have been able to make for myself or them.

I know not however, enough of this subject to decide any Thing.—Is he a Speaker at the Bar? If not he will never be any Thing. But above all I positively forbid any Connection between my Daughter and any Youth upon Earth, who does not totally eradicate every Taste for Gaiety and Expence. I never knew one who had it and indulged it, but what was made a Rascall by it, sooner or later.

This Youth has had a Brother in Europe, and a detestible Specimen he exhibited. Their Father had not all those nice sentiments which I wish, although an Honourable Man.

I think he and you have both advanced too fast, and I should advise both to retreat. Your Family as well as mine have had too much Cause to rue the Qualities which by your own Account have been in him. And if they were ever in him they are not yet out.

This is too serious a subject to equivocate about. I dont like this method of Courting Mothers. There is something too fantastical and affected in all this Business for me. It is not nature, modest, virtuous, noble nature. The Simplicity of Nature is the best Rule with me to judge of every Thing, in Love as well as State and War.

This is all between you and me.

I would give the World to be with you Tomorrow. But there is a vast Ocean.—No Ennemies.—But I have not yet Leave from my Masters. I dont love to go home in a Miff, Pet or Passion nor with an ill Grace, but I hope soon to have leave. I can never stay in Holland—the Air of that Country chills every drop of Blood in my Veins. If I were to stay in Europe another Year I would insist upon your coming with your daughter but this is not to be and I will come home to you.

Adieu ah ah Adieu.

JA to AA

My dearest Friend — Paris January 29. 1783

Your kind Letters of Oct. 25 and November 13 came to hand but to day. A Packet from you is always more than I can bear. It gives me a great Pleasure, the highest Pleasure, and therefore makes me and Leaves me Melancholly, like the highest Strains in Music.

I have written you many times and Ways, that I have written to Congress a Resignation, and that I expect the Acceptance of it by the first ships, and will embark for home as soon as it arrives. There is a Possibility that one Case may happen, vizt. that Congress may accept my Resignation, and send me at the same time a Renewal of my old Commission to make a Treaty of Commerce with Great Britain. There is not in my Opinion the least Probability of this, nor do I desire it, the first desire of my Soul being to go home. But if it should happen, I beg you would come to me with it, for nothing but your Company will make it acceptable. However brillant a Feather it might be in my Cap, to make a Treaty of Commerce with G[reat] Britain, and how much soever malicious Wits may suppose me disappointed by the Extraordinary Resolution of Congress which took from me a distinction, which I had dearly earned by accepting and attempting to execute a Commission which they had given me with so much Unanimity and without any Solicitation of mine, yet I assure you I think I can be employed more agreably to my self in America, if not more usefully to the Public.

However this may be my Resolution is fixed, to return home unless Congress should restore me my Honour, whether they accept of my Resignation or not.

My "Image," my "superscription," my "Princess," take care how you dispose of your Heart.—I hoped to be at home and to have chosen a

Partner for you. Or at least to have given you some good Advice before you should choose.

If I mistake not your Character it is not Gaiety and Superficial Accomplishments alone that will make you happy. It must be a thinking Being, and one who thinks for others good and feels anothers Woe. It must be one who can ride 500 miles upon a trotting Horse and cross the Gulph Stream with a steady Heart.

One may dance or sing, play or ride, without being good for much.

But I must conclude, by my Wishes and Prayers for your Direction in all Things, and by assuring you, that no Words can express the Feelings of my Heart, when I subscribe myself Yours forever.

JA to AA

My dearest Friend Paris Feb. 4. 1783

Your two Letters concerning Mr. T[yler] are never out of my Mind. He is of a very numerous Family and Connection in Boston who have long had great Influence in that Town and therefore if his Education has been regular to the Bar, as it must have been if he followed his Studies regularly, under two such Masters as Mr. Dana and Mr. Angier, if he has been admitted and sworn with the Consent and Recommendation of the Bar, and if he has Health, Talents, and Application and is a Speaker, his Relations will easily introduce him to full Business.

But I dont like the Trait in his Character, his Gaiety. He is but a Prodigal Son, and though a Penitent, has no Right to your Daughter, who deserves a Character without a Spot. That Frivolity of Mind, which breaks out into such Errors in Youth, never gets out of the Man but shews itself in some mean Shape or other through Life.—You seem to me to have favoured this affair much too far, and I wish it off.

Nevertheless, I cannot judge, you have not furnished me with Facts enough for the Purpose. I must submit my Daughters Destiny to her own Judgment and her own Heart, with your Advice and the Advice of our Parents and Brothers and sisters and Uncles and Aunts &c. You must endeavour to know the Opinion of the Family, and I pray a kind Providence to protect my Child.

I had flattered myself with the Hopes of a few Years of the society of this Daughter, at her Fathers House. But if it must be otherwise I must submit.

I am so uneasy about this subject, that I would come instantly home, if I could with decency. But my Dutch Treaty is not yet exchanged, I have not yet taken Leave of their High Mightinesses, nor of the Court, nor have I yet signed all the Obligations for the Loan: so that I dont see how I can possibly, come home without first returning to the Hague. There are other Subjects too about which I am not on a Bed of Roses. The Revocation of my Commission to make a Treaty of Commerce with G[reat] Britain without assigning any Reason, is an affront to me and a Stain upon my Character that I will not wear one Moment longer than is indispensably necessary for the public Good, and therefore I will come home, whether my Resignation is accepted or not, unless my Honour is restored. This can be but one Way in Europe, and that is by sending me a Renewal of the Commission. This I have no Idea will be done: because the Forest is laid wide open for the Game and all the Hounds of Faction will be let loose at the Halloo of the Sportsman. I will have no share in the Chase. I am weary to death of a Residence in Europe, and so would you be. You have no Idea of it. Mrs. Jay can tell you. This Lady is as weary as is possible, and you would be more so.

If it were only an Affair of myself and my Family, I would not accept a Commission if sent. But I consider it a public Point of Honour. An infamous Attack has been made upon me, only for Doing my Duty, or rather an Attack has been made upon the Fisheries, the Mississippi and the Western Lands, through my Sides. I have totally defeated the Attack upon those Great Objects and I Say the Honour the Dignity and future Safety of the United States are interested in restoring that Commission to me, that future Attacks of the same Kind may be discouraged, and future Servants of the Publick protected. And I have sworn that Justice shall be done in this Case somehow or other. The Public Voice shall pronounce the Righteous sentence, if Congress does not.

If therefore Congress should renew my Commission to make a Treaty of Commerce with G.B., come to me, with your Daughter if she is not too much engaged, and master Tommy. Send Charles to his Uncle Shaw or some school and let any Body draw upon me for his support. I do not however believe, Congress will send me such a Commission, and if not I shall have my Daughter by her Hand before she gives it away, at the Blue Hills at the latest by Mid summer. Endeavour to learn what passes upon the subject in Congress and write it to me for my Guidance. You may write by Way of England, Holland, France or Spain. Send under Cover however to some other Friend.

I shall send Johnny home to Colledge, I believe, bring him certainly with me if I come, as I expect and hope.

Yours forever.

SAMUEL ADAMS

JA to AA

My dearest Friend Paris March 28. 1783

On the 30 Nov. our Peace was signed. On the 28. March We dont know that you have yet heard of it. A Packet should have been sent off. I have not yet received the Ratification of my Dutch Treaty.—I know not when I shall be able to embark for home. If I receive the Acceptance of my Resignation, I shall embark in the first ship, the first good ship I mean, for I love you too well, to venture my self in a bad one, and I love my own Ease too well to go in a very small one.

I am sometimes half afraid, that those Persons who procured the Revocation of my Commission to King George, may be afraid I shall do them more harm in America, than in England, and therefore of two Evils choose the least and manoeuvre to get me sent to London. By several Coaxing hints of that Kind, which have been written to me and given me in Conversation, from Persons who I know are employed to do it, I fancy that Something of that is in Contemplation. There is another Motive too—they begin to dread the Appointment of some others whom they like less than me.—I tremble when I think of such a Thing as going to London. If I were to receive orders of that Sort, it would be a dull day to me. No Swiss ever longed for home more than I do. I shall forever be a dull Man in Europe. I cannot bear the Thought of transporting my Family to Europe. It would be the Ruin of my Children forever. And I cannot bear the Thought of living longer seperate from them. Our foreign Affairs, are like to be in future as they have been in times past an eternal Scæne of Faction. The fluctuation of Councils at Philadelphia have encouraged it, and even good Men seem to be seized with the Spirit of it.

The definitive Treaty is yet delayed, and will be for any Thing I can see till Mid Summer. It may however be signed in a few Weeks. If it should be signed I could go home with the Dutch Ambassador, in a Frigate which will sail from the Texel in June. But So many Points are uncertain, that I cannot determine on any thing. Dont think of coming to Europe however, unless you should receive a further desire from me, which is not at all probable. My present Expectations are to pay my Respects to you, at Braintree, before Midsummer.

My dear Daughters happiness employs my Thoughts night and Day. Dont let her form any Connections with any one, who is not devoted entirely to study and to Business, to honour and Virtue. If there is a Trait of Frivolity and Dissipation left, I pray that She may renounce it, forever. I ask not Fortune nor Favour for mine but Prudence, Talents and Labour. She may go with my Consent wherever she can find enough of these.

My Son has been another Source of Distress to me. The terrible Weather has made his Journey from Petersbourg very long. But I have a Letter from him at Hamborough the 14th. and hope he is at the Hague by this day. I am much relieved on his Account.—My Charles and Thomas how are they? Fine Boys I dare say? Let them take Care how they behave if they desire their Fathers approbation. My Mother and your Father enjoy I hope a good Share of Health and Spirits. Mr. Cranch's Health is perfectly restored I hope, and Uncle Quincy and Dr. Tufts as good and as happy as ever.—Why should not my Lot in Life be as easy as theirs? So it would have been if I had been as wise as they and staid at home as they do. But where would have been our Cod and Haddock, our Bever skins, Deer skins and Pine Trees? Alass all lost, perhaps. Indeed I firmly believe so, in a good Conscience. I cannot therefore repent of all my fatigues, Cares, Losses, Escapes, anxious Days and Sleepless nights.

Nothing in Life ever cost me so much Sleep, or made me so many grey Hairs, as the Anxiety I have Suffered for these Three Years on the Score of these Objects. No body knows of it: Nobody cares for it. But I shall be rewarded for it, in Heaven I hope. Where Mayhew, and Thatcher and Warren are rewarded I hope, none of whom however were permitted to suffer so much. They were taken away from the Evil to come.

I have one favour for you to ask of Mr. [Samuel] Adams the President of the Senate. It is that he would make a compleat Collection of his Writings and publish them in Volumes. I know of no greater Service that could be rendered to the Rights of Mankind. At least that he would give you a List of them. They comprize a Period of forty Years, and although they would not find so many Rakes for Purchasers, as the Writings of Voltaire, they would do infinitely more good to mankind especially in our rising Empire. There Posterity will find a Mass of Principles, and Reasonings, suitable for them and for all good Men. The Copy, I fancy would sell to Advantage in Europe.

Yours most affectionatly and eternally.

AA to JA

My dearest Friend April 7 1783

Tis a long a very long time since I had an opportunity of conveying a single line to you. I have upon many accounts been impatient to do it.

I now most sincerely rejoice in the great and important event which sheaths the Hostile Sword and gives a pleasing presage that our Spears may become prunning hooks; that the Lust of Man is restrained, or the powers and revenues of kingdoms become inadequate to the purposes of distruction.

I have had the good fortune to receive several Letters from you of late; I thank you for them; they are always too short, but I do not complain knowing the thousand avocations you must have upon your mind and Hands. Yours of December 4th, gave me the highest pleasure.

"And shall I see his face again
And shall I hear him speak"

are Ideas that have taken full possession of my Heart and mind. I had much rather see you in America, than Europe. I well know that real, true and substantial happiness depend not upon titles, Rank and fortune; the Gay coach, the Brilliant attire, the pomp and Etiquet of Courts, rob the mind of that placid harmony, that social intercourse which is an Enemy to ceremony. My Ambition, my happiness centers in him, who sighs for domestick enjoyments, amidst all the world calls happiness—who partakes not in the jovial Feast, or joins the Luxurious table, without turning his mind to the plain unadulterated food which covers his own frugal Board, and sighs for the Feast of reason and the flow of soul.

Your Letter of Janry. 29 created perturbations, yet allayed anxiety. Your "Image," your "Superscription," Your Emelia would tell you, if she would venture to write to you upon the subject, that it was not the superficial accomplishments of danceing, singing, and playing, that led her to a favorable opinion of Selim; since she knew him not, when those were his favorite amusements—nor has he ever been in the practise of either, since his residence in this Town; even the former Beau has been converted into the plain dressing Man; and the Gay volatile Youth appears to become the studious Lawyer. Yet certain reasons which I do not chuse to enumerate here, have led me to put a present period, as far as advise and desires would go, to the Idea of a connection. To extirpate it from the Hearts and minds of either is not I apprehend in my power, voilent opposition never yet served a cause of this nature. Whilst they believe me their best Friend, and see that their Interest is near my Heart, and that my opposition is founded upon rational principals, they submit to my prohibition, earnestly wishing for your return, and more prosperous days; as without your approbation, they never can conceive themselves happy.

I will be more particular by the first direct conveyance. Mr. Guile who kept Sabbeth with me, tells me he has a vessel which will sail tomorrow for Virgina, and from thence to Europe, yet he knows not for certain to what part, but as this is the only opportunity since December, I would not let it slip.—We are all well, our two Sons go on Monday with Billy Cranch to Haverhill; there to be under the care and tuition of Mr. Shaw who has one in his family which he offers for colledge in july. I have done the best I could with them. They have been without a School ever since Janry. I tried Mr. Shutes but could not get them in, he having seven in his family, and four more engaged to him. Andover was full and so is every other private School. They do not like the thoughts of Mammas going a broad, and my little Neice who has lived 5 years with me prays that her uncle may return, and hopes he will not send her away when he comes.—This day has been our meeting for the choise of a Governour. The vote in this Town was for Genll. Lincoln. There were proposals of chuseing an absent Man, but I discouraged it wherever I heard it mentiond.

Be kind enough to let the young Gentlemen who reside with you know, that their Friends are well and that I will do myself the pleasure of answering their Letters by the first vessel which sails from this port.

Adieu and believe me most affectionately and tenderly yours,

Portia

Mr. Smith is to be my Gaurdian and protector if I cross the Atlantick. He comes whether I do or not. Emelia has spent the winter in Boston, during that time it has been currently reported that *preliminary articles* were setled between this Gentleman and her. She took no pains to discountanance this report—but alass her Heart is drawn an other way—and Mr. S. never entertaind an Idea of the kind.

During the spring of 1783 Abigail Adams held in abeyance a decision to travel to Europe. She did reduce the responsibilities that held her in Braintree, however, by sending Charley and Tommy to Haverhill to live with her sister and study with her sister's husband, the Reverend John Shaw. But she received no news from Philadelphia respecting Congress' determinations on Adams' continuance abroad. Instead, reports came of the storm raised when Adams' "Peace Journal," extracts from his private diary for November–December 1782, by a series of quirks was read before Congress in March.

AA to JA

My dearest Friend — April 28th 1783

At length an opportunity offers after a space of near five Months, of again writing to You. Not a vessel from any port in this state has sailed since Jan'ry, by which I could directly convey you a line. I have written twice by way of Virgina, but fear they will never reach you. From you I have lately received several Letters containing the most pleasing intelligence.

"Peace o'er the world her olive Branch extends. Hail! Goddess heavenly bright, profuse of joy, and pregnant with delight." The Garb of this favorite of America, is woven of an admirable texture and proves the great skill, wisdom, and abilities, of the Master Workmen. It was not fabricated in the Loom of France, nor are the materials english, but they are the product of our own American Soil, raised and nurtured, not by the gentle showers of Heaven, but by the hard Labour and indefatigable industery and firmness of her Sons, and water'd by the Blood of many of them. May its duration be in proportion to its value, and like the Mantle of the prophet descend with blessings to Generations yet to come.

And may you my dearest Friend, return to your much loved solitude with the pleasing reflextion of having contributed to the happiness of Millions.

We have not yet received any account of the signing of the definitive Treaty, so that no publick rejoiceings have taken place as yet. The 5th article in the Treaty has raised the old spirit against the Tories to such a height that it would be at the risk of their lives should they venture here: it may subside after a while; but I Question whether any state in the union will admit them even for 12 Months. What then would have been the concequence if compensation had been granted them?

Your journal has afforded me and your Friends much pleasure and amusement. You will learn, perhaps from Congress that the journal, you meant for Mr. Jackson, was by some mistake enclosed to the Minister for foreign affairs, and concequently came before Congress with other publick papers. The Massachusetts Delegates applied for it, but were refused it. Mr. Jackson was kind enough to wait upon me, and shew me your Letter to him, and the other papers inclosed, and I communicated the journal to him. Mr. Higginson writes that it was moved in congress by Hamilton of Virgina and Wilson of Pensilvana to censure their ministers, for departing from their duty in not adhering to their instructions, and for *giving offence* to the Court of France, by *distrusting their Friendship*; they however could not carry their point. It was said the instruction alluded [to] was founded upon Reciprocity, and that the C.V. [Comte de Vergennes] had not acted upon that principal. When these Gentry found that it would not be considerd in the Light in which they wished, they gave out that if no more was said upon that subject, the other would drop. This is all I have been able to collect—my intelligence is very imperfect since Mr. L[ovel]l left congress. Mr. G[e]r[ry] I believe is determined to go again. I shall then have a Friend and correspondent who will keep me informed. Upon receiving a Letter from you in which you desire me to come to you should you be longer detained abroad, I took the Liberty of writing to Dr. Lee, requesting him to give me the earliest intelligence respecting the acceptance of your resignation. I do not think it will be accepted, by what I have already learnt; if it should not, I shall still feel undetermined what to do. From many of your Letters I was led to suppose you would not return without permission; yet I do not imagine the bare renewal of a former commission would induce you to tarry. I shall not run the risk unless you are appointed minister at the Court of Britain. Mr. Smith is waiting for me to hear from congress. He means to go whether I do or not, but if I do he will take charge of every thing respecting my voyage. Our two sons together with Mr. Cranch's, are placed in the family of Mr. Shaw. He had one young Gentleman before whom he offers this year for Colledg. I doubt not he will contribute every thing in his power towards their instruction and improvement. I last evening received Letters from them, and they appear to be very contented and happy.

With Regard to some domestick affairs which I wrote you about last winter, certain reasons have prevented their proceeding any further, and perhaps it will never again be renewed. I wished to have told you so sooner, but it has not been in my power. Our Friends are all well and desire to be affectionately rememberd to you. Where is our son, I hear no more of him than if he was out of the world. You wrote me in yours of December 4th that he was upon his journey to you, but I have never heard of his arrival.

Need I add how earnestly I long for the day when Heaven will again bless us in the Society of each other—whether upon European or American ground is yet in the Book of uncertainty, but to feel intirely happy and easy, I believe it must be in our own Republican cottage; with the Simplicity which has ever distinguished it—and your ever affectionate Portia

My dearest Friend 29 April

I last Evening received yours of Febry 18th in which you are explicit with Regard to your return. I Shall therefore let Congress renew or create What commission they please, at least wait your further direction tho you should be induced to tarry abroad. I have taken no Step as yet with regard to comeing out, except writing to Dr. Lee as mentiond before. Heaven send you safe to your ever affectionate

Portia

John Quincy Adams' long trip back from Russia ended in April. At The Hague he lived in the household of C. W. F. Dumas, John Adams' friend and agent, until the arrival of the senior Adams in July. Meanwhile, from Paris, John Adams resumed his instruction of his son in morals, sound habits, and penmanship, and told his wife how he occupied himself in his idleness.

John Adams to John Quincy Adams

My dear Child Paris May 14. 1783

Mr. Hardouin has just now called upon me, and delivered me your Letter of the 6 Instant.

I find that, although, your hand Writing is distinct and legible, yet it has not engaged so much of your Attention as to be remarkably neat. I should advise you to be very carefull of it: never to write in a hurry, and never to let a slovenly Word or Letter go from you. If one begins at your Age, it is easier to learn to write well than ill, both in Characters and Style. There are not two prettier accomplishments than a handsome hand and Style, and these are only to be acquired in youth. I have suffered much, through my whole Life, from a Negligence of these Things in my young days, and I wish you to know it. Your hand and Style, are clear enough to shew that you may easily make them manly and beautifull, and when a habit is got, all is easy.

I see your Travells have been expensive, as I expected they would be: but I hope your Improvements have been worth the Money. Have you kept a regular Journal? If you have not, you will be likely to forget most of the Observations you have made. If you have omitted this Usefull Exercise, let me advise you to recommence it, immediately. Let it be your Amusement, to minute every day, whatever you may have seen or heard worth Notice. One contracts a Fondness of Writing by Use. We learn to write readily, and what is of more importance, We think, and improve our Judgments, by committing our Thoughts to Paper.

Your Exercises in Latin and Greek must not be omitted a single day, and you should turn your Mind a little to Mathematicks. There is among my Books a Fennings Algebra. Begin it immediately and go through it, by a small Portion every day. You will find it as entertaining as an Arabean Tale. The Vulgar Fractions with which it begins, is the best extant, and you should make yourself quite familiar with it.

A regular Distribution of your Time, is of great Importance. You must measure out your Hours, for Study, Meals, Amusements, Exercise and Sleep, and suffer nothing to divert you, at least from those devoted to study.

But above all Things, my Son, take Care of your Behaviour and preserve the Character you have acquired, for Prudence and Solidity.

Remember your tender Years and treat all the World with Modesty, Decency and Respect.

The Advantage you have in Mr. Dumas's Attention to you is a very prescious one. He is himself a Walking Library, and so great a Master of Languages ancient and modern is very rarely seen. The Art of asking Questions is the most essential to one who wants to learn. Never be too wise to ask a Question.

Be as frugal as possible, in your Expences.

Write to your Mamma, Sister and Brothers, as often as you have Opportunity. It will be a Grief to me to loose a Spring Passage home, but although I have my fears I dont yet despair.

Every Body gives me a very flattering Character of your Sister, and I am well pleased with what I hear of you: The principal Satisfaction I can expect in Life, in future, will be in your good Behaviour and that of my other Children. My Hopes from all of you are very agreable. God grant, I may not be dissappointed.

Your affectionate Father, John Adams

JA to AA

My dearest Friend Paris June 19. 1783

The Legion of Lauzun has arrived, and We hope has brought the Orders of Congress, for Us, but We have not yet received them, and are as much at a Loss as ever. I know not whether my Resignation is accepted, and consequently can give you no Conjecture, when I shall be able to get away. As the Spring and Summer Passage is lost, I cannot now embark before September or October, or November. Whether I shall embark from France, Holland or England I dont know. It will be according as I shall hear of a convenient Passage. Write me by all these Ways. I have received no Line from you, dated since December.

The definitive Treaty may be signed in three Weeks: and it may as probably be trained on till Christmas. In the last Case, provided the Acceptance of my Resignation should not arrive, it may be Spring before I can embark. In this State of Suspense and Perplexity you may well suppose I do not sleep upon a bed of Roses, especially, as the Public Affairs are as uncertain as our private ones.

I should like very well, to take a short Tour to London before my Return, for the Sake of taking a look at that Country, and seeing some Personages there, because if I waive this Opportunity, it is not likely I shall ever have another. Once more at home, it is not probable, I shall again go abroad. Indeed it is more for the Sake of Mr. John than my own, that I wish to see England, at all.

I was at Versailles, the day before Yesterday and paid my Respects to the King and Queen, Monsieur and Madame his Lady, the Comte D'Artois, Madame Elizabeth and the Mesdames of France Adelaide and Victoire. As the Weather was more like a Spring Equinox than a Summer Solstice, the Number of Ambassadors was smaller than usual, and the Attendant Croud less, so that I had a better Opportunity of viewing the Royal Family at Leisure than ever I had before.

I dined and breakfasted indeed, with the Ambassadors and found them universally more sociable, than ever they were before. They begin now universally to consider and treat Us, as Members of their Body.

It is forbidden I suppose to Princes and Princesses upon these Occasions, to utter a Sentiment least they should betray a secret of S[tate or] say something which might lead a sagacious Ambassador to political Consequences. According No one Word is ever said, except asking a Question about some common Thing, as the Weather, the Spectacles, or have you come from Paris to day.

I know an Ambassador who has been fourteen Years at a Court, who has attended regularly once a Week, who says that a Prince has never failed to ask him the same question, every Time. "Did you come from home to day"—and never any other. This Ambassador too, is of the highest Rank.

Among all the Officers, who come in Play upon these occasions such as Introducers of Ambassadors, Secretary of the Presentations of Ambassadors &c., there ought I think to be one Præceptor to teach the Princes and Princesses, the Art of asking Questions and making Observations upon these Occasions.

The Prince of Orange's Court is a Miniature of that of Versailles. The Ceremonials, and the Conversation of Princes and Princesses is much the Same. The English Gentlemen here, particularly Mr. Hartley tells me, I must be presented at Court, if I should go to London only for a Visit, in my publick Character as a Minister at the Peace. This is rather a discouraging Circumstance, as I should wish to go incog. as much as possible, and my Appearance at Court would make more Talk than I wish. I should be Stared at, as a Sight. I should be treated however complaisantly enough, I doubt not.—The Case is altered.— I had rather make my Court to my Princesses at Pens Hill, than to all the others in the World. This Honour I hope for but cannot promise myself so soon as I wish.

Reports from Philadelphia of actions taken by Congress grew ever more illusory. Abigail Adams' information that Congress had voted a "joint commission" to Adams, Jay, and Franklin to negotiate a commercial treaty with Great Britain seemed as reliable to her as it did to her husband in September, when he received official word of Congress' resolution. By that resolution of May 1, Secretary Livingston had indeed been directed to prepare such a commission. Yet he resigned his office a month later without submitting the required drafts. When reconstituted a year later, the joint commission took a different form.

The numerous problems unresolved at the end of hostilities seemed at the moment more disturbing to Abigail Adams. The economic plight of New England promised chaos, as did the trade "war" between the states. The conflict between Congress and the state legislatures over military pensions and severance pay was ominous. The proper treatment for those, like Thomas Brattle, who were charged with having been loyalists became a political issue that rent the fabric of the State. The solution of these and other issues, for Mrs. Adams, lay in the early return to Massachusetts of one whose abilities demonstrated abroad "should be exerted at home for the publick Safety."

As her husband waited impatiently for the signing of the definitive peace treaties and for new instructions, he viewed New England with all its problems as far more attractive than the allurements of European courts. After rejoining his son in July and bringing him back with him to Paris in early August, Adams saw no insurmountable obstacles to their return home. Letters received from his wife reinforced the decision. She reported word from Arthur Lee, later proved incorrect, that Congress would accept Adams' resignation. Her hints that he was being considered for "a certain office," the Massachusetts governorship, though disquieting, were no hindrance. Her domestic intelligence that the progress of Royall Tyler's courtship of their daughter had been halted, that "what you wish, has taken place, that is that it is done with," was a promise that the family reunion would be unmarred. By the time the definitive treaties were signed in September, Adams had renewed his application to Congress to be recalled as envoy to the Netherlands and promised his wife to come home on the first spring vessel.

AA to JA

My Dearest Friend — Braintree June 20th 1783

If I was certain I should welcome you to your native Land in the course of the Summer, I should not regret Mr. Smiths going abroad without me. Should it be otherways, should you still be detained abroad—I must submit, satisfied that you judge best, and that you would not subject me to so heavy a dissapointment, or yourself to so severe a mortification as I flatter myself it would be, but for the General Good. A European life would, you say, be the ruin of our Children. If so, I should be as loth as you, to hazard their embibeing sentiments and opinions which might make them unhappy in a sphere of Life which tis probable they must fill, not by indulging in Luxuries for which tis more than possible they might contract a taste and inclination, but in Studious and Labourious persuits.

You have before this day, received the joint commission for forming a commercial treaty with Britain. I am at a loss to determine whether you will consider yourself so bound by it, as to tarry longer abroad. Perhaps there has been no juncture in the publick affairs of our country, not even in the hour of our deepest distress, when able statesmen and wise Counsellors were more wanted than at the present day. Peace abroad leaves us at leisure to look into our own domestick affairs. Altho upon an Estimate of our national debt, it appears but as the small dust of the balance, when compared to the object we have obtained, and the benifits we have secured, yet the restless Spirit of man will not be restrained; and we have reason to fear that Domestick Jars and confusions, will take place, of foreign contentions and devastations. Congress have commuted with the Army by engageing to them 5 years pay, in lieu of half pay for Life. With Security for this they will disband contented, but our wise Legislators are about disputing the power of Congress to do either; without considering their hands in the mouth of the Lion, and if the just and necessary food is not supplied, the outragious animal may become so ferocious as to spread horrour, and devastation, or an other Theseus may arise who by his reputation, and exploits of valour, whose personal character and universal popularity, may distroy our Amphictionic System and subjugate our infant republick to Monarchical domination.

Our House of Representitives is this Year composed of more than a hundred New Members, some of whom no doubt are good Men. Near all the able and Skillfull Members who composed the last House, have lost their Seats, by voting for the return of Mr. Brattle; notwithstanding the strongest evidence in his favour, and the many proofs which were produced of his Friendly conduct towards America. For this crime, our worthy Friend Mr. Cranch was droped by this Town. The Senate is a loser this year by the resignation of Some excellent Members. We have in this state an impost of 5 per cent, and an excise act, whilst the Neighbouring States have neither. Foreigners finding this the case, cary their Cargoes to other States. At this the Merchant grumbles, the Farmer groans with his taxes, and the Mechanick for want of employ. Heaven avert that like the Greek Republicks we should by civil discension weaken our power, and crush our rising greatness; that the Blood of our citizens, should be shed in vain: and the labour, and toil of our Statesmen, be finally bafled, through niggardly parsimony, Lavish prodigality, or Ignorance of our real Interest. We want a Soloman in wisdom, to guide and conduct this great people: at this critical ære, when the counsels which are taken, and the measures which are persued, will mark our future Character either with honour, and Fame, or disgrace, and infamy. In adversity, we have conducted with prudence and magninimity. Heaven forbid, that we should grow giddy with prosperity, or the height to which we have soared, render a fall conspicuously fatal.

Thus far I had written when your welcome favour of March 28th reached me; I was not dissapointed in finding you uncertain with regard to the time of your return; should the appointment which I fear, and you have hinted at, take place, it would indeed be a dull day to me. I have not a wish to join in a scene of Life so different from that in which I have been educated, and in which my early and I must suppose, happier days, have been spent; curiosity satisfied and I should sigh for tranquil Scenes,

> "And wish that Heaven had left me still
> The whisp'ring Zephyr, and the purling rill."

Well orderd home is my chief delight, and the affectionate domestick wife with the Relative Duties which accompany that character my highest ambition. It was the disinterested wish of sacrificeing my personal feelings to the publick utility, which first led me to think of unprotectedly hazarding a voyage. I say unprotectedly for so I consider every Lady who is not accompanied by her Husband. This objection could only be surmounted by the earnest wish I had to soften those toils which were not to be dispenced with, and if the publick welfare required your Labours and exertions abroad, I flatterd myself, that if I could be with you, it might be in my power to contribute to your happiness and pleasure. But the day is now arrived, when with honour and well earned Fame, you may return to your native land—When I cannot any longer consider it as my duty to submit to a further Seperation, and when it appears necessary that those abilities which have crownd you with Laurels abroad, should be exerted at home for the publick Safety.

I do not wish you to accept an embassy to England, should you be appointed. This little Cottage has more Heart felt satisfaction for you than the most Brilliant Court can afford, the pure and undiminished tenderness of weded Love, the filial affection of a daughter who will never act contrary to the advise of a Father, or give pain to the Maternal Heart. Be assured that she will never make a choice without your approbation which I know she considers as Essential to her happiness. That she has a partiality I know, and believe, but that she has submitted her opinion to the advise of her Friends, and relinquished the Idea of a connection upon principal, of prudence and duty, I can with equal truth assure you. Yet nothing unbecomeing the Character which I first entertaind has ever appeard in this young gentleman since his residence in this Town, and he now visits in this family with the freedom of an acquaintance, tho not with the intimacy of a nearer connection. It was the request of Emelia who has conducted with the greatest prudence, that she might be permitted to see and treat this Gentleman as an acquaintance whom she valued. "Why said she should I treat a Gentleman who has done nothing to forfeit my esteem, with neglect or contempt, merely because the world have said, that he entertained a preferable regard for me? If his foibles are to be treated with more severity than the vices of others, and I submit my judgment and opinion to the disapprobation of others in a point which so nearly concerns me, I wish to be left at liberty to act in other respects with becomeing decency." And she does and has conducted so as to meet with the approbation of all her Friends. She has conquerd herself.

An extract from a little poetick peice which some months ago fell into my Hands may give you some Idea of the Situation of this matter. You will tell me you do not want a poet, but if there is a mind otherways well furnished, you would have no objection to its being a mere amusement. You ask me if this Gentleman is a speaker at the Bar. He attends Plimouth Court and has spoke there. He is not yet Sworn in to the Superiour court, but is proposed to be sworn in the next court, with his cotemporaries. I cannot say what he will make, but those who most intimately know him say he has talants to make what he pleases, and fluency to become a good Speaker. His buisness encreases here, and I know nothing but what he is well esteemed. His temper and disposition appear to be good. The family in which he boards find no fault with his conduct. He is regular in his liveing, keeps no company with gay companions, seeks no amusement but in the society of two or 3 families in Town, never goes to Boston but when Buisness calls him there. If he has been the gay thoughtless young fellow which he is said to have been and which I believe he was, he has at least practised one year of reformation. Many more will be necessary to establish him in the World. Whether he will make the Man of Worth and Steadiness time must determine.

Our two sons are placed under the care, and in the family of Mr. Shaw. They have been near 3 months absent from me. This week with my daughter and Mr. Smith to accompany us I go to see them.—My dear John. Where is he? I long to see him. I have been very anxious about him. Such a winter journey. I hope he is with you. I want to receive a Letter from him. If you should continue abroad untill fall I should be glad you would make me a small remittance. Goods will not answer. We are glutted with them. I do not wish for any thing more than I want for my family use. In this way a few peices of Irish linnen and a peice of Russia sheeting together with 2 green silk umbrellas I should be glad of as soon as convenient. If you should have an opportunity from France to send me 3 Marsels cotton and silk quilts I should be very glad; they are like the Jacket patterns you sent me by Charles. I want a white, a Blew and a pink. Mr. Dana sent 3 to Mrs. Dana; I think she said Mr. Bonfeild procured them. I mentiond in a former Letter a few other articles. I am going to marry one of my family to a young fellow whom you liberated from jail, a son of Capt. Newcombs, to the Jane Glover who has lived 7 years with me and as she never would receive any wages from me I think myself obligated to find her necessaries for house keeping. I have been buying land, and my last adventure came to so poor a market, that I am quite broke. My letter is an unreasonable long one, yet I may take an other sheet of My paper—not to night however. I will bid you good Night. I seal this least Mr. Smith should sail before I return. Mean to write more. Have a Letter for Mr. T[haxter].

JA to AA

My dearest Friend Paris July 17. 1783

No Letter from you, yet. I believe I shall set off Tomorrow or next day, for the Hague, and shall bring John with me back to Paris in about 3 Weeks. There will be an Interval, before the Signature of the definitive Treaty, and several publick Concerns oblige me to go to the Hague for a short time. When I get my Son with me, I shall be ready to go to any Place, where I may embark for home, as soon as I get Leave.

I am weary beyond all Expression of waiting in this State of Uncertainty about every Thing. It is at this Moment as uncertain as it was six months ago when the definitive Treaty will be signed. Mr. Laurens and Mr. Dana have leave to go home. Mr. Danas is upon a Condition, however, which is not yet fullfilled so that he will not go home for some time. Dr. Franklin says he is determined to go home, and Mr. Jay talks of going next Spring.

In short it is a terrible Life We lead. It wearies out the Patience of Job, and affects the health of Us all.

Mr. Smith writes me that Charles and Thomas are gone or were going to Haverhill, under the Care of Mr. Shaw. I approve of this very much. They will learn no Evil there. With them at Haveril, yourself and Miss Nabby and Mr. John with me, I could bear to live in Europe another Year or two. But I cannot live much longer without my Wife and Daughter and I will not. I want two Nurses at least: and I wont have any, at least female ones but my Wife and Daughter.

I tremble too, least a Voyage and change of Climate should alter your health. I dare not wish you in Holland for there my Charles, Mr. Thaxter, My servants and myself were forever Sick. I am half a Mind to come home with the definitive Treaty, and then if Congress dismiss me, well—. If they send me back again I can take you and your Daughter with me. However I can determine upon nothing. I am now afraid We shall not meet till next Spring. I hear, by Word of Mouth that Congress will not determine upon my Resignation till they have received the definitive Treaty. Heaven knows when this will be. It will be a Mercy to Us all, if they let me come home: for if you and your Daughter come to Europe you will get into your female Imaginations, fantastical Ideas that will never wear out, and will spoil you both.*

I hope New York and Penobscot will be evacuated before this reaches you. That will be some Comfort.—You must pray Mr. Storer or your Unkle Smith to send Your Letters to me, by Way of New York, Philadelphia, London, Bilbao, Holland, France or any way. If they inclose them to any of their Friends in London they will get to me.

Farewell, my dearest Friend Farewell.

* The Question is whether it is possible for a Lady, to be once accustomed to the Dress, Shew &c. of Europe, without having her head turned by it? This is an awfull Problem. If you cannot be Mistress enough of yourself, and be answerable for your Daughter, that you can put on and put off these Fooleries like real Philosophers, I advise you never to come to Europe, but order your husband home, for this you may depend on, your Residence in Europe will be as uncertain as the Wind. It cannot be depended on for one Year no nor for Six Months. You have seen two or three very striking Instances of the Precariousness of Congress Commissions, in my first, second and third. The Bread that is earned on a Farm is simple but sure. That which depends upon Politicks is as uncertain as they.

You know your Man. He will never be a Slave. He will never cringe. He will never accommodate his Principles, Sentiments or Systems, to keep a Place, or to get a Place, no nor to please his Daughter, or his Wife. He will never depart from his Honour, his Duty, no nor his honest Pride for Coaches, Tables, Gold, Power or Glory.—Take the Consequences then.—Take a Voyage to Europe if the Case should so happen that I shall write to you to come. Live [here?] three Months. Let your Man see something in a different Light from his Masters, and give them offence, be recalled. You and he return back to the

JOHN QUINCY ADAMS IN 1783 BY ISAAK SCHMIDT

Blue Hills, to live upon a Farm.—Very good.—Let Lyars and slanderers without [knowing? experiencing?] any of this, write Reports and nourish Factions behind his back, and the same Effect is produced.—I repeat it. It will be a Blessing to Us all, if I am permitted to return.

Be cautious my Friend, how you speak upon these subjects. I know that Congress are bound, from regard to their own honour as well as mine, to send me to England, but it is the most difficult Mission in the Universe, and the most desperate, there is no Reputation to be got by it, but a great deal to be lost. It is the most expensive and extravagant Place in Europe, and all that would be allowed would not enable one to live, as a set of insolent Spenthrifts would demand. I am quite content to come home and go to Farming, be a select Man, and owe no Man any Thing but good Will. There I can get a little health and teach my Boys to be Lawyers.

John Adams to Abigail Adams 2d

My dear Daughter — Paris, August 13th, 1783

I have received your affectionate letter of the 10th of May, with great pleasure, and another from your mother of the 28th and 29th of April, which by mistake I omitted to mention in my letter to her to-day. Your education and your welfare, my dear child, are very near my heart; and nothing in this life would contribute so much to my happiness, next to the company of your mother, as yours. I have reason to say this by the experience I have had of the society of your brother, whom I brought with me from the Hague. He is grown to be a man, and the world says they should take him for my younger brother, if they did not know him to be my son. I have great satisfaction in his behaviour, as well as in the improvements he has made in his travels, and the reputation he has left behind him wherever he has been. He is very studious and delights in nothing but books, which alarms me for his health; because, like me, he is naturally inclined to be fat. His knowledge and his judgment are so far beyond his years, as to be admired by all who have conversed with him. I lament, however, that he could not have his education at Harvard College, where his brothers shall have theirs, if Providence shall afford me the means of supporting the expense of it. If my superiors shall permit me to come home, I hope it will be soon; if they mean I should stay abroad, I am not able to say what I shall do, until I know in what capacity. One thing is certain, that I will not live long without my family, and another is equally so, that I can never consent to see my wife and children croaking with me like frogs in the Fens of Holland, and burning and shivering alternately with fevers, as Mr. Tha[xt]er, Charles, Stephen[s], and myself have done: your brother John alone had the happiness to escape, but I was afraid to trust him long amidst those pestilential steams.

You have reason to wish for a taste for history, which is as entertaining and instructive to the female as to the male sex. My advice to you would be to read the history of your own country, which although it may not afford so splendid objects as some others, before the commencement of the late war, yet since that period, it is the most interesting chapter in the history of the world, and before that period is intensely affecting to every native American. You will find among your own ancestors, by your mother's side at least, characters which deserve your attention. It is by the female world, that the greatest and best characters among men are formed. I have long been of this opinion to such a degree, that when I hear of an extraordinary man, good or bad, I naturally, or habitually inquire who was his mother? There can be nothing in life more honourable for a woman, than to contribute by her virtues, her advice, her example, or her address, to the formation of an husband, a brother, or a son, to be useful to the world.

Heaven has blessed you, my daughter, with an understanding and a consideration, that is not found every day among young women, and with a mother who is an ornament to her sex. You will take care that you preserve your own character, and that you persevere in a course of conduct, worthy of the example that is every day before you. With the most fervent wishes for your happiness, I am your affectionate father,

John Adams

JA to AA

My dearest Friend — Paris August 14. 1783

I have received your two favours of 7 May and 20 June. I had received no Letter from you for so long an Interval that these were really inestimable. I always learn more of Politicks from your Letters, than any others. I have lost all my Correspondents in Congress. I wrote to Mr. Jackson and General Warren supposing they were Members. Mr. Gerry is there now, to my Great Joy. Beg of him to write to me, if I stay in Europe.

I learn with great Satisfaction the Wisdom of my Daughter, whom I long to see. What is to be my Fate I know not. We have not received any joint Commission to make a Treaty of Commerce with Great Britain. I hate to force my self home without Leave, and Congress have not given me Leave as Mr. Lee gave you Reason to expect. My

Son is with me, at present, and you will be as proud of him as I shall be of my Daughter, when I see her. He is grown up a Man, and his Steadiness and Sobriety, with all his Spirits are much to his honour. I will make of him my Secretary while I stay.

I like the Situation of Charles and Tom.

Your Purchase of Land tho of only the Value of 200 Dollars gives me more Pleasure than you are aware. I wish you had described it. I Suppose it to be that fine Grove which I have loved and admired from my Cradle. If it is, I would not part with it, for Gold. If you know of any Woodland or salt Marsh to be sold, purchase them and draw upon me for the Money. Your Bills shall be paid upon Sight. Direct the Bills to be presented if I should be returned home, to Messrs. Wilhem and Jan Willink Merchants Amsterdam, who will accept and pay them for the Honour of the Drawer. Pray dont let a Single Tree be cutt upon that Spot. I expect, very soon, to be a private Man, and to have no other Resource for my Family but my Farm, and therefore it is my Intention when I come home to sell my House in Boston and to collect together all the Debts due to me and all other little Things that I can convert into Money and lay it out in Lands in the Neighbourhood of our Chaumiere. The whole will make but a small Farm,Yet it will be large enough for my Desires if my Children are content. You speak of a high Office. In Gods Name, banish every Idea of such a Thing. It is the Place of the greatest slavery and Drudgery in the World. It would only introduce me to endless Squabbles and Disputes, and expose me to eternal obloquy and Envy. I wish that all Parties would unite in the present one who has the Hearts of that People and will keep them. The Opposition will only weaken and distress his Administration, and if another were chosen in his Place, the Administration of that other would be weakened and distressed by a similar opposition. I have not health to go through the Business, nor have I Patience to endure the Smart. I beg that neither you nor yours would ever encourage in yourselves or others such a Thought. If after my Return home, the state should think proper to send me to Congress and you will go with me, I will go, for a short time, but not a long one. After that if I should be chosen into the Senate or House, I should be willing to contribute my Mite to the publick Service in that Way. At home, upon my Farm and among my Books, assisting in the Education of my Children, and endeavouring to introduce them into Business to get their Bread and do some service in the World, I wish to pass the feeble Remnant of my Days. But I am too much hurt, by those Exertions to which the Times have called me, to wish or to be capable of any great active Employment whatsoever. You know not how much your Friend is altered.

The Fever burnt up half his Memory and more than half his Spirits, and has left him, with scorbutic Disorders about him that are very troublesome. Without Repose, if with it, he can never hope to get the better of them. This is said to you my friend in Confidence and is to be communicated to no one else. After having seen so many of my friends thro Life fall Victims to the great Contest, I think my self very happy to have got through it, in no worse a Condition. Adieu.

Receipt in Paris early in September of official word of Congress' resolution of May 1 authorizing a new "joint commission," with its implicit promise that credentials and instructions would follow, caused a radical shift in Adams' plans. Now he felt able to bring his wife and daughter to Europe. That decision, though based on partly false expectations, was fortunately adhered to until the family was reunited. By the time her husband's firm invitation to Europe reached Abigail Adams in Braintree, the death of her father had freed her from the last of the obligations that had deterred her from undertaking the voyage earlier. But winter intervened.

In this interval John Adams, bemused and frustrated, experienced a renewed fever; after his recovery, father and son traveled to England for the first time. Their breathless sightseeing was cut short by an imperative call to John Adams to rescue the failing credit of the United States in the Netherlands. In the first days of January 1784 he and John Quincy made a perilous crossing of the North Sea and then on through the Dutch islands by iceboat and boor's wagon. In residence again at The Hague and among the capitalists at Amsterdam during the months before his wife and daughter's arrival in England, Adams executed a new Dutch loan to the United States.

JA to AA

My dearest Friend — Paris September 7. 1783

This Morning for the first Time, was delivered me the Resolution of Congress of the first of May, that a Commission and Instructions should be made out, to Me, Dr. Franklin and Mr. Jay to make a Treaty of Commerce with Great Britain. If this Intelligence had been Sent Us by Barney, who sailed from Philadelphia a Month after the 1st of May, and has now been sailed from hence on his return home above a Month it would have saved me and others much Anxiety.—I am now even at a Loss. It is of great Importance that such a Treaty should be well made. The Loan in Holland must be attended to, and when the present one is full, another must be opened, which cannot be done but by me or my Successor. There are other Things too to be done in Europe of great Importance. Mr. Laurens has Leave to go home, and Mr. Dana is gone so that there remain in Service only Mr. Franklin, Mr. Jay and my self. In these Circumstances I must stay another Winter. I cannot justify going home. But what shall I do for Want of my Family. By what I hear, I think Congress will give Us all Leave to come home in the Spring. Will you come to me this fall and go home with me in the Spring? If you will, come with my dear Nabby, leaving the two Boys at Mr. Shaws, and the House and Place under the Care of your Father, Uncle Quincy or Dr. Tufts, or Mr. Cranch. This Letter may reach you by the middle of October, and in November you may embark, and a Passage in November, or all December will be a good Season. You may embark for London, Amsterdam, or any Port in France. On your Arrival, you will find Friends enough. The Moment I hear of it, I will fly with Post Horses to receive you at least, and if the Ballon should be carried to such Perfection in the mean time as to give Mankind the Safe navigation of the Air, I will fly in one of them at the Rate of thirty Knots an hour. This is my sincere Wish, although the Expences will be considerable, the Trouble to you great and you will probably have to return with me in the Spring. I am so unhappy without you that I wish you would come at all Events. You must bring with you at least one Maid and one Man servant.

I must however leave it with your Judgment, you know better than I the real Intentions of Philadelphia, and can determine better than I whether it will be more prudent to wait untill the Spring. I am determined to be with you in America or have you with me in Europe, as soon as it can be accomplished consistent with private Prudence and the publick Good. I am told that Congress intend to recall Us all, as soon as a few Affairs are finished. If this should be the Case, all will be well. I shall go home with infinite Pleasure, But it may be longer than you think of, before all their necessary Affairs will be dispatched. The Treaty of Commerce with G[reat] B[ritain] must take Time. A Treaty will be wanted with Portugal and Denmark if not with the Emperor and Empress. If you come to Europe this Fall, in my Opinion you will be glad to go home in the Spring. If you come in the Spring you will wish to return the next fall. I am sure I shall, but six months of your Company is worth to me, all the Expences and Trouble of the Voyage.

This Resolution of Congress deserves my Gratitude; it is highly honourable to me, and restores me, my Feelings, which a former Proceeding had taken away. I am now perfectly content to be recalled whenever they think fit, or to stay in Europe, untill this Business is finished, provided you will come and live with me. We may spend our Time together in Paris, London or the Hague, for 6 or 12 Months as the Publick Business may call me and then return to our Cottage, with contented Minds. It would be more agreable to my Inclinations to get home and endeavour to get my self and Children into a settled Way, but I think it is more necessary for the Publick that I should stay in Europe, untill this Piece of Business is finished. You dont probably know the Circumstances which attended this Proceeding of Congress. They are so honourable to me, that I cannot in Gratitude or Decency refuse.

I must submit your Voyage to your Discretion and the Advice of your Friends, my most earnest Wishes are to see you but if the Uncertainties are such as to discourage you, I know it will be upon reasonable Considerations and must submit. But if you postpone the Voyage for this Fall, I shall insist on your coming in the Spring, unless there is a certainty of my going home to you. Congress are at such grievous Expences, that I shall have no other Secretary than my son. He however is a very good one. He writes a good hand very fast, and is very steady, to his Pen and his Books. Write me by every Ship to Spain, France, Holland or England, that I may know. You give me more public Intelligence than any body. The only hint in Europe of this Commission was from you to yours forever, John Adams

JA to AA

My dearest Friend Auteuil near Paris Oct. 14. 1783

I have had another Fever, which brought me low, but as it has carried off certain Pains and Lamenesses the Relicks of the Amsterdam Distemper, I am perswaded it will do me much good.

I am going next Week to London, with my son. I may stay six Weeks, if nothing from Congress calls me away sooner.

I have only to repeat my earnest Request that you and our Daughter would come to me, as soon as possible. The Business that is marked out for Us, will detain me in Europe at least another Year, as I conjecture. You may take the Voyage and satisfy your Curiosity and return with me. It is not very material, whether you arrive in Nantes, Amsterdam or London—the Distance from Paris is about the Same.

You once wrote me that Mr. Allen had offered his Place for Sale. Pray what was his Price?

I suppose that Bills upon Europe will now sell for Money or more than Money. If so draw upon me, for what you want, and your Bills shall be paid, upon Sight. I sent you a little by Mr. Thaxter.

I have particular Reasons for wishing to own that Piece of Land where Mr. Hancocks House stood and the Addition which has been made to it. If Coll. Quincy will sell it, at any tollerable Price, and you can sell a Bill upon me, for Cash to pay for it, buy it. Pray Dr. Tufts to do it, if you have not time.

Your Letters by the Way of England have all come to me very regularly and in good order. It is the best Way at present of Writing. You may write however, by the Way of the French Packet from N. York to L'Orient. But Secrets should not be trusted to that Conveyance by you nor me.

The Family affair which has been mentioned in several of your Letters, may be managed very well. The Lady comes to Europe with you. If the Parties preserve their Regard untill they meet again and continue to behave as they ought, they will be still young enough. Lawyers should never marry early. I am quite unqualified to decide upon that matter. To your Judgment, with the Advice of our Friends, I must leave it. One Thing I know, that Knowledge of the Law comes not by Inspiration, and without painfull and obstinate Study no Man will ever have it.

Yours, without Reserve.

AA to JA

My dearest Friend October 19 1783

My last Letter to you was written in Sepbr. I closed it, because I knew not how to think upon any other Subject than the solemn one I had just past through; since that date I have received a Number of Letters from you, written in April, May, june and 2 in july.

To hear from you is a satisfaction, but the whole tenor of your Letters rather added to my melancholy, than mitigated it. The state of your Health gives me great anxiety; and the delay of your return increases it. The Season is now so far advanced, that if you embark I shall have a thousand terrors for you; if you tarry abroad, I fear for your Health.

If Congress should think proper to make you an other appointment, I beg you not to accept it. Call me not to any further trials of the kind! Reflect upon your long absence from your family, and upon the necessity there is, of your returning in order to recover that Health which you have unhappily impaired and lost abroad.

Your Children have a demand upon you, they want your care, your advice and instruction; I mean at all times to consult and promote their interest and happiness, but I may be mistaken in it; I cannot feel so safe or so satisfied as I should if your approbation was added to it.

There was a time when I had brought my mind to be willing to cross the Seas to be with you, but tho one strong tie which held me here, is dissolved, the train of my Ideas for six months past has run wholy upon your return; that I now think nothing short of an assurence from you, that your happiness depended upon it, would induce me to alter my oppinion. The Scenes of anxiety through which you have past, are enough to rack the firmest constitution, and debilitate the strongest faculties. Conscious Rectitude is a grand Support, but it will not ward off the attacks of envy, or secure from the assaults of jealousy. Both ancient and Modern history furnish us with repeated proofs, that virtue must look beyond this shifting theatre for its reward; but the Love of praise is a passion deeply rooted in the mind, and in this we resemble the Supreem Being who is most Gratified with thanksgiving and praise. Those who are most affected with it, partake most of that particle of divinity which distinguishes mankind from the inferiour Creation; no one who deserves commendation can dispise it, but we too frequently see it refused where it is due, and bestowed upon very undeserving characters. "Treachery, venality and villainy must be the effects of dissipation, voluptuousness and impiety, says the Great Dr. Price and adds, these vices sap the foundation of virtue, they render Men necessitous and supple, ready at any time to sacrifice their consciences. Let us remember these Truths in judging of Men. Let us consider that true goodness is uniform and consistant; and learn never to place any great confidence in those pretenders to publick Spirit, who are not men of virtuous Characters. They may boast of their attachment to a publick cause, but they want the living root of virtue, and should not be depended upon."

You call upon me to write you upon a subject which greatly embarrasses me, yet I ought to tell you what I conceive to be the real Truth. The Gentleman whom I formerly mentiond to you, resides here still, and boards in the same family. I wrote you the Truth when I informed you that the connection was broken off—and nothing particular has since past. Yet it is evident to me, as well as to the family where he lives, that his attachment is not lessned. He conducts prudently, and tho nothing is said upon the Subject, I do not immagine that he has given up the Hope, that in some future Day he may be able to obtain your approbation. Your Daughter so highly values your esteem and approbation, that she has frequently said she never could be happy without it. That she will not act contrary to the opinion of her Friends, I am fully satisfied, but her sentiments with regard to this Gentleman she says are not to be changed but upon a conviction of his demerrit. I wish most sincerely wish you was at Home to judge for yourself. I shall never feel safe or happy untill you are. I had rather you should inquire into his conduct and behaviour, his success in Buisness and his attention to it, from the family where he lives, than say any thing upon the Subject myself. I can say with real Truth that no Courtship subsists between them, and that I believe it is in your power to put a final period to every Idea of the kind, if upon your return you think best. There is a young Gentleman, who formerly kept our school, by the Name of Perkings, who is now studying Law with Mr. Tyler. He has been in Virgina for a twelve month past and designs to return there again.

I was very unhappy to find by your Letters that you was so long without any intelligence from America, but I hope you have been amply compensated before this time. Your Letters which were dated in April, May and June did not reach me untill Sep'br. I must request you in future to calculate those you send to Philadelphia for the post office. Every line of yours is invaluable to me, yet blank paper is not so, and the double covers pay as large postage, as if they were wholy written. I have disputed the matter some time with the postmaster, and now he will not deliver a Letter untill the postage is pay'd. I payd 3 dollors the other day for what one sheet of paper would have containd. I do not yet believe that congress mean to make their foreign ministers subject to postage, and I design to write to Mr. Gerry upon the subject.

I hear of a vessel bound to France. I will forward this and write to Mr. Thaxter by way of England. I hear he is there, and that Mr. Smith arrived after a short passage. At this I rejoice tho I was not his companion. Our two Sons are gone to Haverhill. I hope to hear frequently from you if I do not see you, which I now almost dispair of, this winter.

Adieu my dearest Friend ever Yours, Portia

AA to JA

My dearest Friend Braintree November 11 1783

Col. Trumble has been so kind as to visit me, and request a Letter from me to you; I have promised him one. You direct me to write by every opportunity. I very seldom let one slip unimproved, but I find many more conveyances by way of England than any other. I have written twice to you since the recept of your last favour, which was dated July 17th.

I wish you to write by way of England but to send no letters to the Southard.

I pleased myself with the Idea of seeing you here during the summer, but when I found how publick Buisness was delayed I endeavourd to banish the Idea, for one month of daily expectation, is more tedious than a year of certainty. I think it would be a releif to my mind if your next Letter was to assure me, that you had no intention of comeing out till next Spring; yet think not, that I am more reconciled to your absence, or less ardently desire your return. But your Life and Health are too dear to me, to gratify my wishes at the expence of either.

I have but last evening returnd, from a visit to Haverhill, where I was led at this season, by the Sickness of Master Tommy, who has a second time experienced a severe fit of the Rhumatism. It was an unfortunate bequest, but it is so similar to what at his age I was excersised with, that I think it must have descended to him. He lost the use of his Limbs for a fortnight. It was attended with a fever, and stricture across his Breast. I had the Satisfaction to find him upon the recovery, and much better than my fears, for Seazing him at this Season and with so much voilence, I feard he would have been disabled all winter.

Both Mr. and Mrs. Shaw speak very well of our young Lads, who begin to think of a Colledge Life as not more than a year and half distance. Charles is very desirious that he may be ready at 15, and Master Tommy is determined that he shall not out strip him, in his learning, what ever he may do in his entrance at colledge, for which purpose he requests that his lessons may be the same with his Brothers. He took great pains to overtake Charles during his absence and sickness with the Measles, nor did he rest untill he accomplished it. Mr. Shaw is I believe an excellent preceptor and takes great pains with them. Their Morals and Manners are strickly attended to, and I have every satisfaction I can wish with respect to care and tenderness both in Sickness and Health, I wanted for nothing but to see you Mamma, says Master, during my Sickness. Mrs. Shaw is the same amiable good woman you always knew her. She has one son and one daughter, but her Health is feeble and her frame exceedingly delicate and tender, her Spirits lively, her temper placid. The children Love her with a filial affection.

I longed for you to accompany me in this journey, and to have participated the pleasure of seeing our children attentive to their Studies, and promiseing to be wise and good.

While your own Heart dilates, you will tell me, that the season for temptation is not yet arrived, that altho they are carefully guarded against evil communications, and warned of the danger of bad examples, no humane foresight can effectually preserve them from the contagion of vice; true, but I have a great opinion of early impressions of virtue, and believe that they take such hold of the mind, as neither time, or temptations can wholy subdue. They recall the wanderer to a sense of his Duty, tho he has strayed many many times. Attend says the good Ganganalla, more to the Hearts, than the understanding of your pupils. If the Heart is good, all will go well.

I have a thousand fears for my dear Boys as they rise into Life, the most critical period of which is I conceive, at the university; there infidelity abounds, both in example and precepts. There they imbibe the speicious arguments of a Voltaire, a Hume and Mandevill. If not from the fountain, they receive them at second hand. These are well calculated to intice a youth, not yet capable of investigating their principals, or answering their arguments. Thus is a youth puzzeld in Mazes and perplexed with error untill he is led to doubt, and from doubting to disbelief. Christianity gives not such a pleasing latitude to the passions. It is too pure. It teaches moderation, humility and patience, which are incompatable with the high Glow of Health, and the warm blood which riots in their veins. With them, "to enjoy, is to obey." I hope before either of our children are prepaird for colledge you will be able to return and assist by your example and advise, to direct and counsel them; that with undeviating feet they may keep the path of virtue.

I have heitherto been able to obtain their Love, their confidence and obedience, but I feel unequal to the task of guiding them alone, encompassed as I know they must be, with a thousand snares and temptations.

I hope our Dear son abroad will not imbibe any sentiments or principals which will not be agreable to the Laws, the Government and Religion of our own Country. He has been less under your Eye than I could wish, but never I dare say without your advise and instruction. If he does not return this winter, I wish you to remind him, that he has forgotten to use his pen, to his Friends upon this Side the water.

With Regard to what passes in the political world, I hear little said upon the subject. We are anxious to receive official accounts of the signing the definitive Treaty. The Merchants will Clamour if the commercial Treaty is not to their taste. The peace necessitates many of them to a less extravagant mode of living, and they must retrench still more if ever they pay their debts abroad. Bills are now sold at par. If you continue abroad, I shall be under a necessity of drawing upon you, for tho the War is ceased, taxes have not. Since I took my pen, and within this hour, I have been visited by the collector with 3 tax Bills; the amount of which is 29 pounds 6 and 8 pence, the continental tax, State tax, and town tax, beside which, I have just paid a parish tax. I live with all the frugality in my power. I have but two domesticks, yet I find it as much as I can do to muster cash enough to pay our sons Quarter Bills and Cloath them decently.

Of one thing you may rest assured, that I involve you in no debts, nor go one Inch without seeing my way clear; you laugh at me with regard to my Virmont purchase. I still value it, and do not doubt of its becomeing so. I have a Right in about [2?] hundred acers of land some where in Northburry which comes to me from my Mother, I will exchange with you. My Father left to me and Mrs. Shaw his Medford Farm Stock buildings &c. and his medow in Malden, the value of which is estimated at near 800. Now what I wish is to persuade my Sister to sell you her part of the Farm, and make a purchase in the Town where she lives. But I do not chuse to say any thing upon the subject at present. I suppose it will sell for more than the apprizement, and as I hope you will return early in the Spring, that will be as soon as any thing can be done about it. The estate is some cloged in concequence of a numerous family, but the personal estate will clear it and pay the Legacies which amount to about 300 pounds and some small debts.

Adieu my dearest Friend. Heaven preserve your Life and Health, and safely conduct You to Your ever affectionate Portia

John Adams' "pressing invitation" to his wife to join him, expressed in his letters to her in September, was probably reinforced by messages delivered by Francis Dana and John Thaxter on their arrival in America in December. In the meantime, Mrs. Adams, for her guidance, had sought from their friend Elbridge Gerry some hint as to the likelihood of her husband's early return. Gerry replied that though he himself wished for such an event, he thought it improbable and alluded to possible further employments in store in Europe. Congress, it appeared, had not even yet settled its diplomatic arrangements. But Abigail Adams, though she seems then to have determined upon the voyage at winter's end, was still troubled by information that Gerry had earlier provided her. He had enclosed in a letter to her a copy of a letter from Franklin to Secretary Livingston "calculated to give a private Stab to the Reputation of our Friend." In it Franklin, recognizing that in so doing "he hazzarded a mortal Enmity," was severely critical of Adams' vocal suspicions directed against Vergennes and against his own French-dominated policy that had been approved by Congress. Presented with word of this renewed attack upon her husband, Abigail Adams sensed the possibility of his recall from Europe. With suitable circumlocution, she enclosed in the following letter the evidence on which her fears were based.

During the next month she began preparations for the voyage and took steps to insure the care of the family's affairs in her absence, even to providing that her tenants "may have liberty to cut currents out of the Garden but no Children to be permitted to go in to the garden."

AA to JA My Dearest Friend Braintree December 15 1783

I returned last Evening from Boston, where I went at the kind invitation of my uncle and Aunt, to celebrate our Anual festival. Doctor

Cooper being dangerously sick, I went to hear Mr. Clark; who is setled with Dr. Chauncey; this Gentleman gave us an animated, elegant and sensible discourse, from Isaah 55 chapter and 12th verse—"For ye shall go out with joy, and be led forth with peace; the Mountains and the Hills shall break forth before you into singing, and all the Trees of the Field shall clap their Hands."

Whilst he asscribed Glory and praise unto the most high, he considerd the Worthy, disinterested, and undaunted patriots as the instruments in the hand of providence for accomplishing what was marvelous in our Eyes; he recapitulated the dangers they had past through, and the hazards they had run; the firmness which had in a particular manner distinguished some Characters, not only early to engage in so dangerous a contest, but in spight of our gloomy prospects they persevered even unto the end; untill they had obtained a peace Safe and Honorable; large as our designs, Capacious as our wishes, and much beyond our expectations.

How did my heart dilate with pleasure when as each event was particularized, I could trace my Friend as a principal in them; could say, it was he, who was one of the first in joinning the Band of patriots, who formed our first National Counsel. It was he, who tho happy in his domestick attachments, left his wife, his Children, then but Infants, even surrounded with the Horrours of war, terified and distresst, the Week after the memorable 17th of April. Left them, to the protection of that providence which has never forsaken them, and joined himself undismayed, to that Respectable Body, of which he was a member. Trace his conduct through every period, you will find him the same undaunted Character, encountering the dangers of the ocean, risking Captivity and a dungeon, contending with wickedness in high places, jeoparding his Life, endangerd by the intrigues, revenge, and Malice of a potent, tho defeated Nation.

These are not the mere eulogiums of conjugal affection, but certain facts, and solid truths. My anxieties, my distresses, at every period, bear witness to them; tho now by a series of prosperous events, the recollection, is more Sweet than painfull.

Whilst I was in Town, Mr. Dana arrived very unexpectedly, for I had not received your Letters by Mr. Thaxter. My uncle fortunately discoverd him, as he came up into State Street, and instantly engaged him to dine with him, acquainting him that I was in Town, and at his House. The news soon reached my Ears. Mr. Dana arrived, Mr. Dana arrived—from every person you saw. But how was I affected? The Tears involuntary flowed from my eyes. Tho God is my witness, I envyed not the felicity of others, yet my Heart swelled with Grief, and the Idea that I, I only, was left alone, recall'd all the tender Scenes of seperation, and overcame all my fortitude. I retired and reasoned myself into composure sufficient to see him without a childish emotion.

He tarried but a short time, anxious as you may well imagine, to reach Cambridge. He promised me a visit with his Lady, in a few days, to which I look forward with pleasure.

I reach'd home last evening, having left Nabby in Town, to make her winter visit. I found Mr. Thaxter just arrived before me. It was a joyfull meeting to both of us, tho I could not prevail with him only for half an hour. His solicitude to see his parents was great, and tho I wished his continuance with me, yet I checked not the fillial flow of affection. Happy youth! who has parents still alive to visit, parents who can rejoice in a Son returned to them after a long absence; untainted in his morals, improved in his understanding; with a Character fair and unblemished.

But O my dearest Friend what shall I say to You in reply to your pressing invitation [?] I have already written to you in answer to your Letters which were dated Sepbr. 10th and reachd me a month before those by Mr. Thaxter. I related to you all my fears respecting a winters voyage. My Friends are all against it, and Mr. Gerry as you will see, by the Coppy of his Letter inclosed, has given his opinion upon well grounded reasons. If I should leave my affairs in the Hands of my Friends, there would be much to think of, and much to do, to place them in that method and order I would wish to leave them in.

Theory and practise are two very different things; and the object magnifies, as I approach nearer to it. I think if you were abroad in a private Character, and necessitated to continue there, I should not hesitate so much at comeing to you. But a mere American as I am, unacquainted with the Etiquette of courts, taught to say the thing I mean, and to wear my Heart in my countanance, I am sure I should make an awkward figure, and then it would mortify my pride if I should be thought to disgrace you. Yet strip Royalty of its pomp, and power, and what are its votaries more than their fellow worms? I have so little of the Ape about me, that I have refused every publick invitation to figure in the gay World, and sequestered myself in this Humble cottage, content with rural Life and my domestick employments in the midst of which I have sometimes smiled, upon recollecting that I had the Honour of being allied to an Ambassador. Yet I have for an example the chaste Lucretia who was found spinning in the midst of her maidens, when the Brutal Tarquin plotted her distruction.

I am not acquainted with the particular circumstances attending the renewal of your commission; if it is modeled so as to give you satisfaction I am content, and hope you will be able to discharge it, so as to receive the approbation of your Sovereign.

A Friend of yours in Congress some months ago, sent me an extract of a Letter, requesting me to conceal his Name, as he would not chuse to have it known by what means he procured the Coppy. From all your Letters I discoverd that the treatment you had received, and the suspence You was in, was sufficiently irritating without any thing further to add to your vexation. I therefore surpresst the extract, as I knew the author was fully known to you. But seeing a letter from G[e]n. W[arre]n to you, in which this extract is alluded to, and finding by your late Letters, that your Situation is less embarrassing, I inclose it, least you should think it much worse than it really is. At the same time I cannot help adding an observation which appears pertinant to me: that there is an ingredient necessary in a Mans composition towards happiness, which people of feeling would do well to acquire—a certain respect for the follies of Mankind. For there are so many fools whom the opinion of the world entittles to regard, whom accident has placed in heights of which they are unworthy, that he who cannot restrain his contempt or indignation at the sight, will be too often Quarrelling with the disposal of things to realish that share, which is allotted to himself.—And here my paper obliges me to close the subject, without room to say adieu.

JA to AA

My dearest Friend — The Hague Jan. 25. 1784

I was much disappointed, on the Arrival of Mr. Temple in London, at not finding a Letter from you, but last Week at Amsterdam, I had the Happiness to receive your kind favours of Sept. 20. and Oct. 19. Mr. Trumbull is not arrived.

The Loss of my kind Father has very tenderly affected me, but I hope with full Confidence to meet him in a better World. My ever honoured Mother I still hope to see in this.—I feel for you, as I know how justly dear to you, your father was.

You have seen, before now, Mr. Thaxter and I hope Mr. Dana.—The Determinations of Congress, upon the Arrival of the definitive Treaty, will be your best Guide for your own Conduct. You will juge best from thence whether it is worth your while to come to The Hague or to Europe. If Congress should determine to continue me in Europe, I must intreat you to come to me, for I assure you, my Happiness depends so much upon it, that I am determined, if you decline coming to me, to come to you. If Miss Nabby is attached to Braintre, and you think, upon Advizing with your Friends, her Object worthy, marry her if you will and leave her with her Companion in your own House, Office, Furniture, Farm and all. His Profession is the very one I wish. His Connections are respectable, and if he has sown his wild Oats and will study, and mind his Business, he is all I want.

I must at present leave all to your Judgment. If you think it not advizeable to come to Europe, I will come to you, although I should be sorry to break away and return, without Permission from Congress. I should not care a Farthing my self whether it were in England or Holland, if I could preserve my Health, which I should hope to do with my Family in a settled Way of Life, for I am determined not to venture in future upon such Journeys and Wanderings as have heretofore been necessary, and have done me so much harm. Somewhere or other, I am determined to have a regular Habitation and settled Abode.

John is a great Comfort to me. He is every Thing you could wish him. Wholly devoted to his studies he has made a Progress, which gives me intire Satisfaction. Miss N[abby']s Friend must rise very early, or he will be soon overtaken by her worthy Brother. In the Course of two or three Years, John must go home, and go into some Office, and if he should have a Brother in Law of sufficient Merit, why should he wish for any other Master? These Things are but Speculations. Miss hopes I shall approve of her Taste. I can scarcely think it possible for me to disapprove, of her final Judgment, formed with deliberation, upon any Thing which so deeply concerns her whole Happiness. But she will listen to the Advice of her Mother, Grandmother, and her Aunts, in whose Wisdom I have great Confidence.

The next Dispatches from Congress, and from you, after Mr. Thaxters Arrival will determine me and I shall write you more fully.

I have enjoyed better Health, since my Fever last Septr. at Paris. I got poisoned at Amsterdam with the Steams of the Canals, and bad Water in the Cisterns, and my Constitution has been labouring, these two or three Years to throw it off. Two violent Fevers, have not been sufficient, wholly to relieve me, but the last has made me better. I am cured of the Imprudence of living in a great City in hot Weather.

Adieu my dearest Friend. Adieu.

AA to JA

Febry. 11th 1784

Two days only are wanting to compleat six years since my dearest Friend first crost the Atlantick. But three months of the six Years have been spent in America. The airy, delusive phantom Hope, how has she eluded my prospects. And my expectations of your return from month to month, have vanished "like the baseless Fabrick of a vision."

You invite me to you, you call me to follow you, the most earnest wish of my Soul is to be with you—but you can scarcly form an Idea of the conflict of my mind. It appears to me such an enterprize, the Ocean so formidable, the quitting my habitation and my Country, leaving my Children, my Friends, with the Idea that prehaps I may never see them again, without my Husband to console and comfort me under these apprehensions—indeed my dear Friend, there are hours when I feel unequal to the trial. But on the other hand I console myself with the Idea of being joyfully and tenderly received by the best of Husbands and Friends, and of meeting a dear and long absent Son. But the difference is, my fears, and anxieties are present; my hopes, and expectations, distant.

But avaunt ye Idle Specters, the desires and requests of my Friend are a Law to me. I will Sacrifice my present feelings and hope for a blessing in persuit of my duty.

I have already arranged all my family affairs in such a way that I hope nothing will suffer by my absence. I have determined to put into this House my Pheby, to whom my Father gave freedom, by his Will, and the income of a hundred a year during her Life. The Children furnished her to house keeping, and she has ever since lived by herself, until a fortnight ago, she took unto her self a Husband in the person of Mr. Abdee whom you know. As there was no setled minister in Weymouth I gave them the liberty of celebrating their nuptials here, which they did much to their satisfaction.

I proposed to her taking care of this House and furniture in my absence. The trust is very flattering to her, and both her Husband and she seem pleased with it. I have no doubt of their care and faithfullness, and prefer them to any other family. The Farm I continue to let to our old tennant, as no one thinks I shall supply myself better.

I am lucky too in being able to supply myself with an honest faithfull Man Servant. I do not know but you may recollect him, John Brisler, who was brought up in the family of Genll. Palmer, has since lived with Col. Quincy and is recommended by both families as a virtuous, steady, frugal fellow, with a mind much above the vulgar, very handy and attentive. For a maid servant I hope to have a Sister of his, who formerly lived with Mrs. Trott, who gives her a good character. It gave me some pain to refuse the offerd service of an old servant who had lived 7 years with me, and who was married from here. As I wrote you some time ago, both she and her Husband solicited to go, but I could not think it convenient as Babies might be very inconvenient at Sea, tho they offerd to leave it at Nurse if I would consent to their going. But tho I felt gratified at their regard for me I could not think it would answer. On many accounts a Brother and Sister are to be prefered. Thus far have I proceeded but I know not yet what Ship, or what month or what port I shall embark for. I rather think for England.

I wrote you largely by Capt. Love, who saild for England 3 weeks ago. By him I mentiond a set of Bills which I expected to draw in favour of Uncle Smith for 200 dollors. He did not send me the Bills untill yesterday. Instead of 60 pounds Lawfull, he requested me to sign a Bill for 60 Sterling, as that was just the sum he wanted, and that it would oblige him. I have accordingly drawn for that; as I supposed it would not make any great odds with you, whether I drew now, or a Month hence, as I suppose I shall have occasion before I embark. You will be so kind as to honour the Bill.

I have not heard from you since Mr. Robbins arrived. I long to hear how your Health is. Heaven preserve and perfect it. Col. Quincy lies very dangerously ill of the same disorder which proved fatal to my dear and honourd parent. The doctor is apprehensive that it will put a period to his life in a few days.

Your Honourd Mother is as well as usual. The thoughts of my going away is a great Grief to her, but I shall leave her with a particular request to my Sister Cranch, to pay the same attention to her during her Life, which I have done, and to supply my place to her in Sickness and Health.

However kind sons may be disposed to be, they cannot be daughters to a Mother. I hope I shall not leave any thing undone which I ought to do. I would endeavour in the discharge of my duty towards her, to merit from her the same testimony which my own parent gave me, that I was a good, kind, considerate child as ever parent had. However undeserving I may have been of this testimony, it is a dear and valuable Legacy to me and will I hope proove a stimulous to me, to endeavour after those virtues which the affection and partiality of a parent ascribed to me.

Our Sons are well. I hope your young companion is so too. If I should not now be able to write to him please to tell him I am not unmindfull of him.

I have been to day to spend a few Hours with our good uncle [Norton] Quincy, who keeps much confined a winters and says he misses my two Boys almost as much as I do; for they were very fond of visiting him, and used to go as often as once a week when they lived at home.

There is nothing stiring in the political world. The Cincinati makes a Bustle, and will I think be crushed in its Birth.—Adieu my dearest Friend. Yours most affectionately, A.A.

At the end of May, Abigail Adams was able to inform her husband (though he would receive the letter only after she had reached England) of the ship on which she had engaged passage, the approximate date of sailing, and her own likely arrival in London. She was also enabled, through Elbridge Gerry's kindness and promptness, to embark with the knowledge that Congress, now sitting in Annapolis, had "finished the Instructions to their Ministers, and Mr. Adams, Docter Franklin and Mr. Jefferson are appointed in the order mentioned to negotiate a great Number of commercial Treaties, which will detain them about two years in Europe."

What had happened was that, after a full year of confusion and delay, Congress had substituted Jefferson for Jay (now elected secretary of foreign affairs), and the commissioners were authorized to treat with some twenty European and North African commercial powers not including Great Britain. Jefferson, who had had a major role in resolving the matter, traveled north in June and wrote Adams from Boston on the nineteenth that he had "hastened" there "in hopes of having the pleasure of attending Mrs. Adams to Paris and of lessening some of the difficulties to which she may be exposed."

He was too late. Abigail Adams sailed the next day. Her accounts of her voyage, the landing at Deal, and her first sojourn in England, brought together here from one of her diaries and her several journal letters sent to her sisters, prove that she was quite as gifted a travel writer as her husband.

AA to JA

My dearest Friend Boston May 25 1784

I came to Town yesterday and have engaged my passage on Board the Ship Active Capt. Lyde, agreable to the advise of my Friends. She will sail in about a fortnight or 3 Weeks and is the only good vessel now going. Mrs. Jones with whom I hoped to have been a passenger is still in so poor Health that there is no prospect of her going very soon, and my Uncle Smith upon whose judgment and care I place much dependance advises me by no means to delay my passage. It gives me some pain that I can only hear of you by second hand; and that not since the last of Janry. I find Congress have commissiond the Gentlemen now abroad to transact and form all their commercial Treaties, and Mr. Gerry wishes me to give you the earliest notice, and requests that Mr. Jay may be prevented from returning. There was a trial to add Mr. Jefferson to you, but I cannot learn that it is done.

And now my dear Friend let me request you to go to London some time in july that if it please God to conduct me thither in safety I may have the happiness to meet you there. I am embarking on Board a vessel without any Male Friend, connection or acquaintance, my servant excepted, a stranger to the capt[ain] and every person on Board, a situation which I once thought nothing would tempt me to undertake. But let no person say what they would or would not do, since we are not judges for ourselves untill circumstances call us to act. I am assured that I shall have a state room to myself and every accommodation and attention that I can wish for. It is said to be a good vessel, copper Bottom and an able Captain. Should I arrive, I know not where to apply for accommodations. I shall carry with me a Number of Letters and rely upon the Captains care of me. The United States Capt. Scot is not yet arrived tho we are in hourly expectation of it. I hope to hear from you by her. Tis six months since a single line reachd me from you. All communication seems to be shut out between Amsterdam and America. I think after the arrival of the Letters by Capt. Love, that you would write as you would not then look for me untill july. I have given you my reasons for not going with Capt. Callihan. I could get no Satisfaction from Mr. Gerry with regard to the movements of Congress untill this month.

Our children are all well. Charles and Tommy are both at home now but will return to Haverhill next week. The expence attending my voyage will be great I find. The Captains have got into a method of finding every thing and have from 20 to 25 Guineys a person. I shall draw Bills upon you for this purpose but in whose favour I do not yet know. I shall embark with a much lighter Heart if I can receive Letters from you. I dare not trust my self with anticipating the happiness of meeting you; least I should unhappily meet with a bitter alloy. I have to combat my own feelings in leaving my Friends, and I have to combat, encourage and sooth the mind of my young companion whose passions militate with acknowledged Duty and judgment.—I pray Heaven conduct me in safety and give me a joyful and happy meeting with my long long seperated best Friend and ever dear companion and long absent son to whom my affectionate Regards. I hope to be benefitted by the voyage as my Health has been very infirm and I have just recoverd from a slow fever. I have one anxiety on account of the Maid who attends me. She has never had the small pox. The one I expected to have come with me undertook to get married and dissapointed me. The one I have is a daughter of our Neighbour Feilds and has lived with me ever since Jinny was married. I shall be very happy in two excellent servants.—Adieu my dear Friend, Heaven preserve [us] to each other.

Yours with the tenderest affection, A. Adams

ABIGAIL ADAMS IN 1785 BY MATHER BROWN

The Book of Abigail and John

From Abigail Adams' Diary

SUNDAY JUNE 20 1784.

Embarked on Board the ship Active Capt. Lyde commander, with my daughter and 2 servants for London. To go back to the painfull Scenes I endured in taking leave of my Friends and Neighbours will but excite them over again. Suffice it to say that I left my own House the 18 of june. Truly a house of mourning; full of my Neighbours. Not of unmeaning complimenters, but the Honest yeomanary, their wifes and daughters like a funeral procession, all come to wish me well and to pray for a speedy return.—Good Heaven, what were my sensations? Heitherto I had fortified my mind. Knowing I had to act my little part alone, I had possessd myself with calmness, but this was too much for me, so I shook them by the hand mingling my tears with theirs, and left them. I had after this to bid my neices, adieu. And then another scene still more afflictive, an aged Parent from whom I had kept the day of my departure a secret knowing the agony she would be in. I calld at her door. As soon as the good old Lady beheld me, the tears rolled down her aged cheek, and she cried out O! why did you not tell me you was going so soon? Fatal day! I take my last leave; I shall never see you again. Carry my last blessing to my son.—I was obliged to leave her in an agony of distress, myself in no less. My good Sister Cranch who accompanied me to Town endeavourd to amuse me and to console me. I was glad to shut myself up the remainder of the day and to be denied to company. Saturday I had recoverd some from my fatigue and employed the day in writing to several of my Friends and in getting my baggage on Board. Several of the Passengers calld upon me, amongst whom was a Col. Norton from Marthas Vinyard a Member of our Senate, a grave sedate Man about 50 Years of age. A Mr. Green an english Gentleman who was Seceretary to Admiral Arbuthnot when he was at Charlestown, a high monarckacal man you may easily discover but he behaves like a Gentleman. A Dr. Clark and Mr. Foster, Mr. Spear and a Capt. Mellicot make up the number of our male passengers. We have one Lady a name sake of mine, Mrs. Adams Daughter of the late Revd. Mr. Laurence of Lincoln whose Husband has been absent ever since the War, is a physician and setled abroad. A modest, amiable woman well educated with whom I had a passing acquaintance before I came on Board. Sund[ay] at 12 oclock Mr. Foster sent his carriage for myself and daughter. We bid adieu to our Friends and were drove to Rows Wharf, from whence we alighted amidst an 100 Gentlemen who were upon the Wharf, to receive us. Mr. Smith handed me from the Carriage and I hastned into the ship from amidst the throng. The ship was soon under sail and we went of with a fine wind. About 2 oclock we reachd the light when the Capt. sent word to all the Ladies to put on their Sea cloaths and prepare for sickness. We had only time to follow his directions before we found ourselves all sick. To those who have never been at Sea or experienced this disspiriting malady tis impossible to discribe it, the Nausia arising from the smell of the Ship, the continual rolling, tossing and tumbling contribute to keep up this Disorder, and when once it seazeis a person it levels Sex and condition. My Servant Man was very attentive the first day, not sick at all, made our beds and did what I should not have put him upon in any other Situation for my maid was wholy useless and the sickest of either. Monday mor[nin]g very fogy every Body on Board Sick except the Dr. and 3 or 4 old sea men. My Servant as bad as any. I was obliged to send a petition to the Capt. to release to me Jobe Feild whose place on board the ship I had procured for him. He came and amply supplied the others place. Handy, attentive, obligeing and kind, an excellent Nurse, we all prized him. He continued untill tuesday when we had a fine mor'g. Our sickness abated and we went upon Deck, beheld the vast and boundless ocean before us with astonishment, and wonder. How great, how Excellent, how stupendous He who formed, governs, and directs it.

Abigail Adams to Elizabeth Smith Shaw

On Board the Ship Active
Latitude 34, Long. 35
[*10? July 1784*]

My dear Sister

This day 3 weeks I came on Board this Ship; and Heaven be praised, have hietherto had a favourable passage. Upon the Banks of Newfoundland we had an easterly Storm, I thought, but the Sailors say it was only a Brieze. We could not however sit without being held into our chairs, and every thing that was moveable was in motion, plates Mugs bottles all crashing to peices: the Sea roaring and lashing the Ship, and when worn down with the fatigue of the voilent, and incessant motion, we were assisted into our Cabbins; we were obliged to hold ourselves in, with our utmost Strength, without once thinking of closeing our Eyes, every thing wet, dirty and cold, ourselves Sick; you will not envy our Situation: yet the returning sone, a smooth sea and a mild Sky dispelld our fears, and raised our languid heads.

"Ye too, ye Winds, I raise my voice to you
In what far distant region of the Sky
Hushed in deep Silence, Sleep you when tis calm?"

There is not an object in Nature, better calculated to raise in our minds sublime Ideas of the Deity than the boundless ocean. Who can contemplate it, without admiration and wonder.

> "And thou Majestick Main,
> A secret world of wonders in thyself
> Sound his stupendous praise; whose greater voice
> or bids your roar, or bids your roarings fall."

I have contemplated it in its various appearences since I came to Sea, smooth as a Glass, then Gently agitated with a light Brieze, then lifting wave upon wave, moveing on with rapidity, then rising to the Skyes, and in majestick force tossing our Ship to and fro, alternately riseing and sinking; in the Night I have behold it Blaizing and Sparkling with ten thousand Gems—untill with the devoute psalmist I have exclamed, Great and Marvellous are thy Works, Lord God Almighty, In Wisdom hast thou made them all.

It is very difficult to write at Sea, in the serenest Weather the vessel rolls; and exceeds the moderate rocking of a cradle, and a calm gives one more motion, than a Side wind going at 7 and 8 knots an hour: I am now setting in my *State room*, which is about 8 foot square, with two Cabbins, and a chair, which compleatly fills it, and I write leaning one Arm upon my cabbin, with a peice of Board in my lap, whilst I steady myself by holding my other hand upon the opposite Cabbin; from this you will judge what accommodations we have for writing; the door of my room opens into the Great Cabbin where we set, dine, and the Gentlemen sleep: we cannot Breath with our door shut, so that except when we dress and undress, we live in common. A sweet Situation for a delicate Lady, but necessity has no law: and we are very fortunate, in our company.

We have 6 Gentlemen passengers and a lad, Brother to Mrs. Adams whom I find a very agreeable modest woman. There are two State rooms; one of which I occupy with my Maid, the other Mrs. Adams and Nabby; when we first came on Board, we sufferd exceedingly from Sea Sickness, which is a most disheartning disorder. This held us in some degree for ten days, and a more than ordinary motion will still affect us. The Ship was very tight, and consequently very loathsome, in addition to this our cargo was not of the most odorifferous kind consisting of oil, and potash, one of which leaked, and the other fermented, so that we had that in concert with the Sea Smell. Our cook and Steward is a laizy dirty Negro, with no more knowledge of his Buisness than a Savage; untill I was well enough to exert my

Authority, I was daily obliged to send my Shoes upon deck to have them scraped: but the first time we were all able to go upon deck, I summoned my own Man Servant, who before had been as sick as any of us; and sent him down with all the Boys I could muster, with Scrapers, mops, Brushes, infusions of vinegar &c. and in a few hours we found there *was Boards for a floor.* When we returnd, we scarcly knew our former habitation; since which I have taken upon me the whole direction of our cabbin, taught the cook to dress his victuals, and have made several puddings with my own hands. We met with a great misfortune in the loss of our cow, which has deprived us of many conveniences; the poor creature was so bruized in the Storm which we had, that they were obliged to kill her the next day.

Our Captain is the very Man, one would wish to go to Sea with, always upon deck a nights, never sleeps but 6 hours in the 24, attentive to the clouds, to the wind and weather; anxious for his Ship, constantly watchfull of his Sails and his rigging, humane and kind to his Men, who are all quiet and still as a private family, nor do I recollect hearing him swear but once since I came on board, and that was at a vessel which spoke with us, and by imprudent conduct were in danger of running on Board of us, to them he gave a Broadside. Since that I have not wished to see a vessel near us. At a distance we have seen several Sail. We came on Board mere Strangers to the passengers, but we have found them obligeing and kind, polite and civil, particularly so a Dr. Clark, who has been as attentive to us as if we were all his Sisters; we have profitted by his care, and advice, during our Sea Sickness when he was Nurse, as well as physician; doctors you know have an advantage over other gentlemen, and we soon grow fond of those who interest themselves in our welfare, and particularly so of those who show tenderness towards us in our Sickness.

We have a Mr. Foster on Board, who is a very agreeable Man, whose manners are soft and modest, indeed we have not a dissagreeable companion amongst them, all except one are married Men. Dr. Clark is a great favorite of Nabbys. He found I believe, that the mind wanted soothing, and tenderness, as well as attention to the Body. Nobody said a Word, nor do I know from any thing but his manner of treating her, that he suspected it, but he has the art of diverting and amuseing her, without seeming to try for it. She has behaved with a Dignity and Decorum worthy of her.

I have often my dear Sister lookd towards your habitation, since I left America; and fancied you watching the wind, and the weather, rejoiceing, when a favourable Brieze was like to favour our passage, and lifting up a pious Ejaculation to Heaven for the Safety of your Friends, then looking upon the children committed to your care with additional tenderness. Aya why drops the tear as I write? Why these tender emotions of a Mothers Breast, is it not folly to be thus agitated with a thought?—Nature all powerfull Nature! How is my dear Brother? He too is kindly interested in my welfare. "Says, here they are" and there they go. Well when is it likely we shall hear from them? Of a safe arrival I hope to inform you in ten days from the present; I will not seal my Letter but keep it open for that happy period, as I hope it will prove.

You must excuse every inaccuracy and be thankfull if you can pick out my meaning. The confinement on Board Ship is as urksome as any circumstance I have yet met with; it is what we know there is no remedy for. The weather is so cold and damp, that in the pleasantest day we can set but a little while upon deck. There has been no time so warm, but what we could bear our Baize Gowns over our double calico, and cloaks upon them whilst you I imagine are panting under the mid Summer heat. Tell Brother Shaw I could realish a fine plate of his Sallet, and when his hand is in a few of his peas; but not to day; I would not have him send them, as I am now upon a low Diet, for yesterday my dear Sister I was seazed with a severe fit of the Rheumatism, which had threatned me for several Days before, occasiond I suppose from the constant dampness of the ship. I was very sick, full of pain, a good deal of fever and very lame, so that I could not dress myself, but good nursing and a good Physician, with rubbing, and flannel, has relieved me.

Abigail Adams to Mary Smith Cranch

Deal July 20 [*1784*]

Heaven be praised I have safely landed upon the British coast. How flattering, how smooth the ocean, how delightfull was Sunday the 18 of July. We flatterd ourselves with the prospect of a gentle Breeze to carry us on shore at Portsmouth where we agreed to land, as going up the channel always proves tedious, but on Sunday night the wind shifted to the South west, which upon this coast, is the same with our north East winds: it blew a gale on Sunday night, on Monday and Monday night equal to an Equinoctial. We were obliged to carry double reef top Sails only, and what added to our misfortune was: that, tho we had made land the day before it was so thick that we could not certainly determine what land it was. It is now Twesday and I have slept only four hours since Saturday night. Such was the tossing and tumbling on Board our Ship. The Captain never left the deck the whole time either to eat or Sleep, tho they told me there was no danger, nor do I suppose that there realy was any, as we had Sea room enough. Yet the great number of vessels constantly comeing out of the channel and the apprehension of being run down, or being nearer the land than we imagined kept me constantly agitated. Added to this I had a voilent sick head ack. O! what would I have given to have been quiet upon the land. You will hardly wonder then at the joy we felt this day in seeing the cliffs of Dover: Dover castle and town. The wind was in Some measure subsided. It raind, however; and was as squaly as the month of March, the Sea ran very high. A pilot boat came on Board at about ten oclock this morning; the Captain came to anchor with his Ship in the Downs and the little town of Deal lay before us. Some of the Gentlemen talkd of going on Shore with the pilot Boat, and sending for us if the wind subsided. The boat was about as large as a Charlstown ferry boat and the distance from the Ship about twice as far as from Boston, to Charlstown. A Shore as bald as Nantasket Beach, no wharf, but you must be run right on Shore by a wave where a number of Men stand to catch hold of the Boat and draw it up. The Surf ran Six foot high. But this we did not know untill driven on by a Wave, for the pilots eager to get money assured the Gentlemen they could land us safe without our being wet, and we saw no prospect of its being better through the day. We accordingly agre'd to go. We were wraped up and lowerd from the ship into the boat; the whole Ships crew eager to assist us, the Gentlemen attentive and kind as tho we were all Brothers and Sisters: we have spent a month together, and were as happy as the Sea would permit us to be. We set of from the vessel now mounting upon the top of a wave high as a Steeple, and then so low that the boat was not to be seen. I could keep myself up no other way than as one of the Gentleman stood braced up against the Boat, fast hold of me and I with both my Arms round him. The other ladies were held, in the same manner whilst every wave gave us a Broad Side, and finally a Wave landed us with the utmost force upon the Beach; the Broad Side of the Boat right against the Shore, which was oweing to the bad management of the men, and the high Sea.

(Thus far I had proceeded in my account when a Summons to tea prevented my adding more; since which I have not been able to take my pen; tho now [23 *July*] at my Lodgings in London I will take up the thread where I left it, untill the whole Ball is unwound: every particular will be interesting to my Friends I presume, and to no others expose this incorrect Scral.)

We concequently all pressd upon the Side next the Shore to get out as quick as possible, which we need not have done, if we had known what I afterwards found to be the case, that it was the only way in which we could be landed, and not as I at first supposed oweing to the bad management of the Boatmen; we should have set still for a Succession of waves to have carried us up higher, but the roar of them terrified us all, and we expected the next would fill our Boat; so out we sprang as fast as possible sinking every Step into the Sand, and looking like a parcel of Naiades just rising from the Sea. A publick house was fortunately just at hand, into which we thankfully enterd, changed our cloathing, dried ourselves and not being able to procure carriages that day we engaged them for Six oclock the next morning, and took lodgings there, all of us; ten in Number. Mr. Green Set of immediately for London—no body mourn'd. We were all glad to retire early to rest. For myself I was so faint and fatigued that I could get but little; we rose by 5 and our post Chaise being all at the door we set of in the following order. Mr. Foster myself and Ester in one, Dr. Clark and Nabby in the second, Col. Norton, Mrs. Adams and Brother in the 3 and Mr. Spear and Lieut. Millicot brought up the rear. Our first Stage was 18 miles from Deal, to Canteburry where we Breakfasted, the roads are fine, and a Stone a Novelty. I do not recollect to have seen one, except the pavements of Canteburry, and other Towns, from Deal to London which is 72 miles. Vast Feilds of wheat, oats, english, Beans, and the horse Bean, with hops: are the produce of the country through which we past; which is cultivated like a Garden down to the very edges of the road, and what surprized me was, that very little was inclosed within fences. Hedg fence are almost the only kind you see, no Cattle at large without a herdsman, the oxen are small, but the Cows and Sheep very large, such as I never saw before. When we arrived at the end of our Stage, we discharge the first carriages. Call for New ones which will be ready in a few moments after you issue your orders. Call for Breakfast. You have it perhaps in ten moments for ten people, with the best of Attendance and at a reasonable price. Canteburry is a larger town than Boston, it contains a Number of old Gothick Cathedrals, which are all of Stone very heavy, with but few windows which are grated with large Bars of Iron, and look more like jails for criminals, than places designd for the worship of the deity, one would suppose from the manner in which they are Gaurded, that they apprehend devotion would be Stolen. They have a most gloomy appearence and realy made me shudder. The Houses too have a heavy look being chiefly thatched roofs or coverd with crooked brick tile, now and then you would see upon the road a large woods looking like a Forest, for a whole mile inclosed with a high Brick Wall or cemented Stone. An enormous Iron gate would give one a peep as we passt of a large pile of Building, which lookd like the castles of some of the ancient Barons; but as we were strangers in the Country, we could only conjecture what they were, and what they might have been; we proceeded from Cantuburry to Rochester about 15 miles, an other pretty town, not so large as the former, from thence to Chatam where we stoped at a very Elegant Inn to dine. As soon as you drive into the yard you have at these places as many footmen round you as you have Carriages, who with their politest airs take down the Step of your Carriage, assist you out, inquire if you want fresh horses or carriages; will supply you directly, Sir, is the answer. A well dresst hostess steps forward, making a Lady like appearence and wishes your commands, if you desire a chamber, the Chamber maid attends; you request dinner, say in half an hour, the Bill of Fare is directly brought, you mark what you wish to have, and suppose it to be a variety of fish, fowl, meat, all of which we had, up to 8 different dishes; besides vegetables. The moment the time you stated, is out, you will have your dinner upon table in as elegant a Stile, as at any Gentleman's table, with your powderd waiters, and the master or Mistress always brings the first Dish upon table themselves. But you must know that travelling in a post Chaise, is what intitles you to all this respect. From Chatham we proceeded, on our way as fast as possible wishing to pass Black Heath before dark. Upon this road, a Gentleman alone in a chaise past us, and very soon a coach before us stoped, and there was a hue and cry, a Robbery a Robbery. The Man in the chaise was the person robbed and this in open day with carriages constantly passing. We were not a little allarmed and every one were concealing their money, every place we past, and every, post chaise we met were crying out a Robbery. Where the thing is so common I was surprized to see such an allarm. The Robber was pursued and taken in about two miles, and we saw the poor wretch gastly and horible, brought along on foot, his horse rode by a person who took him; who also had his pistol. He looked like a youth of 20 only, attempted to lift his hat, and looked Dispair. You can form some Idea of my feelings when they told him aya, you have but a short time, the assise set next Month, and then my Lad you Swing. Tho every robber may deserve Death yet to exult over the wretched is what *our* Country is not accustomed to, long may it be free of such villianies and long may it preserve a commisiration for the wretched. We proceeded untill about 8 oclock. I was set down at Lows Hotel in Covent Gardens, the court end of the Town. These Lodgings I only took for one night untill others more private could be procured as I found Mr. Adams was not here, I did not wish such expensive appartments. It was the Hotel at which he kept when he resided here. Mr. Spear set out in quest of Mr. Smith but he had received intelligence of my comeing out with Capt. Lyde and had been in quest of me but half an hour before at this very place; Mr. Spear was obliged to go first to the custom house, and as good fortune would have it, Mr. Smith and Mr. Storer were near it and saw him allight from the coach, upon which he informd them of my arrival. Tho a mile distant, they set out upon a full run (they say) and very soon to our mutual Satisfaction we met in the Hotel. How do you and how do ye? We rejoice to see you here, and a thousand such kind of inquiries as take place between Friends who have not seen each other for a long time naturally occured.

My first inquiry was for Mr. Adams. I found that my Son had been a month waiting for my arrival in London, expecting me in Callighan, but that upon getting Letters by him, he returnd to the Hague. Mr. Smith had received a Letter from his Father acquainting him that I had taken passage in Capt. Lyde, this intelligence he forwarded three days before I came, so that I hourly expect either Mr. Adams or Master John. I should have mentiond that Mr. Smith had engaged lodgings for me; to which Mr. Storer and he accompanied me this morning after paying a Guiney and half for tea last evening and Lodging and Breakfast, a coach included; not however to carry me a further distance than from your House to our own; the Gentlemen all took less expensive lodgings than mine, excepting Dr. Clark who tarried with us, said he would not quit us untill we were fixed in our present Hotel, the direction to which is Osbornes new family Hotel, Adelphi at Mrs. Sheffields No. 6. Here we have a handsome drawing room Genteely furnished, and a large Lodging room. We are furnished with a cook, chamber maid, waiter &c. for 3 Guineys per week—but in this is not included a mouthfull of vituals or drink all of which is to be paid seperately for.

London july 23. 1784
Osbornes new family Hotel
Adelphi at Mrs. Sheffields No. 6

AA to JA

My Dearest Friend

At length Heaven be praised I am with our daughter Safely landed upon the British Shore after a passage of 30 days from Boston to the Downs. We landed at Deal the 20 instant, rejoiced at any rate to set our feet again upon the land. What is past, and what we sufferd by sickness and fatigue, I will think no more of. It is all done away in the joyfull hope of soon holding to my Bosom the dearest best of Friends.

We had 11 passengers. We travelled from Deal to London all in company, and tho thrown together by chance, we had a most agreeable Set, 7 Gentlemen all except one, American, and marri'd Men, every one of whom strove to render the passage agreeable and pleasent to us. In a more particular manner I feel myself obliged to Mr. Foster who is a part owner of the Ship, a modest, kind, obliging Man, who paid me every Service in his power, and to a Dr. Clark who served his time with Dr. Loyd and is now in partnership with him. He took a kind charge of Nabby in a most Friendly and Brotherly way, shewed us every attention both as a Gentleman, physician, and sometimes Nurss, for we all stood in great want of both. My Maid was unfortunately sick the whole passage, my Man servant was so sometimes, in short for 2 or 3 days the Captain and Dr. who had frequently been to sea before, were the only persons who were not sea sick. Capt. Lyde is a Son of Neptune, rather rough in his manners, but a most excellent Sea man, never leaving his deck through the passage for one Night He was very obligeing to me. As I had no particular direction to any Hotel when I first arrived a Gentleman passenger who had formerly been in London advised me to Lows Hotel in Covent Garden, where we stoped. My first inquiry was to find out Mr. Smith, who I presumed could inform me with respect to you. Mr. Spear a passenger undertook this inquiry for me, and in less than half an hour, both he and Mr. Storer were with me. They had kindly provided lodgings for me to which I removed in the morning after paying a Guiney and half for tea after I arrived and lodging and Breakfast, a coach included to carry me to my lodgings. I am now at lodgings at 34 and 6 pence per week for myself, daughter, and two Servants. My Man servant I left on Board the Ship to come up with it, but it has not yet got up. I drew upon you before I left America one Bill in favour of Dr. Tufts of an hundred pound Lawfull Money, 98 of which I paid for our passages. This Bill is to be paid to Mr. Elworthy. I drew for two hundred more in favour of Natll. Austin to be paid in Holland, one hundred and 80 pounds of this money I shall bring with me to the Hague as I cannot use it here without loss, it being partly Dollors partly french crowns and French Guineys. Mr. Smith has advised me to this and tells me that what money I have occasion for he can procure me here. My expences in landing, travelling and my first Nights entertainment have amounted to 8 Guineys. I had a few english Guineys with me. I shall wish to shelter myself under your wing immediately, for the expences frighten me. We shall be dear to you in more Senses than one. Mr. Jefferson I left in Boston going to Portsmouth where he designd spending a week and then to return to Newyork to take passage from thence to

France. He urged me to wait his return and go with him to New York, but my passage was paid on Board Capt. Lyde. The season of the Year was the best I could wish for and I had no desire to take such a journey in the Heat of summer. I thanked him for his politeness, but having taken my Measures, I was determined to abide by them. He said Col. Humphries the Secretary to the commercial commission had sailed before he left Philadelphia, and that he did not doubt I should find you in France. I have a Letter from him which I inclose and several other Letters from your Friends. Mr. Smith thinks Master John will be here to Night from the intelligence he forwarded to you before I arrived. I do not wish to tarry a day here without You, so that if he comes I shall immediately set out, provided I have not to wait for the Ship to come up. How often did I reflect during my voyage upon what I once heard you say, that no object in Nature was more dissagreeable than a Lady at sea. It realy reconciled me to the thought of being without you, for heaven be my witness, in no situation would I be willing to appear thus to you. I will add an observation of my own, that I think no inducement less than that of comeing to the tenderest of Friends could ever prevail with me to cross the ocean, nor do I ever wish to try it but once more. I was otherways very sick, beside Sea Sickness but you must not expect to see me pined, for nothing less than death will carry away my flesh, tho I do not think I eat more the whole passage than would have sufficed for one week. My fatigue is in some measure gone off and every hour I am impatient to be with you.

Heaven give us a happy meeting prays your ever affectionate

A. Adams

At The Hague John Adams remained uncertain about the plans of his wife and daughter. And at this late juncture he altered his initial brusque rejection of Royall Tyler's suit for young Abigail's hand. In letters to his wife and the young man—letters which did not reach the recipients before mother and daughter embarked—Adams gave the couple his consent to any arrangements that accorded with their "own Judgments" and empowered his wife to "marry your Daughter" whether or not the voyage to England materialized. At the end of that voyage and on the eve of their reunion, Adams wrote that the couple "shall be asunder no longer than they choose." But the affair was not to be so concluded. Both the young people eventually made other matches.

Earlier, while still unaware what ship was bearing his family, Adams had sent John Quincy to London in mid-May to await them. He remained there a month or more, returning to The Hague within days of the ladies' actual arrival.

When Adams received his wife's first and heart-warming letter from

London, he had already had word of Congress' final diplomatic arrangements. But he still had business to complete in the Netherlands, and so he turned John Quincy right around for London, where he arrived on July 30. The plan was for the family to meet at The Hague and proceed by coach (the "Imperial" that John Quincy was to purchase in London) in a leisurely, sightseeing way through the Low Countries and France to Paris. "It is the first time in Europe," Adams remarked, "that I [have] looked forward to a Journey with Pleasure."

News of Jefferson's remarkably fast voyage from Boston changed all this. From "On board the Ceres off Scilly," July 24, Jefferson wrote Adams that he would be in Paris in a fortnight and looked forward to seeing the Adamses there. Adams was delighted. He cut short all business and formalities and followed his son posthaste to London.

JA to AA

My dearest Friend — The Hague July 26 1784

Your Letter of the 23d has made me the happiest Man upon Earth. I am twenty Years younger than I was Yesterday. It is a cruel Mortification to me that I cannot go to meet you in London, but there are a Variety of Reasons decisive against it, which I will communicate to you here. Meantime, I send you a son who is the greatest Traveller of his age, and without Partiality, I think as promising and manly a youth as is in the World.

He will purchase a Coach, in which We four must travel to Paris. Let it be large and strong, with an Imperial, and accommodations for travelling. I wish you to see the Hague before you go to France. The season is beautifull both here and in England. The Journey here will be pleasant excepting an Hour or two of Sea sickness between Harwich and Helvoet Sluis. You may come conveniently with your two children and your Maid, in the Coach, and your Man may ride on Horseback, or in the Stage Coach.

I can give you no Council about Cloaths. Mr. Puller will furnish the Money you want, upon your Order or Receipt. Expences I know will be high but they must be born, and as to Cloaths for yourself and Daughter, I beg you to do what is proper let the Expence be what it will.

Every Hour to me will be a Day, but dont you hurry, or fatigue or disquiet yourself upon the Journey. Be carefull of your Health.

After spending a Week or two here, you will have to set out with me to France, but there are no Seas between, a good Road, a fine season and We will make moderate Journeys and see the Curiosities of several Cities in our Way.—Utrecht, Breda, Antwerp, Brussells &c. &c.

It is the first time in Europe that I looked forward to a Journey with Pleasure. Now, I promise myself a great deal. I think it lucky that I am to go to Paris where you will have an Opportunity to see that City, to acquire its Language &c. It will be more agreable to you to be there, than here perhaps for some time.

For my own Part I think myself made for this World. But this very Idea makes me feel for a young Pair who have lately seperated. If my Consent only is wanting they shall be asunder no longer than they choose. But We must consult upon Plans about this.—They have discovered a Prudence. Let this Prudence continue and all will be right by and by.

Yours with more ardor than ever, John Adams

Abigail Adams to Elizabeth Smith Shaw

[*London*] Thursday morning [*29 July 1784*]

I went out yesterday as I told you I should; I had never been out before but in a Coach. Mr. Storer advised me to walk as it was a fine morning and the Sides of the Streets here are laid with flat Stone as large as tile. The London Ladies walk a vast deal and very fast. I accordingly agreed to go out with him, and he led me a jaunt of full four miles, I never was more fatigued in my life, and to day am unable to walk across the room; having been on Board Ship for some time, and never being used to walking: it was two miles too far for my first excursion; but if I was to live here I would practice Walking every day when the weather was pleasent. I went out at Nine and did not return untill one, when I was obliged to lye upon the bed an hour before I could dress me. In the mean time Mrs. Copely called upon me; and the Servant came up and asked me if *I was at Home*? The replie ought to have been no, but Ester not being yet accustomede to London Stile, replied yes. Fortunately Nabby was near dresst, so we past off Miss Adams, for Mrs. Adams, one being at home, the other not. You must know, having brought a concience from America with me, I could not reconcile this to it, but I am told not [to be at] home, means no more, than that you are not at home to company. [In L]ondon visitors call, leave a card, without even an intention, or des[ire of becomin]g company. I went to see a Lady; the Gentleman inquired of the Servant if his Mistress was at home, the Servant replied no Sir, upon which he questiond the Servant again (this Gentleman was Husband to the Lady), upon which he stept out and return'd, *realy* Mrs. Adams, says he, she is gone out, and I am very sorry for it.

Well, say you, but have you been yet to dine as you told me, with my old Friend? Yes I have: and was much pleased. This Gentleman retains all that pleasing Softness of Manners which he formerly possesst. In addition to these, he has all the politeness and ease of address which distinguish the Gentleman. He has been Married to a Yorkshire Lady about 3 Months, a Lady of fortune I am told. She has been Educated in the Country, and has none of the London airs about her. She is small, delicate as a Lily and Blushing as a rose, diffident as the Sensitive plant which shrinks at the touch. Their looks declare a unison of Hearts; Mr. Joy has made a great deal of money during the War and lives Elegantly, the dinning room and morning room were the most elegant of any I have seen, the furniture all New, and had an air of neatness which pleased me. I am in Love with what I have seen of the London Stile of entertaining company. There were 4 American Gentlemen who dinned with us. I would mention that fish and poultry of all kinds are extravagantly high here; we had a table neatly set, fish of a small kind, at the head; a ham in the middle, and a roast fillet of veal at the foot, peas and collyflower, an almond pudding and a pair of roast ducks were brought on. When the fish was removed, cherries and coosberries. One Servant only to attend, but he a thorough master of his Buisness. This I am told was a much higher entertainment than you will commonly meet with at a Gentlemans table who has an income of 10 thousand a year. I have dined out Six times by invitation and have never met with so much as or so great a variety as yesterday at Mr. Joys table. This is a day set apart for publick thanksgiving for the peace. The Shops are all shut and there is more the appearence of Solemnity than on the Sabbeth, yet that is kept with more Decency and Decorum than I expected to find it. The Churches which I attended last Sunday were large, yet were they crouded. I was to have attended divine Service to day at the Assylum or orphan House where Mr. Duchee formerly of Philadelphia, and chaplin to Congress, officiates. But my walk yesterday and a bad head ack prevents me, for in this country they keep the doors and windows Shut; this in a crouded assembly is not only prejudicial to Health, but I soon grow faint. Nabby has taken a sad cold by comeing out last Sunday from the Magdelin, tho we were in a coach; but tis the fashion they say for all Stranger[s] to have colds and coughs. I wonder not at it if they attend publick assemblies. It has not been warm enough, since I came into the city, to set with the windows open, and for two Nights past I have had my bed warmed. Mr. and Mrs. Atkinson would not excuse us from dinning with them to day. Charles Storer calld for us about 3 oclock. This is a fine young fellow, uncorrupted amidst all the licentiousness of the age. He seems like a child to me; is as attentive and obligeing as possible. There is not a day when I do not have 10 to a dozen Americans to see me, many of the refugees amongst them. Mr. Leonard of

Taunton made me a visit to day, assured me Mrs. Leonard would call upon me. Col. Norton, Mr. Foster, Mr. Spear, Mr. Appleton, Mr. Mason, Mr. Parker have been our morning visitors. Dr. Clark comes 2 miles twice a day to see us, and is like one of our family. When say you do you write; why I rise early in the morning and devote that part of the day to my pen. I have not attempted writing to many of my Friends. The Bugget is pretty much together. I have no leisure to coppy or correct, on that account beg I may not be exposed, for you know if one has a little credit and reputation we hate to part with it, and nothing but the interest which my Friends take in my welfare can possible excuse such a Scrible.

In the afternoon I called and drank tea with Mr. and Mrs. Elworthy to whom I had letters, and who very early called upon me. Mrs. Elworthy is a Neice of Brother Cranchs. They are Buisness folk, worthy good people, make no pretentions to fine living, but are of the obligeing Hospitable kind. He lives near a publick Building call'd Drapers Hall, the tradesmen of this Country are all formed into companys, and have publick Buildings belonging to them, this is a magnificent Eddifice at the end of which is a most Beautifull Garden surrounded by a very high wall, with four alcoves and rows of trees placed upon each side the walks: in the middle of the Garden is a fountain of circulour form, in the midst of which is a large Swan, out of whose mouth the water pours, and is convey'd there by means of pipes under ground, flowers of Various Sorts ornament this Beautifull Spot: when you get into these appartments and others which I have seen similar, you are ready to fancy yourself in Fairy land, and the representations which you have seen of these places through Glassess, is very little hightned.

Whilst we were at dinner to day a Letter was brought to Nabby from her Cousin Betsy. You can form an Idea how pleasing it was to hear from home only 25 Days since. Dear Romantick Girl, her little narative of her visit to the deserted cottage made me weep; my affection for which is not lessned by all the Magnificent Scenes of the city, tho vastly beyond what our country can boast. Mr. Jefferson had a very quick passage, and tho he saild a fortnight after me, arrived here only six days after me. He landed at Portsmouth and is gone on for France; this I imagine will make an alteration in my excursion to the Hague, as my Friends here advise me not to go on, untill Mr. Adams is acquainted with Mr. Jeffersons arrival. I know he must go to Paris, and by going directly there much time, fatigue and expence will be saved. Either Master John or his Pappa will be here to day, unless detained by the wind. Mr. Smith sets off tomorrow in order to embark for America, so that my Letter must soon come to a close. I send a

Book for my little Nephew, and as I am going to France, I think to purchase your lace there where it can be bought upon better terms than here. Remember me to Mr. Thaxter. Tell him he must write to me, and he will find me punctual in return.

My dear Boys I will write them if I can possibly. My Love to them. Remember me to Mr. Whites family and to Judge Sergants, to good Mrs. Marsh and all others who inquire after Your ever affectionate Sister,

A. Adams

London 30 of july Hotel Adelphi Adams Street at Mrs. Sheffields

Abigail Adams to Mary Smith Cranch

Fryday [30 *July 1784*]

To day my dear Sister I have determined upon tarrying at home in hopes of seeing my Son; or his Pappa; but from a hint dropt by Mr. Murray I rather think it will be my Son, as political reasons will prevent Mr. Adams'es journey here. Whilst I am writing a Servant in the family runs puffing in, as if he was realy interested in the Matter. Young Mr. Adams is come. O Where where is he, We all cried out? In the other house Madam, he stoped to get his Hair drisst. Impatient enough I was, yet when he enterd (we have so many Strangers) that I drew back not realy believing my Eyes—till he cried out, Oh my Mamma! and my Dear Sister. Nothing but the Eyes at first sight appeard what he once was. His appearence is that of a Man, and in his countanance the most perfect good humour. His conversation by no means denies his Stature; I think you do not approve the word *feelings*, but I know not what to Substitute in lieu, or even to discribe mine. His Sister he says he should have known in any part of the World. He inquired if his Cousin Betsy had received a long letter of Several pages which he wrote her in April.

Mr. Adams chuses I should come to the Hague, and travell with him from thence. Says it is the first journey he ever lookd forward to with pleasure since he came abroad; I wish to set out on fryday, but as we are obliged to purchase a Carriage and many other Matters to do, Master John thinks we cannot go untill the twesday after. In the mean time I shall visit the curiositys of the city, not feeling 20 years younger, as my best Friends says he does, but feeling myself exceedingly Matronly with a grown up Son on one hand, and Daughter upon the other, and were I not their Mother, I would say a likelier pair you will seldom see in a Summers day.

AA to JA

My dearest Friend *[London, 30 July 1784]*

I was this day made very happy by the arrival of a son in whom I can trace the strongest likeness of a parent every way dear to me. I had thought before I saw him, that I could not be mistaken in him, but I might have set with him for some time without knowing him.

I am at a loss to know what you would wish me to do, as Mr. Jefferson arrived last week at Portsmouth, immediately from Boston, altho he saild a fortnight after me, and went on to Paris.

Some of my Friends suppose that you would rather I should proceed from hence; and agree upon meeting at Brussels than make the journey first to the Hague. If I was to follow my own inclinations I should set off next twesday, but our son thinks I cannot come with convenience untill fryday. We have concluded upon this, to wait your replie to these Letters untill this day week, and come to the Hague or set off for Paris as you think best, or meet you at any place you may appoint. As to the article of cloathing I am full as much at a loss as you can possibly be. I have bought a Lutestring for myself and Nabby which I have had made, and Nabby is equipt with a rideing dress, but I thought the fewer I purchased here the better, as I was so soon to go to Paris, where I suppose it will be necessary to conform to the fashion. If by comeing on first to the Hague, I could relieve you from any trouble, or render you any assistance, I will most cheerfully perform the journey, but Mr. Storer thinks it will be attended with less trouble and expence; which is a matter worth considering, to proceed with my family to Paris. The sooner we meet the more agreeable it will be to me, for I cannot patiently bear any circumstance which detains me from the most desirable object in my estimation that hope has in store for me. I hardly dared flatter myself with the prospect of your comeing for me yourself, and was the less dissapointed when Master John arrived. I shall feel myself perfectly safe under his care. There are many Americans in this city most of whom I believe have called upon me, some of whom were quite strangers to me. I have not been to any publick entertainment or even seen the curiositys of the city. I chose to wait yours or my Sons comeing. I have not sent on the Letters which I have for you as they contain no particular intelligence, are mere Letters of Friendship.

Nabby has had Letters from Boston, from Dr. Welch and her Cousin Betsy written only 25 days since. Mr. Tracy came out with Mr. Jefferson. Adieu and believe me most affectionately, most tenderly yours and only yours and wholly yours,

A. Adams

JA to AA

My dearest Friend The Hague Aug. 1. 1784

Your favour without a Date, just now received and Mr. Jeffersons Arrival, a Month sooner than he expected, have indeed changed my Plan. Stay where you are, and amuse yourself, by seeing what you can, untill you see me. I will be with you in Eight Days at farthest, and sooner, if possible.—I will cross from Helvoet to Harwich, by the Packet of the day after tomorrow if I can. If this is impossible, by the next. I must take Leave, here, and write to Paris and arrange my Household, as well as I can before I depart. But I will join you in London. Let your Son buy his Coach, and have every Thing ready, to depart for Dover, for I cannot stay a Day in London. I must join my Colleagues in Paris without Loss of Time. Your Daughter may write her Friend as favourably as she pleases. I wrote him on the 3 of April my Approbation of his Views, and hoped he had the Letter before you sailed. Yours without Reserves, John Adams

Neither of the principals recorded with any particularity the reunion at the Adelphi in London on August 7. Five months later, Abigail Adams wrote in a letter to Mrs. Cranch, "You will chide me" for not recounting the event, "but you know my dear Sister, that poets and painters wisely draw a veil over those Scenes which surpass the pen of the one and the pencil of the other; we were indeed a very very happy family once more met together after a Seperation of 4 years."

The one surviving account that permits us some penetration into the scene is that entered by Nabby, the younger Abigail, in her journal. Meager and pedestrian for the most part, the journal here rises to a dramatic moment in the history of the Adams family. Neither Miss Burney nor Mr. Sheridan could have done better.

From Abigail Adams 2d's Diary

LONDON, AUG. 7TH, 1784.

At 12, returned to our own apartments; when I entered, I saw upon the table a hat with two books in it; every thing around appeared altered, without my knowing in what particular. I went into my own room, the things were moved; I looked around—"Has mamma received letters, that have determined her departure?—When does she go?—Why are these things moved?" All in a breath to Esther.

"No, ma'm, she has recieved no letter, but goes to-morrow morning."

"Why is all this appearance of strangeness?—Whose hat is that in the other room?—Whose trunk is this?—Whose sword and cane?—It is my father's," said I. "Where is he?"

"In the room above."

Up I flew, and to his chamber, where he was lying down, he raised himself upon my knocking softly at the door, and received me with all the tenderness of an affectionate parent after so long an absence. Sure I am, I never felt more agitation of spirits in my life; it will not do to describe.

INDEX

NOTE ON THE INDEX

Since the present volume is not intended as a research tool, the reader is referred, for more detailed entries, to the indexes in volumes 2 and 4 of *Adams Family Correspondence* and to the index in volume 4 of the *Diary and Autobiography of John Adams*, all in the Belknap Press edition of *The Adams Papers.*

Proper names are indexed in the form in which they first appear in the text. Where this form of the name is not the correct form, the correct spelling follows in parentheses. When the first mention is the correct form but subsequent mentions introduce variant spellings, the variants appear in parentheses.

The editors have tried (not always successfully) to supply forenames for persons who appear in the text only with surnames, to identify by residence or occupation those persons whose forenames are either unknown or not known with certainty, and to distinguish by dates persons with identical or nearly identical names.

Wives' names follow their husbands' names. Maiden names and pseudonyms are supplied in parentheses where needed.

INDEX

Index